Ubuntu: Up and Running

Robin Nixon

O'REILLY®

Beijing · Cambridge · Farnham · Köln · Sebastopol · Taipei · Tokyo

Ubuntu: Up and Running
by Robin Nixon

Published by O'Reilly Media, Inc., 1005 Gravenstein Highway North, Sebastopol, CA 95472.

O'Reilly books may be purchased for educational, business, or sales promotional use. Online editions are also available for most titles (*http://my.safaribooksonline.com*). For more information, contact our corporate/institutional sales department: 800-998-9938 or *corporate@oreilly.com*.

Editor: Andy Oram	**Indexer:** Ellen Troutman Zaig
Production Editor: Loranah Dimant	**Cover Designer:** Karen Montgomery
Copyeditor: Genevieve d'Entremont	**Interior Designer:** David Futato
Proofreader: Kiel Van Horn	**Illustrator:** Robert Romano

Printing History:

April 2010:	First Edition.

RepKover™

This book uses RepKover™, a durable and flexible lay-flat binding.

ISBN: 978-0-596-80484-8

[M]

1270749739

For Julie.

Table of Contents

8. Installing and Removing Software 257

Foreword

When I first heard about Ubuntu back in 2004, a few years before becoming the Ubuntu Community Manager, I was captivated by the approach that Mark Shuttleworth, the founder of Ubuntu, was taking with his new venture. Not only did he have a firm commitment to rock-solid technology, forged by a team of open source rock stars with Debian as a foundation, but he underlined his vision with similarly rock-solid commitment to community.

At the time, the industry growing up around open source was still fairly new, Linux was beginning to be commercialized, and community was increasingly seen as an impediment in companies with a traditional software development culture. Corporations and community were beginning to clash, and it was easier for many companies to merely tolerate community rather than embrace it.

Things seemed different with Ubuntu and its primary sponsor, Canonical. Ubuntu took a confident and adventurous approach to their new operating system. They made opinionated decisions about the best tools to satisfy given use cases, integrated exciting new technologies before others were willing to do so, and delivered the whole shebang on a single CD to make distribution and installation easy.

Ubuntu was compelling from a technical and usability standpoint—which in itself was exciting—but as a community management dork, what really excited me was the open and transparent approach to community that Shuttleworth adopted from the project's very launch. Right out of the gate, Ubuntu provided open communication and development resources, an openly governed community council and technical board, public meetings, and even open specification tracking for each new release. This was stunning. Most companies at that time were regressing in the areas of openness and transparency, not progressing. This is when that cheeky young upstart called Ubuntu came screaming into my own consciousness, first as a curiosity, then as an interest, and ultimately as a passion to grow a global, inclusive, and energized community around an ethos of openness and rocking software.

At the time this book is published, I will have been at Canonical for over three and a half years, and the journey we have been on has been remarkable. We have seen our small community grow into global, sprawling user and contributor bases that transcend the borders of countries, languages, and cultures. As our community has grown, we have been united by a shared set of values and energized by a vision of just what could be possible if we came together to change the status quo. What excited me three and a half years ago about Ubuntu was its willingness to question and challenge the norms of the time, underlined by a code of ethics that put community at the heart of the approach. That sense of adventure has never been so effervescent as it is today, and we now have a diverse global movement united by the same spirit; each set of eyes, ears, and fingers putting their brick in the wall to effect change in the way we approach computers, information, and freedom. This is what community is all about: a shared dream in which we all play a part.

This book is one such contribution to that dream. Robin has taken on quite a challenge and put together a comprehensive guide to the ins and outs of Ubuntu. As Robin was writing this book, we were in the thick of our latest release cycle. Robin worked hard to stay ahead of the curve, writing and explaining the operation of functionality that was sometimes only a few days old. I did this once myself when I wrote a book, and it is a complex, time-consuming, and sometimes frustrating process, but Robin took to it with grace and elegance. Robin's efforts, combined with the reputation and publishing prowess of O'Reilly, contribute another brick in the wall toward mainstream Ubuntu success.

I am hugely proud of the progress that we have made so far in our journey, but we still have plenty of road ahead of us. While our global Ubuntu family has broken down many barriers and achieved many things, the fast-changing world of technology brings forward new challenges and opportunities. Fortunately, the firm foundation of our community and drive to succeed will help us to scale these challenges and celebrate the opportunities. Before we step into the future, though, let us celebrate our achievements of today by exploring the many features and nuances in Ubuntu outlined and explained in Robin's book. I hope to see you all joining us on our continued journey!

—Jono Bacon
Ubuntu community manager

Preface

Ubuntu is far and away the most popular version (or distribution) of the Linux operating system. Dreamed up by a dot-com billionaire and ex-cosmonaut, and based on years of work by thousands of dedicated programmers, Ubuntu is a serious contender in both the desktop and the web server worlds.

It is based on the philosophy that software should be free, both economically and legally, in that you should be able to install it at no cost, and should also be allowed to modify and/or distribute it without paying any fees or royalties, which is achieved by releasing Ubuntu under a special license that protects these rights.

This means you may install Ubuntu on any computer on which it will run, and can upgrade to the latest version as often as you like, without worrying about licenses, product activation, or special keys you have to enter. You can give it to your friends and family too.

Ubuntu is also very easy to install, automatically recognizing and setting up the best drivers for the devices you use. And, with other operating systems taking anything from one hour to half a day to install, Ubuntu really shines with an average installation time of under an hour.

For over a decade, Linux has provided the computing power behind millions of web servers, so it's no surprise with the amount of work that has been put into developing graphical frontends, desktop installations of Linux now exceed 1% of the total (a figure that is rapidly growing), with Ubuntu taking the lion's share of that amount.

Everything you need to know to become a seasoned Ubuntu user is in this book, which also covers upgrading to and using the latest 10.04 Lucid Lynx release. What's more, it also shows you how to easily and quickly upgrade to the even newer versions that are released every six months.

Audience

This book is for people interested in learning about Ubuntu, the most popular Linux distribution. This includes students, home and business users, hobbyists, professionals, and all other types of user. Because this book takes you from the first steps of installing the operating system, through configuration, maintenance, and security, and on to topics such as networking, it provides a complete resource for all beginning to intermediate users.

Assumptions This Book Makes

This book assumes that you have a basic understanding of your computer and are comfortable using either Windows or Mac OS X, but no prior knowledge of Unix, Linux, or Ubuntu is required.

Organization of This Book

The chapters in this book are carefully ordered so that different aspects of the operating system are fully introduced before moving on to the next step. To get the best results from this book, you are therefore recommended to read the chapters in sequence.

For example, to get you started, the first chapter introduces Ubuntu, explains its background, and explores the different parts that make up the operating system. Then, with introductions out of the way, the second chapter takes you straight into installing Ubuntu. The process is fully explained in simple terms with plenty of screen grabs to guide you.

After that, the next chapter shows how to configure Ubuntu to your computer, including setting up your keyboard, mouse, and monitor, and managing peripherals such as printers, sound cards, and webcams.

With your setup now configured, the next chapters introduce the Linux filesystem and how to use it, both with the desktop and via the command line. You are then shown how to install and remove programs with the easy-to-use built-in tools, as well as how to maintain your system and keep it secure.

The following two chapters then cover networking functions such as file and folder sharing and accessing the Internet.

By this time, you will have a solid understanding of Ubuntu, so the remaining chapters show you what you can do with it, such as using the OpenOffice.org office suite of programs, installing and playing games, connecting peripherals such as scanners and Bluetooth devices, running Windows programs, and how to install other flavors of Ubuntu.

Along the way, each new topic is introduced using plain English, with the absolute minimum of jargon, and is supported by screen grabs showing exactly what you should see on your computer.

Supporting Books

Once you have mastered Ubuntu Linux, you may be interested in learning more about Linux and its other distributions. You can take your skills to the next level using the following books, which range from beginner to advanced level:

- *Linux in a Nutshell, Sixth Edition* (*http://oreilly.com/catalog/9780596154493*) by Ellen Siever, Stephen Figgins, Robert Love, and Arnold Robbins (O'Reilly)
- *Bash Cookbook: Solutions and Examples for bash Users* (*http://oreilly.com/catalog/9780596526788*) by Carl Albing, JP Vossen, and Cameron Newham (O'Reilly)
- *Linux System Administration* (*http://oreilly.com/catalog/9780596009526*) by Tom Adelstein and Bill Lubanovic (O'Reilly)
- *Linux System Programming* (*http://oreilly.com/catalog/9780596009588*) by Robert Love (O'Reilly)

Conventions Used in This Book

The following typographical conventions are used in this book:

Italic
> Indicates new terms, URLs, email addresses, filenames, file extensions, pathnames, directories, and Unix utilities.

`Constant width`
> Indicates command-line options, variables and other code elements, HTML tags, macros, the contents of files, and the output from commands.

`Constant width bold`
> Shows commands or other text that should be typed literally by the user.

`Constant width italic`
> Shows text that should be replaced with user-supplied values.

 This icon signifies a tip, suggestion, or general note.

 This icon indicates a warning or caution.

Using Code Examples

This book is here to help you get your job done. In general, you may use the code in this book in your programs and documentation. You do not need to contact us for permission unless you're reproducing a significant portion of the code. For example, writing a program that uses several chunks of code from this book does not require permission. Selling or distributing a CD-ROM of examples from O'Reilly books does require permission. Answering a question by citing this book and quoting example code does not require permission. Incorporating a significant amount of example code from this book into your product's documentation does require permission.

We appreciate, but do not require, attribution. An attribution usually includes the title, author, publisher, and ISBN. For example: "*Ubuntu: Up and Running*, by Robin Nixon. Copyright 2010 Robin Nixon, 978-0-596-80484-8."

If you feel your use of code examples falls outside fair use or the permission given here, feel free to contact us at *permissions@oreilly.com*.

How to Contact Us

Please address comments and questions concerning this book to the publisher:

> O'Reilly Media, Inc.
> 1005 Gravenstein Highway North
> Sebastopol, CA 95472
> 800-998-9938 (in the United States or Canada)
> 707-829-0515 (international or local)
> 707-829-0104 (fax)

We have a web page for this book, where we list errata, examples, and any additional information. You can access this page at:

> *http://www.oreilly.com/catalog/9780596804848*

There is also a companion website to this book available online at:

> *http://ubuntubook.net*

There you can see all the examples with color-highlighted syntax. To comment or ask technical questions about this book, send email to the following, quoting its ISBN number (9780596804848):

> *bookquestions@oreilly.com*

For more information about our books, conferences, Resource Centers, and the O'Reilly Network, see our website at:

> *http://www.oreilly.com*

Safari® Books Online

Safari Books Online is an on-demand digital library that lets you easily search over 7,500 technology and creative reference books and videos to find the answers you need quickly.

With a subscription, you can read any page and watch any video from our library online. Read books on your cell phone and mobile devices. Access new titles before they are available for print, and get exclusive access to manuscripts in development and post feedback for the authors. Copy and paste code samples, organize your favorites, download chapters, bookmark key sections, create notes, print out pages, and benefit from tons of other time-saving features.

O'Reilly Media has uploaded this book to the Safari Books Online service. To have full digital access to this book and others on similar topics from O'Reilly and other publishers, sign up for free at *http://my.safaribooksonline.com*.

Acknowledgments

A huge thank you goes to my editor, Andy Oram, for all his guidance and the tremendous amount of work and all the extra snippets of advice and information he put into making this book such a useful guide. And, as usual, the production staff at O'Reilly also did a magnificent job copyediting the text and designing the book's format and layout. It's a pleasure to work with you all.

With a book introducing something as complex as an operating system, it's essential for it to be as accurate as possible, so I am also very grateful to the team of eagle-eyed technical reviewers: Lesley Harrison, Matthew Helmke, and Jeff Kite, who provided many excellent suggestions for improving the manuscript.

And, of course, this book wouldn't exist without Canonical, GNU, Linux, and the many other organizations that have worked tirelessly for the best part of two decades to integrate a myriad of different parts into the whole known as Ubuntu. Because they number in the thousands, I don't want to single out just a few of the contributors; instead, on behalf of all Ubuntu users, I would simply like to thank each and every person who has participated in creating such an amazing piece of software.

CHAPTER 1

About Ubuntu

Some people say South African entrepreneur Mark Shuttleworth is a very lucky man. Others say he's an astute businessman and talented software engineer. But whichever way you look at it, there's no denying that he has twice helped steer the course of technological development throughout the world.

In 1995, he founded Thawte, the first company outside the United States to produce a fully encrypted, commercially available web server, and a leading provider of server certification, that he sold for a cool half billion dollars just four years later.

Using the proceeds, not only did Shuttleworth achieve his ambition of blasting into space on a Russian Soyuz and spending over a week in the International Space Station, he also funded the development of Ubuntu, now the largest Linux distribution by a long way.

Since its release in 2004, Ubuntu has consistently topped the chart of the most popular Linux distributions, and it currently accounts for over a third of all installations. In 2009, according to *Dimensional Research/KACE*, Ubuntu was the second most likely operating system companies intended to deploy in place of Windows Vista or 7. And if it continues its phenomenal growth, 2010 should see Ubuntu knock OS X out of first place in that poll.

So this book is about Mark Shuttleworth's second major technology hit because, with an estimated 10 million users and growing, a hit it surely is. But to understand what Ubuntu is you need to know a little of its development because it's the result of combining many different unique parts, whose roots can be traced back over 25 years.

Why Ubuntu?

The one question I am most asked is, "Why Ubuntu?" There's no single answer to this. Instead, I offer a selection of reasons depending on the asker's computing requirements. So here, in no particular order, are my reasons why you should choose Ubuntu as your operating system.

Its development is open

The whole philosophy behind the GNU project of which Linux is a part (and Ubuntu is a flavor of Linux) is that "software should be free." Although that often means the software is free of charge (not always, as you can see in the successful marketing of Red Hat products and Novell's SUSE products, both based on Linux), it means more importantly that all development is visible and shared.

Downloads and upgrades are free

So whether you are a personal user running Ubuntu at home or one of hundreds of people in a company running Ubuntu, you pay nothing for the software. People around the world, of every economic class, so long as they have access to a computer, can use everything offered as part of Ubuntu. And not only is the original download free but so is every upgrade that follows.

It's quick to install

If you haven't installed Ubuntu before but have installed an operating system such as Windows XP, Vista, or 7, you'll be amazed at how quick and easy Ubuntu is to install.

Upgrading is easy

Whenever a new version is released, Ubuntu will tell you and offer to upgrade automatically, at no cost, as long as you have an Internet connection.

Support is readily available

For home and private users, a wealth of support is available at the Ubuntu website and in forums across the Internet. If you have a problem, you can usually get an answer within hours (if not minutes). This is because Ubuntu is written by volunteers all around the globe who maintain contact with each other via these forums, and they are always happy to help out if they can.

Enterprise support is priced modestly

Although free support is available, businesses will probably find it much more convenient to take out a multi-installation license for a Long Term Support version of Ubuntu (such as 10.04). This brings a whole new level of assistance to the enterprise user, while still keeping the overall running costs of Ubuntu far cheaper than proprietary operating systems such as Windows.

You can modify it

If you have programmers who are familiar with Linux in your organization, they can obtain the Ubuntu source code totally free of charge and can then modify it in any way necessary, as long as they release the new code under the same terms. This can drastically speed up a company's development cycle by relying on software that's already been written. This is, in fact, how new features often get added to Linux, and how parts of the operating system are improved.

It's portable

You can run Ubuntu from a CD-ROM or USB thumb drive without installing it.

It comes with office applications

Ubuntu comes with OpenOffice.org preinstalled so that you can get up and running straight away, writing documents, spreadsheets, and presentations, and your files will be compatible with Microsoft Office.

Of course, there are many other reasons, but these are probably the main ones.

The Parts That Make Up Ubuntu

Ubuntu, named after a South African word meaning "humanity toward others," is a free operating system (OS) with a strong focus on usability and ease of installation. It is sponsored by the UK company Canonical Ltd., owned by Mark Shuttleworth.

By keeping Ubuntu free and open source (I'll define these terms in a moment), Canonical says it is able to utilize the talents of a community of developers. Canonical makes its profit from selling technical support and from creating other services related to Ubuntu.

In 2005 Shuttleworth also created the Ubuntu Foundation, kicking it off with a 10 million dollar grant, which he calls insurance for the project should he ever cease his involvement. The foundation's purpose is to ensure the support and development for all future versions of Ubuntu. In December 2009, Shuttleworth stepped down as CEO of Canonical to "focus on product design, partnerships, and customers."

Ubuntu (whose logo you can see in Figure 1-1) strongly relies on other developers, too, as it's a fork of the Debian project's code base, itself a popular Linux distribution.

Figure 1-1. The official Ubuntu logo

Debian

Initially developed in 1993, Debian—a contraction of the first name of the developer, Ian Murdock, along with that of Debra Lynn, a former girlfriend—is not backed by any company, yet it still manages to provide the basis of over a dozen other Linux distributions, and is available as both a desktop and a server operating system.

The Debian project is a volunteer organization with over a 1,000 member developers, each working on different aspects of the OS.

GNU

Both Debian and Ubuntu, and most of their constituent parts, are released under the GNU General Public License (GPL) and the Lesser General Public License (LGPL). This is a free software license, meaning that anyone can share the software with other people and any derived works must be available under the same terms.

The term GNU is a recursive acronym (a kind of joke that is popular among software hackers); it stands for GNU's Not Unix. The GNU project was started in 1984 at MIT by Richard Stallman, who had the goal of making a totally free operating system. This was finally achieved in 1992 with the appearance of the Linux kernel, itself released under the GPL.

The Linux Kernel

The Linux kernel is the core operating system used by all distributions of Linux, and is generally pronounced *lin-ucks*. It was created in 1991 by Linus Torvalds, a Finnish software engineer, who also had a vision of creating a free operating system.

Because Linux filled a critical gap in the GNU project by providing a working kernel, the total package is often called GNU/Linux. But most people just refer to it as Linux, which I'll do for the rest of this book.

So far, thousands of programmers have worked on the Linux kernel, with even Microsoft contributing 20,000 lines of code. In fact, so much work has gone into it that in 2006 a European Union study put the redevelopment cost of the kernel at over a billion U.S. dollars.

Tux

You may often see a penguin character called Tux used as the Linux logo (see Figure 1-2). It was created by Larry Ewing using GIMP (the GNU Image Manipulation Program) as an entry to a Linux competition. Surprisingly, it didn't win, but it has since become the official mascot.

Linux Distributions

Linux comes in a variety of different versions called *distributions*, or *distros* for short. Generally each distribution consists of the Linux kernel along with libraries and utilities from the GNU project, as well as a variety of applications such as word processors, spreadsheets, media players, and so on.

Unbelievably, there are estimated to be over 600 distributions of Linux, of which 300 are actively maintained. Of course, the vast majority of them are quite specialized and don't have many users. However, a significant number of distributions are relatively popular, although none of them comes close to the usage of Ubuntu.

Figure 1-2. Tux, the friendly Linux mascot

Table 1-1 lists some of the more common distributions, roughly in order of popularity according to the *http://distrowatch.com* website. Of course there are too many to list them all, so please don't be disappointed if you don't see all of your favorites.

Table 1-1. Some of the more popular Linux distributions

Name	Type of distribution
Ubuntu	A Linux distribution using the GNOME desktop environment
Fedora	A community distribution sponsored by Red Hat
Mint	A distribution based on and compatible with Ubuntu
openSUSE	Originally derived from Slackware and sponsored by Novell
Debian	A volunteer-driven, noncommercial distribution
Mandriva	A Red Hat derivative popular in France and Brazil
PCLinuxOS	A derivative of Mandriva
Puppy	A very small distribution that fits in 64 MB of memory
Sabayon	A Gentoo-based distribution
Arch	An independent distribution targeted at competent Linux users
CentOS	A 100% compatible rebuild of Red Hat Enterprise Linux
MEPIS	A Debian-based desktop Linux distribution
Slackware	One of the first Linux distributions
Kubuntu	A version of Ubuntu using the KDE desktop environment
Gentoo	A distribution with FreeBSD similarities, targeted at power users
Ubuntu Studio	A version of Ubuntu modified for intensive audiovisual work
Xubuntu	A version of Ubuntu using the Xfce Desktop environment
Red Hat	A derivative of Fedora maintained by Red Hat
Edubuntu	A derivative of Ubuntu designed for use in classrooms and schools

One reason for all these different distributions is that they are usually tailored for specific purposes, such as types of users, ranging from beginner to power user, or for types of computers, ranging from low- to high-end. There are also distributions that focus on education, music, graphics, office, or other tasks.

Some distributions come with the absolute minimum of additional software and a tightly reduced kernel, making them suitable for use in embedded environments such as cell phones or routers, whereas others include every conceivable feature.

Ubuntu Versions

Ubuntu treads the middle line. As can be seen from browsing through Table 1-1, there are only a few officially sanctioned versions of Ubuntu, of which the following are covered in this book:

Ubuntu
> The main Ubuntu Linux distribution

Kubuntu
> A version that uses the KDE desktop instead of GNOME

Xubuntu
> A version that uses the Xfce desktop instead of GNOME

Mythbuntu
> A version tailored for use as a personal video recorder (PVR)

Netbook Edition
> A version redesigned for use on Netbook computers (previously known as Netbook Remix)

X Window System

Graphics in Ubuntu are displayed thanks to the X Window System, which is separate from Linux and runs on many other operating systems as well. It's free and open source, like Ubuntu.

The X Window System was invented in the 1980s at MIT, explaining the terse name. Computer programmers sometimes avoid fanciful labels, to the point where two of the most popular programming languages are named C and R. The X Window System was derived from another one called W, which ran on an operating system from Stanford called V.

Although X has powered the graphics on nearly all Unix systems (and Unix-like systems, including Linux) for over two decades, its development faltered for a while during debates over licensing and leadership. Luckily, a group of dedicated developers reinvigorated the window with the nonprofit X.org, which was responsible for the code on a new, community-centered footing.

In testimony to the importance of healthy community support for free software, X has undergone a pretty thorough rewrite from the ground up and now supports quite a range of sophisticated graphics hardware. It lies at the basis of all the desktops described in the next section.

Linux Desktop Environments

If you use Windows or a Mac, you will generally access your computer from a graphical desktop environment such as Windows XP, Vista, or 7, or Mac OS X. On Ubuntu Linux, there are three main desktop environments to choose from: GNOME, KDE, and Xfce.

GNOME

GNOME is the default desktop used by Ubuntu. It was designed to provide a working environment with a heavy emphasis on simplicity, usability, and "making things just work."

The GNOME project arose because the more popular desktop environment at the time, KDE, was built on a development framework called Qt. At the time, this framework wasn't licensed under the GPL, and presented potential conflicts of interest.

Therefore, GNOME was built entirely using GPL- and LGPL-licensed software and is an example of many different projects being brought together. Based on the GTK+ toolkit, its look and feel is not too dissimilar from Windows or Mac OS X, with moveable windows that can be resized, a launcher menu, taskbar, and notification area (see Figure 1-3). Other distributions that use GNOME include Debian and Fedora.

KDE

The KDE desktop is based on the Qt framework, which now *is* licensed under the LGPL. It is the desktop environment used by Kubuntu and was first released in 1998 as a modern Unix desktop that gave all applications a consistent look and feel. In 2006 Mark Shuttleworth became the first patron of KDE, the highest level of sponsorship available.

The main difference between Ubuntu and Kubuntu is that, by default, Ubuntu uses GNOME applications, such as the Evolution Personal Information Manager (PIM) and the Synaptic Package Manager, whereas Kubuntu uses the KDE equivalents, such as the Kontact PIM and KPackageKit package manager. There are also numerous programs written for KDE, but you can usually run them from GNOME if you prefer.

However, it is possible to run both KDE and GNOME on the same machine, because Kubuntu and Ubuntu share all the same repositories. You can even install Ubuntu and then add KDE to it, as shown in Figure 1-4. This also has the effect of adding several KDE programs to your GNOME menus, and vice versa.

Figure 1-3. A typical Ubuntu desktop using GNOME

Although your desktop of choice is a personal matter, many users feel that KDE provides a little more power in terms of options and configuration than GNOME, but at the slight expense of organization and user simplicity. Hence KDE is more likely to be installed by more experienced users. Windows users may also find its "K" menu system, located in the bottom-lefthand corner, reminiscent of the Start Menu.

Xfce

The Xfce desktop environment is used by Xubuntu Linux (as well as two other Unix-based operating systems: Solaris and BSD) and is based on the same GTK+ toolkit as GNOME, but it uses the Xfwm window manager.

The Xfce philosophy is "small is simple," as you can see in Figure 1-5. Due to its ability to run on low specification equipment, it is most commonly implemented on systems with old or resource-limited hardware. Its configuration is mouse-driven, with all advanced options hidden from casual users.

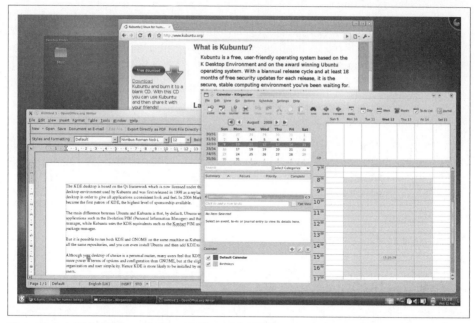

Figure 1-4. A typical Ubuntu desktop running under KDE

Figure 1-5. Ubuntu after adding the Xfce desktop environment

Xfce does, however, include an option to preload the libraries for GNOME and KDE, resulting in the ability to mix applications more quickly than the other major desktops. Although it's extremely fast, some have noted that the Xubuntu desktop is slower than other Xfce implementations.

Xfce is the least used of the three environments, with less than 10% of all Linux desktop installations. That said, it is quite similar to the Windows XP "Classic" desktop and probably deserves more users than it has.

In the same way that KDE is available with Kubuntu, Xfce comes with Xubuntu. But either can be quite easily added to the main Ubuntu distribution, and I'll show you how to do this in Chapter 2.

Linux Packages

Each distribution is usually split up into smaller packages, some of which become optional add-ons that can be installed using a package manager. There are different managers for different flavors of Linux; Ubuntu uses the Synaptic Package Manager (see Figure 1-6) and, more recently, the Ubuntu Software Center.

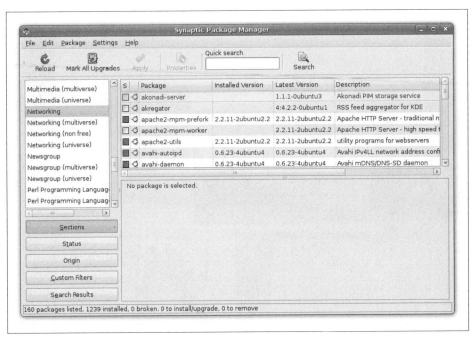

Figure 1-6. The Synaptic Package Manager

If you have heard of people having difficulty installing Linux software, don't be put off, because package managers have changed all that. You can now install almost any program available for Ubuntu with only a few mouse clicks.

The Ubuntu Community

One of the great things about Ubuntu is that it is open source, meaning that not only is it free to use, it's also free to modify, as long as any modifications you make are released under the same license. This means that the thousands of independent developers working on it have a vested interest in sharing all the latest information with one another. When one developer has a problem, another steps in to help, and vice versa.

But more than that, there's a vibrant and growing community that includes Ubuntu's millions of users. Of course they all communicate with each other via email, instant messages, and list servers, etc., but one of the main meeting points is the Ubuntu Community at *http://ubuntu.com/community* (see Figure 1-7), where everyone is welcome to join in. Many members also sign the Ubuntu Code of Conduct (*http://ubuntu.com/community/conduct*), in which they agree to be considerate and respectful of all Ubuntu users and to collaborate with them. So you won't simply be told to "refer to the documentation" when you ask a question in a forum.

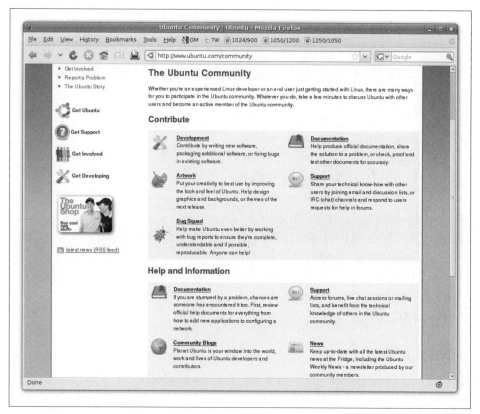

Figure 1-7. The Ubuntu Community website

On the website, you'll find forums covering every aspect of using Ubuntu you can imagine and where, due to its popularity, you can often get an answer to a problem within just a few minutes. There's also full documentation for all the latest releases, the Planet Ubuntu blog, and The Fridge news website.

You can also get more involved in the community and participate by adding to the program code or documentation, or by contributing artwork, user support, or bug reports. Whatever it is, the Ubuntu Community will welcome you.

Ubuntu Versions

There are two releases of Ubuntu each year, generally around April and October. Each release has a major number based on the year and a minor one based on the month. Ubuntu releases are also given code names based on animals, which since the third release have progressed in alphabetical order. A lot of fun precedes each launch, with Ubuntu users everywhere trying to guess whether the next version will be Observant Ostrich or Obvious Otter, and so on. The release history so far is shown in Table 1-2.

Table 1-2. The Ubuntu release history

Version	Code name	Release date	Supported until	
			Desktop	Server
4.10	Warty Warthog	October 2004	April 2006	
5.04	Hoary Hedgehog	April 2005	October 2006	
5.10	Breezy Badger	October 2005	April 2007	
6.06 LTS	Dapper Drake	June 2006	July 2009	June 2011
6.10	Edgy Eft	October 2006	April 2008	
7.04	Feisty Fawn	April 2007	October 2008	
7.10	Gutsy Gibbon	October 2007	April 2009	
8.04 LTS	Hardy Heron	April 2008	April 2011	April 2013
8.10	Intrepid Ibex	October 2008	April 2010	
9.04	Jaunty Jackalope	April 2009	October 2010	
9.10	Karmic Koala	October 2009	April 2011	
10.04 LTS	Lucid Lynx	April 2010	April 2013	April 2015

Things You See

When using Ubuntu, the things you will see on the desktop include applications such as the OpenOffice.org suite of programs (which are compatible with Microsoft Office), the Firefox web browser, or the Terminal (used for entering command-line instructions).

There are also loads of games, graphic manipulation tools, instant messaging utilities, audio-visual applications, and a lot more that I will introduce over the following chapters.

Things You Don't See

What you won't see by default in Ubuntu are important operating system files, program source code, configuration files, and the like. Of course, these are all necessary parts of an operating system and are all there, but they are hidden from casual view, unless you know where to look—in which case, you will be more than a casual user.

This means that on the whole you can rummage around and play with what you find in the Ubuntu desktop, update programs, configure peripherals, and so on, all from easy-to-use graphical frontends. This doesn't mean that you can't make major changes to your computer, because you can, just as you can with Windows or OS X. But it does mean you won't need to roll up your sleeves and get under the desktop's hood too often to configure Ubuntu.

Summary

If any of the information in this chapter has confused you, don't worry. The most important aspect of Ubuntu, and possibly the greatest contribution to its success, is the operating system's usability. It really is as easy as Windows or OS X to install and set up (in fact, it's usually a lot quicker), and you don't actually need to know most of the preceding details.

As the following chapters will show, Ubuntu is a very friendly OS that will not only save you money (because it is free), but will also grow with you due to the tremendous user support and frequent upgrades provided.

I promise that by the time you finish this book, using Ubuntu will be second nature.

CHAPTER 2

Installing and Upgrading Ubuntu

In this chapter, we'll take a look at the companion DVD for this book, which is attached to the inside back cover, and I'll also show readers without access to the DVD how to get the same software by downloading and burning ISO disc images.

Unlike most program discs you may have used, this DVD is unusual in that you don't actually have to install anything if you don't wish to, because it's been set up as a *Live DVD*.

This means that the DVD itself is a fully working installation of Ubuntu 9.10 that will run from the disc without the need to install anything. Therefore you can test Ubuntu to ensure it will work properly on your computer before installing it. It achieves this trick by creating a RAM disc out of system memory, which it then treats as if it were the hard disk.

The disc also contains the installer for Ubuntu 9.10 desktop edition and a set of ISO files for several of the other popular editions of Ubuntu, such as Kubuntu and Xubuntu. This chapter shows you how to use and install these files.

 To access the disc, you must have a DVD-compatible optical drive. If you don't, you cannot use the disc and should refer to the section "Downloading a Distribution" on page 24.

The Live DVD

The great thing about the Live DVD system is that you can insert the disc into most PCs and run Ubuntu without installing anything. Once you've verified that all is in order, you can then choose to install Ubuntu, either as the only operating system or as an additional OS (alongside Microsoft Windows, for example). Or you can simply run the Live DVD if you choose.

The downside of running from the Live DVD is that it is much slower than a hard disk installation because DVD drives are not as fast. Also, because the operating system exists only in RAM, any settings you make or documents you save locally will be lost when you close a session (although there are techniques you can use to keep session data on a USB drive, explained at *https://help.ubuntu.com/community/LiveCD/Persis tence*). But I recommend you perform a full installation as soon as you're ready. First, however, let's look at simply running Ubuntu from the disc.

To do this, you should ensure that your BIOS settings allow booting from your CD/ DVD drive. Systems usually do this by default. If not, the manual that came with your PC will have advice on how to change it. Sometimes you can simply watch the messages that come up on your screen as you boot your system, and they will tell you how to enter BIOS and change your boot settings by pressing a certain key combination.

 The DVD will work on an Intel Macintosh computer, but you will need to force it to boot from the DVD by either setting the System Preference for the startup disk, or shutting down and turning off your Mac and then holding down the C key while you turn it on again.

Now insert the disc into your drive and restart your computer. You should be presented with the screen shown in Figure 2-1.

This is where you select the language that should be used for the Live DVD (or during installation if you select that option). Only the main language type is required. For example, as long as English is your native language, go ahead and select it, regardless of which country you are in. Don't worry about local differences such as keyboard layout. In the next section you'll see how you can further tailor the language to your locale.

So either select the language of your choice or, if you wait 30 seconds, English will be chosen by default. Upon selection, the screen shown in Figure 2-2 will appear.

The Main Menu

From here, you have five main choices and a range of options selectable via the function keys. The choices are:

Try Ubuntu without any change to your computer
    As it sounds, this choice launches Ubuntu ready for you to use. It then runs from the DVD without modifying your computer's hard disk.

Install Ubuntu
    Select this choice when you wish to install Ubuntu on your computer.

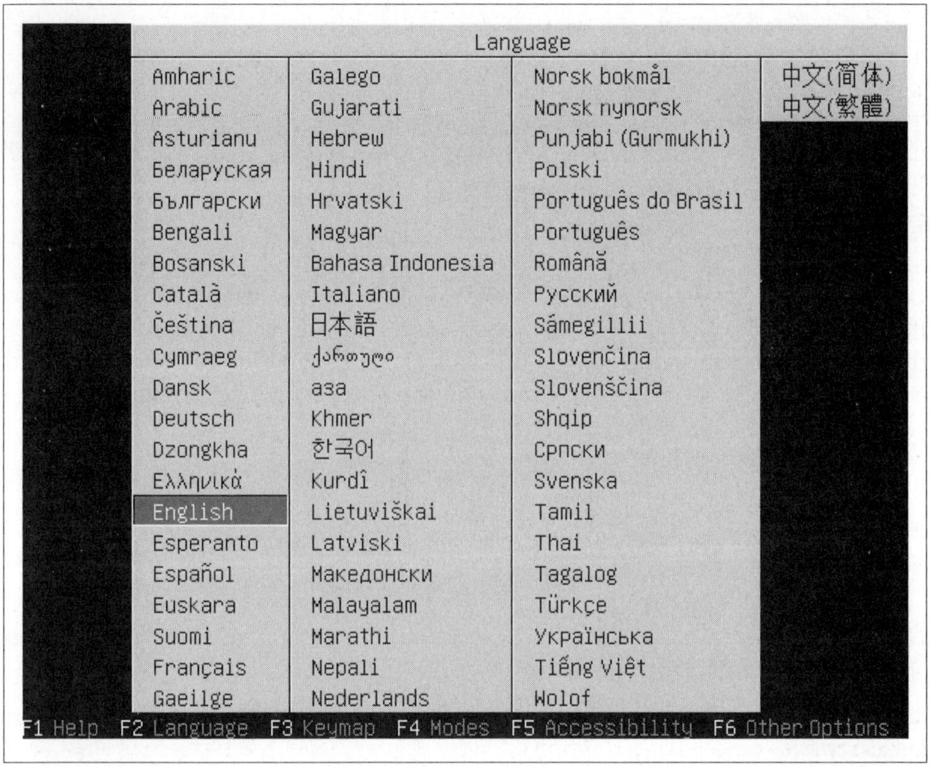

Language			
Amharic	Galego	Norsk bokmål	中文(简体)
Arabic	Gujarati	Norsk nynorsk	中文(繁體)
Asturianu	Hebrew	Punjabi (Gurmukhi)	
Беларуская	Hindi	Polski	
Български	Hrvatski	Português do Brasil	
Bengali	Magyar	Português	
Bosanski	Bahasa Indonesia	Română	
Català	Italiano	Русский	
Čeština	日本語	Sámegillii	
Cymraeg	ქართული	Slovenčina	
Dansk	аза	Slovenščina	
Deutsch	Khmer	Shqip	
Dzongkha	한국어	Српски	
Ελληνικά	Kurdî	Svenska	
English	Lietuviškai	Tamil	
Esperanto	Latviski	Thai	
Español	Македонски	Tagalog	
Euskara	Malayalam	Türkçe	
Suomi	Marathi	Українська	
Français	Nepali	Tiếng Việt	
Gaeilge	Nederlands	Wolof	

F1 Help F2 Language F3 Keymap F4 Modes F5 Accessibility F6 Other Options

Figure 2-1. The first screen you see after the Live DVD boots

Check disc for defects
> If you are experiencing problems with the DVD and suspect it may be faulty, you can test it using this choice.

Test memory
> Using this choice, you can check that all your computer's memory is in working order.

Boot from first hard disk
> You will most likely use this choice if you accidentally leave the DVD in your hard drive during a reboot but actually intended to run the operating system installed on your hard drive. With this choice you can quit from the DVD and commence a regular boot from your hard disk.

The Function Key Options

Using these options, you can set up various features before selecting one of the main five menu choices. Most of these options either let you revisit options that were presented to you already or provide workarounds for unusual situations advanced users

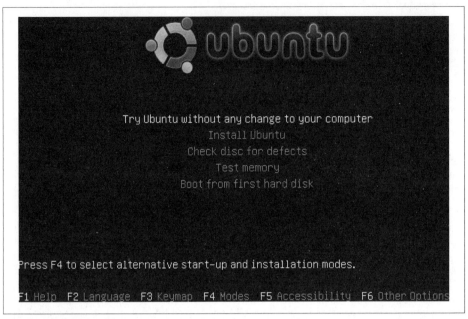

Figure 2-2. The Live DVD main menu screen

face, so I'll just point you in the right direction and let you investigate further if necessary.

F1 Help
>   This brings up a comprehensive help system, the top screen for which is shown in Figure 2-3. From within the help system, you use the function keys shown to select different sections, which you can scroll through with the cursor keys. To exit, press the Esc key.

F2 Language
>   This option redisplays the language selection menu shown in Figure 2-1.

F3 Keymap
>   This option is where you can tell Ubuntu about the country in which you live, and therefore which keyboard type you are using, as shown in Figure 2-4.

F4 Modes
>   With this option you can tell Ubuntu the graphic mode to use, as shown in Figure 2-5. Normally you should leave the default selected unless you experience problems, in which case try the Safe graphics mode. You are unlikely to need either of the remaining two options.

F5 Accessibility
>   This option provides a number of assistive features such as high contrast, a magnifier, use of a screen reader or Braille terminal, and more. You can see the options available in Figure 2-6.

F6 Other Options

You are extremely unlikely to need this option, which provides a range of different parameters for booting Ubuntu, as shown in Figure 2-7. If you are curious, the help system provides more information on what they do. Purists who do not want to run any proprietary software at all, such as binary device drivers, may wish to select the "Free software only" option.

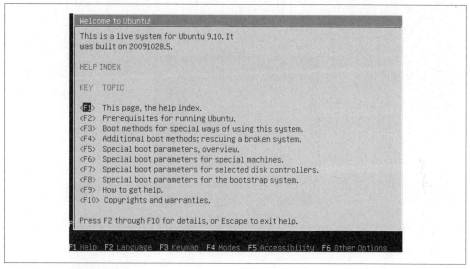

```
Welcome to Ubuntu!

This is a live system for Ubuntu 9.10. It
was built on 20091028.5.

HELP INDEX

KEY  TOPIC

<F1>  This page, the help index.
<F2>  Prerequisites for running Ubuntu.
<F3>  Boot methods for special ways of using this system.
<F4>  Additional boot methods; rescuing a broken system.
<F5>  Special boot parameters, overview.
<F6>  Special boot parameters for special machines.
<F7>  Special boot parameters for selected disk controllers.
<F8>  Special boot parameters for the bootstrap system.
<F9>  How to get help.
<F10> Copyrights and warranties.

Press F2 through F10 for details, or Escape to exit help.

F1 Help  F2 Language  F3 Keymap  F4 Modes  F5 Accessibility  F6 Other Options
```

Figure 2-3. The help system

```
                              Keymap
   Afghanistan  Denmark    Israel      Nepal         Swiss German
   Albania      Dvorak     Italy       Netherlands   Syria
   Andorra      Esperanto  Japan       Nigeria       Tajikistan
   Arabic       Estonia    Kannada     Norway        Tamil
   Armenia      Ethiopia   Kazakhstan  Pakistan      Telugu
   Asturian     Faroes     Korea       Poland        Thailand
   Azerbaijan   Finland    Kurdish     Portugal      Turkey
   Bangladesh   France     Kyrgyzstan  Romania       Turkey (F)
   Belarus      Georgia    Laos        Russia        Turkmenistan
   Belgium      Germany    Latin Amer. Saami (Fin.)  UK
   Bhutan       Ghana      Latvia      Saami (Nor.)  USA
   Bosnia       Greece     Lithuania   Saami (Swe.)  USA Intl.
   Brazil       Guinea     Macedonia   Senegal       Ukraine
   Bulgaria     Gujarati   Malayalam   Serbia        Uzbekistan
   Cambodia     Gurmukhi   Maldives    Slovakia      Vietnam
   Canada       Hungary    Malta       Slovenia
   Catalan      Iceland    Maori       South Africa
   China        India      Mongolia    Spain
   Congo        Iran       Montenegro  Sri Lanka
Press F4 Croatia  Iraq     Morocco     Sweden
   Czechia      Ireland    Myanmar     Swiss French
F1 Help  F2 Language  F3 Keymap  F4 Modes  F5 Accessibility  F6 Other Options
```

Figure 2-4. Choosing your country

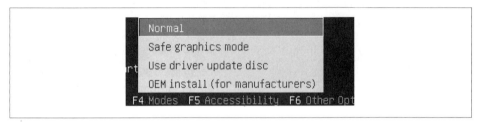

Figure 2-5. Selecting the graphics mode to use

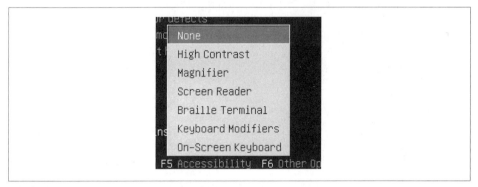

Figure 2-6. The accessibility features available

Figure 2-7. The Other Options menu

You can back out of any screen by pressing the Esc key.

Starting the Live DVD

Select the first choice from the menu, "Try Ubuntu without any change to your computer," to start loading the operating system. When you do this, the screen will show a small Ubuntu logo in white, followed by a large, animated version.

In between you may see some text scroll by, but you can generally ignore this, even if you see what look like warning messages, as they usually are just generated when the operating system checks your PC for certain types of nonessential hardware and does not find them.

After that, a small, animated disc will appear while Ubuntu loads the operating system drivers and other files into memory. Then, you'll see the screen shown in Figure 2-8, which is the Ubuntu desktop.

Figure 2-8. Ubuntu, up and running from the Live DVD

The various parts of the desktop are explained in the following chapters, but you may want to double-click the Examples icon to bring up a folder of examples and *readme* files that are worth browsing through (see Figure 2-9).

For example, the file *Welcome_to_Ubuntu.odt* is a document that you can double-click to view, as shown in Figure 2-10. You can safely open all the files in this folder and its subfolders by double-clicking them. These include documents, spreadsheets, images, music, presentations, and more.

By opening a range of files from the *Examples* folder, you'll also be able to ensure that Ubuntu works properly on your computer, including whether your audio is functioning.

To determine whether your networking is operational, check for an icon in the top panel that looks like two plugs connecting together. If instead you see an icon that looks

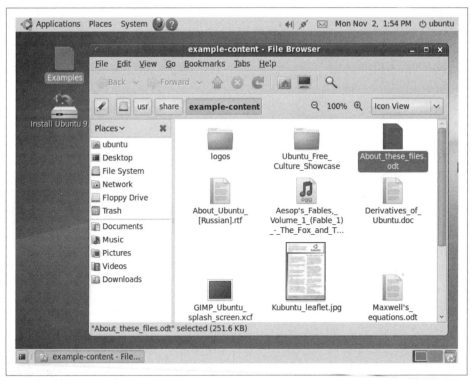

Figure 2-9. Browsing the Examples folder

like the "no signal" symbol on mobile phones (an antenna next to five dots), your networking is not currently working. Try right-clicking that icon and then ensure that the Enable Networking checkbox is checked. If it is and you have an Ethernet cable connected, the symbol showing two plugs should appear. If not, left-click the symbol and select "Auto eth0" to enable your networking card.

If you have a wireless networking card and it isn't shown when you left-click that icon, you will need to establish a wired Ethernet connection in order to search for and locate a suitable driver. Details on how to do this are in Chapter 3.

 A long as you can connect via Ethernet and your mouse, keyboard, monitor, sound card, and other peripherals work using the Live DVD, installing Ubuntu shouldn't present any problems. But as a newcomer to Ubuntu, you may want to install it alongside your computer's original operating system until the time comes that you find you can do everything you need with it, and are prepared to delete your original OS to reclaim the space it uses.

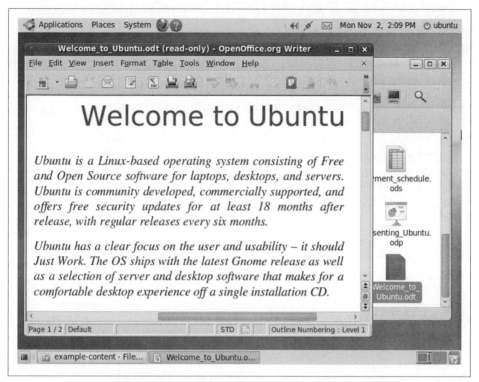

Figure 2-10. Viewing a document in OpenOffice.org

Alternative Editions

The DVD supplied with this book also contains a number of other Ubuntu editions that are saved as ISO files—representations of an entire CD-ROM that can be easily transferred across networks and the Internet. They will take up an entire CD when copied, and can also be opened and treated like optical discs if you have the right software.

 Although the installation procedures for other varieties of Ubuntu are similar, they are not identical to the directions in this chapter for installing the standard desktop edition. In fact, there are so many distros that there's simply not enough room in this book to detail the installation process for each. Therefore, when installing an alternative edition, you should keep your eyes open, carefully read all the prompts and information provided during the process, and use your common sense when making choices and entering information.

The ISO files are located in the *distros* folder and are detailed in Table 2-1.

Table 2-1. The distributions provided on the DVD

Filename	MD5 hash	Distribution
ubuntu-9.10-desktop-i386.iso	8790491bfa9d00f283ed9dd2d77b3906	Ubuntu: the main release that uses the GNOME desktop
kubuntu-9.10-desktop-i386.iso	18ecb71bff567ce7a91443720a86473e	Kubuntu: the version of Ubuntu that uses the KDE desktop in place of GNOME
xubuntu-9.10-desktop-i386.iso	dbcde7bcfcf3d03cedb309e6856d39a4	Xubuntu: the version of Ubuntu that uses the Xfce desktop in place of GNOME
mythbuntu-9.10-desktop-i386.iso	e7ae3d48092c89b31ffbfc4bd7652ca4	Mythbuntu: a version of Ubuntu configured to act as a standalone Myth TV Personal Video Recorder
ubuntu-9.10-netbook-remix-i386.iso	ed6e77587b87fe0d92a2f21855869f00	Ubuntu Netbook Remix: a version of Ubuntu enhanced specifically for running on Netbook PCs

About the MD5 Hashes

In order for you to verify that the ISO files are uncorrupted, Table 2-1 also contains the MD5 hash values for each one. These are unique strings that will be quite different if even one single byte of an ISO file is changed, compared to the original file.

To check the files using Windows, you can download a utility such as *winMD5sum* from *http://www.nullriver.com/index/products/winmd5sum*. After installation, you can compare a file's hash value against the string value for the original ISO shown in Table 2-1. If the values are the same, you can be sure that the file is an exact copy of the original.

On Mac OS X, you can use the Disk Utility program, located in the *Utilities* folder, by dragging an ISO file to Disk Utility's dock icon. Then select the ISO file and go to the Images menu, where you should select Checksum → MD5.

If you wish to install any of these alternative distros, you can do so either by using a virtualization program such as VirtualBox (see the section "Virtual Installation" on page 28) or by burning them to CD or DVD and performing a full installation (see the section "Full Installation" on page 38).

Downloading a Distribution

If you are reading an electronic version of this book, you won't have access to the DVD and will need to download the ISO image file that you want to install. This will also be the case if the edition you need isn't on the DVD.

In either case, Table 2-2 lists the main URLs for downloading the various ISO distributions.

Table 2-2. List of URLs for downloading different editions of Ubuntu

Distribution	URL
Edubuntu	http://www.edubuntu.org/download
Eeebuntu	http://eeebuntu.virginmedia.com
Kubuntu	http://www.kubuntu.org/getkubuntu/download
Mythbuntu	http://www.mythbuntu.org/downloads
Ubuntu	http://www.ubuntu.com/getubuntu/download
Ubuntu MID Edition	http://www.ubuntu.com/products/mobile
Ubuntu Netbook Edition	http://www.ubuntu.com/getubuntu/download-netbook
Ubuntu on ARM	http://www.ubuntu.com/products/whatisubuntu/arm
Ubuntu Server	http://www.ubuntu.com/getubuntu/download-server
Ubuntu Studio	http://ubuntustudio.org/downloads
Xubuntu	http://www.xubuntu.org/get

You can also access all past and present releases (since version 6.06) at *http://releases .ubuntu.com*.

In case you're wondering, the MID edition is a version of Ubuntu specially tailored for use on very small PCs. It uses a different desktop and icon layout that is more suitable for the small screen size. Netbook Remix (renamed to Netbook Edition beginning with version 10.04) is a version created to run well on Netbooks such as the Eee PC range, which also has its own edition. And the ARM version is for use on ARM processor technology. None of these is covered in this book, so you will need to refer to their internal and online documentation. However, there are more details on the other versions in Chapter 15.

If you wish to try out either Kubuntu or Xubuntu in particular, Chapter 15 shows how you can easily add either (or both) onto a standard Ubuntu desktop installation with a few simple commands, which can save you a lot of time compared with installing them separately. You will then be able to choose between the different distributions when you log in.

Once you've downloaded the ISO file you need, you should burn it to a disc (see the following section) or perform a virtual installation from the ISO file (see the section "Virtual Installation" on page 28).

Burning a CD or DVD

If you are using Windows and don't already have a CD/DVD-burning utility, the *distros* folder contains the subfolder *Active ISO Burner*, which contains a program for installing Active ISO Burner, a utility for burning ISO files to CD or DVD. Mac OS X and Ubuntu users have solutions already built in.

 If you intend to use the Wubi installer (see "Installing Ubuntu Under Windows" on page 36), you must burn the ISO file to CD, as the program functions only with CDs and ISO files and doesn't support DVDs.

Using Active ISO Burner for Windows

Locate the *Active ISO Burner* folder within the *distros* folder of the DVD, and then double-click the file within it called *IsoBurner-Setup.exe* to commence installation. After clicking the Next button on the initial welcome screen (see Figure 2-11), you'll be shown the License screen. Click to accept the agreement, and then click Next.

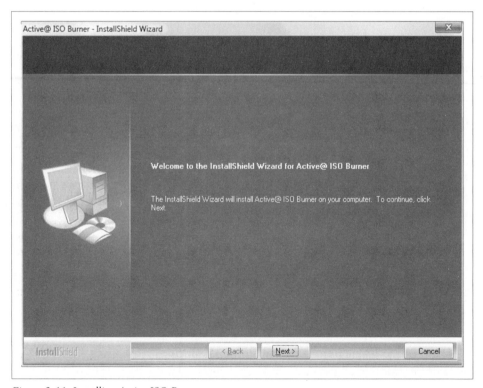

Figure 2-11. Installing Active ISO Burner

On the third screen, you are given a choice between a Complete and Custom setup. I recommend you select Complete and then click Next, and then click Install on the screen that follows. A progress bar will then appear.

After the program completes installation, you can click Finish and the program will launch, presenting a screen such as the one shown in Figure 2-12.

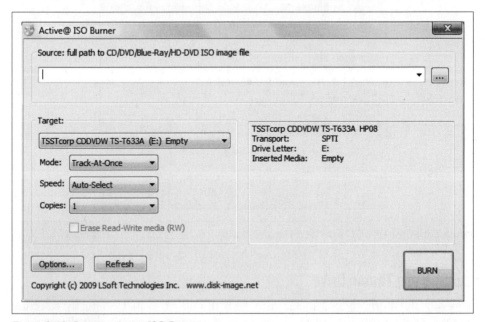

Figure 2-12. Running Active ISO Burner

To burn one of the ISO files to disc, click the Browse button at the top right to select it. Then make sure that the correct optical drive is shown under the Target heading and that you have inserted a blank disc.

You can also choose the speed at which to write within a range between 1 and 24 times (if your drive can handle it). I recommend using Auto-Select to let the program choose an optimum speed.

All that's left is to decide how many copies you need and then to click the BURN button.

Burning an ISO Image Using OS X

To burn an ISO image to disc using OS X, simply select Applications → Utilities → Disk Utility. Then go to Images → Burn and locate the ISO file.

Burning an ISO Image Using Ubuntu

With Ubuntu, burning an ISO file to disc is as easy as right-clicking it, selecting Open with Brasero, inserting a blank disc, and then clicking Burn, as shown in Figure 2-13.

Figure 2-13. Creating a CD from an ISO with Brasero

Burning to a Thumb Drive

You can also burn an ISO image to a USB thumb drive in Ubuntu by selecting System → Administration → USB Startup Disk Creator. Just ensure that the memory capacity of the USB device is equal to or greater than the ISO image size. When the utility's window opens, select the ISO image as the source and the USB device for the destination, and then click Make Startup Disk.

You can then use the USB drive as if it were a Live CD, by inserting it into a target computer that is configured so it is able to boot from such a device. This is the perfect way to try out Ubuntu or install it on a laptop without an optical drive. You can also use the USB drive as a handy, portable Ubuntu environment that lets you boot up on any computer that you are allowed to access.

Virtual Installation

One of the easiest ways to install Ubuntu alongside another operating system, or even another installation of Ubuntu, is to use virtualization software. This is a technology that creates a virtual PC that, to the operating system being installed, looks exactly like a physical PC.

You can create virtual hard drives and CD-ROM drives, as well as specify the amount of RAM to provide, among various other configuration options. There are a number of products that offer this technology. The following sections outline just a few.

Microsoft Virtual PC

I generally don't recommend Microsoft's Virtual PC for virtualizing Ubuntu, as it is supported only on Windows XP Professional and Tablet PC, Windows Vista Business, Enterprise and Ultimate, or Windows 7. Users of operating systems such as XP Home or Vista Home Premium are left out.

That said, I have had a modicum of success with it, even when the installer warns that it may not work, so you might find that it runs adequately for you. However, if you choose to use it, I apologize in advance that you'll have to figure out on your own any Ubuntu customization issues whose configuration lies outside of Ubuntu and must be performed in Virtual PC.

VMware

VMware comprises a set of powerful virtualization systems that will run on Linux and Max OS X, as well as most Windows platforms. It's a proprietary system, but one version (VMware Player) is available for download free of charge. It's quite popular and meets many people's needs. Its cousin, VMware Workstation, which is not free, offers even more.

Please refer to the documentation supplied with the VMware software if you are using it to run Ubuntu and need to perform any customizations that cannot be made within Ubuntu itself. The only task most people need to do with VMware desktop virtualization is find the version of Ubuntu (or other operating systems) appropriate for them and install it. VMware offers a number of preconfigured "appliances" that you can download.

Sun VirtualBox

This is far and away my favorite virtualization system. It's open source, is available for Windows, OS X, Ubuntu, and Solaris, and is the most robust yet easy to use system I have seen. Even better, it's free of charge for personal and academic use.

There are two ways you can use VirtualBox to install or run a Live CD or DVD: insert a physical disc into the drive, or provide an ISO image file.

So let's look at using the DVD supplied with this book from within VirtualBox. Once you've seen how it works, you'll be able to do the same with any other Ubuntu edition.

Getting started

The first thing to do is visit *http://www.virtualbox.org* and download the program using the Downloads link, located in the lefthand panel of the web page. Then, choose the version to download from the choices of Windows, Intel Macs, Linux, or Solaris. For example, as I write this, the Windows version is 3.1.4 and is 71 MB in size.

Once you have downloaded the file, you should run it to bring up the installer, as shown in Figure 2-14.

Figure 2-14. Installing VirtualBox

Click Next, and then agree to the license before clicking Next again. After that you can choose the support and networking features you want. If in doubt, just click Next to continue using the defaults. Then click Next one more time, followed by clicking Yes and then Install to start the installation.

A window with a progress bar will appear to keep you up-to-date on the installation. When finished, click the Finish button. After that, the program will run, presenting the window shown in Figure 2-15.

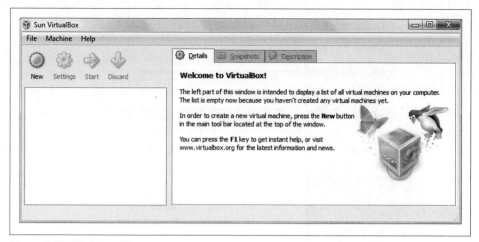

Figure 2-15. The VirtualBox main screen

When you run VirtualBox, a registration window may also pop up asking you to create and/or enter a Sun account, but sometimes the Sun registration server doesn't appear to work correctly. Don't worry if you can't create a new Sun account when requested. Just close the registration window, and you can proceed with using VirtualBox without registering.

Creating a virtual machine

You are now ready to create a virtual machine, so click the New icon at the top left. Then, when the New Virtual Machine Wizard window opens, click Next to bring up the window shown in Figure 2-16.

For name, enter the name of the operating system, such as Ubuntu 9.10, and then select Linux for the operating system. The version of Linux will then default to Ubuntu, which is what you want, so click Next to get to the Memory screen (see Figure 2-17).

I recommend you accept the default of 384 MB shown here. However, if you have plenty of memory (say, 2 GB or more), you could increase that to 1000 MB or thereabouts. Then click Next to move on to the hard disk screen shown in Figure 2-18.

Ensure that "Boot Hard Disk" and "Create new hard disk" are both checked, and then click Next, then Next again on the following screen, to get to the Hard Disk Storage Type screen (see Figure 2-19).

Figure 2-16. Creating a virtual machine

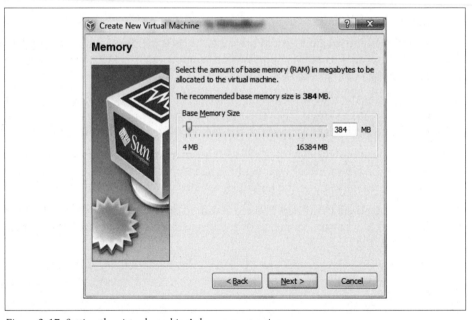

Figure 2-17. Setting the virtual machine's base memory size

Figure 2-18. Creating a virtual hard disk

Figure 2-19. Selecting Dynamically expanding storage

Here, I recommended you select the "Dynamically expanding storage" option, and then click Next. The reason for this is that you don't actually need to create a large hard disk in VirtualBox, because it has the ability to increase a hard disk's size as necessary. The only downside to this is that the upper limit to how large it can grow is your physical hard disk's size. If you think you will be using a lot of disk space in your virtual machine and this may impinge on the space you need for your original operating system, you may wish to choose "Fixed-size storage" instead. This will ensure that the virtual hard disk will never grow any larger than a set size.

On the next screen (see Figure 2-20), you get to choose the virtual hard disk's starting size (or exact size if you chose "Fixed-size storage").

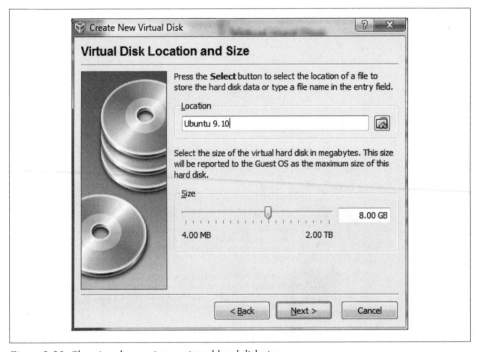

Figure 2-20. Choosing the maximum virtual hard disk size

Here, you can also choose the location and filename for this disc, which by default will have the same name as the virtual machine. Click Next when you are done, and then click Finish to complete the creation of the virtual hard disk. If you enter a location and filename that is already in use, you will receive an error message and should enter a different one instead.

Otherwise, click the Finish button that will be displayed on the summary screen that appears. Your virtual machine will now be created and ready to use (but powered off), as shown in Figure 2-21.

Figure 2-21. The virtual machine Ubuntu 9.10 is now created

Running a virtual machine

To start up your new virtual machine, double-click its icon in the lefthand pane. The first time you do this, it will call up the First Run Wizard (see Figure 2-22).

Click the Next button to start the wizard and bring up the screen shown in Figure 2-23, where you have the opportunity to choose to install an operating system on the virtual machine from either the optical drive or an ISO file.

If you click Next at this point (while Host Drive is selected), the CD or DVD in the drive will be used as the installation media.

Alternatively, you can choose an ISO file to boot from by selecting the Image File option. You must then click the Browse button, locate the required file, and click the Add button at the top left of the next screen (see Figure 2-24).

Here, you can see I have added the image file *ubuntu-9.10-desktop-i386.iso*. Once you have added an ISO file, click the Select button to return to the previous media selection screen, and then click Next, followed by Finish to commence the installation process.

The familiar Ubuntu startup screen shown earlier in Figure 2-1 will then be displayed, waiting for you to select a language.

Figure 2-22. The First Run Wizard

Figure 2-23. Selecting the installation media

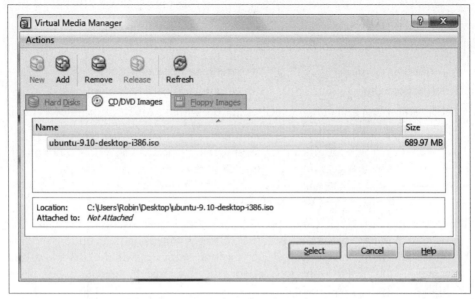

Figure 2-24. Adding a disc ISO image

From here onward, you can consider the new "machine" to be a complete PC in its own right, and you can either run the ISO or disc in Live mode or go right ahead and install the operating system. I recommend the latter because you can then power up the virtual machine any time you like and start up where you left off work before.

There's more information on using VirtualBox in Chapter 3.

 You can use your keyboard and mouse in the VirtualBox window, but often the guest machine will capture the mouse and you may have to press the righthand Ctrl key to release it.

Other Virtualizers

Of course, there are other virtualizers available, such as the free Bochs and QEMU systems. If one of these is your preferred choice, go ahead and use it; running software that you already know is usually preferable when you have a lot of new things to learn. However, you may need to refer to the supplied documentation or use a search engine if you encounter any difficulties.

Full Installation

There are three main types of full installation you can make (other than via a virtualizer):

1. As the sole operating system, taking over all hard disk partitions
2. As part of a dual- or multi-boot setup with its own hard disk partition
3. Using the Wubi program to run Ubuntu from within a Microsoft Windows virtual disk, without any hard disk repartitioning

The most efficient way to run Ubuntu together with Windows is option 2. But installation can take a very long time to complete because the Ubuntu installer needs to repartition the hard disk to make room for the new operating system, potentially moving hundreds of gigabytes of data around.

Wubi offers the fastest installation possible, because Ubuntu installs in just a few files within your Windows filesystem. Wubi also changes your boot menu options, adding Ubuntu as an alternative operating system that you can select with the cursor keys and Enter at boot time, just as with a full dual- or multi-boot install. Therefore, I will cover Wubi first.

Installing Ubuntu Under Windows

Wubi is a powerful program that creates a virtual hard disk under Windows and runs Ubuntu from there as part of a dual- or multi-boot operating system.

Performing the installation

To perform the installation, as it will not run directly from the DVD, drag and drop the following two files from the *distros* folder of the DVD onto your Windows desktop:

- *wubi.exe*
- *ubuntu-9.10-desktop-i386.iso*

Once they are on your desktop, remove the DVD from the drive (this is important; if you leave the disc in the drive, Wubi will not run correctly), and double-click *wubi.exe* to commence installation.

Important considerations

There are a number of things to consider when using Wubi, as follows:

- There appears to be a bug in the Wubi program, which can occur after a disc is inserted and then removed (such as when copying the preceding files). Sometimes the program will ask you to reinsert the disc in the drive because it thinks it needs access to it. In fact, Wubi doesn't, and it must *not* gain access, so don't reinsert the disc, or the program will not work correctly. If this happens to you, the only way to get a functioning installation is to click the Continue button several times until the program starts. You may also have to do this during the installation process if the disc is again requested.

- If you burn the ISO file to CD (or otherwise have access to an Ubuntu CD), you can insert it into a Windows CD-ROM drive and Wubi will offer the option to install Ubuntu inside Windows without you having to copy an ISO file to your computer—but this only works with CDs, not DVDs.

- If you have Windows configured so that it doesn't display file extensions, you will see only the filenames *wubi* and *ubuntu-9.10-desktop-i386*, without the *.exe* and *.iso* extensions. This is normal, and you can still drag and drop the icons to make copies and double-click the Wubi program icon to run it (after removing the disc from the drive).

- If you wish, you can copy a different ISO file to the desktop in place of the standard Ubuntu one. You can then select that edition from Wubi's menu to have it installed instead of regular Ubuntu.

Once the program is running, the next screen you'll see will be the one shown in Figure 2-25.

Figure 2-25. The Wubi installation screen

From this screen, you can choose the drive to which Ubuntu should be installed, the language to use, the size of virtual hard disk to create, and your Ubuntu username and password.

I recommend you keep the installation size large enough to make it unlikely for you to run out of room. The default is usually 17 GB, but if you have a 100 or more gigabytes of free space, you may wish to change this to the maximum of 30 GB.

It is important to choose both a username and a password, even though Wubi will let you continue without entering a password, because I have encountered a number of difficulties using Ubuntu/Wubi without one. To ensure you enter it correctly, you must type in the password twice.

If your computer will contain private information, I suggest you choose a difficult-to-guess password, possibly consisting of both uppercase and lowercase letters as well as numerals and punctuation. But make sure that you can remember whatever password you choose. I discuss the creation of good passwords in Chapter 9.

The installation process will then begin, continuously showing you how far the installation has progressed. Typically, for any fairly recent PC, the initial installation should take less than 10 minutes (see Figure 2-26).

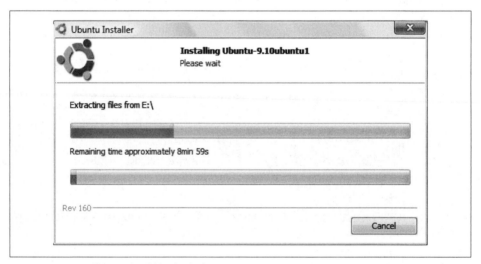

Figure 2-26. Installation should be fairly fast

If Wubi detects any problems with the disc, it may try to download the ISO over the Internet. If this happens, it is usually because the ISO you copied to the desktop is corrupted. To prevent this from happening, you can first check the MD5 hash for a file, as described in the section "About the MD5 Hashes" on page 24, to ensure that it's a true copy of the original.

When installation is complete, you will see the window shown in Figure 2-27. If you are ready to start using Ubuntu now, select "Reboot now." Otherwise, select "I want to manually reboot later" if you have work that needs saving. Either way, click Finish to end the installation.

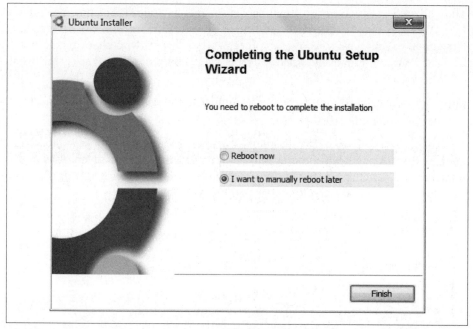

Figure 2-27. Ubuntu has been installed and just awaits a reboot

Whenever you reboot from now onward, Ubuntu will be displayed as a selectable operating system alongside your usual Windows OS. The first time you start Ubuntu, it will spend a few minutes performing some additional installation functions and will then reboot when it has finished.

If you wish, the next time you load Windows you can delete the two files that you copied to your Windows desktop.

You are now ready to move on to Chapter 3 to continue your exploration of Ubuntu, although I recommend you complete this chapter first, since there's a lot of useful information in the following sections.

 In the same way that you cannot install Wubi using the DVD supplied with this book, it also will not work if you burn an ISO to DVD. This is because Wubi currently supports only ISO files and CDs, not DVDs.

Installing Ubuntu As a Standalone OS

Wubi is great for getting Ubuntu installed quickly, but the overhead it imposes for managing the virtual hard disk causes a slight performance hit.

To create a native Ubuntu installation that uses your hard disk directly, and is therefore as fast as it can be, you will need to perform some partitioning of your hard disk during the installation process (explained a little further on).

There are two ways you can go about natively installing Ubuntu. The first is to run the Live DVD and then double-click the Install Ubuntu 9.10 icon on the desktop (see Figure 2-8) to start a six-screen setup process, which begins with choosing the installation language. Alternatively, when you reboot your computer, simply select the Install Ubuntu option.

Either way, the installation screens will be similar to those starting at Figure 2-28.

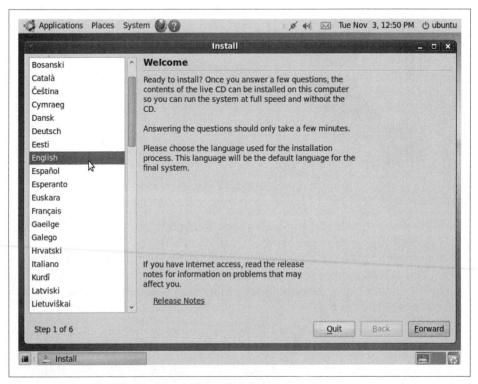

Figure 2-28. Installing Ubuntu from the Live DVD desktop

Don't concern yourself with keyboard layouts or countries at this point; just choose the language you wish to use for the installation process. You will be given other options to customize your installation later. Once you have selected your language, click the Forward button to move on to the location screen, shown in Figure 2-29.

Here, you can either click the part of the map where you are or use the drop-down inputs to select your region and zone. When done, click the Forward button to move on to the keyboard selection screen (see Figure 2-30).

Normally you can just click Forward at this point, but if your keyboard layout is different from the one shown, click "Choose your own" and select the right keyboard. You can test your selection by typing text into the white box. When you click Forward, you'll be taken to the disk-partitioning screen.

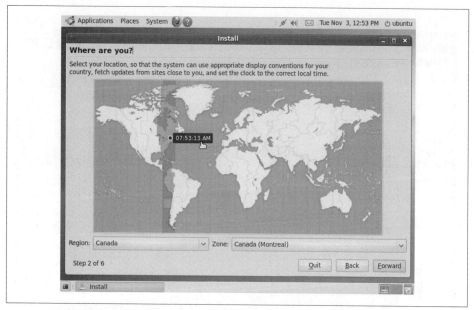

Figure 2-29. Selecting your location

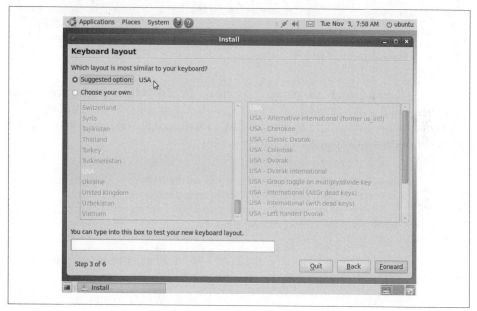

Figure 2-30. Choosing a keyboard type

If your computer doesn't already have an operating system, the partitioning screen will look like Figure 2-31, in which case, you will most likely wish to select the "Erase and use the Entire disk" option to turn your entire hard disk over to Ubuntu.

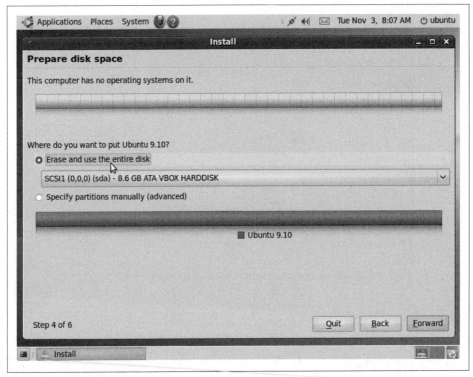

Figure 2-31. The disk partition screen

However, if there is already an operating system on the disk (which, depending on your computer, could be Windows, OS X, or even another installation of Ubuntu), as shown in Figure 2-32, you now have to decide whether to install the operating systems side by side or overwrite the original operating system.

 Be careful here. If you choose "Erase and use the entire disk," it will not be retrievable. So I recommend that you make doubly sure that you have working backups of all programs and data you need from the original operating system before removing it.

If you choose the "Erase and use the entire disk" option, all you need to do now is press Forward for the disk partitioner to do its work.

But if you have decided to add Ubuntu alongside your previous operating system (by selecting "Install them side by side, choosing between them each startup"), you can now slide the partition division icon left or right along the bottom bar. As you move it to the left, you will reduce the space used by the original operating system, leaving more space available for the new one. Conversely, by moving the division to the right, you will decrease the size of the new OS and allocate more space to the original one.

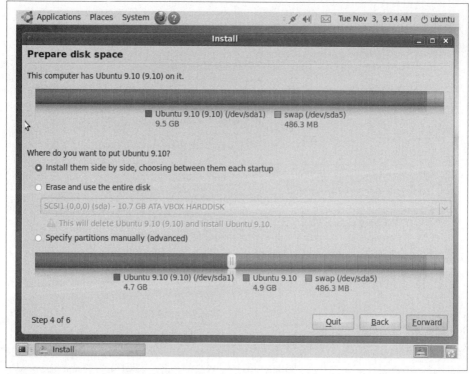

Figure 2-32. Disk partitioning with a preexisting operating system

Either way, you will divide up the available space and share it between the two operating systems.

 If you are an advanced Linux user, you can also choose to manually specify the partitions. However, I strongly recommend that newcomers bypass that option.

Sharing the hard disk

If you decide to install Ubuntu alongside an existing operating system, after choosing the sizes that each will have, click Forward. The dialog in Figure 2-33 will display to remind you that what you plan to do is irrevocable. It will also tell you that the resizing operation might take a long time.

When you click Continue, one or more windows will pop up explaining what's going on until the installation process eventually gets to the screen shown later in Figure 2-34.

Figure 2-33. This dialog reminds you that there's no going back

 Depending on where data is stored on the hard disk, once the resizing process starts, you should be prepared to leave the computer to the repartitioning and installation for a couple of hours or more, although it usually takes a lot less time than that. Compared to how long it can take to install some major operating systems, this is actually not that bad.

Using the entire hard disk

If you choose to have the Ubuntu installation take up the entire hard disk, partitioning will be very quick because there will be no data to move about during a resize operation. So, a few seconds after you click the Forward button, the user information screen should be displayed.

Entering your user details

The next screen to be displayed asks you to enter your user details, such as your name, username, password, and computer name (see Figure 2-34).

Here, you should enter your name, which could be your full name, just your first or last name, or whatever you prefer. You can use uppercase characters if you like. Your username will then be created for you based on the name you give, but it will be set to all lowercase.

You can change the username if you wish, as long as you keep it to lowercase letters and numbers. However, I don't recommend doing so, because it could then be confusing to tell which user has what username, especially on a system with several users.

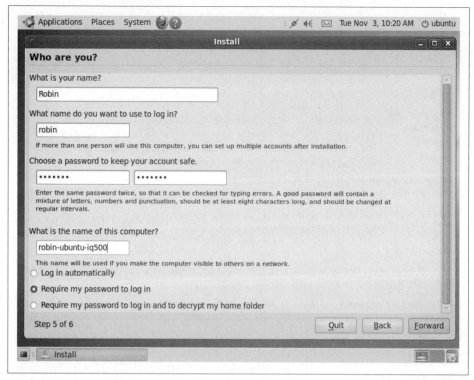

Figure 2-34. The user details installation screen

You must then choose a password for your computer (without setting a password, you will not be able to progress to the next screen). If you will have sensitive data in your account, I recommend that you create a strong password comprising both uppercase and lowercase letters, as well as numbers and punctuation; just make sure you can remember it. You will have to type the password in twice to ensure you didn't make a typo.

If you choose a password that Ubuntu considers weak, it will tell you so and offer to let you choose a different one, or you can confirm that you do want the one you chose.

For computer names, I generally choose to combine the username, the operating system name, and the computer model. That way, it's easy to see exactly which computer is what over a network, and it's especially useful when building dual- and multi-boot systems with different operating systems. In this case, I ended up with a computer name of *robin-ubuntu-iq500* for the installation, although you can enter any name you like here.

Finally, on this screen, you can decide whether to have Ubuntu log you in automatically. If you won't have any sensitive data on the computer and are not concerned about other people using it, then go ahead.

But generally I would recommend you choose the second option to require a password. If someone else wants to use the computer, you can simply create a new account. That way you never have to think about it again. To be ultra secure, you can require a password to be used both for logging in and to decrypt the contents of your home folder.

 If you choose the option to have your home folder encrypted, the first time you run Ubuntu after installation a special password will be generated, and you will need to keep a note of it should you ever need to manually recover the folder. You can also run the command `ecryptfs-unwrap-passphrase` from the Terminal at any time to retrieve this passphrase if you forget it.

Once you have filled in all the details, click the Forward button to continue to the final summary screen, which will look like Figure 2-35.

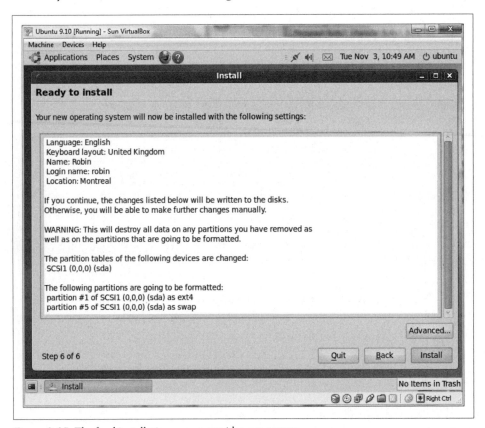

Figure 2-35. The final installation screen provides a summary

If everything looks correct, click the Install button to commence the installation process, which should proceed uninterrupted—so now's the time to go and make a pot of coffee.

 Don't worry if the installation appears to hang at various points during the process. It's almost certainly still installing—even when you can't see anything. If you have a hard disk indicator light, you can check that it is flickering, or just place your ear to the PC and listen for the clicking of the disk being accessed to assure yourself that your computer hasn't hung.

Once installation is complete, a window will pop up asking you to click the Restart Now button. If you ran the installer from the Live DVD, you'll also see a Continue Testing button (see Figure 2-36). So go ahead, remove the DVD from the drive, and prepare to enjoy your new operating system by clicking Restart Now.

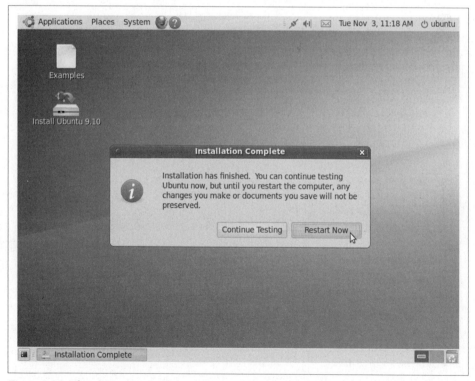

Figure 2-36. Ubuntu is now installed

Sometimes the eject button on an optical disc drive fails to work with Ubuntu. If that happens, you can usually eject a disc by calling up a Terminal window (select Applications → Accessories → Terminal). Then type eject at the prompt and press Return.

After rebooting

If you have installed Ubuntu as the computer's only operating system, rebooting will display a couple of lines of text that will quickly disappear, to be replaced with the official Ubuntu logo, followed by the Ubuntu login screen.

Dual- and multi-boot setups

On dual- or multi-boot computers, you will be offered a choice each time your computer boots up. This will vary according to the operating systems installed, but will look something like Figure 2-37.

```
              GNU GRUB  version 1.97~beta4

Ubuntu, Linux 2.6.31-14-generic
Ubuntu, Linux 2.6.31-14-generic (recovery mode)
Memory test (memtest86+)
Memory test (memtest86+, serial console 115200)
Ubuntu, Linux 2.6.31-14-generic (on /dev/sda1)
Ubuntu, Linux 2.6.31-14-generic (recovery mode) (on /dev/sda1)




    Use the ↑ and ↓ keys to select which entry is highlighted.
    Press enter to boot the selected OS, 'e' to edit the
    commands before booting or 'c' for a command-line.
```

Figure 2-37. Selecting an operating system to start up

In this case, there are two installations of Ubuntu. The first entry shown is one of them, and the fifth entry is the other.

Dual- and multi-boot setups can also include many more operating systems, which could include Windows and OS X, as well as the *recovery mode* and *memtest86+* options shown in the screen grab.

Recovery mode

The recovery mode entries boot the associated Ubuntu operating system into a command mode from which you can perform various repair functions that are quite technical and therefore beyond the scope of this book.

Instead, I recommend you keep your Ubuntu Live DVD on hand so that you can use it to recover from various problems, using the information supplied on the Ubuntu website: *https://help.ubuntu.com/community/LiveCdRecovery*.

If all else fails and nobody at the Ubuntu forums has been able to provide a solution to fixing a broken installation, you can always reinstall Ubuntu from this DVD. You do keep regular backups of important files, don't you?

Memory testing

The memtest86+ option is very useful when you suspect you may have a problem with your computer's system memory. When run, it performs a sequence of stringent tests, reporting any errors it finds (see Figure 2-38).

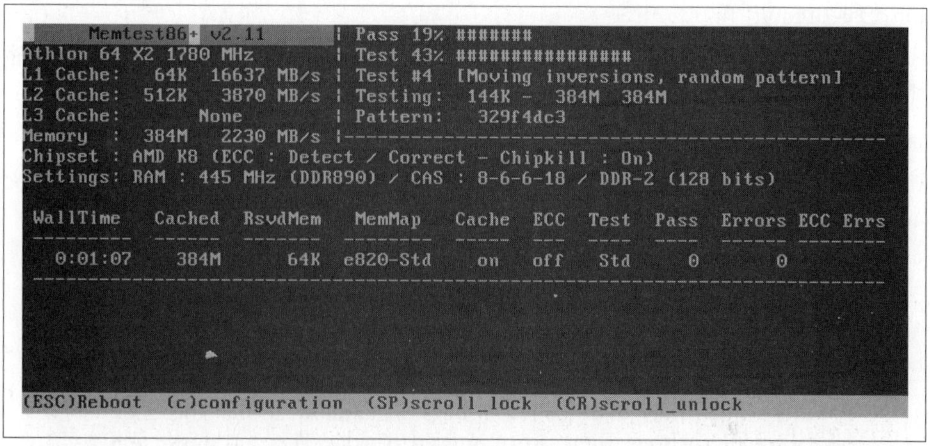

Figure 2-38. Testing the computer's system memory

The tests take a few minutes to run, but you can keep track of how far the program has progressed by watching the Pass and Test lines at the top of the screen. The program will continue running these tests indefinitely, but once one complete pass has been made, the program will either display one or more error messages or tell you that there are no errors.

To exit at any time and reboot back to the operating system selection menu, press the Esc key.

What's New in 10.04

One of the major goals of Ubuntu 10.04 was to substantially decrease the time it takes to boot into the operating system to under 10 seconds. This book went to test during the beta tests, and even by then boot times on my test machines had already been reduced from between 30 to 60 (or more) seconds to between 10 and 20 seconds, with a couple of the machines usually arriving at the desktop within 12 seconds. This is a major breakthrough and is way faster than any other operating systems, by a huge margin. If you are interested in keeping track of your boot times and would like to compare the results before and after upgrading to 10.04, *https://wiki.ubuntu.com/Boot Charting* has advice on installing a simple program to keep a record of your reboot times, and display them using charts.

Upgrading to New Releases

Ubuntu 9.10 was the most current release when this book went to print, but due to the six-month upgrade cycle, Ubuntu 10.04 was already on the horizon and 10.10 was being planned. With such a release cycle, it's important that you know how you can upgrade Ubuntu to take advantage of new and better features, and to keep your computer secure.

Before upgrading, though, it is always a good idea to acquaint yourself with everything that's new in the upgrade by visiting the following URL:

> *http://www.ubuntu.com/getubuntu/releasenotes*

Click the More » link next to the release for full details. That way there shouldn't be any major surprises.

 By participating in the Alpha and Beta tests, I was able to include in this book the new features and improvements the Ubuntu 10.04 release offers. In fact, the Beta is so good that we considered putting a copy on the companion DVD. However, in the end we agreed that beta tests are just that: tests, and unforeseen bugs might show up that this book couldn't help you with—so we dropped that idea. Therefore this section shows you how to upgrade over the Internet to the fully tested, final release of Ubuntu 10.04. The same procedure will let you upgrade to all other future versions, too.

Installing from CD

There are two ways that you can upgrade your installation of Ubuntu. First, you can download the latest ISO file, burn it to CD, and perform a fresh installation. The download locations you need are listed in the section "Downloading a Distribution" on page 24. Immediately following that, the section "Burning a CD or DVD" on page 26 provides all the information you need to burn the ISO to disc.

This method is probably your best choice when you want to set up new Ubuntu installations or provide copies of the latest release to friends and colleagues, or if you have a version of Ubuntu more than one release behind the current release.

However, there's a much easier way to upgrade an existing installation, as explained in the following section.

Upgrading an Existing Installation

Instead of upgrading from disc, you can upgrade Ubuntu directly from the desktop. But before you start, it's important to ensure that you have applied all the latest updates. To do this, select System → Administration → Update Manager to bring up a window like the one shown in Figure 2-39.

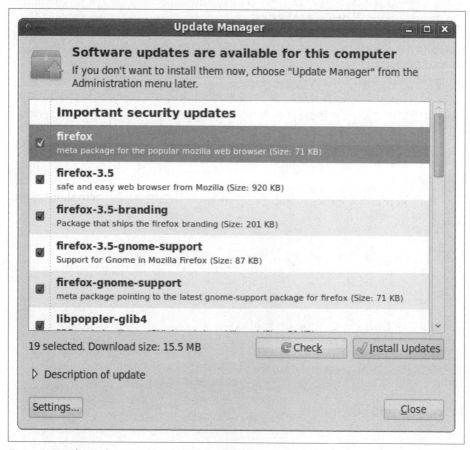

Figure 2-39. The Update Manager

The contents of this window will vary. You may have different upgrades or no upgrades shown, depending on how up-to-date your installation is. But to make absolutely sure that your computer is aware of all the latest available updates, you should click the Check button.

After downloading all the latest information, you may see the same or different updates in the window. If any updates are displayed, click the Install Updates button to install them. If you are asked for your password at any point, you should enter it. You may also be prompted to restart your computer.

On the other hand if, after clicking Check, there are still no new updates, the Install Updates button will be grayed out, indicating that the release of Ubuntu installed is already fully up-to-date.

Upgrade availability

When a new distribution is available (which usually happens twice a year, generally in April and October), the top of the Update Manager screen will show the text "New Distribution release '*xx.xx*' is available," where *xx.xx* will be the release number, as shown in Figure 2-40. If there is no release newer than your current version, this screen will not be shown.

Figure 2-40. A new distribution is available

To upgrade to the new distribution, click the Upgrade button and follow the simple instructions on the screen, entering your password if requested and rebooting when necessary.

If your current release is more than one version older than the latest one, you will need to keep repeating the preceding process to upgrade through all the intermediate releases in turn, until you get to the latest one. When no newer release is available, you have finished.

Skipping versions

If your installed release is more than one behind the latest and you wish to avoid upgrading through a number of intermediate versions, you will need to download the ISO image file of the latest version, burn it to disc, and perform a full installation from it. Make sure all your data is fully backed up first, though, because a full installation creates a brand new environment, either replacing your original one or creating a new one alongside it (depending on the option you choose). If you decide to overwrite your current installation, you'll need to back up and restore all your data and configuration options.

What's New in 10.04

Ubuntu 10.04 uses new programs to improve the bootup experience, removing unwanted messages and replacing them with clean graphical animations. In particular the version of GRUB (Grand Unified Bootloader) that is used is now version 2 which, by default, does not display a screen of options. Therefore when you want to choose whether to boot directly into Ubuntu, or into a repair mode, or previous kernel and so on, you need to hold down the Shift key while booting. This causes GRUB 2 to display the standard menu and wait for a key press.

Summary

Ubuntu is generally very fast to install, unless you make it part of a dual- or multi-boot setup and therefore have to resize partitions. And even then it's a lot quicker to install Ubuntu than some other major operating systems.

So, by the time you finish this chapter, you should have Ubuntu installed on your computer in one form or another: alongside another operating system, within a virtualizing application, or as your computer's only operating system.

Whichever type of installation you have, the next chapter will show you how to fully configure it to your requirements, and how to get it working with the peripherals you have connected to your computer, such as printers, webcams, and the like.

CHAPTER 3

Configuring

Before exploring Ubuntu in depth in Chapter 4, I think it's best to first ensure that your Ubuntu setup is properly installed and configured to your requirements.

Luckily, this is very easy to do due to the huge amount of work Ubuntu's developers have put in. In fact, as a result of the open source approach in which users write the features they want themselves, some drivers are faster and more feature-packed than their Windows equivalents. They also tend to be simpler to manage because of the user feedback built into the development process.

So whatever keyboard, mouse, graphics card, monitor, and network card you have, there is almost certainly already a Linux driver for it, and this chapter will show you how to install it, if it hasn't been already. I also think that by reading this chapter you'll learn about using the Ubuntu desktop by osmosis, and will pick up how things work while learning how to perform useful and essential configurations of your new installation.

By the way, Ubuntu supports multiple users, so by default the changes you make to preferences will apply only to you.

Keyboard

Once you've installed Ubuntu following the advice in Chapter 2—whether you are running it within Windows, as part of a dual-boot system, or standalone—you can now further tweak your setup to match your keyboard, mouse, and other peripherals.

Generally, the way to reconfigure your environment using Ubuntu's GNOME desktop is to select the System menu at the top left of your screen, followed by Preferences, and then choose one of the options in that submenu. Figure 3-1 shows the Keyboard Preferences being selected in this manner. From now on, I'll describe a sequence of menu selections in the style System → Preferences → Keyboard.

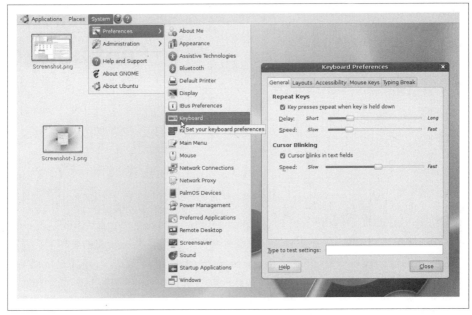

Figure 3-1. Using the GNOME desktop to call up the System menu

The Keyboard Preferences dialog that comes up looks similar to Figure 3-2. Five tabs across the top of the window represent the main options. The following subsections describe what each tab offers.

Ubuntu is ever evolving, and during the life of this book there may be a number of new releases, so some options may be labeled differently or even move from one menu or screen to another. If you find that an option you want is not in the location that I give in this book, just browse the menus and look for other possible candidates. It's extremely unlikely that the Ubuntu developers would remove any of the essential options I describe in this book, but they could decide to put it under a different menu or dialog box.

General

As can be seen in Figure 3-2, the General tab allows you to change the delay before a key repeats and the speed of repeating using the Repeat Keys section. If you don't wish to allow keys to repeat, you should uncheck the box. Otherwise, move the two sliders left and right, and then enter text in the "Type to test settings" box to try out the settings.

You can also choose whether or not the cursor should blink when in a text field and, if so, the speed at which it should blink. Again, you can test the result in the input box at the bottom of the window.

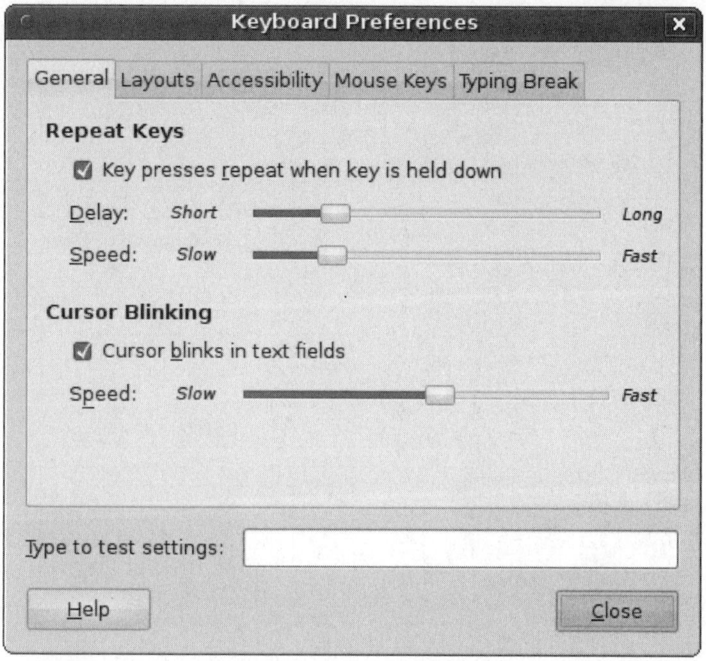

Figure 3-2. The Keyboard Preferences window

If you need assistance at any time, you can click the Help button. When you are finished setting the current options, don't click the Close button yet, as there are more settings to look at first.

Layouts

During installation of the version of Ubuntu used for these screen grabs, I chose to use a UK keyboard by default, as can be seen in Figure 3-3 (although if you are using Ubuntu 10.04 or higher, the screen layout will be slightly different).

But let's assume that you don't have the correct settings here and need to change them. First of all, to ensure that you have the correct keyboard installed, click the button to the right of "Keyboard model." This opens up a new window in which you can see a range of keyboard models from a wide variety of vendors, as Figure 3-4 shows.

If in doubt, or if you can't find your keyboard manufacturer listed, you should choose Generic for the vendor and then select the model most similar to yours. Click OK when you are done.

If you use more than one keyboard, you can check the "Separate layout for each window" box to match different keyboards to different windows.

Figure 3-3. The Layouts tab showing a UK keyboard

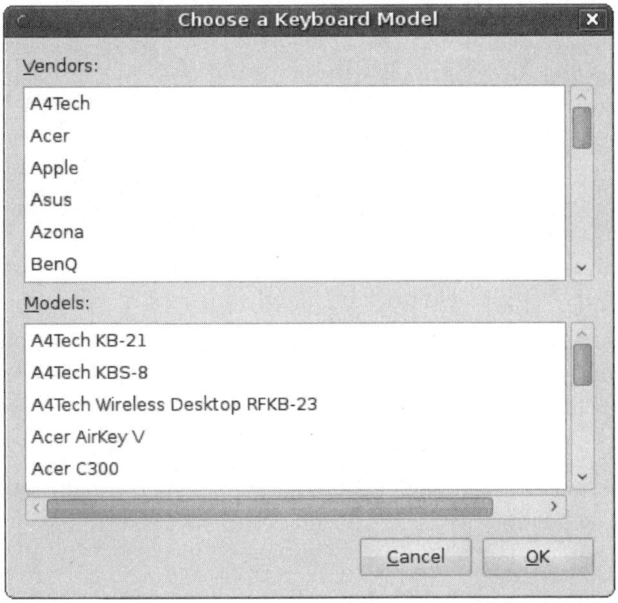

Figure 3-4. Choosing your keyboard from the supplied list

If you need to change the country layout of your keyboard, the best way is to click the Add button to create a new one. This will bring up a new window, such as the one in Figure 3-5, in which the full layout is displayed, making it very easy to select the one that matches your keyboard.

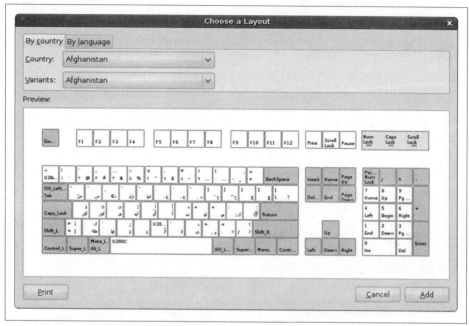

Figure 3-5. You can choose the exact layout to match your keyboard

So, for example, to choose a U.S. keyboard layout, you could click the "By country" tab, then select United States for the country, and then USA for the variant from the options provided. Alternatively, you can click the "By language" tab, then select English, followed by USA for the variant, or, for example, Spanish; Castilian followed by Latin American, and so on.

When you have the right keyboard layout selected, click the Add button and you will see it listed in the Layout section. At this point, if you want to remove a keyboard, you can now highlight it and click the Remove button.

Incidentally, on Ubuntu 9.10, once you have more than one layout installed, if you check the "Separate layout for each window" box, the Layout section will show a radio button next to each layout, which you can use to choose one of the layouts as the default.

If you decide you don't want to keep the changes you have made, you can always click the Reset to Defaults button, or you can make your changes apply to all users on your system by clicking on the Apply System-Wide button.

You can also further customize your layout by clicking the Layout Options button to bring up the window shown in Figure 3-6. Here, you have all manner of options relating to the handling of Esperanto, the Euro monetary sign, the Caps Lock and Ctrl keys, the numeric keypad, and much more. Just click on a heading to open up its available options.

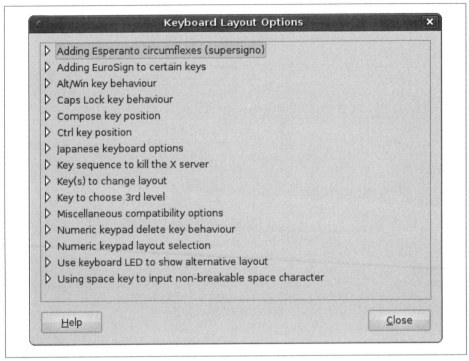

Figure 3-6. The Keyboard Layout Options dialog allows configuring down to the minutest detail

Accessibility

As you would expect from a good operating system, Ubuntu offers some useful accessibility features under the Accessibility tab (see Figure 3-7). The options available include Sticky Keys, which lets you press Ctrl and Shift keys before the key being controlled instead of simultaneously; Slow Keys, which ignores brief key presses; and Bounce Keys, which ignores fast duplicate key presses. These are all enabled or disabled by checking or unchecking the associated boxes.

You can also choose to provide audio and visual feedback for these actions by clicking on the Audio Feedback button, which brings up the window in Figure 3-8. Just check or uncheck the boxes provided to enable or disable beeps for the actions shown, as well as to flash the title bar or screen if needed.

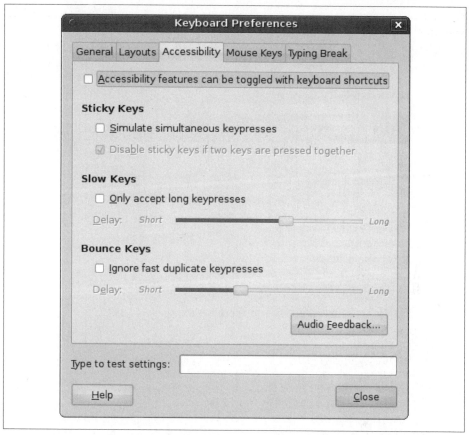

Figure 3-7. The Accessibility tab is invaluable for people with impaired keyboard ability

Mouse Keys

Sometimes it can be useful to be able to control the mouse using the keyboard. You can do just that with the Mouse Keys tab, shown in Figure 3-9.

Click the checkbox to activate the feature, and you can then choose your desired acceleration, speed, and delay for the simulated mouse by moving the sliders left and right. You can test the settings by pressing the keypad arrow keys.

Typing Break

Are you or someone else who uses your computer a workaholic, or someone susceptible to carpal tunnel or tendinitis problems, who must be forced to take a break? If so, Ubuntu comes to the rescue with the Typing Break tab (see Figure 3-10).

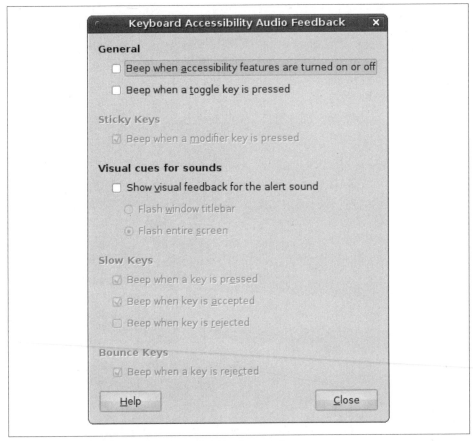

Figure 3-8. Audio and visual alerts are available if required

Enable the feature by clicking in the checkbox. Then you can choose the lengths of the work and break periods, and whether to allow the user to postpone breaks should something important come up.

This facility is smart about timings. If you stop using the keyboard and mouse for any period equal to or longer than the break interval, you'll get a new, full work interval when you next use the computer again.

Assuming you have now been through all the tabs and set up all the keyboard options the way you want them, you can click the Close button to close the window.

Keyboard Shortcuts

While you're at it, now is a good time to set up or edit your keyboard shortcuts. To do this, select System → Preferences → Keyboard Shortcuts, and the window in Figure 3-11 will appear.

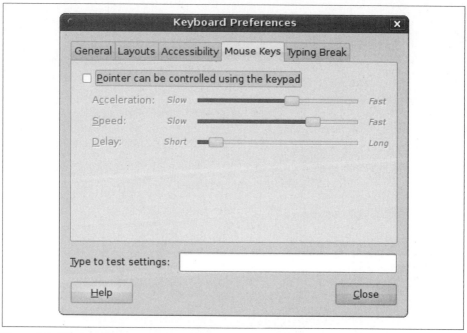

Figure 3-9. Ubuntu allows you to control the mouse with the keyboard

To change the shortcut for a specified action, select it with the mouse and then press the key (or combination of keys) you want to initiate that action. For example, if you would like Ctrl-PgUp to increase the volume, click on "Volume up" and then hold down the Ctrl key and press the PgUp key.

If you have one of those fancy advanced keyboards that has special keys for actions such as volume control, web surfing, or fetching email, and Ubuntu doesn't appear to recognize them, you can attach them in the same way by clicking on an action and pressing the associated key.

You can also add custom shortcuts for actions that aren't listed by clicking the Add button. But be aware that you'll need to enter details about the program to call up by entering a Linux (shell) command, so it's best to leave such advanced configuration until you've mastered how to use these commands (see Chapter 7).

When you have finished with the shortcuts, click the Close button.

Mouse

Configuring your mouse is a little easier than the keyboard, as there are fewer options. To start the process, select System → Preferences → Mouse to call up the window in Figure 3-12, which offers two sets of options: General and Accessibility.

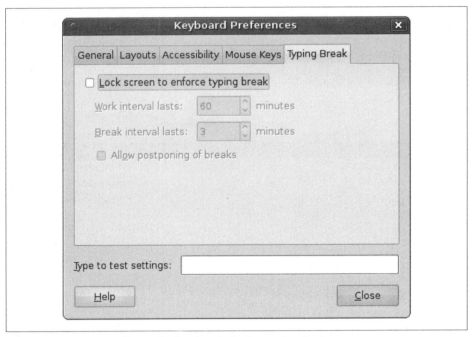

Figure 3-10. Give yourself a regular break with the Typing Break tab

General

Under the General tab you can choose whether you will use your mouse left- or right-handed, and whether to highlight the location of the mouse pointer when the Ctrl key is pressed. You also can adjust various settings such as the Acceleration speed and Sensitivity, the Drag and Drop Threshold, and the Double-Click Timeout.

Adjust the settings to your preference, and then click the light bulb image. A single click will make it light dimly for a while and then go out. This length of time is the Double-Click Timeout, which increases as you move the slider to the right.

The Acceleration setting determines the speed at which the pointer will move as you move the mouse, whereas the Sensitivity determines the responsiveness. If you find the mouse pointer is a little jerky, move the slider to the left; if it seems sluggish, move the slider to the right.

The Drag and Drop Threshold specifies the distance you have to move an item before Ubuntu decides you are conducting a drag-and-drop operation.

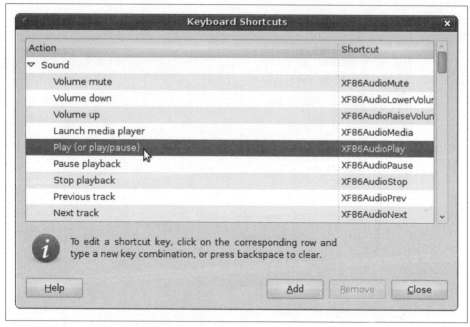

Figure 3-11. You can define keyboard shortcuts for many actions

Accessibility

The Accessibility tab provides enhanced features to provide assistance when a user's mouse control is limited. The options available, Simulated Secondary Click and Dwell Click, are shown in Figure 3-13.

If you can't use the second button on your mouse, you can enable the Simulated Secondary Click feature to invoke the function of a second button, which generally opens a menu. This feature invokes the right-click function when you hold down your primary button (usually the left button) for the period of time specified.

However, for this feature to work, the system has to enable Assistive Technology Support, which is disabled by default. So if you haven't already enabled the support, when you click in the checkbox, a new window will open up, as shown in Figure 3-14. This window will ask you to enable Assistive Technology Support and then log out so that you can log back in again with everything correctly set up.

If you want this support, click the Enable and Log Out button and Ubuntu will return to the login screen, where you should re-enter your username and password. Having done this, try moving your mouse pointer to an open area of the desktop and hold down the left button. As you hold it, you will see the mouse pointer icon slowly fill with a different color.

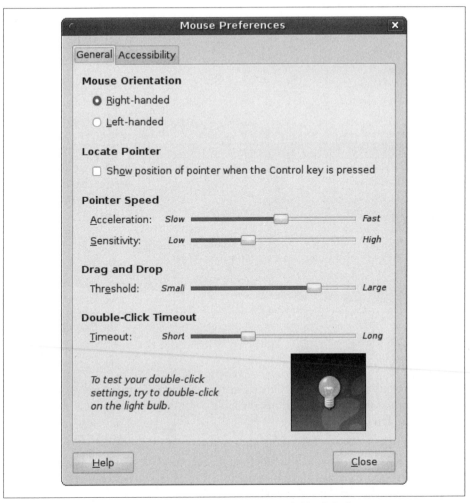

Figure 3-12. The Mouse Preferences window, set to right-handed by default

If you leave the button held down until the pointer has fully changed color, a right mouse click event will be generated, and you'll see the context menu you'd expect as a result of right-clicking the desktop. Set the delay before the secondary click is activated by returning to the Mouse Accessibility dialog and sliding the delay timer left or right.

With Assistive Technology Support enabled, the Mouse Accessibility dialog also lets you try out the Dwell Click option. This performs a click for you, even if you are unable to depress the mouse button. It does this by noticing that the pointer has stopped moving, and then starts to fill the mouse pointer icon with a different color.

If you leave the pointer still and the cursor fills up, it will then change to a crosshair symbol. If you then move the cursor a little bit to the left (while the crosshair is visible),

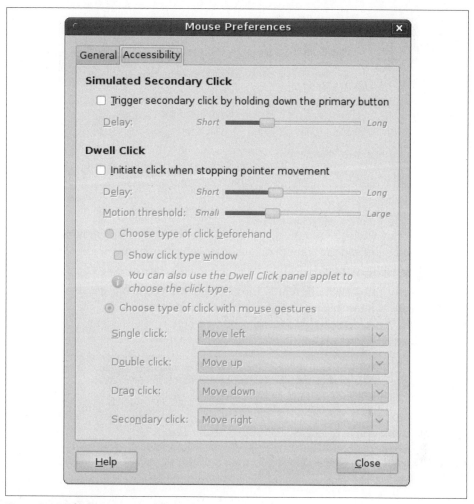

Figure 3-13. The Mouse Accessibility settings

a mouse click will be generated at the position at which the mouse was just resting. In fact, you can generate four different types of mouse events according to the direction in which you choose to move the mouse while the crosshair is visible:

- Move left: single click
- Move up: double click
- Move down: drag click
- Move right: secondary click

You can modify these directions and behaviors if you like, using the drop-down boxes provided in the Mouse Accessibility window.

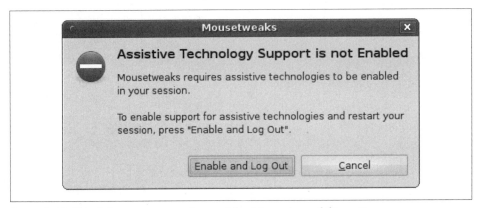

Figure 3-14. This dialog may appear when enabling Mouse Accessibility options

The initial delay while the mouse cursor fills up can be changed by moving the delay slider left and right, and the amount of cursor movement required to initiate an action can be set using the motion threshold slider.

If this behavior turns out to be a little too complicated, you can use a simpler system by clicking the "Choose type of click beforehand" option and ensuring that "Show click type window" is checked. A new control window will pop up (see Figure 3-15) that lets you rest the mouse over the action that you want to happen next.

Figure 3-15. Resting the mouse pointer over one of these icons will make that the default action for the next mouse event

So, to create a right-click, you would pass the mouse pointer over the Right Click icon and leave it there until the mouse pointer fills up with the new color. Now move the mouse pointer to a clear part of the desktop and leave it there to call up the desktop right-click context menu.

To disable either of these options, just uncheck their associated radio buttons or boxes.

Graphics

In the early years of Linux desktops, sections such as this one on setting up graphics tended to be much longer, showering the reader with potential problems to solve and pitfalls to avoid. But over the years, more and more work has gone into making the Linux graphics drivers as bulletproof as possible.

For a long time, a Linux installation might not have been able to call up a graphical desktop at all without strenuous configuration work. Nowadays you are almost certain to be able to open up a desktop of 800 × 600 (or at the very least, 640 × 480) pixels. This is because a lot of effort has been put into developing a very robust set of basic drivers.

However, that doesn't mean that your new high-resolution widescreen monitor is guaranteed to display its top resolution mode straight "out of the box," and less standard graphics cards and monitors may also have difficulties displaying some graphic resolutions. So some hints and tips follow to help you achieve the best possible results from your graphics card and monitor.

Display Preferences

You can call up the Display Preferences window by selecting System → Preferences → Display, which will present a window similar to that shown in Figure 3-16.

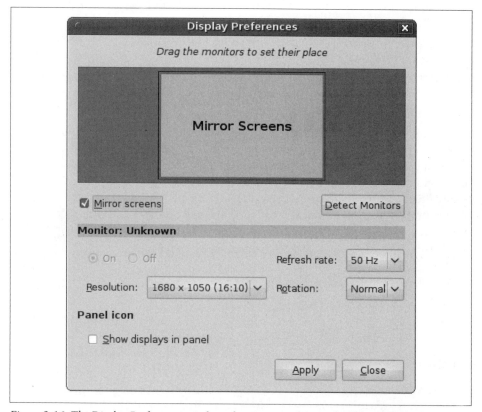

Figure 3-16. The Display Preferences window, showing a resolution of 1680 × 1050 pixels

There are a number of options available in this window, but the most important to you at this moment is probably the Resolution drop-down menu. When you click on it, you will be shown all the different display resolutions that Ubuntu thinks your graphics card and monitor are capable of displaying.

In this window, you can also change the refresh rate of your monitor (generally not necessary) and the screen rotation (if supported), and decide whether to echo (or mirror) the display from your main monitor onto any others you have attached. If you have more than one monitor and turn mirroring off, you can drag the monitors to the positions relative to each other that you prefer. If you do have multiple monitors but not all of them are shown, you can click Detect Monitors, which should make Ubuntu find them all.

I tend to check the box called "Show displays in panel" after a new Ubuntu install. This places a small icon resembling a computer monitor at the top right of the desktop top panel, and you can use this icon to quickly change display settings.

As I mentioned, the main option of interest here after installing Ubuntu is probably the Resolution, which sometimes isn't set to the width and height you prefer. Figure 3-17 shows the resolutions available for a widescreen monitor, with a maximum resolution of 1680 × 1050 pixels. Currently, 1024 × 768 is selected. A click on 1680 × 1050 will put Ubuntu into the desired widescreen mode.

However, sometimes the resolution you require isn't displayed in this window because the right drivers haven't been loaded yet. If you load these drivers, they will show up on the list and you can choose them.

The reason Ubuntu doesn't load some drivers is that they are proprietary and not open source. Proprietary drivers do not provide source code publicly and therefore have not undergone the full scrutiny of the Linux community. However, companies sometimes have legitimate reasons for keeping source code secret—for instance, they may have licensed part of the code from another company and lack the rights to make it open— but the proprietary drivers that you can load using the procedure in this section have been tested by the Ubuntu team, so they can be considered safe enough to use.

Therefore, if you have installed Ubuntu either as a standalone installation or as part of a dual- or multi-boot system, you may be able to install proprietary drivers for your hardware. These need to be downloaded from development sites, so your system must be connected to the Internet.

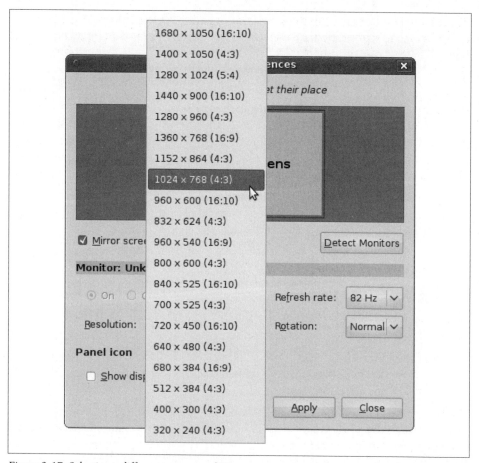

Figure 3-17. Selecting a different screen resolution

 If you are running Ubuntu directly from the DVD, you will not be able to select any screen resolutions except those shown in the Display Preferences window. So if you are not yet ready to perform a full Ubuntu installation, I recommend you either use the Wubi program for installing Ubuntu alongside a Windows setup or install Ubuntu inside a Sun VirtualBox virtual machine. Either way, you will keep your original operating system on your computer. Both of these types of installation are fully detailed in Chapter 2.

To find out whether there are any such drivers available on your computer, select System → Administration → Hardware Drivers, and you'll be presented with a window similar to that in Figure 3-18. Any proprietary drivers that are available for your computer will be listed there. In the case of the system I used for the Figure 3-18 screen

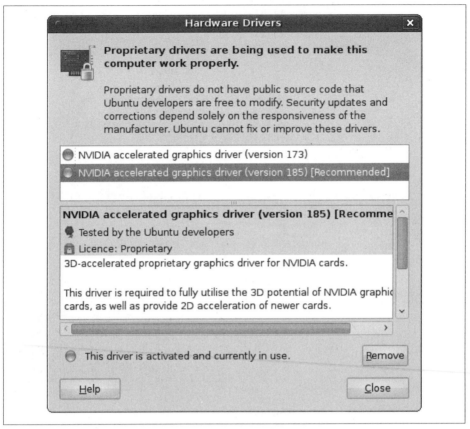

Figure 3-18. Ubuntu is showing that various proprietary Nvidia drivers are available

grab, some Nvidia graphics drivers can be enabled to provide additional functionality and possibly a wider range of screen resolutions.

Starting with Ubuntu 10.04, the latest drivers are marked as "version current," making it obvious which is the best one to select. If you find any graphics drivers listed here, you can try enabling one by highlighting it and clicking on the Activate button. You will be prompted for your password, and the driver will then be downloaded and installed. After installation completes, you should reboot Ubuntu, and you may find that you now have additional screen resolutions available.

If there is more than one driver, you might want to try them in turn to find out which supports the most features on your monitor. You can determine this by trying the three options available in System → Preferences → Appearance → Visual Effects, ranging from "No extra features," to Normal, and Extra.

Once you have installed a proprietary driver, you may also be offered use of a different Display Preferences window (see Figure 3-19). If you select No, you will be shown the standard window, which may or may not work fully, due to the proprietary driver.

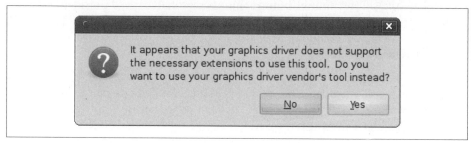

Figure 3-19. Message displayed when using a proprietary graphics driver

If you select Yes, you'll be presented with a different window, such as the one in Figure 3-20, which is for an Nvidia driver.

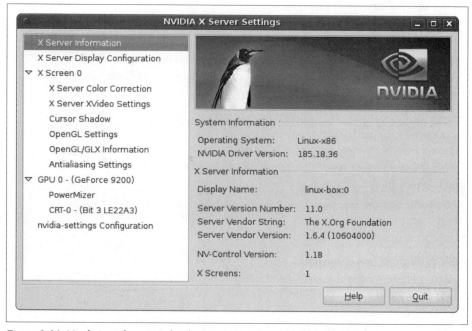

Figure 3-20. Nvidia's replacement for the Display Preferences window

Because of the wide variety of proprietary driver software, you will be on your own at this point, as it's beyond the scope of this book to detail each one. That said, though, you'll generally find the tools provided to be intuitive and easy to use and comparable with (if not more fully featured than) the Ubuntu default.

Sun VirtualBox

As I explained in Chapter 2, Sun's VirtualBox virtual machine software is my preferred virtualization solution because it's extremely robust software that I have found almost impossible to crash, and it runs Ubuntu at quite a reasonable speed considering it's not running natively. What's more, it's available for all of Windows NT 4.0, 2000, XP, Server 2003, Vista, and Windows 7, as well as for DOS/Windows 3.x, Linux, Solaris, OpenSolaris, and OpenBSD.

However, if you are running Ubuntu inside a Sun VirtualBox virtual machine, then you may have only 640 × 480 and 800 × 600 resolutions available to you by default. To increase these dimensions, you will need to make sure you have a clear Ubuntu desktop that is fully visible. Then, press the Ctrl key on the right of your keyboard to ensure you are controlling your computer (not the virtual machine), and select Devices → Install Guest Additions from the VirtualBox menu (as shown in Figure 3-21).

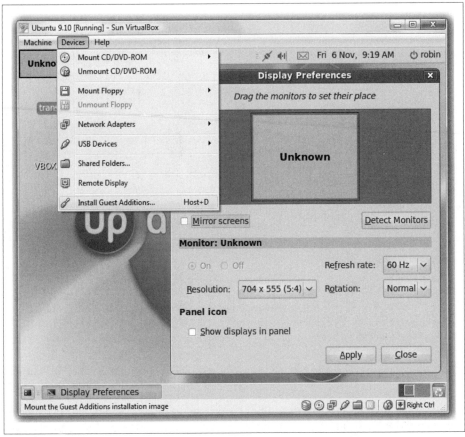

Figure 3-21. You can add more screen resolutions by installing Guest Additions to VirtualBox

Now click again inside the window to regain control of the virtual machine and, if a new CD-ROM icon has not been added to your desktop, restart Ubuntu by clicking the broken circle icon at the top right of the desktop.

Once you have the new virtual CD-ROM icon on your Ubuntu desktop (with a name similar to *VBOXADDITIONS_5_3*, although this may change for different versions), double-click it to open up the disc. You will see that one of the new icons displayed is called *autorun.sh*. Double-click this icon and then select either Run in Terminal or simply Run, and follow any prompts, inputting your Ubuntu password if it is requested. Figure 3-22 shows what the installation process will look like.

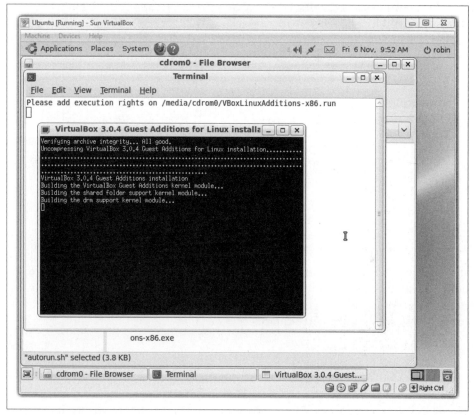

Figure 3-22. Installing the VirtualBox Guest Additions

If a message appears asking you to add execution rights to a particular file, you should be able to ignore it, as the installation appears to proceed without problems anyway.

Once installation is complete, you can press Return (in the virtual machine) to exit the install, and then restart Ubuntu. When it has rebooted, you can select the display preferences again from within Ubuntu and should now be presented with more available screen resolutions from which to choose (see Figure 3-23).

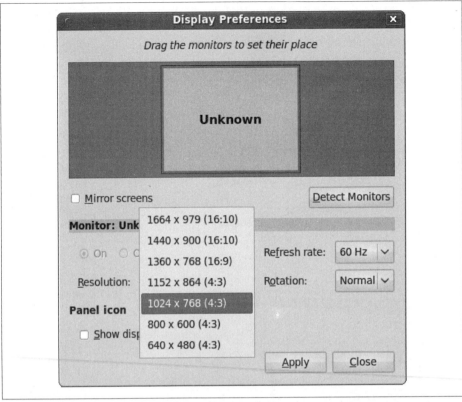

Figure 3-23. This VirtualBox installation of Ubuntu can now use resolutions up to 1664 × 979

It is important when using virtualization software to save the state of your guest operating system when you aren't using it. Otherwise, any updates may be completely lost next time you run the virtual machine. With VirtualBox, you can click on the Close icon and you will be given three choices:

- Save the machine state
- Send the shutdown signal
- Power off the machine

Normally you should check the first option to ensure that next time you use it the guest operating system will be fully up-to-date. However, if it has hung and become unresponsive, you may have no choice other than to select one of the other two options. You may then have to reinstall any software added since the last time you saved the machine's state.

Sound

Sound cards these days generally stick to rigidly defined protocols, so you'll rarely have problems with them. However, you may still wish to configure certain sound options to your taste. You can do this using the Sound Preferences window, available by selecting System → Preferences → Sound, which results in the window shown in Figure 3-24.

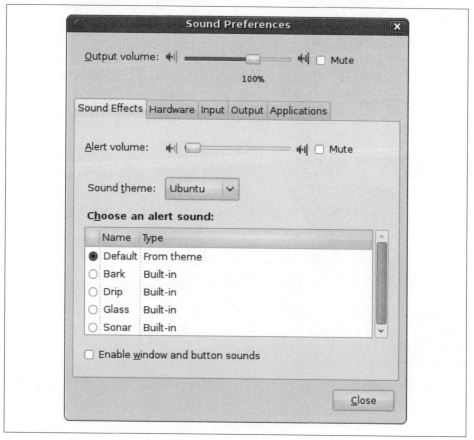

Figure 3-24. The Sound Preferences window

In addition to a volume slider and a checkbox for muting audio, this window displays five main tabs. We'll look at each one in the following subsections.

Sound Effects

This tab lets you choose the sound theme. By default, the theme will be Ubuntu. If other themes are available you can select them (or choose to not use a theme and so turn sounds off) using the "Sound theme" drop-down menu. Underneath there you can also choose your preferred alert sound and choose whether to enable window and button sounds by checking the associated box.

Hardware

If you don't know what sound hardware you computer uses, you are best advised to avoid this tab for now, but if you still have sound problems after trying everything else, you can try changing the settings here to see whether that helps. To do this, select a device to configure and then use the Profile drop-down menu to configure it.

Input

Here, you can specify the input volume with a slider, or mute input entirely by checking the Mute checkbox. You can also test sound levels by checking the lights next to "Input level" (see Figure 3-25).

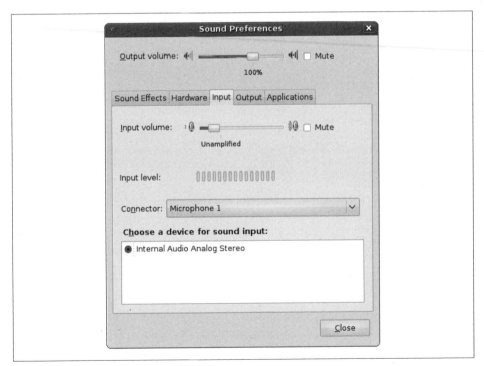

Figure 3-25. Configuring sound input

Underneath that you can choose which connection to use for input through the Connector drop-down menu (the most common choices are line in and microphone input), and use the radio buttons in the bottom area to select between different input devices.

Output

This tab lets you specify the device to use for output by selecting the radio buttons in the top area of the window, or you can set the balance using the slider underneath (see Figure 3-26).

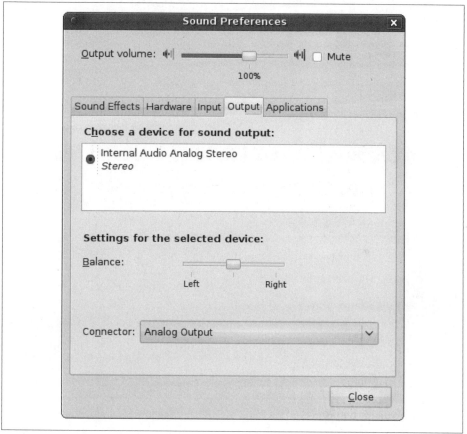

Figure 3-26. Configuring sound output

Below that you can select the output method using the Connector drop-down menu. The usual choices here will be either headphones or general analog output.

Applications

Whenever you have any applications using sound on your computer, the Applications tab will show the application and enable you to alter the sound level or mute it (see Figure 3-27). By the way, some sound drivers have a bug where the action of the mute checkbox is reversed. So if it is unchecked and you cannot hear any sound, try checking it.

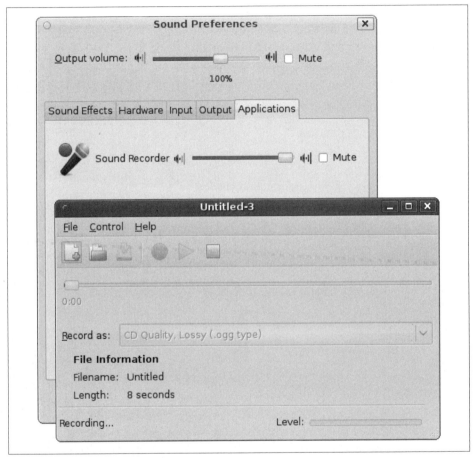

Figure 3-27. Programs making use of sound appear in the Applications tab of the Sound Preferences window

If no sound is in use (either recording or playing), this tab will simply display the message "No application is currently playing or recording audio."

PulseAudio

The standard sound server in Ubuntu is PulseAudio, a background process that takes input from multiple sources, processes it, and outputs it to multiple sound cards, servers, or other processes. The idea is to allow all audio streams to integrate seamlessly with each other to provide crystal-clear sound, no matter how the input streams are combined.

Although it's not essential to have it installed in order to play sound, PulseAudio features, among many other things, per-application volume controls, compatibility with most popular audio applications, and high-quality resampling, and it even handles network audio. So it's a very useful and powerful program to have installed.

However, there have been reports of sound problems on certain setups, such as scratchy sound and random pops, or even no sound at all. So if you've tried everything else and still can't get the sound to work correctly in Ubuntu, you may be able to solve the problem by uninstalling PulseAudio.

To do this, make sure that you do not have Synaptic running, and then open a Terminal window by selecting Applications → Accessories → Terminal. Then enter the following, providing your password when asked:

```
sudo apt-get remove pulseaudio
```

Hopefully the issue will now be solved, but you may still wish to try reinstalling a future release of PulseAudio (which may now work for you) in order to gain use of the features it offers. To do this, you would enter the following from a Terminal window prompt:

```
sudo apt-get install pulseaudio
```

You can always uninstall it again if it still doesn't work for you.

Basic Networking

There's a lot more about networking in Chapter 10, but for now you'll just want to ensure your new Ubuntu installation is able to reach the network in your own home or office, and from there the Internet. To find out if that's the case, double-click on the Firefox icon right next to the system menu at the top left of the screen, or select Applications → Internet → Firefox Web Browser. When the browser opens, it should display the default Google/Ubuntu home page, as shown in Figure 3-28.

If the home page doesn't open and you get an error such as "Offline Mode, This document cannot be displayed while offline...", then you need to check your network configuration options.

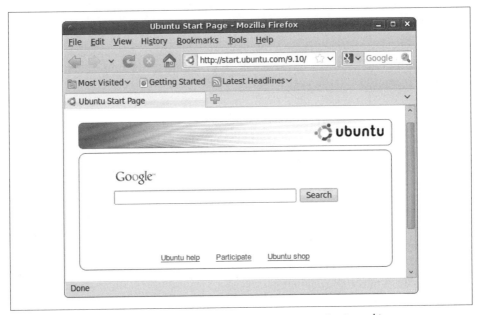

Figure 3-28. If Firefox displays its home page, your Internet connection is working

To see what might be the problem, take a look at Figure 3-29. You can call up this menu by clicking on the network settings icon at the top right of the desktop. The icon will usually look like a pair of plugs connecting to each other diagonally or, as in this case because a wireless network is connected, a set of signal strength bars.

Normally you will see "Auto eth0" under Wired Network if you have an Ethernet cable plugged into the computer. Furthermore, if your machine has a wireless card and there's a wireless hub within range, you'll see the name of the network to which you are connected under Wireless Networks. In this case, my computer isn't plugged into a wired network, but it is connected to a wireless network called *The Dunes*. If you're not connected to either type of network, or wish to connect to one that you can see in the box but isn't connected, just click it to activate it.

You also need to be aware that either or both types of network connection may be disabled. To check this, right-click on the network connections icon and make sure that you have checked all the boxes that need to be enabled, as shown in Figure 3-30.

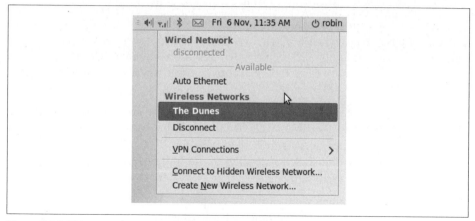

Figure 3-29. The network connections drop-down menu

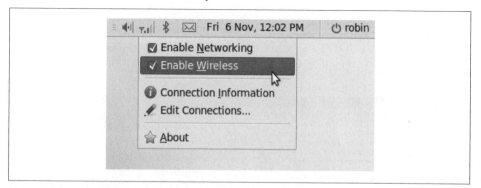

Figure 3-30. Make sure the connections you are using are enabled

Wired Connections

In the case of a wired (or Ethernet) connection, select "Auto eth0" (or "Auto eth1", etc., if you have more than one network card). The icon will show an animation while the connection attempt is made, and if successful, will be replaced with the diagonal-pair-of-plugs Ethernet icon I mentioned earlier. You will also know whether this has worked because a black message box will appear saying "Auto eth0 connection established." If you ever unplug your Ethernet lead, this message will become "Auto eth0 disconnected."

If you don't have an Ethernet cable connected, all that will appear under Wired Network is the word "disconnected," and you will be unable to select a wired network. Likewise, if there are no wireless networks within range, then the word "disconnected" will appear underneath the Wireless Networks section.

Installing suitable drivers

You should also bear in mind that if you do not have a network card (either wired or wireless) or it is not correctly installed, then Ubuntu will not show any option at all, as only the cards it finds connected are provided as options. Therefore, if you do have a wired network card but none is listed, then you may need to use a search engine to find a suitable driver and install it.

For example, I discovered from a Google search that one of my computers experiencing networking problems uses the RALink 2790 chipset—which is not installed by default. After performing another quick search, I located the RT2860STA driver software, which I downloaded and installed according to the supplied instructions. After a reboot, the menu was properly activated.

Due to the wide variety of network cards, it's not practical to list them and their drivers here. However, you can usually determine what hardware is connected by opening up the Terminal (by selecting Applications → Accessories → Terminal), typing `lspci` (the command to list all PCI devices), and then pressing Enter. The result of running this command can be seen in Figure 3-31. Look for the words Network or Ethernet, and you should see which devices are used for networking. You can then use a search engine to get more information and download drivers.

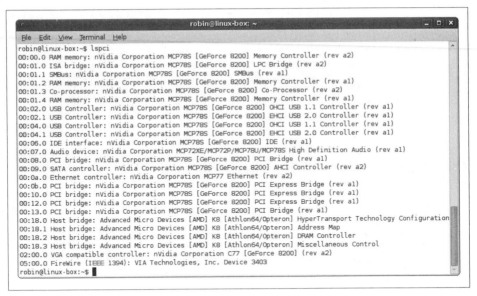

Figure 3-31. Listing all PCI devices

Wireless Connections

The same advice for installing drivers given in the previous section also applies here. If your wireless network card is not detected, follow the advice in that section for looking up the card's details and installing the correct driver for it.

The first step is always to ensure that you can see the name of the wireless connection you want and that you can click on it. When you do so, if no password is required you should be connected automatically. Otherwise, Ubuntu will determine the type of encryption used and prompt for the right type of password. In the case of Figure 3-32, a WEP 40/128-bit key is being requested.

Figure 3-32. Connecting to a secured wireless network

If you wish to ensure you have entered the correct characters, you can click the "Show key" box before you enter them, but for security reasons, you should uncheck the box afterward.

When you click the Connect button, the network connections icon will animate for a while, and assuming you are successful, you will see a black message box appear saying "connection established."

Using an Ethernet Bridge

When trying to get wireless networking to connect, if all else fails there is a solution that should work every time: using an Ethernet bridge, which is a wireless device that features a socket for connecting to the Ethernet card in your computer. When you do this, as far as your computer is concerned it's using a wired connection to your network via its Ethernet card.

There are two types of bridge available. One uses the wiring in your electrical sockets to connect two devices together, just as if you had run a long Ethernet cable between them. They usually come in pairs, and you connect one to your computer and the other to your router or access point.

The other type of bridge uses an antenna to connect your computer to your wireless network. You configure the device with your network's name and security details, and it remembers this information, even when it's switched off. You then plug it into the Ethernet socket of any computer (running Ubuntu, Windows, OS X, or any other operating system) within range of an access point. This kind of device is often called a Wireless Ethernet Bridge or a Wireless Gaming Adapter.

This solution always seems to work because wired networking has been around much longer than wireless, and the drivers required are now refined to such a level that just about all Ethernet cards are supported—which isn't something that can be said about all wireless networking devices.

Printing

To install your printer, select System → Administration → Printing, which will call up the printer configuration window. Then click the New button, or select Server → New → Printer, and a Searching message will appear for a few seconds, which is then replaced by a list of any network or other printers found by Ubuntu (see Figure 3-33).

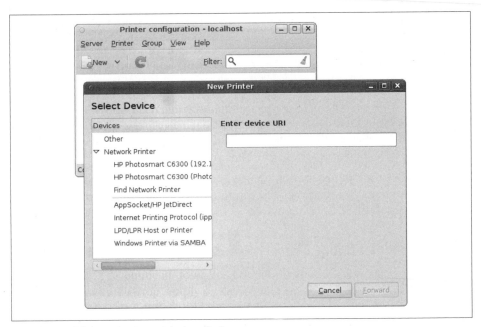

Figure 3-33. Selecting a printer to be installed

If your printer is shown, select it and click the Forward button. A box will then pop up telling you that Ubuntu is searching for available drivers. If it finds the right one, it will prompt you to install it. Otherwise, it will call up the dialog shown in Figure 3-34. Here, you should manually select the manufacturer and model of the printer. Using a little more technical sophistication, you can provide a PPD (printer driver) file, or search the Web for a driver to download.

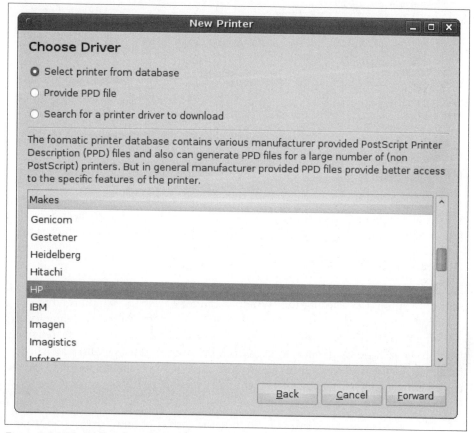

Figure 3-34. Manually selecting a printer

If you manually select the driver, submenus will appear until you narrow it down enough and the driver you want is listed in the Drivers window. Select the driver, click Forward, and you'll be prompted to provide a printer name, description, and location (see Figure 3-35).

After clicking Apply, you will be asked whether you would like to print a test page. I recommend you click Yes, just to make sure everything installed correctly.

Upon successful installation, your printer will appear in the printer configuration window. You can also add other printers to this window.

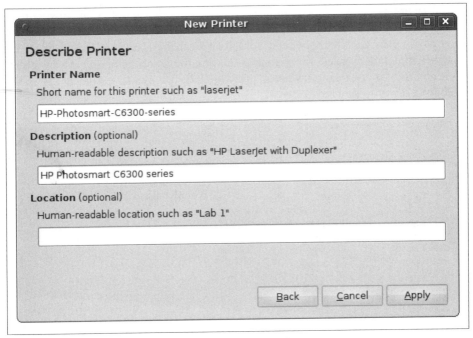

Figure 3-35. The driver has been found and is ready to install

Finding Unreported Printers

If your network printer is not automatically discovered by Ubuntu and it is a Windows printer, you should try selecting the "Windows Printer via SAMBA" option and entering the server/printer details in the "smb://" input box. These will be the name of the computer to which the printer is connected, followed by a /, and then the shared name that computer has provided for it. Then click Browse to list any printers attached to that server. In the case of my local network, I know there's a shared printer using the name *Samsung* attached to a machine identified by the name *IQ500*, so I entered those details, and Ubuntu found the printer, as shown in Figure 3-36.

From there it was simply a matter of choosing the correct printer driver as before and then printing out a test page, all of which worked smoothly.

Other Printers

Of course, there are hundreds (if not thousands) of different makes and models of printer, and so you may still be having difficulty installing yours under Ubuntu. If this is the case, I suggest you visit *https://help.ubuntu.com/community/Printers* (make sure you use a capital P for *Printers*), where there's advice on installing most of the Brother, HP, Lexmark, Samsung, and Xerox printers.

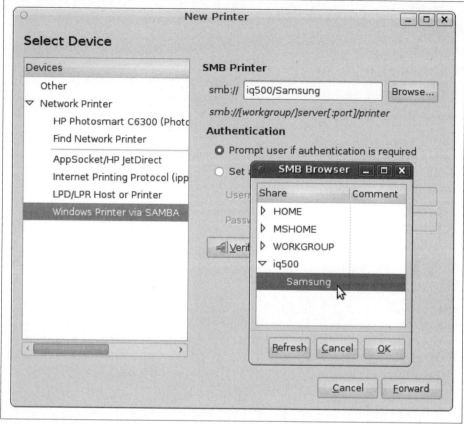

Figure 3-36. Informing Ubuntu where to find a network printer

There's also *http://wiki.ubuntu.com/HardwareSupportComponentsPrinters* for information on the entire range of Ubuntu supported printers. If yours isn't there, unfortunately there's probably no Ubuntu driver available for it...yet. I say yet because if your printer is very new, keep checking back. A driver could be available soon.

TV Tuners

A wide variety of TV tuner cards (both analog and digital) are supported by Ubuntu, and the best way to use them is with the MythTV program, the Linux equivalent of Windows Media Center. To install it you can either visit *apt://mythtv* in the Firefox web browser (making sure you select *apturl* as the application launcher if a pop-up window requests it) or select Applications → Accessories → Terminal and enter:

```
sudo apt-get install mythtv
```

If you are prompted for your password, you should enter it and then wait a few minutes for installation to complete, as there are a number of other programs it depends on that may also require installing.

During the process you may be advised to set a password for the MySQL *root* user. If so, type one in and make sure you remember it, as you'll be using it later on in the installation. Alternatively, if you are behind a firewall and running a personal computer, you may wish to just press Enter here to leave the password unset; you can always create a root password for MySQL later if you need one.

You will also have the opportunity to allow remote computers running MythTV to connect to this service. If your computers are all behind a firewall, this is a reasonably safe thing to allow and you can go ahead and select Yes. If not, I don't recommend this option, as you may expose both MythTV and MySQL services to the Web.

Restarting and Setup

Although you may not be asked to, I recommend restarting your computer after installing MythTV to be absolutely sure that installation is complete. You will now be ready to configure the system.

First you will need to tell the program about your TV card by selecting System → Administration → MythTV Backend Setup, which will present the screen shown in Figure 3-37. The first time you do so, you may be asked if you wish to be added to the *mythtv* group. If you do, click OK and enter your Ubuntu password when prompted. After that you will need to log in to Ubuntu again, so click log out, then log back in again, and then re-run the MythTV program.

Once up and running, you may not see your mouse on the screen. If this is the case, you will have to use the cursor keys and Enter to select and change options. The first option you'll need to use is "Capture cards," with which you will tell MythTV what capture card you have connected to your computer.

Capture Cards

Select "Capture cards" by pressing the down cursor key a few times and pressing Enter, followed by (New Capture card). There may be a delay of several seconds while the configuration software searches your machine's hardware, after which a screen similar to Figure 3-38 will appear.

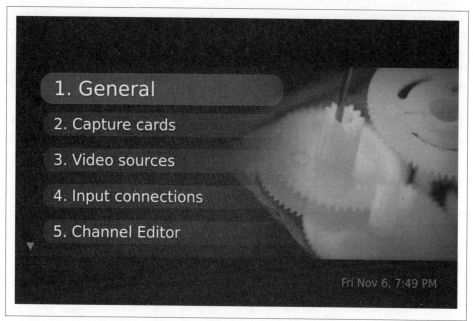

Figure 3-37. The MythTV configuration menu

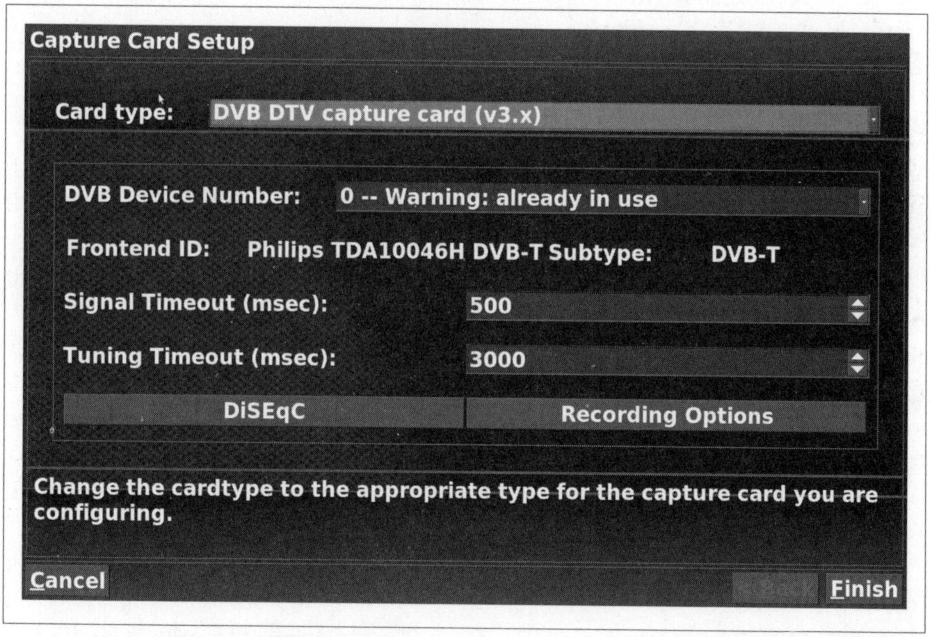

Capture Card Setup

Card type: DVB DTV capture card (v3.x)

DVB Device Number: 0 -- Warning: already in use

Frontend ID: Philips TDA10046H DVB-T Subtype: DVB-T

Signal Timeout (msec):   500

Tuning Timeout (msec):   3000

DiSEqC   Recording Options

Change the cardtype to the appropriate type for the capture card you are configuring.

Cancel   Back   Finish

Figure 3-38. Identifying your TV tuner card

Use the cursor keys to move to the "Card type" field, and press the right cursor key to scroll through the types of cards shown until yours is listed, ignoring any USB cameras or other input devices. For example, the computer used for the screen grab in Figure 3-38 has a Philips digital tuner card, so once the program displayed that one, I selected Finish by pressing Alt-F. To go back a level you can press Alt-B, or to discard any changes you can press Alt-C or the Escape key.

At this point, though, you should be back at the "Capture cards" menu and should now press Escape to return to the Main menu.

 If you find that MythTV doesn't find all your channels when performing a scan (which we'll get to shortly), you can tweak the configuration here to help by changing either or both of the Signal Timeout and Tuning Timeout fields to a larger number, such as 5,000 milliseconds instead of 500 (or whatever the default value shows).

Video Sources

Next you need to select the "Video sources" menu and then select (New video source) to bring up the screen shown in Figure 3-39. To keep things simple, I have chosen to use only TV listings supplied along with the television channels by setting the "Listings grabber" field to "Transmitted guide only (EIT)." I therefore entered the name *EIT* in the "Video source name" field and then selected Finish.

To return back to the Main menu, press Escape.

Input Connections

You are now ready for the final essential step, which is the "Input connections" menu. Select it, and then select the single connection that should be listed to enter the setup screen shown in Figure 3-40.

Here, I chose to give a display name of *Digital TV*, and then moved onto the "Video source" field and pressed the right cursor key to call up the previously created video source, *EIT*.

Once the video source has been selected, you can then click "Scan for channels," followed by selecting Next, to set up all the TV channels your card can receive. Be prepared to wait for some time while all possible channels are scanned. It will take even longer if you have increased any of the Timeout settings for your card, but higher settings help you stand a greater chance of finding all receivable channels.

Once the scanning is complete, your main configuration work is done, but you can then go ahead and configure other options if you like and, when you are ready, exit from the program. When you exit, you'll be asked whether you wish to run *mythfilldatabase* to update MythTV. If you will be using the EIT program information rather than obtaining listings information over the Internet, just click Cancel.

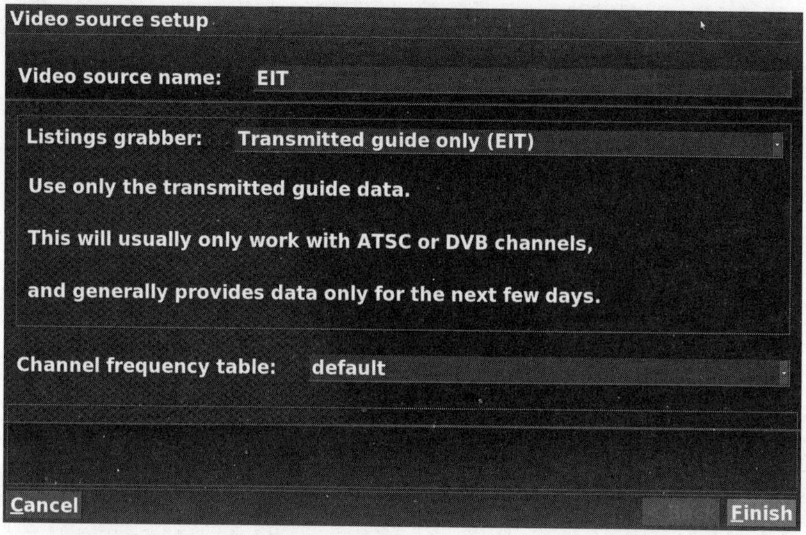

Figure 3-39. Selecting the video and listing source

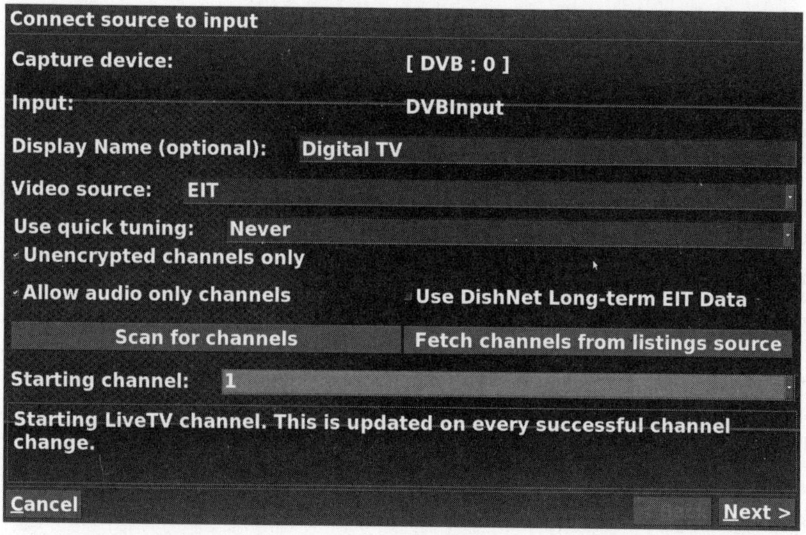

Figure 3-40. Connecting the EIT video source to the input

Once you have completed installation and configuration, you are ready to call up MythTV itself by selecting Applications → Sound & Video → MythTV Frontend. Your screen should now look like Figure 3-41.

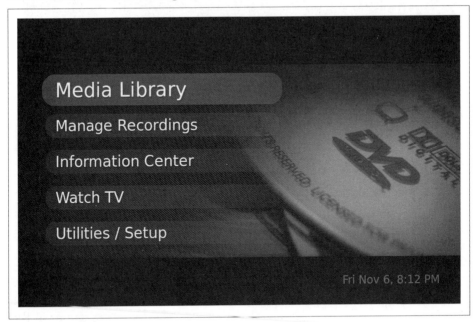

Figure 3-41. The MythTV frontend using the mythbuntu theme

Running MythTV

You are now ready to test out MythTV by selecting Watch TV. All being well, you'll get a screen such as the one shown in Figure 3-42. You should also be able to pause live TV and record and play back various TV programs and other media. Just experiment with the options to get the hang of them.

Webcams

There's a USB standard called UVC that defines streaming video, which makes webcams as easy to use as memory sticks and hard drives by allowing one driver to work with many webcams. Therefore, most (if not all) webcams work automatically in Ubuntu.

For a quick way to ensure that your webcam is working, you can install and run the Cheese program by selecting the Terminal (Applications → Accessories → Terminal) and then entering:

```
sudo apt-get install cheese
cheese
```

Figure 3-42. MythTV up and running

The first command installs the program (and will prompt you for your Ubuntu password), whereas the second (which you should issue only after installation finishes) will run the webcam program and bring up a window similar to the one shown in Figure 3-43. Once you have satisfied yourself that your webcam works, you can close Cheese, but it's worth leaving on your computer because it's a great utility for recording video and taking photos.

USB Media

You may have various storage devices connected (or sometimes connected) to your computer via USB, such as cameras, thumb drives, hard disk drives, and so on. All of these should be recognized by Ubuntu as soon as you connect them, after which they are then mounted in the filesystem and on the desktop.

You can usually drag and drop files in and out of the device's folders, and in the case of cameras, you can delete the photos on the camera once you have copied them to your hard disk.

Figure 3-43. Testing a webcam using the Cheese program—and yes, I do need to tidy up my office!

A note about iPhones. In versions of Ubuntu prior to 10.04, iPhones only mounted the photo part of their memory because the iPod media files are encrypted. To handle them, some people have had success installing the Wine Windows interface and then installing the iTunes software. However, results vary due to different versions of iTunes, and often this method results in iTunes hanging or simply not recognizing the iPhone. The most success seems to come from running VirtualBox on Ubuntu, and then installing both Windows XP and iTunes. This is a long-winded approach just to run a single program, but see the following section.

What's New in 10.04

Starting with Ubuntu 10.04, as well as mounting your iPhone's photo folders using Nautilus, it will also let you browse the entire contents of your iPhone, including your apps, music and videos. What's more, the Rhythmbox music player now integrates with iPhones, working in a similar manner to the iTunes program. Hopefully this integration will stay and won't be interrupted by any future iPhone firmware upgrades. It's one more good reason to upgrade to 10.04 soon after you've installed 9.10.

Summary

I know this chapter covered a lot of material, but by throwing you in the deep end and getting your installation properly configured, I hope you now have a good feel for what Ubuntu is like, how easy it is to use, and what it can do for you.

In the next chapter, we'll look at the desktop in more depth and learn how to modify its layout via the various personalization options, as well as how to add more users to the system (and manage them), how to perform searches, and other useful features.

CHAPTER 4

The Desktop: Accessing Applications and Features

Long gone are the days when Linux was considered the exclusive domain of highly technical and skilled programmers. Nowadays, we have desktops that provide easy and intuitive interfaces to all their functions, in much the same way as we now expect from any other modern OS, such as Windows or Mac OS X. Xfce, KDE, and the default Ubuntu desktop, GNOME, have been developed through many years of cooperative labor and take advantage of the most advanced graphics cards.

In particular, the GNOME environment of Ubuntu 10.04 represents the leading edge of Linux desktops, and this chapter will help you to thoroughly familiarize yourself with how it works and what it has to offer.

Logging In

You may wonder why there's a whole section on logging in. Well, it's because you can do more than just log in at this screen, as you can see from Figure 4-1. I've set up my system so the login screen already shows the user *Robin* and is waiting for a password to be entered. But at the bottom of the screen are a number of options you can use to modify your login session. So,s before getting on with the logging in itself, let's look at them in turn.

Language

By clicking the Language drop-down menu at the bottom left of the screen (displaying the country United States in the screen grab,) you can change the language you will be using, which is useful if you need to work in more than one language. For example, Canadians might need to use both English and French, or Belgians might need to switch between Flemish and French, and so on. Or, as shown in Figure 4-2, you may simply wish to have a variety of different versions of English available to you.

robin-ubuntu-iq500
Robin
Password:
Cancel
Log In
Language:
English (United States)
Keyboard:
United Kingdom
Sessions:
GNOME
Sun Nov 8, 4:24 AM

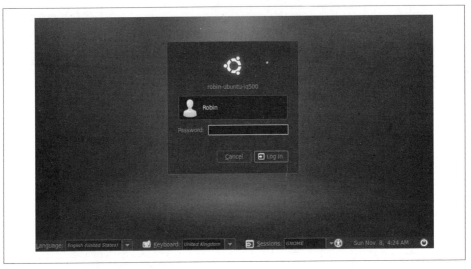

Figure 4-1. The Ubuntu login screen

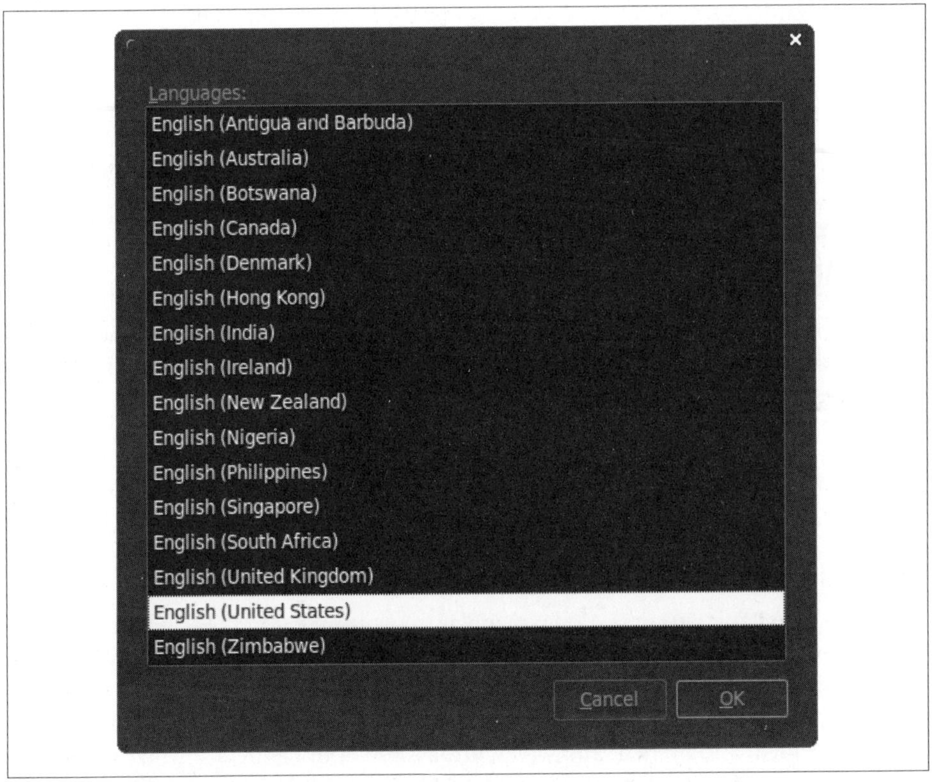

Languages:
English (Antigua and Barbuda)
English (Australia)
English (Botswana)
English (Canada)
English (Denmark)
English (Hong Kong)
English (India)
English (Ireland)
English (New Zealand)
English (Nigeria)
English (Philippines)
English (Singapore)
English (South Africa)
English (United Kingdom)
English (United States)
English (Zimbabwe)
Cancel
OK

Figure 4-2. Selecting U.S. English for the language

By default, all supported variations of the installed language(s) are offered for selection. To obtain access to additional languages, you first select System → Administration → Language Support from the Ubuntu Desktop, and then click Install / Remove Languages, as shown in Figure 4-3. The first time you do so, you may be informed that language support is not completely installed and may have to click the Install button.

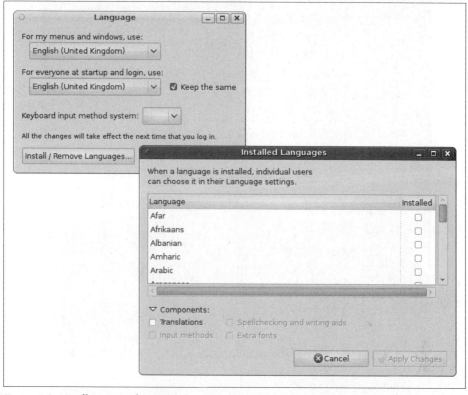

Figure 4-3. Installing a new language

Make sure you check the boxes for the translations and/or writing aids you need before clicking Apply Changes. You will also most likely need to follow the instructions provided in the section "Layouts" on page 59 for installing new keyboard layouts.

Keyboard

If you change the language, you can also change your keyboard layout to match it by clicking the Keyboard drop-down menu and choosing the layout you need, as shown by Figure 4-4. If, when using Ubuntu, you press a key and an unexpected character appears on the screen, you can probably fix the problem right there: you just have to figure out which keyboard matches your language and make the change. Once you have chosen the right one, click OK to continue.

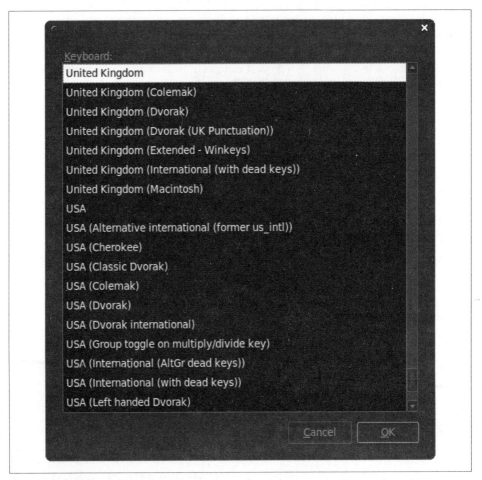

Figure 4-4. Choosing the keyboard layout

Sessions

This option lets you choose the type of desktop to open (see Figure 4-5). By default, it will be the GNOME desktop, but later on, in Chapter 15, I'll show how you can add the KDE or Xfce desktop environments to Ubuntu. And if you do, they will also be listed here as selectable sessions, alongside GNOME.

There is also the Failsafe GNOME option that you can choose if you have display problems when using the regular GNOME desktop. The other option available here is xterm, which opens up a Terminal instead of the Ubuntu desktop. This is useful for situations when the desktop seems to crash or won't even open, perhaps because of changing a graphic driver. With it, you can use text commands to fix the problem. But generally you will not need to use it.

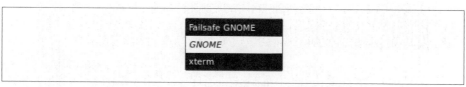

Figure 4-5. Selecting the type of session

Accessibility

If you need it, the Accessibility menu (or as Ubuntu calls it, Universal Access Preferences) can be called up by clicking the icon of a person with his arms and legs extended. You can then enable any or all of the following options:

- Use onscreen keyboard
- Use screen reader
- Use screen magnifier
- Enhance contrast in colors
- Make text larger and easier to read
- Use sticky keys
- Use bounce keys
- Use slow keys

Chapter 3 describes the last three items in the list.

Desktop Layout

One of the best things about Ubuntu is the care and attention that's gone into developing its desktop layout. Based on the GNOME desktop environment (unless you are using Kubuntu or Xubuntu), it provides a slick and intuitive interface to your computer (as do both Xfce and KDE).

The screen grab in Figure 4-6 shows a typical Ubuntu desktop soon after installation. The only minor difference between the screen grab and what you will see on your computer is the wallpaper, which was produced especially for this book.

So, let's take a look at the various parts by taking a clockwise tour, starting at the top left where there are the three main menus. If you are used to using Windows, you can think of these menus as being three Start menus instead of one; rather than having to drill down through a single tree of menu items, Ubuntu divides the options into things dealing with applications, places, and the system itself.

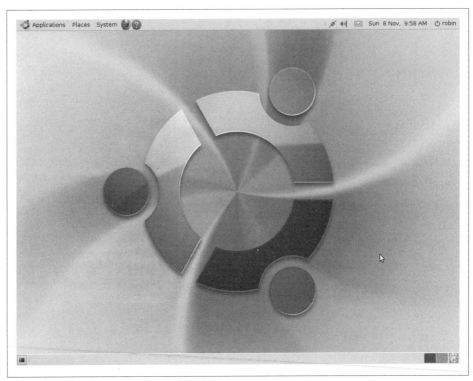

Figure 4-6. Ubuntu's default GNOME desktop environment, featuring a new wallpaper

The Applications Menu

The Applications menu (see Figure 4-7) contains the main programs and accessories you use. This includes things such as Calculator, CD/DVD Creator, and Terminal under the Accessories subheading; over a dozen games under Games; the GIMP image editor and F-Spot Photo Manager under Graphics; the Firefox web browser and Empathy instant messenger (IM) program under Internet; Dictionary and the OpenOffice.org applications under Office; and Sound Recorder, Brasero Disc Burner, and Movie Player under Sound & Video. The Ubuntu Software Center (see Chapter 8) can also be accessed from here. This is where you can easily install and uninstall new software.

As you use Ubuntu and start to install more applications, they will usually appear in this menu under new subheadings such as Education, System Tools, Universal Access, and so on. So, if you can't find a program, the Applications menu is the first place to look.

Figure 4-7. The default Applications menu

The Places Menu

The Places menu (see Figure 4-8) is where you can browse and search all the folders on your computer, as well as any external drives or USB memory sticks. It is also the place for connecting to other computers on the network.

The Home Folder group

The first group of entries in this menu relate to your local computer, as follows:

Home Folder

Each user on the computer has a different home folder, so this is your main folder on the computer. In my case the path to the folder is */home/robin*. For a user named *hannah*, it would be */home/hannah*. All the folders referred to in this group are subfolders of this main one. So, in my case, my Desktop is at */home/robin/Desktop*. Note the capital letter D. Linux is case-sensitive, so you must use the capital letter when referring to this folder.

Desktop

This folder contains all your desktop items, excluding mounted drives.

Documents

This is the place where you'll find your documents as stored by default by applications such as OpenOffice.org.

Music

Music applications will usually use this folder for storing music you download, record, or edit.

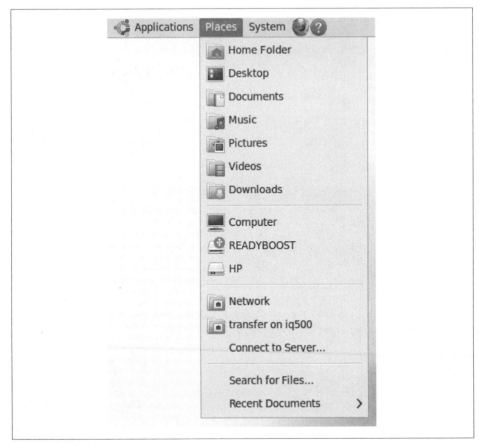

Figure 4-8. The Places menu

Pictures
> Your photos and other images as handled by programs such as the GIMP will be stored here.

Videos
> Videos will generally reside in this folder.

Downloads
> By default, downloaded files are saved in this folder.

The Storage Devices group

The second group of entries relates to your computer's hard disk drives and any attached USB memory sticks or external hard drives. In Figure 4-8, you can see the first item is called Computer. When you click it, a new window similar to the one shown in Figure 4-9 will appear showing all the storage devices and networks attached to your computer or connected to the network.

Figure 4-9. The File Browser open at the top level, showing attached storage devices

In both the Places menu and the File Browser, you may have noticed that this computer has a USB memory stick attached called *READYBOOST*, which is used to provide additional memory caching to Windows Vista. Because that computer has Ubuntu installed alongside Vista in a dual-boot system, I have left that device alone so that it's ready for use whenever I need to reboot into Windows (not that I use it that often anymore).

Speaking of Windows, on that computer the *HP* drive is the name of the Windows partition. Such partitions can be accessed from Ubuntu. When you click one (either in the File Browser or the Places menu) you may be prompted for your password; if so, enter it. A window such as the one in Figure 4-10 will then open, and as long as the folders and files have the required permissions, you can copy files between the Ubuntu and Windows partitions.

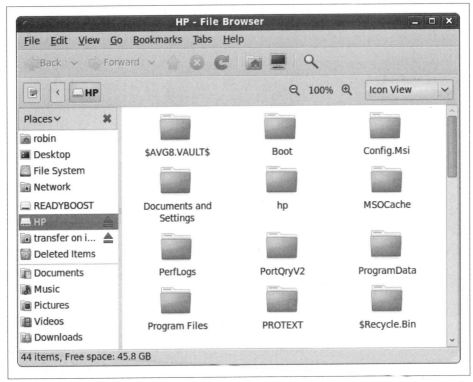

Figure 4-10. Browsing the computer's Windows partition

Whenever you click a storage device, Ubuntu will mount it as an icon on the desktop so that you can quickly reference it from there in the future, until you unmount it or log off.

The Network group

In Figure 4-8, you can see that I have mounted a network folder called *transfer on iq500* in the Network group of the Places menu. This name means the folder called *transfer* on the computer called *iq500*. To access other computers and folders on the network, you click the Network entry to bring up a File Browser window such as the one in Figure 4-11, where two computers on the local network have been found (*AMADEUS* and *MATTHEW*), and a Windows network has also been detected.

Clicking *AMADEUS* takes me to the shared folders on another Linux computer on my desk, whereas clicking *Windows Network* first brings up the workgroups Ubuntu has detected within the Windows network. In my case, as shown in Figure 4-12, three workgroups have been found: *HOME*, *MSHOME*, and *WORKGROUP*.

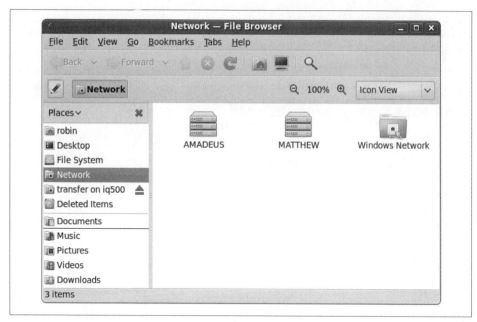

Figure 4-11. Browsing the network

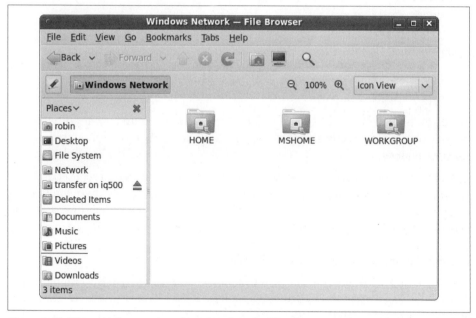

Figure 4-12. Three workgroups have been found on the Windows network

Clicking any of these will bring up another window showing all the computers within that network. So, for example, clicking *MSHOME* brings up five computers in the workgroup, as shown in Figure 4-13. From here on in, you can choose a computer and then select available folders on that machine, although you will have to enter the right passwords for computers that require them.

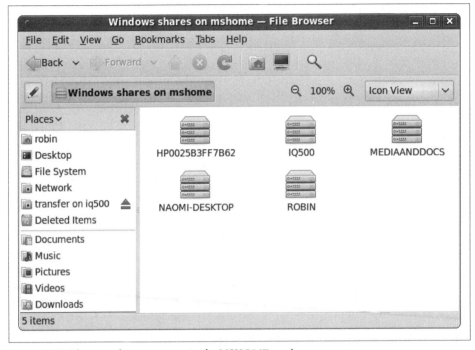

Figure 4-13. There are four computers in the MSHOME workgroup

Once you have connected to another computer and opened up a folder, it will then become accessible directly from the Places menu, and will also be mounted on the desktop as an icon.

Of course, if your computer isn't part of a network or you have a different set of workgroups, what you see when you use the Networks group of the Places menu may be quite different. In any case, you should be able to access whatever Windows and Mac systems that your site can access.

The Search for Files... and Recent Documents groups

The final group in the Places menu is for searching for files or selecting recently accessed documents. Figure 4-14 shows both the Search for Files window and the Recent Documents submenu of the Places menu.

When searching for files you can tell Ubuntu where to look by clicking the "Look in folder" drop-down list and selecting the folders and/or computers or external drives to search.

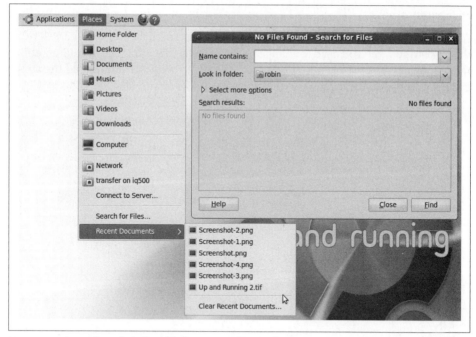

Figure 4-14. Searching for Files and the Recent Documents menu

If you wish to search for specific text within your files, click "Select more options" and you'll be able to enter text to search for, and also narrow down results by date, file size, and several other specifiers.

The System Menu

The System menu (see Figure 4-15) has two groups of items.

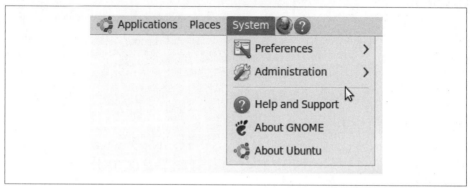

Figure 4-15. The System menu

We'll explore the first group in this section.

Preferences

As you will recall from Chapter 3, the System → Preferences menu (see Figure 4-16) is the place to go when you need to change various settings in your Ubuntu configuration, ranging from the keyboard and display to power management, sound, and the applications to run automatically when the computer boots up.

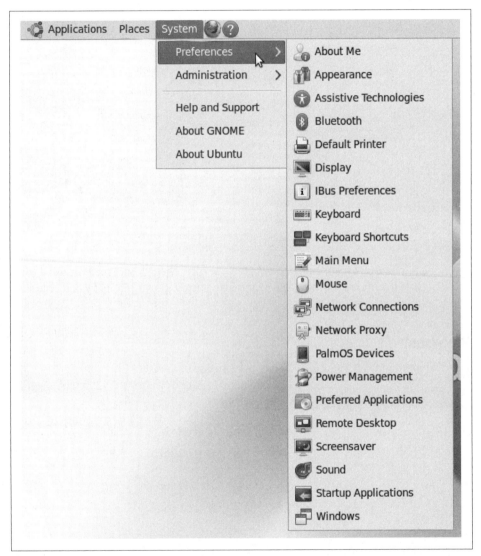

Figure 4-16. The System Preferences menu

There's plenty of information on customizing your computer in the rest of this chapter and throughout this book, so I won't go into further details in this section.

Administration

The System → Administration menu (see Figure 4-17) is where you make more fundamental changes to your computer, such as installing hardware device drivers, setting up TV tuners or webcams, and installing new packages.

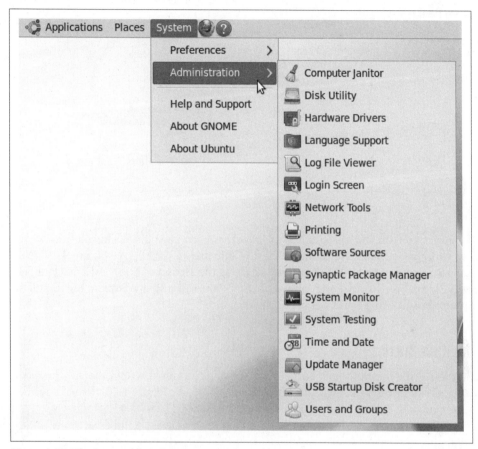

Figure 4-17. The System Administration menu

All of these operations and more are fully explained throughout this chapter and the rest of this book.

The bottom three menu entries

The second group of menu items provides support through built-in web pages, specific information on Ubuntu, and GNOME's online help.

The Top-Left Icons

As you move your eyes past the menus at the top-left side of the GNOME screen, you'll see icons to their immediate right. These are intended to represent some of the most frequently used programs and features. By default, the icons are likely to be for *Firefox* and *Help*, but you can remove any of them by right-clicking and selecting Remove from Panel (see Figure 4-18).

Figure 4-18. Removing an icon from the top panel

Likewise, you can add a program to the panel as an icon by right-clicking it from within the various menus and selecting "Add this launcher to panel" (see Figure 4-19). You can also add an icon to the desktop by selecting the second option, "Add this launcher to desktop." Or by selecting "Entire menu," you can add a complete menu and its suboptions to either the panel or the desktop.

The Quit Button

Starting at the top-righthand corner and working from right to left, the very first icon is the Quit button, which will display your username (see Figure 4-20). When you click it, a menu will come up with various options, described next.

Set Status

If you are logged into the Pidgin or Empathy messaging programs, the first thing you can do is set your user presence by selecting the Set Status submenu. You can then choose to set your presence status to any of the following:

Available
    I am available to be contacted.

Away
    I am not at my computer.

Busy
    I am busy; please don't try to contact me.

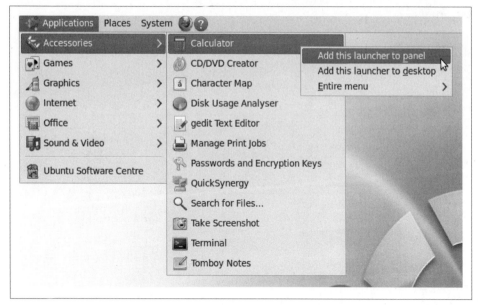

Figure 4-19. Adding the Calculator launcher to the panel

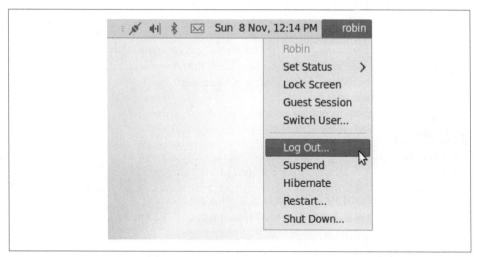

Figure 4-20. The Log Out... entry under the Quit button

Invisible

You can't see me; effectively, I'm not here.

Offline

My computer is offline.

If you are not logged into either IM program, these options will be grayed out and unselectable.

Lock Screen

This blanks out the screen, leaving only a password entry box, which is woken up only when a key is pressed or the mouse is moved (see Figure 4-21). To resume working on your computer, enter your password and click the Unlock button. Alternatively, you can use Switch User to log in as another user.

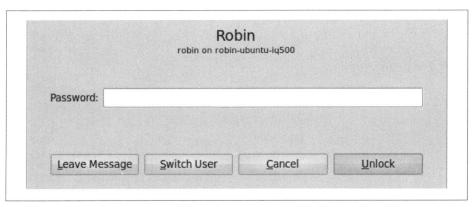

Figure 4-21. The Lock Screen command window

Other people can also leave you a message while you're away with the Leave Message button. The Cancel button is there to darken the screen again without waiting for the blanking timeout delay. In Figure 4-21, you'll see that the box reminds you which user you are on which computer. In this instance, I am user *robin* on the machine identified as *robin-ubuntu-iq500*.

Guest Session

This option lets you commence a guest session, which creates a new desktop with the user *Guest* logged in. Guest users have severely restricted permissions and are prevented from making any major changes. To exit from this session, click the icon again and select Log Out.... You will then be prompted for your password in order to resume using the account from which the *Guest* user desktop was called up.

Switch User...

This takes you back to the login screen shown earlier in Figure 4-1, where you can log in as another user or log back into your previous session.

Log Out...

This option logs you out of your current session and returns you to the login screen, where you can choose to log in again as another (or the same) user, reboot the computer, or turn it off. The difference between Switch User... and Log Out... is that the former keeps your programs open when returning to the Login screen, whereas the latter closes them all first.

Suspend

With the Suspend option you can put the computer to sleep so that all processing is suspended until you reawaken it by pressing a key or by using the mouse. A word of caution here though, because Ubuntu has a known history of occasional problems with this feature, and sometimes, depending on your hardware, it may crash and won't reawaken (or Resume) in a usable state. I recommend that you test it without any important programs open before deciding whether to use it in the future.

Hibernate

The Hibernate option goes a step further because it saves the current configuration to hard disk and then completely turns the computer off. This is the best method for saving electricity while being able to return to exactly where you left off the next time you turn the computer on. Again, testing is recommended before relying on this feature.

Restart

When you select this option, your computer starts a 60-second countdown timer in a window on the desktop, leading to the restarting of your computer. You can choose to click the Cancel button if you didn't intend to restart your PC, or the Restart button to bypass the timer and restart immediately.

However, if other users are logged into the computer, another window will pop up requesting your password before allowing the restart to occur. You can either type in your password and click the Authenticate button to force a restart, or click the Cancel button to halt the process.

Shutdown

This option works identically to Restart, except that the computer is turned off and does not turn on again until you press its on button.

What's new in 10.04

Starting with Ubuntu 10.04, the Quit menu has been divided in two, with all the status indicators now having their own Me Menu on the left and the current username shown next to a speech bubble as the heading/drop-down menu button. The Me Menu lists your username at the top, alongside a thumbnail image which you can personalize by clicking it. Underneath that is an input box where you can enter updates to Twitter, Facebook, and/or other similar sites once you have configured Ubuntu to access them. You can also directly enter any Chat or Broadcast accounts you have set up, or open Ubuntu One from here. To the right, all the user functions such as shutdown and restart are now selectable from the universal broken circle power button.

The Remaining Top-Right Icons

The remaining icons to the left of the Quit button will vary from computer to computer, but generally there will be some or all of the following.

The date and time

Although it shows as text, as soon as you pass your mouse over it, you'll see that the date and time display is actually part of a button that brings up a calendar when clicked, as shown in Figure 4-22.

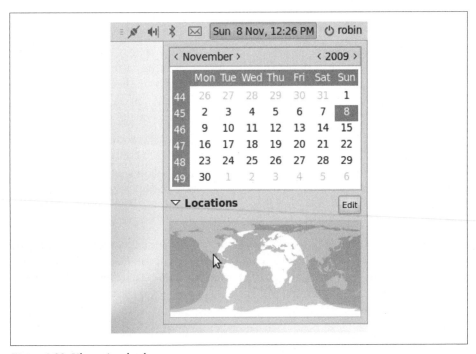

Figure 4-22. Ubuntu's calendar

When you click any dates, the *Evolution* email groupware application is called up to help you manage appointments, tasks, and so on. If it's the first time you've used it, you'll be taken through a setup process before it opens.

If you just want to insert today's date or time into a document, you can right-click the button and select either Copy Time or Copy Date.

If the time and/or date is incorrect on your computer, you can fix it by selecting System → Administration → Time and Date. To change any settings, select "Click to make changes" and, after requesting your password, this will bring up a new window in which you can specify your local time zone and the time and date where you are.

New mail

The new mail icon (which looks like an unopened letter) is likely to be displayed immediately after installing Ubuntu because there is a friendly email from the *Evolution* email program developers waiting to be read. Once you have set up the program by providing your email account details, you'll be able to view the welcome message, as well as your other emails.

Sound volume

Whether or not the sound volume icon is displayed seems to depend on your sound hardware. When it is visible, you can click it to slide the volume up and down, and right-clicking provides access to the Mute checkbox and the Sound Preferences window. If you did not hear an introductory tune when Ubuntu booted up and you have a working sound card, then most likely this checkbox will be selected, so look there first before investigating whether you have a hardware or driver issue.

Bluetooth

If your computer has Bluetooth capability, you may also see a Bluetooth icon. You can click it to bring up a menu with which you can turn it on and off, send files and browse devices, set up new devices, and change your Bluetooth preferences (see Figure 4-23). For this icon, both the left and right mouse buttons pull up the same menu.

Figure 4-23. The Bluetooth menu

Network connection

This icon changes according to the network hardware you have:

- If you don't have a networking device, the icon will show a symbol similar to the one for a mobile phone's connectivity, but with the four bars showing no signal, which indicates that there is no connection.

- If you are using a WiFi card and it is working, the four ascending bars will show your signal level. If it's unconnected, no signal level will be shown.

- If you have a wired connection that is working, the icon will resemble two plugs connected to each other diagonally.

When you click the icon, a menu will open in which you can select the connections you require activated (see Figure 4-24). You can also configure VPN (Virtual Private Networking) from here, as well as connect to hidden wireless networks (those that do not broadcast their name) or create a new wireless network.

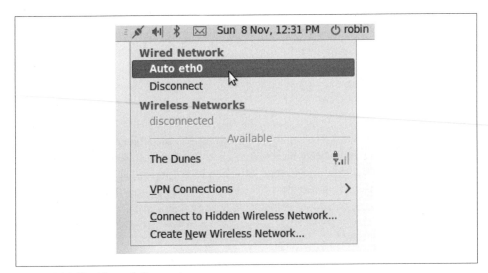

Figure 4-24. The Network Connections menu

Right-clicking brings up a different menu with which you can turn all networking (or just wireless networking) on and off. You can also view information about your connection and edit your connection settings. See Chapter 3 for more on this icon.

The Bottom-Right Icons

Down at the far right of your desktop, you'll find a couple more icons, including the Trash, as shown in Figure 4-25.

Figure 4-25. Emptying the Trash

 Users of non-American English will see this referred to using the word Wastebasket instead of Trash.

The Trash

Whenever you wish to delete a file, just drag and drop it into the Trash and it will be deleted. But there's a failsafe to prevent you from accidentally deleting files you didn't mean to: erased files are stored in the Trash until you empty it by right-clicking the icon and selecting Empty Trash.

To restore or undelete a file, click the Trash icon and a window will open up displaying its contents (see Figure 4-26). You can then drag and drop the files shown to other places in the computer's filesystem, or right-click any item for a list of further features, including options to permanently delete or restore a file. There is also an Empty Trash button in this window.

The workspace switcher

Using the workspace switcher, you can have multiple desktops (up to 36, in fact), each displaying different programs and windows. Each workspace is represented by an icon showing where the various windows are located within it. To switch between them, you can:

- Click the icon representing the workspace you wish to access.
- Use the keyboard shortcut alternatives of Ctrl-Alt-Left arrow to select the workspace to the left or Ctrl-Alt-Right arrow to select the one to the right. When you do this, a grid will appear in the center of the screen showing which workspace you are currently viewing, where the other ones are located relative to it, and the windows each one contains.

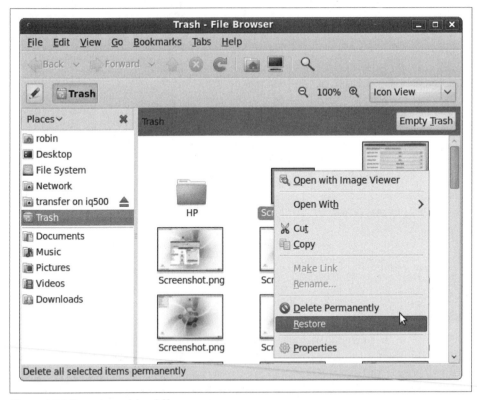

Figure 4-26. Restoring a deleted file

- Place the mouse pointer over the workspace switcher and scroll the middle mouse wheel.

The icons on your desktop will remain where they are, but the open windows and programs will change.

There are also a number of ways you can move a window from one workspace to another. You can:

- Right-click the title bar (or left-click the small dot at the far left of the title bar) and select Move to Workspace Right, Move to Workspace Left, or Move to Another Workspace. The former two will move the window one place to the left or right, whereas the latter opens up a submenu from which you can choose which workspace the window should be moved to.

- Locate the miniature representation of the window to move within the workspace icons at the bottom right of the desktop, and then click and drag it to another workspace.

- Select the window to move by clicking it or its title bar, and then press Ctrl-Alt-Shift-Left arrow to move it to the workspace on the left of the current one (if there is one) or Ctrl-Alt-Shift-Right arrow to move it to the workspace immediately to the right (if there is one).

- Drag any window by its title bar to any workspace of your choice. (For this to work, you need to have a suitable Nvidia graphics card and the Nvidia proprietary drivers installed, as discussed in the section "Display Preferences" on page 71 of Chapter 3.)

You can change the way your workspaces are laid out by right-clicking one of the workspace switcher icons in the bottom-righthand corner and selecting Preferences. A new Workspace Switcher Preferences window will then appear (see Figure 4-27). From here, you can effectively disable all additional workspaces by choosing to display only the current one, or change the number of rows and the total number of workspaces available.

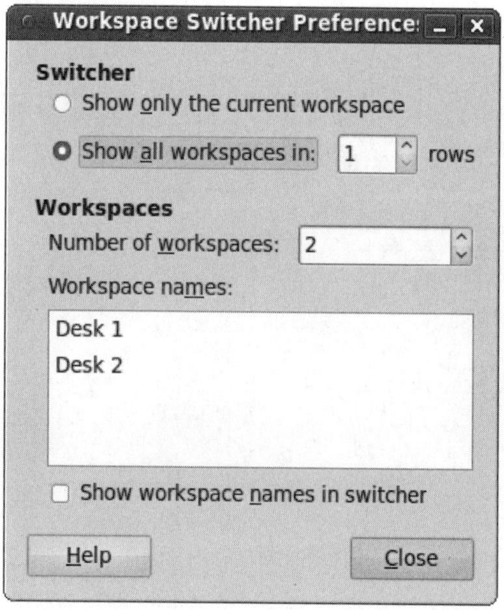

Figure 4-27. The Workspace Switcher Preferences window

If you choose to have more than one row of workspaces, you'll also find that all the previous key presses mentioned are augmented with Up arrow and Down arrow shortcuts to move or select workspaces above and/or below the current one. For example, you'll be able to move a window up by pressing Ctrl-Alt-Shift-Up arrow.

You can also give each workspace different names from the rather inexpressive defaults, such as *Desk 1* and *Desk 2*, and can choose between displaying either the icons or the workspace names.

The Bottom Panel

The bottom panel holds the previously discussed workspace switcher and Trash, as well as all the buttons for controlling the open programs and windows. Figure 4-28 shows three programs open (*Four-in-a-Row*, *Calculator*, and *Firefox*, which is minimized), with matching entries in the bottom panel, which I'll call *tabs* for want of a better name.

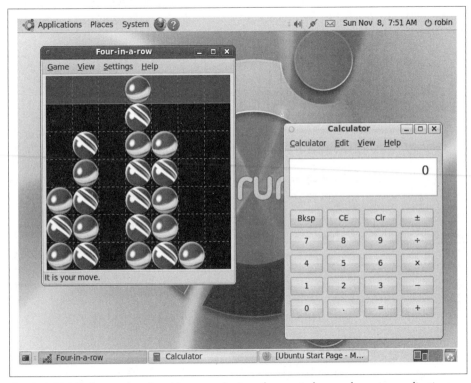

Figure 4-28. The bottom panel enables easy selection of open windows and running applications

Clicking a program or a window's tab toggles between displaying and hiding it. By right-clicking, you can call up a context menu with which you can move and resize the window, set its attributes, such as On Top status or Visibility, and move the window to another workspace (see Figure 4-29).

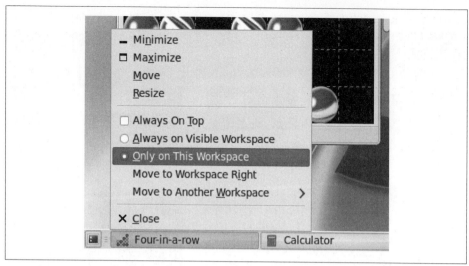

Figure 4-29. Right-clicking a tab brings up its context menu

Show desktop

The final icon in this desktop roundup is in the bottom-left corner, looking like a miniature representation of a monitor showing a desktop. You can click this icon to hide or reveal all the windows on the desktop at once. Each time you click it, Ubuntu toggles the desktop between the two states. This is a great feature when you need to quickly remove all windows to access an icon on the desktop, and then restore the windows back to where they were in order to continue working with them.

Personalization

Now that you've been introduced to the default desktop and have a good feel for where everything is, what it does, and how it works, you may wish to customize it to your own preferences—and personalization is something at which Ubuntu excels, due to its tremendous range of customization options and preference settings.

Appearance

The place to start when customizing Ubuntu is the Appearance Preferences window, which you get to by selecting System → Preferences → Appearance. As Figure 4-30 shows, there are five main sections divided into tabs.

Theme

The Theme tab lets you choose between a selection of predefined themes, of which *Human* is the default. Try clicking different ones, and the desktop will change after a

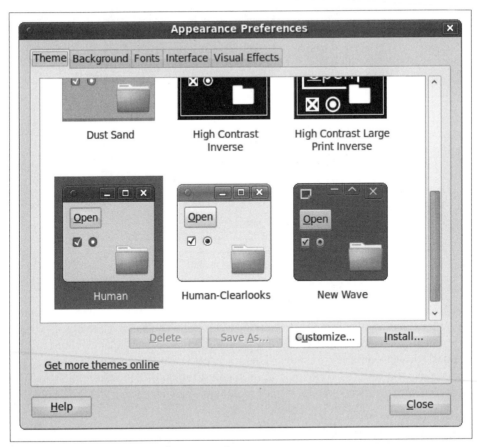

Figure 4-30. The Appearance Preferences window

few seconds. For example, a good theme to choose for people with visual difficulties would be High Contrast Large Print Inverse. Whichever theme you choose will stay selected.

You can further modify a theme by clicking the Customize button, which brings up another window with five options (see Figure 4-31).

Controls
   Lets you choose how you want items such as checkboxes and buttons to appear. Just click the example you want to use.

Colors
   Lets you choose the text and background colors for windows, input boxes, selected items, and tooltips.

Window Border
   Lets you can choose a variety of border types for your windows.

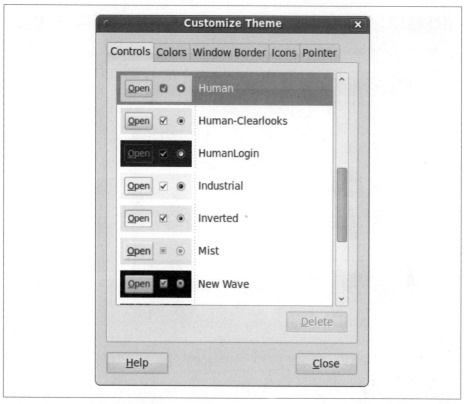

Figure 4-31. The Customize Theme window

Icons

Lets you choose the icon set you prefer most.

Pointer

Lets you choose the type of mouse pointer you prefer to use.

Background

The Background tab chooses which wallpaper (if any) to use, how to display it, and which color to use for the desktop background. Some wallpapers include transparency, so these choices are not mutually exclusive and can be combined. Figure 4-32 shows some of the several backgrounds supplied by default.

You can choose between having the wallpaper tiled, zoomed, centered, scaled, or shown full screen by clicking the Style drop-down menu. Or you can choose a different image by either clicking one of the other wallpapers or clicking Add and browsing through the filesystem to locate a picture to use. Programs such as Firefox and the Image Viewer also have options to set the current image as the desktop background.

Figure 4-32. Changing the desktop background

The Colors drop-down menu allows you to choose between a solid color and either a horizontal or vertical gradient for the background. A gradient shades gradually from one color to another. The box to the right can be clicked to select the actual color to use with a color picker, or you can type in its hexadecimal value (see Figure 4-33).

If you choose one of the gradients, two color boxes will be displayed next to the drop-down menu, one for each color in the gradient.

By the way, any background whose icon shows up as several images in a stack is just that: a group of images that will rotate at 30-minute intervals.

Fonts

With the Fonts tab (see Figure 4-34), you can choose the default face and size of font to use for your applications, documents, desktop, window titles, and fixed-width text. Just click a font name and choose the new one. A window will then appear in which you can choose the font you want, whether it should appear by default in regular, bold, italic, or combined bold and italic style, and the size of the font. Click Cancel to return without making a change, or OK to make the change and go back.

Figure 4-33. The color picker

Figure 4-34. The Fonts tab

There's also quite a clever feature below the fonts with which you can specify the type of font rendering you prefer. Not all monitors are the same, so try clicking the various choices to see which you prefer.

For even finer control, you can then click the Details button (see Figure 4-35) to tell Ubuntu the number of dots per inch your monitor displays, the type of smoothing to use, what hinting setting you prefer, and the subpixel order. The latter is a setting you make to match the order of the red, green, and blue components of each pixel on your monitor, as this varies by manufacturer.

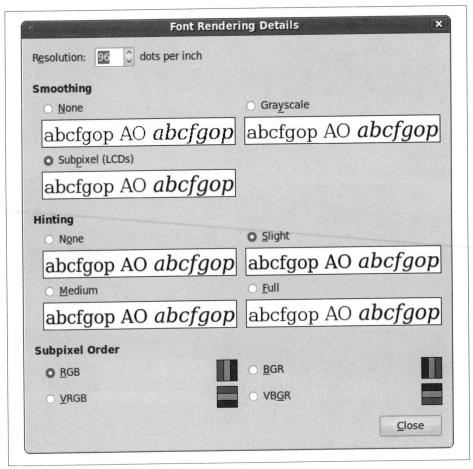

Figure 4-35. Fine-tuning the rendering of fonts

Interface

The Interface tab (see Figure 4-36) lets you change the way some icons and menus appear. In the Menus and Toolbars section, you can check the "Show icons in menus" box to place an icon before each menu item.

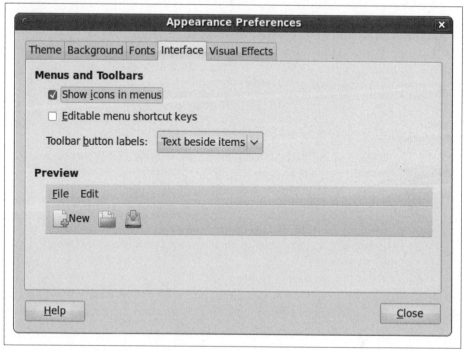

Figure 4-36. Configuring the display of icons, menus, and toolbars

For example, Figure 4-37 shows what the Trash menu shown earlier in Figure 4-25 looks like with this box unchecked—notice how it's a lot plainer. To my mind, the tiny amount of speed increase you might see by removing the icons is outweighed by the better look and feel and quicker comprehension that the icons' visual cues provide.

If you check the "Editable menu shortcut keys" box you can define new keyboard shortcuts for menu items. To change an application shortcut key, open the menu, and with the mouse pointer on the menu item you wish to change, press the new combination of keys. To remove a shortcut key, press Backspace or Delete.

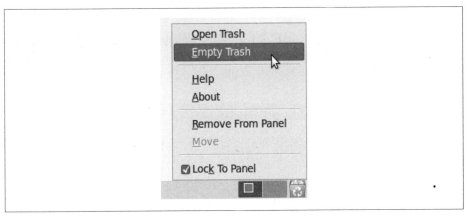

Figure 4-37. The menu items in the Trash menu have been disabled

 When using the "Editable menu shortcut keys" feature, you won't be warned if assigning a new shortcut key to a command will also remove it from another command, and there is no way to restore the default keyboard shortcut for a command. You can also inadvertently assign a normal keyboard key, such as the letter e, to a function, making it so that typing the letter e would no longer result in that letter being sent to the application you are using. For this reason I recommend you keep this option disabled.

Using the drop-down menu next to "Toolbar button labels," you can further specify the appearance of toolbars by choosing whether text should appear below or beside items, and whether to display only text or only icons.

What's new in 10.04

With the release of Ubuntu 10.04, the Interface tab is completely removed from the Appearance Preferences window. This was a decision taken by the GNOME development team, which decided that such options should be provided only by third-party user interface tweaking tools. However, you are able to access the setting directly with the GNOME Configuration Editor by pressing Alt-F2 and then entering gconf-edi tor. When the editor opens, drill down to desktop → gnome → interface and then either check or uncheck the box next to the entry "menus_have_icons". You can also modify many other aspects of GNOME with this interface, but be very careful in case you mess up your desktop.

Visual effects

Depending on your hardware and the drivers installed, Ubuntu may be capable of providing enhanced visual effects (see Figure 4-38).

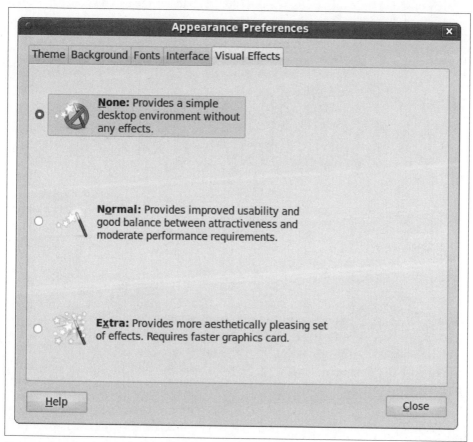

Figure 4-38. Setting the level of visual effects to use

The three levels of effects are:

None

This setting doesn't make use of any special effects and is best suited to slower machines or older graphics hardware.

Normal

This is the most common setting that should suit the widest range of computers and graphics cards. With it, you'll see shadows around windows, windows will gracefully zoom as you minimize and maximize them, and opacity will be enabled, giving an effect similar to Windows Vista and 7's Aero Glass.

Extra

This setting gives you a set of ultra cool effects, such as wobbly windows when you shake them, but you need a fast graphics card and a suitable driver installed. For a great example effect (if your computer lets you select this setting), try opening a

few programs and then press WindowsKey-Tab to see the task switcher shown in
Figure 4-39.

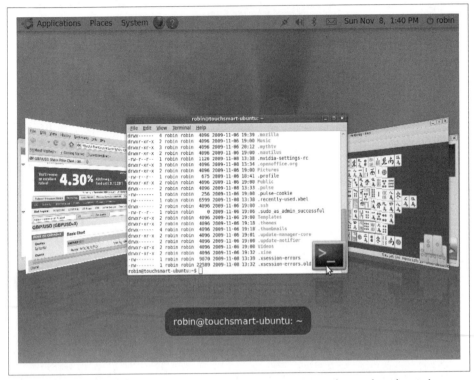

Figure 4-39. Using the Extra Visual Effects setting gives you a Cover Flow–style task switcher

If you choose a setting that requires a graphics driver that isn't already installed, Ubuntu
will attempt to locate and install it. If it can't do so, that setting won't be available to you.

 Should you experience problems in one of the higher settings, your card
may not be quite fast enough or fully compatible, or the driver may not
have all the required features. Try changing down a level and your computer should then be OK.

Managing Panels

Although I don't recommend doing so, you can remove the top and bottom panels
from your Ubuntu desktop simply by right-clicking them and selecting "Delete this
panel." In the same way, you can add more panels by right-clicking a panel and selecting
New Panel. By default, the first new panel you add will be placed on the righthand side
of the screen and the second will go on the left.

If you ever remove the default panels, you won't have access to the programs required to restore them. To fix this, press Alt-F2 and then type gnome-terminal and click Run. Next enter the following commands into the Terminal window:

```
gconftool --recursive-unset /apps/panel
rm -rf/.gconf/apps/panel
pkill gnome-panel
```

Note that there are two dashes preceding the word recursive.

If you add more than two extra panels, new ones will be added underneath the top panel, but you can change the location by right-clicking a panel, selecting Properties, and using the Orientation drop-down menu.

Adding an item to a panel

To add an item to a panel, right-click it and then select Add to Panel to bring up the Add to Panel window. Here, you can select from a wide range of launchers and applets, as shown in Figure 4-40.

The first two options let you add an application of your choosing to the panel, either by creating a new launcher or by copying a launcher from the Applications menu. Alternatively, scroll down through the list of preselected applications and you may find the one you want already listed.

In fact, you can add more than applications using this window because it supports items such as a keyboard status indicator, a custom menu bar, a file searcher, Shut Down and Restart buttons, and many more.

There's also an easy way to add any menu item to the top panel. Just locate the item using the mouse, right-click it, and select "Add this launcher to panel."

Removing an item from a panel

To remove an item from the panel, right-click it and select Remove from Panel. Be careful, though, because you can remove the Quit menu and other important items that are not easy to restore using this feature.

Moving an item within a panel

To move an item to a different location in a panel, select Move and then use the mouse to move it left and right (or up and down) along the panel until you reach the desired destination, then click the left mouse button. Alternatively, you can drag and drop the icon into its new location.

If you wish to insert an item between two others that are right against each other, you will have to move them apart first to make room. Otherwise, you may end up dropping an item onto another, which would have the unwanted effect of opening up the latter item, passing the item dropped to it as if it were data to be acted on.

Figure 4-40. The Add to Panel window

If you wish to prevent an item from being moved, right-click it and select "Lock to Panel." Dragging and dropping that item will then be disabled. You may also need to uncheck this option to move items in the first place.

Changing a launcher's icon

If you want to display a different icon for an item (or launcher) in a panel, right-click it and select Properties to bring up the launcher's properties window. Now click the icon to bring up the icon browser, as shown in Figure 4-41. To reach the state shown in that figure, I created a new *Calculator* launcher in the top panel, opened up its properties window, and clicked its icon.

After browsing through the icons and selecting the one you want, click OK to change the launcher's icon. Otherwise, click Cancel to back out again without making any changes.

Incidentally, as you can see, this window also lets you change a panel item's type, name, command (the command to issue or program to run), and tooltip comment.

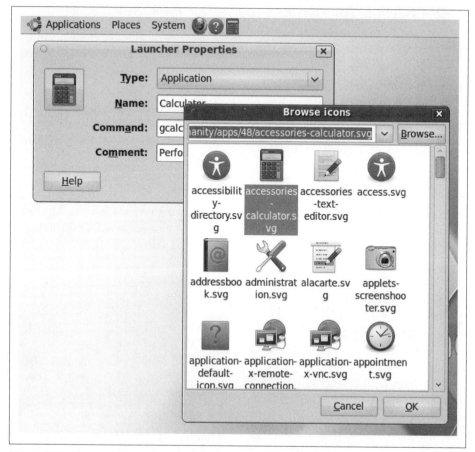

Figure 4-41. Changing a Launcher's icon

Adding a drawer

Ubuntu's panels are already powerful and versatile tools, but you can make them even more useful by adding *drawers* to them. These are drop-down menus in which you can store other items. To add a drawer to a panel, right-click it and select Add to Panel, then scroll down to the Drawer entry, select it, and click the Add button. A small icon that looks like an open drawer will then appear on the panel. If you click this icon, it will drop down an empty box, as there's nothing in it.

To add items to the drawer, as you can probably guess, right-click it and select Add to Drawer. This will bring up a window almost exactly the same as the one shown in Figure 4-40, except it will have the title Add to Drawer, and that includes featuring the Drawer entry again so that you can add drawers within other drawers and so on. Mostly, though, you'll want to add a selection of related items to a drawer.

Items added to a drawer will appear only as icons without any associated text.

Changing a drawer's icon

To change a drawer's icon, right-click it and select Properties. Then, click the Choose Icon button and proceed in the same way as described in the earlier section "Changing a launcher's icon" on page 138. You can also change the drawer icon's size and background color or image.

Adding a menu to a panel

But that's not all, because you can also add complete menus to the top panel by right-clicking a single item within a menu and then selecting "Entire menu." From here, you can then choose to add the menu to the panel, either as a drawer or as a menu, as you can see from Figure 4-42.

Figure 4-42. Adding an entire menu to a panel

Hiding a panel

If you want to obtain a bit more desktop space, you can hide one or more of your panels by right-clicking one and selecting Properties, followed by checking the Autohide box. Then, click the Close button. The panel will disappear, but it can be brought back whenever you need it by moving your mouse to the edge of the screen and leaving it there. The panel will then slide into view and slide back again when you move the mouse away.

If you prefer, instead of checking the Autohide box, check the "Show hide buttons" box instead. This will place an arrow icon at the edge of the panel that, if you click it, will make the panel slide away lengthways to the screen's edge, leaving only the arrow icon behind. Click it again to restore the panel.

Other panel properties

When you right-click a panel and select Properties, you can also uncheck the Expand box, which will make the panel only as big as it needs to be to contain its contents. Or you can set the edge of the desktop (top, bottom, left, or right) to which the panel should be attached, and its width in pixels. Also, if you click the Background tab, you can change the panel's background color and transparency or image.

Editing Menus

Ubuntu comes with a sophisticated menu-editing program that makes it easy for you to customize your menus exactly to your preference. To use it, right-click any of the top panel menus out of System, Places, or Applications (it makes no difference which) and select Edit Menus. As you can see in Figure 4-43, this brings up the Main Menu editor window.

In the lefthand pane of the window you can see the two main menus, Applications and System, as they appear on your desktop, along with the items within them. In the righthand pane all the menu items are displayed, including some that have been set to invisible by unchecking their associated Show boxes.

Whichever item you click in the left pane is opened up in the right one. In the case of a new Ubuntu installation, the Debian, Education, and Science submenus have yet to be populated, and so they are shown in italics. Because they are empty, even if you check their Show boxes in the righthand pane, they will not be enabled on your desktop.

However, you may have items in one or more of the Programming, System Tools, or Universal Access menus, but they will have been set to hidden so that beginners won't stumble across the programs in them and possibly mess up their Ubuntu installation.

Nevertheless, you can verify that they contain items by clicking them in the lefthand pane, so go ahead and click some of them, and you may see the righthand pane change to something like the one shown in Figure 4-44. At this point, I don't recommend checking the Show boxes for any of these items unless you know what you're doing.

Figure 4-43. The Main Menu editor window

Changing menu entry icons

To change the icon for a menu entry, first select the menu in the lefthand pane of the editor, and then select the entry within that menu in the righthand pane. You can now click the Properties button (or right-click the item and select Properties) to bring up the Launcher Properties window shown in Figure 4-41. To edit the icon, follow the procedure outlined in the earlier section "Changing a launcher's icon" on page 138.

In this window, you can also edit the launcher's type, name, the command used to launch a program, and the tooltip comment for the entry.

Moving and deleting entries

To move an entry, select it in the righthand pane and then click the Move Up or Move Down button until it is in the desired location.

If you wish to delete an entry, simply select it and click the Delete button. Be careful, though, as there is no "Are you sure?" warning for this action.

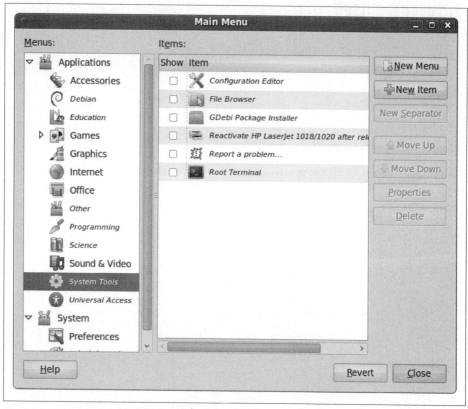

Figure 4-44. Viewing the contents of the hidden System Tools submenu

Adding new menus and items

To add a new submenu, highlight the position where you want it to be inserted and click the New Menu button. A window will pop up asking you to enter a name and comment to be displayed as a tooltip, which you should fill in before clicking OK to create the menu. Click Cancel to return without making a change.

To add a new item to a menu, move to the place where you want it inserted and click the New Item button. A new window will pop up entitled Create Launcher, which is identical to the one shown in Figure 4-41, except that all of the fields are blank and need to be filled in. To complete the process, you will need to enter the entry's type, name, and comment, as well as the command required to launch the item. The command is the critical piece of information you need to know; if you don't have that information, click Cancel and see whether you can figure out the command after reading Chapter 7. Otherwise, enter the information and click the OK button to add the item.

The Desktop Itself

So far I've talked a lot about things relating to the desktop but not so much about the desktop itself and what you can do with it.

After a new install, your desktop will likely have nothing on it, unless you have a CD-ROM or other drive mounted, in which case you might see an icon for it that you can click to browse its files.

Creating Folders, Launchers, and Files

So, let's put something on the desktop by right-clicking it to bring up the context menu shown in Figure 4-45. Click Create Folder, and when the new folder appears with the words "untitled folder" highlighted, replace that text with something meaningful, such as "Test Folder."

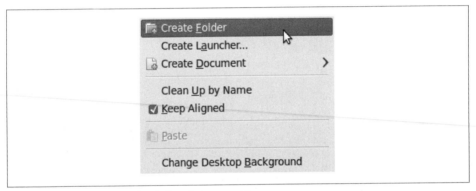

Figure 4-45. Right-clicking the desktop brings up this context menu

Now double-click the folder to open it up, and an empty file browser window will open. The first thing you might want to do at this point is something I always do after a fresh install: enable Ubuntu to respond to single-clicks instead of always requiring double-clicks.

If you want to make your installation work this way, click the Edit menu and select Preferences to bring up the window shown in Figure 4-46. Several options become available to you here under various tabs, which I'll explain in Chapter 6, but for now just select the Behavior tab, check "Single-click to open items," and then click Close. If you won't be using it, you may wish to delete the test folder by dragging it into the Trash.

Other things you can do after right-clicking the desktop include creating a new launcher and creating a new, empty file.

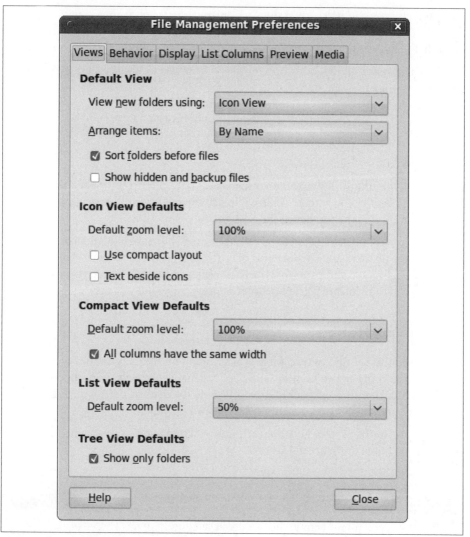

Figure 4-46. The File Management Preferences window

Managing Desktop Icons

To move desktop icons around, all you have to do is drag them to their new locations. If you want to move more than one item, you can lasso a group by clicking and holding the mouse button on a clear area of the desktop and then dragging it so that a rectangle surrounds the icons you are interested in. This groups the enclosed icons, which then can be dragged about as a group.

Alternatively, you can hold down the Ctrl key and click each icon you wish to add to a group. This technique is great when the icons you want are not all next to each other and other icons you don't want selected are among them.

You can also select all the icons on your desktop by clicking once on a clear area of desktop and then pressing Ctrl-A.

 Be careful when deleting or moving icons because a large number of grouped icons can be dragged to the Trash or transferred to other folders in a single action.

If you want Ubuntu to tidy up all your icons for you, you can right-click the desktop and select "Clean Up by Name." This will place them all in alphabetical order in neat columns, starting at the top left of the desktop.

You can also right-click and check the "Keep aligned" box if you would like your icons to always line up along an invisible grid of horizontal and vertical lines. This will keep them in straight rows and columns. If you move icons roughly where you want them, they will snap to the nearest grid line intersection.

Adding New Users

Now that you've set up your desktop exactly how you like it, you may want to give access to your computer to friends, family, or colleagues. Luckily, you can do this very securely using Ubuntu, and each user will be able to customize her working environment to her preferences (or you can do it for them).

The place to start is System → Administration → Users and Groups, which brings up the window shown in Figure 4-47.

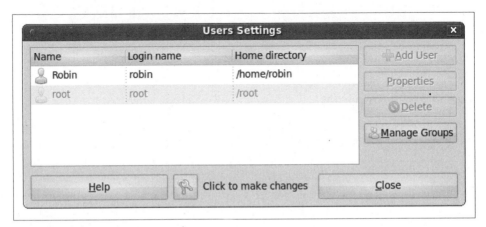

Figure 4-47. The Users Settings window

In this figure, you can see there are two users, *Robin* and *root*. The user *root* is the main and most important user as far as managing your computer goes, as will be explained later, but for now you can ignore it. The other user is me, *Robin*. Because administrating users is a potential security risk, I can edit my own details at this point by clicking my name, followed by the Properties button (which becomes enabled at that point). However, I cannot edit the *root* user or add new users.

To enable these features, you need to click the key icon next to "Click to make changes." You will then be asked for your password, and after you enter it the various grayed-out options will become enabled.

Once you have entered your password and the Add User button becomes accessible, you should click it to bring up the "New user account" window, shown in Figure 4-48.

Figure 4-48. Creating a new user account

Here, you need to enter the Username and Real name of the new account. The username is the short, single-word text that is used to name the Home folder and for other information about the user on the system. The real name is a longer string that can contain spaces and is used to display the user's name on the desktop; if you fail to provide one, the desktop will just display the username. Then, either enter the new user's password manually or ask the computer to generate a random one for you. You should leave the user's profile as "Desktop user" unless you have a reason for changing it.

That's all you need to do to create a new account, but don't press OK yet, though. I recommend you click the other tabs first to fill in other information you may wish to save, such as the user's contact details, their privileges (such as whether they can use printers and video devices, and so on), and advanced settings, such as their Home directory. But unless you know what you're doing, I recommend you ignore the Advanced tab for now.

When you click OK, the new user will be added to the computer and become available at the login screen. Now you can click the Close button and test the new account by logging out and then back in as the new user, or by starting a new session. Both of these options are available from the Quit button.

What's New in 10.04

The 10.04 Lucid Lynx release of Ubuntu sees a switch from the Humanity theme that has been used for many years to one based on Light. The first impressions of Ubuntu forum users was that the new look is "sharp" and "impressive." I think so, too. But you will need to get used to a few things such as the minimize, maximize, and close buttons being at the top left of each window (rather than the top right), as shown in Figures 4-49 and 4-50 (which reveal two versions of the new themes, Ambiance and Radiance).

Figure 4-49. The brand new Ubuntu Ambiance theme used in Ubuntu 10.04

Figure 4-50. All themes are configurable and this is a lighter version of Ambiance called Radiance

Although the Ubuntu forum users loved the new styling, only about 8% were in favor of the buttons being moved (as of this writing, that is). Therefore, by the time the final version of 10.04 is released, it is possible that some things may have changed again. If you find the new styling too different for your tastes, you can easily change it by selecting System → Preferences → Appearance and then either choosing a new theme (perhaps, the old Human theme), or you can click the Customize button and refine a theme to your preferences.

You can also press Alt-F2 and enter the command gconf-editor `gconf-editor`. Then, in the lefthand frame of the editor, click the + symbol next to the "apps" entry to open it up. Scroll down to the "metacity" entry and click its + symbol. Now click the "general" subsection and find the entry in the righthand pane with the name "button_layout." This will be a string such as `maximize,minimize,close:` with the colon representing the opposite window edge from the buttons, and the order of the button names indicating the order in which they should appear. You will need to change this value by right-clicking it and choosing Edit Key. Then, to change the location and order of the buttons, you should edit the entry to give it a new value of `menu:minimize,maximize,close` and click the OK button to store the value. You should then see the buttons immediately return to their previous top-right position (and in the previous order) on all, as shown in Figure 4-51.

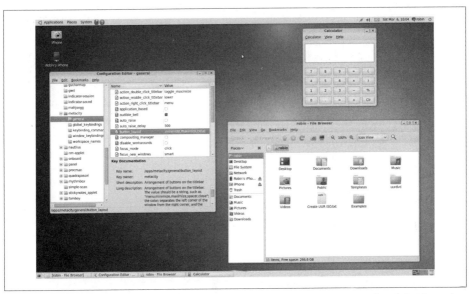

Figure 4-51. The location and positions of the window buttons are now restored and the theme has been changed to Human

Summary

You should now be very proficient at using the Ubuntu GNOME desktop environment, so in the next chapter, we'll start to explore Ubuntu's filesystem in more depth.

CHAPTER 5

The Filesystem, File Attributes, and Permissions

If you come from a Windows background, in which hard disks, CD-ROMs, USB thumb drives, and other storage media are assigned drive letters, then you'll find Ubuntu a little unusual. Mac OS X users, though, will find themselves right at home. The reason for this is that OS X is based on Unix, which uses the same filesystem model to encompass all media available to the operating system.

On a Windows computer, the root of the main hard disk will often be `C:\`, but in Ubuntu, (as with OS X, Unix, and Linux in general) the root of the filesystem is simply /, a forward slash. And that / is not just the root for the main hard disk, it's the root of absolutely everything, so if you have more than one storage device attached, they will also be mounted as extensions to the filesystem (I'll explain how later). Don't confuse the filesystem root with the user named *root*.

> On Ubuntu this filesystem is sometimes also known as *Filesystem*, but whether you see *file system*, *File System*, or *Filesystem*, they all refer to the same thing.

The Directory Tree

Right under the root / lies a handful of system files and several subfolders that make up the next level of the Ubuntu filesystem.

> The terms *folder* and *directory* are generally interchangeable, although you'll mostly see the word directory used when discussing using the command line, whereas the word folder is mainly used when referring to the desktop. For the sake of simplicity, I've chosen to use the term "folder" in both instances throughout most of this book.

Here is a short list of some of the folders and subfolders (out of the thousands) that exist in an Ubuntu filesystem:

```
/
/bin
/boot/
/cdrom
/dev
/etc
/etc/X11
/home
/home/user1/Desktop
/home/user2/Desktop
/lib
/lost+found
/media
/media/cdrom
/mnt
/opt
/proc
/root
/sbin
/selinux
/srv
/sys
/tmp
/usr
/usr/bin
/var
```

Figure 5-1 shows what the first level looks like when viewed with Ubuntu's file browser. In it you can see all the root folders from the preceding list.

At the first level, the filesystem root, there are several folders and a few system files. Many of the folders are reserved mostly for system use, but here are a few that you are likely to access:

/etc

> This folder stores most of the configuration files that control how Ubuntu works. For example, the name of your Ubuntu computer is stored in the file */etc/hostname*.

/home

> This is the folder in which all the main user files are stored, separated into sub-folders with each user's name. For example, the user *robin*'s files are all located in */home/robin*, as shown in Figure 5-2.

> Within this folder are also several subfolders used for sorting files and documents by type:

> *Desktop*
>> Contains all the items that appear on the user's desktop.

> *Documents*
>> Contains all the documents created by OpenOffice.org and other applications.

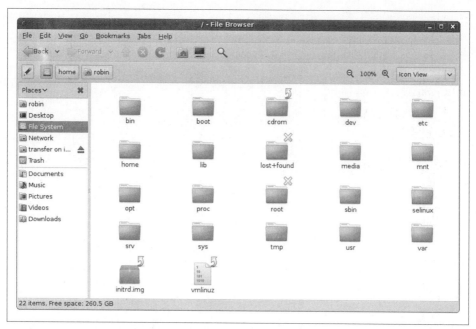

Figure 5-1. Browsing Ubuntu's filesystem

Pictures, Music, and Videos
> For audio and visual media.

Public
> A place where you can copy or move files to be shared.

Templates
> Presaved files with the information and formatting for creating new files of particular document types; see Chapter 6 for more.

Examples
> Contains a range of documents created with the applications supplied with Ubuntu, illustrating things you can do using them.

/media
> All your media devices will show up here, not with drive letters as they would under Windows, but using the name of the media. So, for example, if you insert a CD-ROM or DVD-ROM, an icon appears here using that disc's name. Mounted media also appear in the Places menu and will be displayed as a main item when you select the Computer option from the Places menu. What's more, an icon will also be placed on the desktop, so you should always be able to find your removable media easily.

/tmp
> This folder is used by the system and other applications for storing temporary files. You can use it too, as long as you don't overwrite any files or folders already in use.

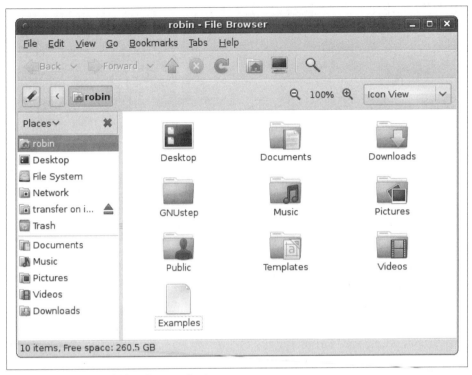

Figure 5-2. The home folder of user "robin"

Case Sensitivity and Special Characters

Newcomers to Linux can sometimes run into problems, particularly if they come from a Windows background in which all three of the folders *Business, business*, and *BUSINESS* refer to the same directory. This is because Linux (like Unix) is case-sensitive when it comes to files and folders. So, to avoid confusion, you may wish to always use lowercase file and folder names, at least until you are used to this system.

Also, if you ever want easy access to your filesystem from the command line, I recommend you steer clear of using spaces in your file and folder names because you would then have to use quotation marks to surround them. Instead, try using underscore or hyphen characters.

You should also avoid using special characters such as *, ?, >, and | in your filenames because each has a different meaning to Ubuntu (explained in Chapter 7), and using them will give you unexpected results.

Mounting Media

When you need access to data, whether on a CD or DVD, another computer, an external USB drive, and so on, you must mount it as part of your Ubuntu filesystem. Mostly this happens automatically as part of the process of accessing the media, for example, by inserting a CD-ROM into the drive.

Drive Mounting

I mentioned the */media* folder a little earlier, which is where external media gets mounted as part of the Linux filesystem. Generally, you simply need to insert a USB thumb drive, other storage device, or a CD or DVD, and it will automatically show up in the */media* folder and the Places menu, as well as on the desktop.

Mounting ISO Files

You can also mount ISO files, which represent the raw contents of a CD-ROM or DVD-ROM in the form of a single file, typically using the file extension *.iso*. To do this, right-click the ISO file's icon and select "Open with Archive Mounter." This will have the same effect as if you had actually inserted a CD or DVD into your drive, except that you access the ISO image at the speed of the media on which it is saved. So, for example, an ISO image on your hard drive will access at the speed of the drive, which will be many times faster than an optical device reading a CD or DVD.

ISO images can be located anywhere there is space for them, such as the main hard disk, USB hard disks, thumb drives, and even CDs and DVDs. In fact, as you saw in Chapter 2, the DVD-ROM that comes with this book includes a few ISO images of various Ubuntu installation CD-ROMs.

ISO images are set to read-only; you can list, view the contents of, and run files, but you cannot change any or add new ones.

Mounting Network Folders

To mount a folder on another computer on your network, select Places → Network, browse through the connected workgroups and computers, and click the appropriate icons to descend through them to the item you want.

If the computer or folder you click on is password protected, you will be asked to provide the correct username and password for an account on that computer that is able to access the folder. Once a folder opens up, it will look just like folders on your own system, as shown by the screen grab in Figure 5-3 in which the folder *media* is being browsed on the computer *mediaanddocs*.

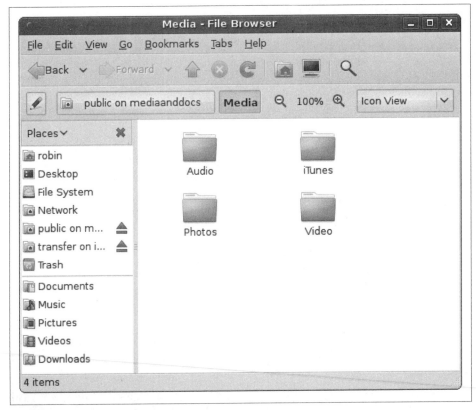

Figure 5-3. Browsing a folder on another computer

If you have browsed your network and cannot find a computer that you are certain is connected to the network, select Places → Connect to Server..., and a new window, as shown in Figure 5-4, will open up.

For a standard Windows share, you should then change the "Service type" from Public FTP to "Windows share" and enter the name of the computer in the Server field. You can enter other optional details, such as the folder under which it should open, and then click the Connect button.

Sharing must be enabled on the computer you connect to, and the folders and files you access must have been specified as being shared. Chapter 10 explains how to do this in detail.

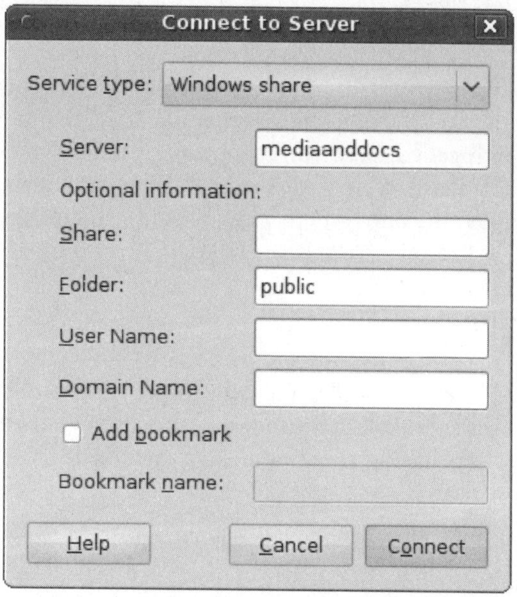

Figure 5-4. Manually connecting to a server

Unmounting

When you have finished using a mounted drive (whether a physical one or a logical one, such as an ISO image), you can unmount it from your system by right-clicking on it and selecting the Unmount option.

If, however, it's a CD or DVD, you may wish to instead select the Eject option, which will both unmount and eject the CD. The Unmount option would leave you with an unmounted disc that you can't right-click on to eject. The disc will, however, remain listed in the Places menu, and if you access it, the disc will automatically be remounted. You can also unmount and eject discs from the Places menu.

Hidden Files and Folders

As with other operating systems, Ubuntu can make certain folders and files invisible. The purpose is to protect important system files from being accidentally modified or deleted by casual users. Hidden files and folders are ones whose filenames start with a period or dot (.) character.

Although the next chapter will cover Nautilus, the file browsing program, in detail, it's worth mentioning here that you can look at hidden files when you need to by selecting Edit → Preferences from any file browser and then clicking the Views tab. This brings up a dialog where, among other features, you can check or uncheck the "Show hidden and backup files" box to reveal or conceal files and folders marked as hidden. But remember that they are hidden for a reason, and you should access these files and folders only if you know what you are doing.

On the other hand, if you would like to make a file or folder of your own hidden from casual view, you can do so by creating it (or renaming it) so that it starts with a period. So, if the file is currently called *diary*, you can hide it by renaming it *.diary*. The file will temporarily stay visible in the current file browser, but if you navigate away and come back it will be gone, and the only way to view it again will be to enable the display of hidden files.

Symbolic Links

Sometimes you need easy access to a file or a folder from a different location. For example, if you have the username *mary* and work mostly in your home folder, it would be inconvenient to keep having to browse to a document stored at the following location:

> */home/mary/Documents/freelance/invoicing/template.odt*

But with a symbolic link to the file as follows, you can always access it directly from your home folder:

> */home/mary/invtemp.odt*

Whenever you open the linked file *invtemp.odt* (also known as an alias or shortcut), you will actually be accessing the original file *template.odt*, several folders down the filesystem. It is also possible to create a symbolic link to an entire folder (and its subfolders).

Creating such links is covered in Chapter 6, and is easily done with a couple of mouse clicks.

File Extensions

Another difference between Linux and Windows files is that Linux imposes no requirement for program files to use any particular extension, such as *.exe* or *.dll*. Instead, each file has an extended set of attributes that tell the operating system what it can do with the file. So, as well as having attributes for read-only, hidden, and system, such as you would use on Windows, there is also an executable attribute.

However, Linux does make good use of file extensions for data files, and they often use full terms such as *.html* and *.jpeg* instead the truncated, three-letter versions *.htm* and *.jpg* that grew up because of restrictions imposed by early Windows systems. Graphic files such as *.gif*, *.tif*, and *.png* files also retain their extensions, as do many other file types. Table 5-1 lists the main extension types and what they are generally used for in Ubuntu.

Table 5-1. Typical file extensions used in Ubuntu Linux

Extension	Type of file
.0–.9	Help pages for the *man* program, and old logfiles
.asm	Assembly language program
.au	Audio file
.bmp	Graphic image
.bz2	A file compressed using the bzip2 program
.c	C language program
.class	Java language compiled program
.cfg / .conf	Configuration file
.cc / .cpp	C++ language program
.css	Cascading style sheet
.csv	Comma-separated value data file
.db	Berkeley DB data file
.deb	Debian application package
.diff	File of differences generated by the *diff* program
.dtd	Document type definition for XML data
.gif	Graphic image
.gz	File compressed using the gzip program
.h	Header file used by the C or C++ program languages
.jar	Java program archive file containing classes and sources
.java	Source file for the Java language
.kwd	Document file for the Kword word processor
.ksp	Document file for the Kspread spreadsheet application
.kss	KDE screensaver
.m3u	MP3 playlist file
.md5	File containing checksum data
.mpg / .mpeg	Mpeg movie
.mp3	Audio file
.o	Compiled source code from the C or C++ languages
.odt	OpenOffice.org document file
.ods	OpenOffice.org spreadsheet file
.odp	OpenOffice.org presentation file
.ogg	Sound file
.pdf	Adobe portable document file
.php	PHP program

Extension	Type of file
.pl	Perl program
.png	Graphic image
.py	Python program
.rpm	Red Hat Linux package manager file
.rtf	Rich-text format file
.s	Assembly language source code
.sh	Shell script
.tar	File archived with the tar program
.tgz	A file archived with both the tar and gzip programs
.tga	Graphic image
.ttf	True type font file
.txt	Plain-text file
.wav	Audio file
.xml	XML data file

File Permissions

From the very start, Unix was designed as a multiuser environment in which different users are given different permissions. But more than that, users can be assigned to groups too, and files and programs can then be made accessible either by user or by group. All this rich multiuser support and precision control over the filesystem has been brought into Linux, making it one of the most robust and secure computing environments. It's achieved by combining all the different concepts of users, groups, and file permissions.

Taking file permissions first, all files have a set of attributes that define what can and can't be done with a file, and who has permission to access it. These are known as permissions, of which there are three main types:

Read
> A file with only this permission set can be read but cannot be written to or executed.

Write
> A file with this permission set can be written to.

Execute
> A file with this permission set can be executed. In other words, this permission is applied to applications.

These permissions can be combined with each other to provide the eight possibilities in Table 5-2. The permissions are numbered from 0 through 7 because these are the numbers that you will use when manually changing a file's permissions using the command line (see Chapter 7).

Table 5-2. Combinations of file permissions

Number	Meaning
0	No permissions
1	Execute only
2	Write only
3	Execute and write
4	Read only
5	Execute and read
6	Write and read
7	Execute and write and read

Users and Groups

Each file has two additional attributes that are string values: one for the *Owner* and one for the *Group* the file belongs to. There is also a third attribute known as *World* (or sometimes *Others*) that is automatically assumed when a user is not in either of a file's Owner or Group attributes.

In Figure 5-5, I have right-clicked the file *rn.png* and then selected the Permissions tab. In it you can see the Owner, Group, and Others sections, within which my username is applied to both the Owner and Group attributes. As Owner I am allowed to read from and write to the file, as a group member (if I were not the Owner) I could only read from it, and everyone else is also limited to only reading the file. A checkbox below this allows you to enable the file as executable.

When you installed Ubuntu and it asked you for a username, it then went and gave your user account membership in a new group it also created, with the same name as your username. So, if your username is *joesmith*, you will also be a member of the group called *joesmith*. This is because you must be a member of at least one group. But you can also be a member of other groups.

For example, an Ubuntu multiuser installation might offer several different user accounts for accessing different parts of a company's data. One group able to access the accounts might be called *finance*, and another responsible for PR and advertising might be called *marketing*. Indeed there might also be a group for web server files called *internet*, and another for *telesales*, and so on. And members of some of these groups can also belong to others. Table 5-3 shows a group of six employees working in such a company.

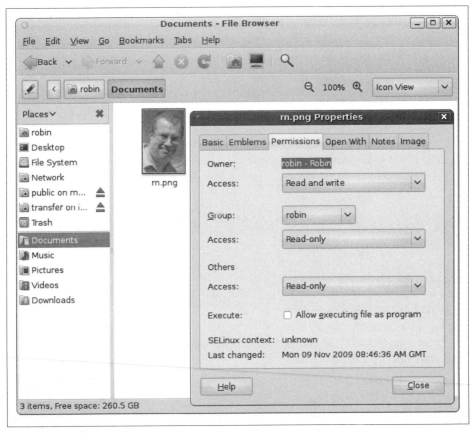

Figure 5-5. Modifying a file's permission settings

Table 5-3. An example of users being members of different groups

Username	Position	Member of group			
		Finance	Internet	Marketing	Telesales
joesmith	CEO	✓	✓	✓	✓
marywhite	CFO	✓		✓	✓
harryjones	Sales exec				✓
paulharvey	Ad manager			✓	✓
annwatson	Payroll exec	✓			
jennywilson	Web admin		✓		

Each username, in addition to being a member of the group with his or her own name, is a member of one or more other groups. For example, Joe Smith, the chief executive officer, is a member of all groups, whereas Paul Harvey, the advertising manager, needs to be a member of only the *marketing* and *telesales* groups.

With people properly allocated to the right groups, sensitive financial information can be restricted to only those employees who need access to it, the website can be set to allow updating only by the webmaster, and so on.

Managing Users

To manage groups, select System → Administration → Users and Groups, which brings up the Users Settings window shown in Figure 5-6. You must then click the key next to "Click to make changes" and enter your password in order to enable the various buttons. Once you've done that, you can click Add User to add a new user account to the computer, as described in the section "Adding New Users" on page 146.

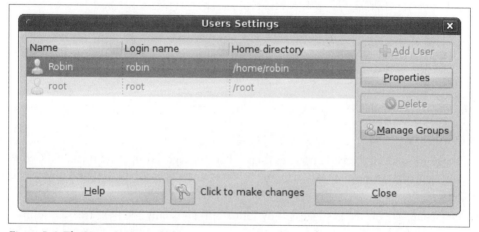

Figure 5-6. The Users Settings window

You can also modify a user's details by selecting the user and then clicking the Properties button to bring up the Account Properties window shown in Figure 5-7. Here, you can change the user's real name or password, or modify the user's contact information using the Contact Information tab. You can also change the privileges that have been granted and other information, such as the user's home directory, using the final two tabs, User Privileges and Advanced.

When using the Users Settings window for more than a few minutes, you may be re-prompted for your password. This is a security measure: changing user and group permissions modifies a computer's entire security settings, so the time delay before revalidating a user is short. Just re-enter your password if asked.

To remove a user from the computer, click the Delete button in the Users Settings window, and then confirm the deletion by clicking the second Delete button that is displayed. Be careful, as this cannot be undone. Furthermore, any files owned by the user you've deleted stay around without an owner.

Figure 5-7. The Account Properties window for user "robin"

Managing Groups

To add groups and then add users to them, click Manage Groups and then Add Group to bring up the window shown in Figure 5-8. Here, I have chosen to create a new group called *internet* and added the user *Robin* to it.

The Group ID you see is suggested by Linux and is usually the next free ID number (starting from 1000). You are not recommended to change this unless you know why you are doing so.

Instead of clicking Add Group, you can also click Properties in the Users Settings window to add and remove users to and from a preexisting group. The Properties window that appears is identical to the New group window, except that you cannot change the group's name. If you need to rename a group, you should create a new group and add all the users to it who need to be there; then you can delete the old one.

By the way, you never need to add the user *root* to a group, because that user can access absolutely every file and folder in the filesystem anyway, regardless of which owner the file has or which group it belongs to.

Other File Attributes

As if all that weren't enough, a number of other file attributes are available to you. To view them, right-click on a file and select Properties to bring up a window such as the

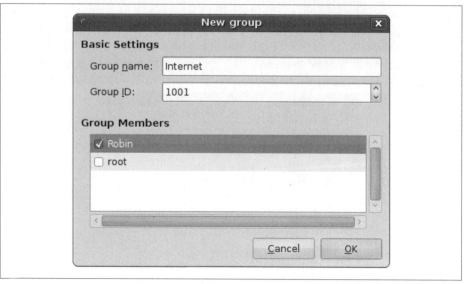

Figure 5-8. Creating the new group "Internet"

one shown in Figure 5-9. Here, you can see a number of tabs, which vary according to the file type or folder selected.

The tabs provide even more control over what you can do with your files and how they are displayed, and include the following:

Basic

Lists basic details about a file or folder, such as its type, size, and location, whether it is a link to another file or folder, and statistics about when the file was last accessed or modified. You can also change the file or folder's name here.

Emblems

Ubuntu icons are great because you can attach secondary icons called emblems that appear above and to the right of them. Figure 5-10 shows the Desktop emblem being attached to *swirl2.png* (because it is being used for the desktop wallpaper). You can choose emblems representing hobbies, finance, games, important files, photos, social networking, and more.

Permissions

I already covered the Permissions tab in the earlier section "Users and Groups" on page 161, which contained a screenshot of the options shown earlier in Figure 5-5. But, to recap, this is where you set a file's users, groups, and read, write and executable attributes.

Open With

Many types of file can be opened with more than one type of program. For example, as Figure 5-11 illustrates, by default Ubuntu offers a choice of four different programs to open the file *swirl2.png*, with Image Viewer being the default choice. Now the Image Viewer is well and good if you mostly just want to browse your image files. But, for example, if you generally need to edit them, you might prefer to make the GIMP Image Editor the default application for PNG files by clicking the circle next to that program's icon.

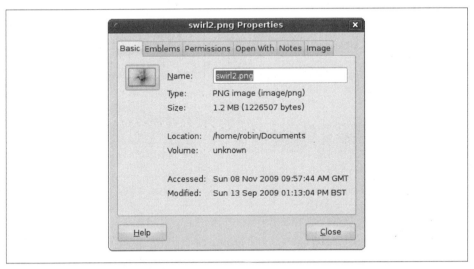

Figure 5-9. Changing a file's properties

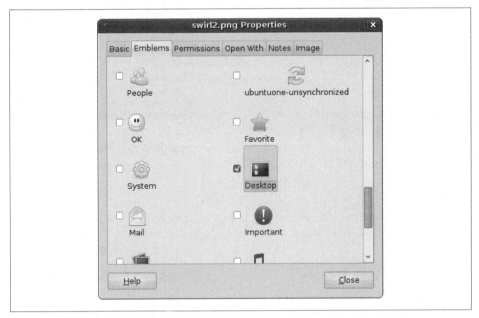

Figure 5-10. Attaching an emblem to a file's icon

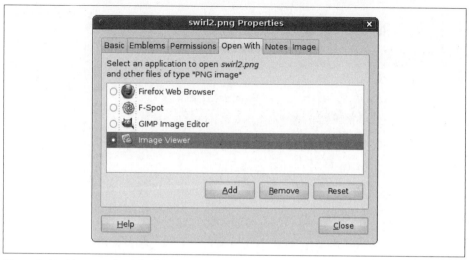

Figure 5-11. Choosing the default application to use with PNG files

Notes
> This tab lets you add a page of notes to a file or folder detailing what it is about. If you do this, an extra emblem, which looks like a pencil and notepad, is added to the right of the icon to indicate the presence of a note.

Image
> This tab is available only for image files, in which case it will display the file's type, width, and height.

Share
> This tab is visible only when you call up the properties for a folder, as shown in Figure 5-12. If you have installed the sharing service (see Chapter 10), you can then check the box next to "Share this folder" and select the name by which to share it, along with an optional comment. Or, the first time you try to share a file or folder, Ubuntu will offer to install the Sharing service for you. Underneath this option, you can also choose whether others can create and delete files in the folder files, and whether guest users (who don't have an account) are also granted access.

The Trash

Whenever you have finished with a file, you can drag and drop it into the Trash at the bottom right of the desktop. Selecting multiple files as well as folders (including their subfolders) is allowed, and they will be immediately removed from the filesystem.

But if you make a mistake, all is not lost. You can open up the Trash and either drag any items you didn't want deleted back to their rightful places, or right-click them and select the Restore option.

Figure 5-12. The Share tab is where you can opt to share a folder's contents

When you are certain that the files are indeed trash, you can either right-click the Trash icon and select Empty Trash or open up the folder and delete them separately, by right-clicking each and selecting Delete Permanently. This allows you to delete files you definitely don't need anymore, while holding on to others you're not totally certain you want completely erased.

Summary

This chapter gave you an in-depth introduction to the basics of the GNU/Ubuntu Linux filesystem, which will stand you in good stead when installing new programs or working with files and data. In the following chapter, I will show you all the things you can do with the Nautilus file browser to increase your productivity and your enjoyment of using Ubuntu.

The Nautilus File Browser

In the preceding chapters, we've had some occasions to use the Nautilus file browser built into Ubuntu. Now I'll cover some of the powerful features it provides, such as file searching, creating symbolic links (which are like Windows shortcuts), compressing and decompressing files, using templates for creating new files, and more.

On the way, you'll discover how well integrated Ubuntu is and how different parts work seamlessly with one another. For example, because Nautilus is the silent power behind the Ubuntu desktop (something of which many users are unaware), many things I'll show you how to do with the Nautilus file browser can also be done directly to files and folders on the desktop.

What's more, items on the desktop can be copied or moved into the location displayed by the file browser, and vice versa, and when you open a folder from the desktop its contents appear within the file browser.

Opening Files and Folders

When you move your pointer over anything that you can manipulate through the use of the pointer, either within the Nautilus file browser or on the desktop, the icon will usually change to a lighter color to show that it's clickable, as shown in Figure 6-1.

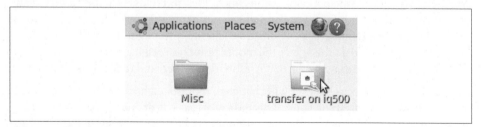

Figure 6-1. Passing the mouse over an openable object

But if you have enabled single-clicking, as discussed in the section "Creating Folders, Launchers, and Files" on page 144, then the mouse pointer will also change into a pointing finger icon to remind you of this, as shown in Figure 6-2.

Figure 6-2. Pointing to a file with single-clicking enabled

 Reminder: to enable single-clicking, open up a file browser window and select Edit → Preferences → Behavior → "Single click to open items."

When you open a folder (by either a single- or double-click), a file browser window is called up, displaying the items it contains.

However, if you open a file, then one of two things will happen:

- If the file has an application associated with it, the application is opened and the file is loaded into it ready to be edited, displayed, or otherwise used.
- If there is no associated application, a warning window will appear telling you that the file is of an unknown type. If this happens but you know the file is openable by a certain application, you can right-click the file and select Open with Other Application, and then choose the right one to open that file.

Dragging and Dropping

As long as you have sufficient permissions, most files and folders can be moved to any part of your filesystem by dragging and dropping them (although I recommend doing so only with nonsystem files; by moving a system file, you might disrupt the operation of some programs). To do this, place the mouse pointer over a file, press and hold down the left mouse button, drag the file to its destination folder, and then release the mouse.

As you do this, the mouse pointer will change to represent a hand grabbing something with an arrow pointing at the hand. This indicates that you are using the move feature, as shown in Figure 6-3 where the file *inventory.txt* has just been grabbed, ready for moving somewhere else.

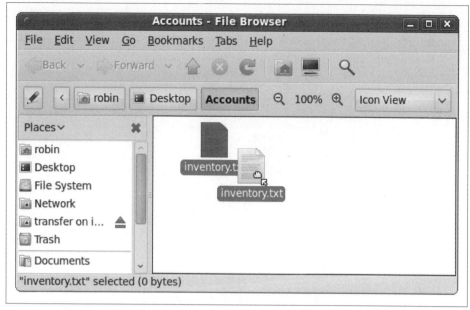

Figure 6-3. Moving a file by dragging and dropping it

Copying Files and Folders

But you can also copy a file or folder by holding down the Ctrl key before you start a drag-and-drop operation. When you do this, the mouse cursor will change to represent a hand dragging something, with a plus sign at its bottom right, as shown in Figure 6-4. Keep the Ctrl key held down until you release the mouse button, or the operation will return to being a simple move, rather than a copy operation.

Copying a folder results in all its subfolders also being copied; if these folders contain very large files, this could take a while and use a lot of disk space.

Copying with External Media

There is no need to hold down the Ctrl key when copying files from one media device to another—whether from a CD-ROM to your hard disk, or vice versa, or between a DVD-ROM and a USB thumb drive, and so on.

Just drag and drop the files you want to copy, and Ubuntu will know that this is a copy operation, so your original files will not be deleted. However, they will remain highlighted so that you can more easily delete them should you wish (if the media is writeable), without having to select them again—which I'll talk about next.

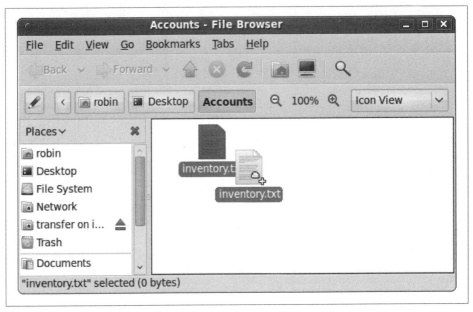

Figure 6-4. Copying a file using the mouse

Selecting Files and Folders

All the previous operations are well and good if you are only copying a single file or folder (even if the folder has subfolders). But often you need to select groups of items for copying, moving, and even deleting, and there are several ways to highlight multiple selections.

Lassoing Items

If all the items you are interested in are located within a rectangular area, you can click the file browser background and then drag a lasso around them. When you release the mouse the selected files will be highlighted. In Figure 6-5, I have chosen to lasso the four items to the right. Notice how a rectangular shape (like an elastic band stretched around four points) outlines the selected area, which itself now has a slightly darkened background color.

Individually Selecting Items

For even more control over selecting files and folders, you can hold down the Ctrl key and click each item once to add to the selection group. If you make a mistake, don't worry, because each time you click the item's state will toggle between being selected

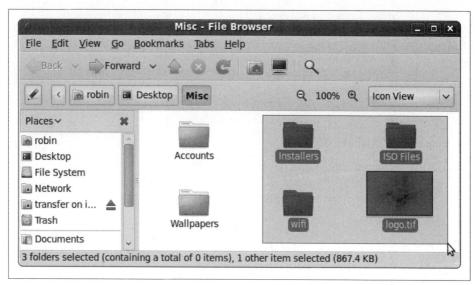

Figure 6-5. Lassoing a group of files and folders

and unselected. Figure 6-6 shows three items that have been selected in this manner, which couldn't have been achieved any other way.

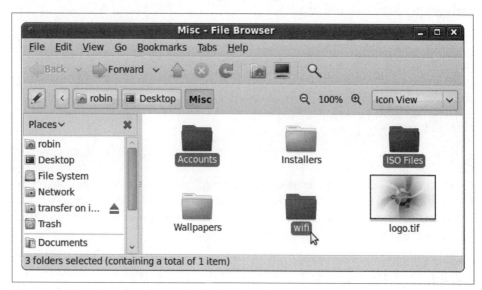

Figure 6-6. Three items have been individually selected

Windows users should note that if you are used to the Windows single-click setting, it works differently on Ubuntu when selecting files. With Windows, when in single-click mode you can simply hover over a file or folder to select it. But Ubuntu doesn't support this behavior. Personally I think Ubuntu does it better because it's so easy to accidentally lose a carefully selected group of files in Windows by hovering a moment too long over another file without the Ctrl key depressed.

Selecting Items in Sequence

If you wish to select a sequence of items, press Ctrl and single-click the first item in the group, then locate the final item and press the Shift key and click. This will highlight all the folders from the first to the last selected.

The way Shift-selecting works depends on how you have arranged the items in a folder. If you right-click the file browser background and select the Arrange Items submenu, you can specify how all the items in the folder should be arranged, out of the following choices:

- Manually
- By Name
- By Size
- By Type
- By Modification Date
- By Emblems

Additionally, you can choose whether to use a compact layout and whether to reverse the order of all items. Whichever order you choose will be the one used for selecting a sequence, as shown in Figure 6-7.

Selecting All Items

Click a blank area of the file browser to clear any current selections, and then press Ctrl-A to select all the files shown in the browser. They will now all change to a darker color, and the text underneath each one will be given a dark background to show that they have been grouped together, as shown in Figure 6-8.

At the bottom of the file browser, the status bar will tell you all the files and folders that have been selected in this manner and how much disk space they take up.

Sometimes you want most of the items but not all. After pressing Ctrl-A, you can keep the Ctrl key held down or depress it again, and then left-click individual items to deselect them.

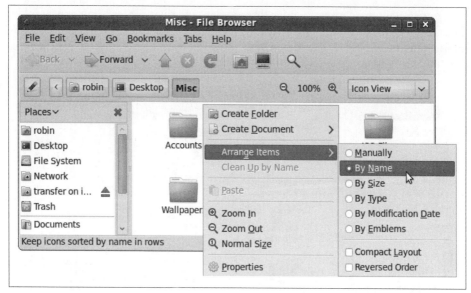

Figure 6-7. Choosing how you want items to be arranged

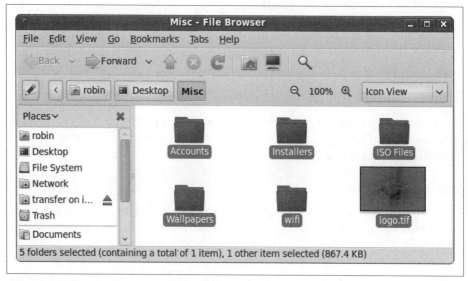

Figure 6-8. Selecting all files in a folder by pressing Ctrl-A

Moving or Deleting with Selections

Once you have selected a group of files or folders, all the items that are highlighted can be treated as though they are a single item for most operations. For example, when you initiate a drag-and-drop operation on one of the highlighted items, all the others in the group come along for the ride (whether they're being copied, moved, or deleted).

In Figure 6-9, I have chosen to move three folders and their contents into a new folder I just made called *Destination*. I did this by highlighting the three folders, grabbing one of them, and dragging it. The screen grab shows all three being dragged and dropped into the new folder.

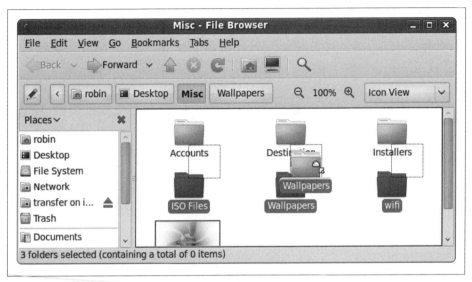

Figure 6-9. Moving a group of folders to a new location

Opening Multiple Items

The same applies to opening a group of files, but with a difference. To open multiple files at once, you need to right-click a group and select the Open With option. The default action for each file type will then be used to open each file.

Opening multiple folders

If the group of files is made up entirely of folders on the desktop, you can right-click and choose Browse Folders to open up several file browser windows at once, one for each folder. If the folders are in a file browser window already, you should right-click and choose between using Open in New Tabs or Open in New Windows. The latter has the same effect as right-clicking on a group of folders on the desktop and then selecting Browse Folders; several new file browsers will open up, displaying each folder's contents.

Using Tabs

The tabs option keeps your screen space usage at a minimum by making the file browser work like a web browser, with tabs at the top; just click the tab you want in order to view its contents. For example, Figure 6-10 shows three folders opened up as tabs. The left and right arrows on the tab line enable you to scroll through the tabs when there are too many to display at once. Click the X icon at the right to close tabs.

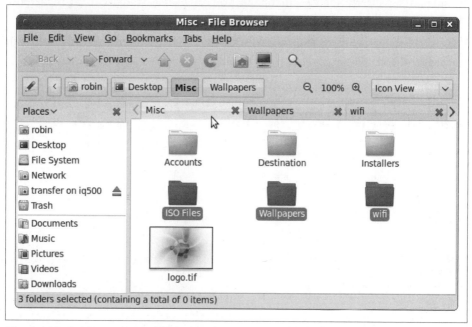

Figure 6-10. Opening a group of folders inside tabs

Deselecting

As I mentioned before, your selections remain in place until you deselect them. This means that if you make a mistake when performing a drag-and-drop operation, you can undo it by dragging files back again. In the case of the Trash, you can also drag them back out of there as a ready-selected group.

When you have finished with a selection, the simplest way to deselect it is to click the background next to a selection group. If you are in a file browser window, click its background; on the desktop, click a clear area of the desktop.

Zooming In and Out

Have you ever used the Zoom facility in Firefox and other browsers to view a web page in larger or smaller type? Well, you can do exactly the same thing with Ubuntu, which offers seven different levels of zoom control over the display of items in the file browser (but not of the desktop icons).

This makes it easy to locate documents even if you have limited visibility, and it is also a great feature for using Ubuntu on a device with a small screen, such as a MID, UMPC, or Netbook. You might want to reduce the size of icons or text so you can see more of them on a small screen, or because you have the luxury of a large monitor that lets you see small things clearly. On the other hand, you can increase the size to see them more clearly on a small screen, at the cost of viewing fewer at one time.

Figure 6-11 shows the icons reduced to their next-to-smallest size so more of them can fit in the file browser.

Figure 6-11. The result of zooming out a few times

Zooming in

To zoom in or enlarge the file browser icons, you can use any of the following controls:

- Hold down Ctrl and press the + (plus sign) key
- Hold down Ctrl and scroll the mouse wheel forward
- Right-click the file browser background and select Zoom In

Zooming out

To zoom out or decrease the size of file browser icons, use one of the following combinations:

- Hold Down Ctrl and press the – (hyphen) key
- Hold down Ctrl and scroll the mouse wheel backward
- Right-click the file browser background and select Zoom Out

Restoring the default size

To return the icons to their default size, you can use one of the following combinations:

- Hold down the Ctrl key and press the 0 (zero) key
- Right-click the file browser background and select Normal Size

The File Browser Menus

I know that we've covered a few of the menu options provided with the Nautilus file browser over the last few chapters, but those features only scratch the surface of what's on offer. So, let's look at these menus in a little more detail, starting with the File menu, as shown in Figure 6-12.

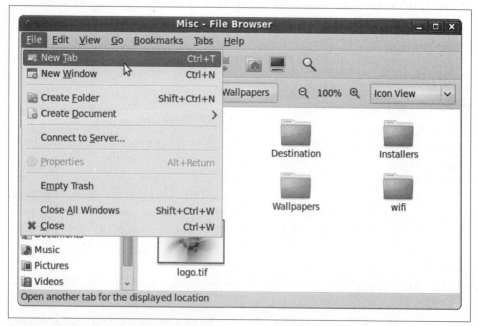

Figure 6-12. The file browser basic File menu

File Menu

The file menu is context-sensitive, so you will have different options available depending on whether you have selected an item or not, and some will be grayed out if you have insufficient permission. When no files or folders have been selected, the options on offer are:

New Tab

This option creates a new tab within the file browser. Initially, it will show the same files and folders as the original window. You can then switch between the different tabs, using them as though they were separate windows.

New Window

Select this option to open a new file browser window. In contrast to the New Tab option, this one will always open up your home folder.

Create Folder

Select this option to create a new empty folder within the current one being viewed. The new folder will be given the default filename of *untitled folder*, but the text will be selected so that you can easily rename it.

Create Document

When you select this option, an empty text file will be created with the name *new file* highlighted so that you can rename it. This file will then be editable in whichever application has been set to handle text documents. By default, this is the *gedit* program.

Connect to Server

This option has the same functionality as selecting Places → Connect to Server..., as covered in the section "Mounting Network Folders" on page 155.

Empty Trash

This option is available only when there are items in the Trash. When you select it, you are prompted to confirm whether you wish to delete the files. In non-American English installations, the word Trash will be replaced with Deleted Items or Wastebasket.

Close All Windows

This option immediately closes all file browser windows without prompting. If you merely want them out of the way temporarily so that you can see the desktop, you may prefer to use the Hide/Show Desktop icon at the bottom-lefthand corner of your desktop instead.

Close

This option closes the current window in the same way as clicking the close icon on the title bar.

If you have one or more items selected, the File menu will include the following options:

Open

If a file has been selected and it has an associated application, this option will appear as "Open with" followed by the application's name. Clicking it will open the application and load in the file. If more than one file of the same type is selected, they will all be passed to the application, which may or may not open them all, depending on the program. If the selected item is a folder, it will be opened as though it had been clicked. If the selection contains two or more folders, they will be opened up in new tabs.

Open in New Tab

This option is available only when a folder has been selected. If two folders have been selected, the menu will say Open in 2 New Tabs, and so on.

Open in New Window

> This is the same as the previous option except that the folders will be opened up in new windows instead of tabs.

Open with Other Application

> Sometimes you will have more than one application that can use a particular type of file. For example, GIMP, F-Spot, and the OpenOffice.org Drawing program can all handle graphic files. For each type of file, one program is the default "Open with" program on the menu, but this option lets you choose a different application.

Properties

> This option brings up the files and folders properties window, as covered in the section "Other File Attributes" on page 164 of Chapter 5. If more than one item is selected, you can change all their properties at once.

 Almost all the menu options in all the file browser menus have keyboard shortcuts. For example, Ctrl-T creates a new tab and Alt-Return opens up an item's properties. If you find yourself frequently using an option, you may find it worthwhile to memorize its shortcut.

Edit Menu

Like the File menu, the Edit menu is context-sensitive. By default, when no files or folders have been selected it will look like Figure 6-13. This is quite a powerful menu with a number of options you haven't yet seen:

Select All

> This option has the same effect as pressing Ctrl-A, discussed in the earlier section "Selecting All Items" on page 174. All folders and files in the current folder will be selected.

Select Items Matching...

> This is an interesting option for narrowing down a large selection of items. When you select it, a new window pops up requesting a pattern. You can enter filenames containing special characters, such as the * (asterisk), for use as wildcards. For example, the pattern *.jpg will select all the files in the current folder with any combination of characters followed by the file extension *.jpg*. Similarly, to find all files beginning with *temp*, use the pattern temp*. You can also search for files containing the word *memo* anywhere in their filename through the pattern *memo*, and so on.

Invert Selection

> This option changes the selection state of all files and folders. In other words, any that are selected become unselected, and those that are unselected become selected.

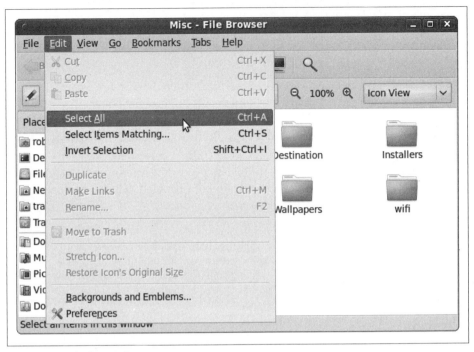

Figure 6-13. The basic Edit menu

Backgrounds and Emblems...

Using this option, you can drag a background of your choice onto a folder to replace the default white background color. If you keep a lot of windows open in the file browser, setting different colors can help you find a folder quickly. The background can be a solid color or a textured pattern, as shown by Figure 6-14, in which the camouflage background is being dragged and dropped onto the folder's background. To remove a patterned background (and restore the original), you will need to drop the color white on top of it.

The Emblems option offers a way of attaching an emblem to an icon, as detailed in the section "Other File Attributes" on page 164. As long as you have selected an item, you can drag and drop an emblem onto it, rather than having to right-click the item and select Preferences. Figure 6-15 shows a folder with the Camouflage texture applied to the background. To remove an emblem, you can uncheck it.

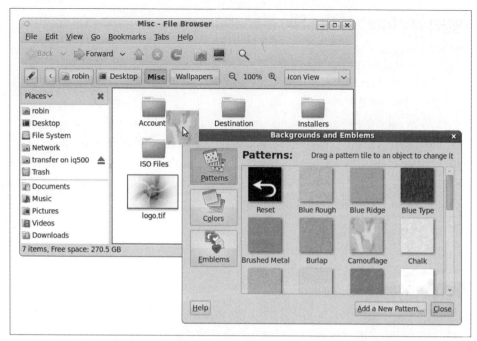

Figure 6-14. Changing the background of a folder

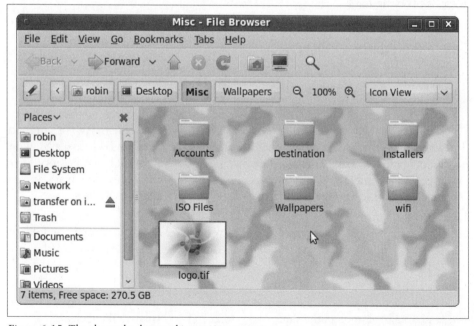

Figure 6-15. The chosen background is now in use

Other Features of the File Manager

The Nautilus file manager offers many useful features to make handling files and folders as easy as possible. In the next few sections, we'll look at the file manager's Edit → Preferences window and its tabs, as well as the file manager's menu bar features. In these sections, you will learn:

- How to use the tree and bookmarks to navigate quickly through your system
- The difference between icon, list, and compact views, and what each offers
- What you normally see, such as names, dates, and so on
- How to view attached devices in the *Computer* folder
- How to preview files, including sound files
- How to zoom in and out
- How to browse a compressed archive

Preferences

This is an important part of the Nautilus file browser if you intend to customize it to your own liking. You already have seen how one of its options lets you change the default clicking action from double-clicking to single-clicking. Here, you'll find a lot of other things you can change. Figure 6-16 shows the Edit → Preferences window, with six tabs of configurable options.

Edit → Preferences → Views

This tab contains the following options:

Default View
> With this section of the Views tab, you can set up defaults for a number of things, such as whether folders should be viewed in an icon view, list view, or compact view. You can also decide whether items should be arranged by name, size, type, modification date, or emblems. Both of these options are available from drop-down menus. Underneath, you can check a box if you want folders to always appear before files, and another if you want to view hidden and backup files.

Icon View Defaults
> This section allows you to specify which zoom level to use when opening folders, to select a compact layout, and whether to view text beside icons instead of underneath them.

Compact View Defaults
> In this section, you can choose the zoom level from a drop-down box, and also restrain all columns to the same width to keep the display looking clean.

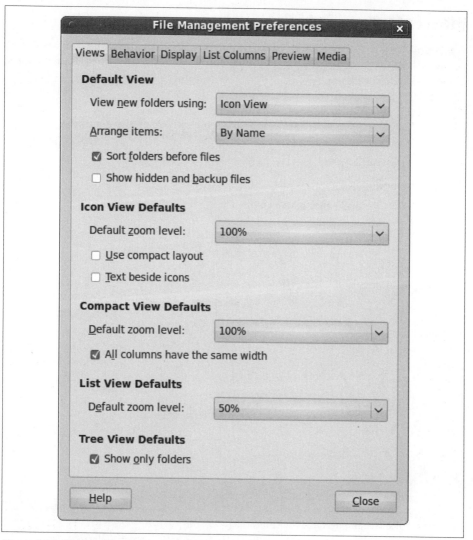

Figure 6-16. The File Management Preferences Views tab

List View Defaults

This drop-down input allows you to choose the default zoom level for icons.

Tree View Defaults

This section has a single option you can check if you want to display only folders in the lefthand pane.

Edit → Preferences → Behavior

This tab covers settings for controlling how you open items, whether you should be prompted by the system before it executes certain actions, and how to manage the Trash, as shown in Figure 6-17.

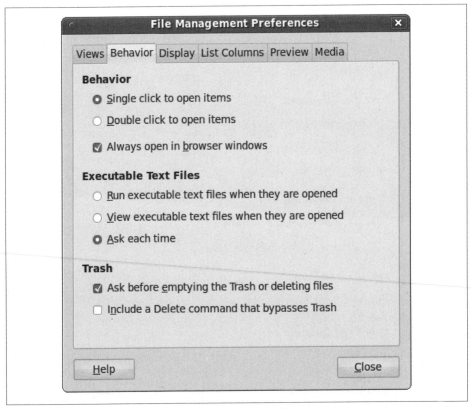

Figure 6-17. The File Management Preferences Behavior tab

Behavior

As mentioned in Chapter 4, you can use this section to change the default click behavior from double-click to single-click for opening a file or folder. You can also choose to always open folders in browser windows, which is the default for a new install. This means that when the box is checked, file browser windows will include the directory tree pane on the left. But if you uncheck the box, the lefthand pane will be omitted and the top toolbars will not appear. The former case (i.e., the box is checked) is called Browser mode, and the latter is known as Spatial mode. This checkbox applies only to folders that have not yet been opened.

Executable Text Files

Some text files can contain executable programs called *shell scripts*, which are similar to batch files on Windows. Using the options in this tab, you can choose whether such files should execute when opened or if they should only be viewed. If neither of these options is selected, the default will be used, which means the computer will ask you each time what it should do with executable files.

Trash

In this section, you can uncheck the first box to remove the confirm dialog that normally appears when you empty the Trash. You can also add a new command to the right-click context menu that lets you immediately delete a file, bypassing the Trash. If you are a new Ubuntu user, I strongly suggest you leave these two options alone because they will make it impossible to recover from any accidental file deletions.

Edit → Preferences → Display

This tab lets you choose what information appears next to your icons and how you wish the date to be formatted. Not all of the selected icon captions appear all the time. When you are zoomed out, there will be no captions, but the more you zoom in, the more are displayed, until all three captions are visible. Figure 6-18 shows the three caption selection menus and the long date format being selected:

Icon Captions

The drop-down boxes in this section let you select three options you would like displayed next to your icons, in the order of how soon they will appear as you zoom in. At the default zoom level, only the first caption will appear next to the file or folder's name. However, after a new install the first caption is set to None, so you will need to change it if you want more than just the file or folder names displayed. The types of information you can display in a caption include a file or folder's size, date modified, last-accessed date, owner, and location. A few other options will appear, such as Permissions and SELinux Context, which you probably won't need unless you become an advanced Linux user, so you can safely ignore them for now.

Date

If one or more of your chosen captions displays the date, you can choose between three formats, from a comprehensive one including the day name, date, year, time, and time zone, to a simple day and time format.

Edit → Preferences → List Columns

This tab selects the columns displayed when you set the file browser to List mode. By default, the file or folder's name, size, type, and modification date are displayed, but you can choose to change that or add up to eight more columns of information. Figure 6-19 shows the Owner column being added to the list.

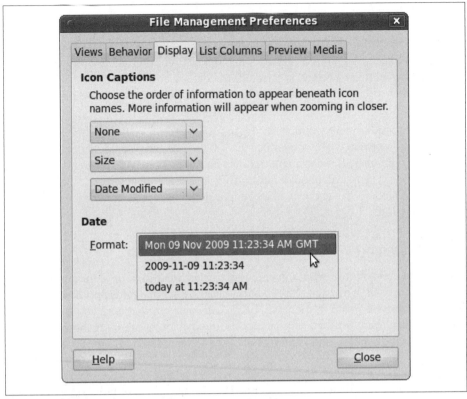

Figure 6-18. The File Management Preferences Display tab

Edit → Preferences → Preview

Using this tab, you can choose how you want your icons to display, including whether to display thumbnail icons (tiny versions of the real file), whether to show tiny text thumbnail icons for text files, whether to preview sounds, and more. Figure 6-20 shows the Folders section being set to count only the items on the local filesystem:

Text Files

Retrieving information from files on a low-speed hard disk or over a network can sometimes be annoyingly slow, especially if there are a lot of them, so Ubuntu gives you control over what level of work it should put into providing you with information about files. In this section, you can choose whether to have the system create thumbnail images of text files to use as icon images all the time, only for local files, or never. The fastest option is Never.

Other Previewable Files

Some other files, such as images and videos, are also previewable, but with this option you can modify how their icons are displayed: always create a thumbnail, create one only for local files, or not at all. If you choose either of the two thumbnail

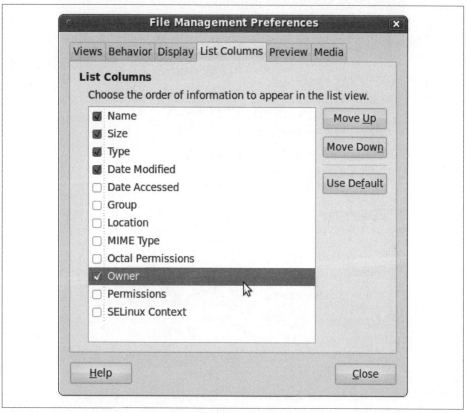

Figure 6-19. The File Management Preferences List Columns tab

settings, you can use the drop-down menu underneath to limit thumbnail creation to files less than a specified file size of your choosing. As with text files, this option can make the file manager display windows faster.

Sound Files

Just as visual files can be previewed, so can sound files. This section gives you the option to enable this for all files, local files, or none.

Folders

Just counting all the files in a folder and its subfolders can take time, so you can decide whether to make this happen all the time, only with local folders, or not at all. Remember that you will see the number of files in a folder only when you have selected to see that as a caption within the Display tab, and only when you have zoomed in sufficiently to view that caption.

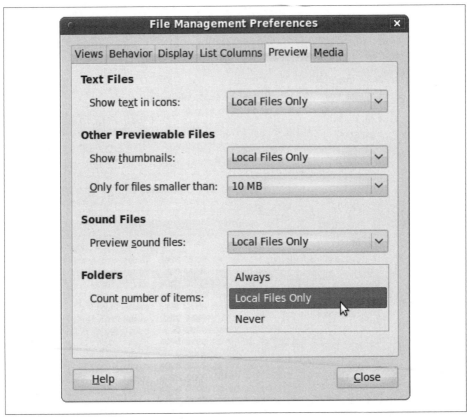

Figure 6-20. The File Management Preferences Preview tab

Edit → Preferences → Media

When you insert a CD or DVD or connect a USB thumb or other drive, you can have Ubuntu perform a default action on the media, such as playing an audio CD or displaying a collection of photos. This tab enables you to precisely specify which actions are performed for which media types. Figure 6-21 shows the Media tab selected, where I have enabled the "Browse media when inserted" option at the window's bottom.

Media Handling

In this section, you can specify what will happen when any audio, video, graphic, or software files are inserted in the drive or attached via USB. The options available are:

Ask what to do
  A prompt will be displayed asking how you want the media handled.

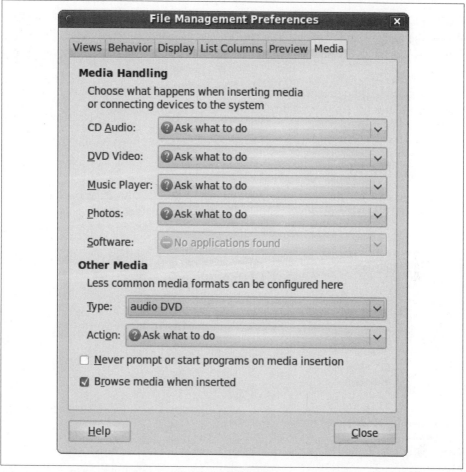

Figure 6-21. *The File Management Preferences Media tab*

Do Nothing

The operating system will ignore the media and leave the manner of access up to you.

Open Folder

The folder or drive containing the media will be opened in a file browser window.

Open in programname

The program shown in the menu as programname will be used to open the media. If more than one application can handle the media, these will also become choices.

Open with other Application…

If the application in which you wish the media to be opened is not listed, you can select this option to add a new application as a handler for that type of data, and set it to the default for inserted media.

Other Media

Using this section you can add additional media types, such as Audio DVDs and Blu-ray, to the media-handling list. Click the Type drop-down menu to select the media type, and then click the Action drop-down menu to choose which application should handle it.

The final two checkboxes allow you to turn off automatic handling of inserted media, and to make the system automatically open up a file browser window for any unrecognized media types.

The View Menu

With the View menu, you can decide how you would like Nautilus to lay out and display your files and folders. Figure 6-22 shows the options available.

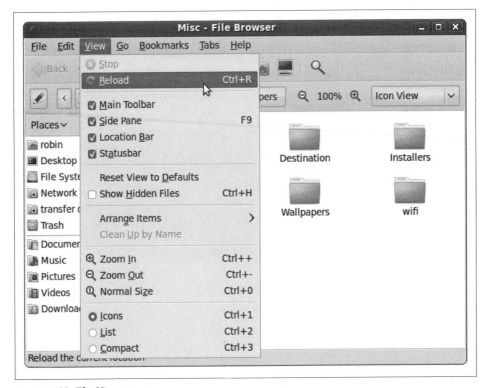

Figure 6-22. The View menu

Stop

This option will stop the current file browser if it is spending too long getting information from a slow local or network drive.

Reload

> This refreshes the file browser to bring it up-to-date with any changes to the folder and its contents.

Hide/view checkboxes

> This section offers four checkboxes with which you can show or hide various toolbars and panes, including the main toolbar, the side pane, the location bar, and the status bar. Removing the top three and leaving the status bar has the same effect as changing the file browser view to Spatial mode, as described in "Edit → Preferences → Media" on page 190.

Reset View to Defaults

> If you change the file browser's layout but decide you don't want the changes, you can quickly set it back to its display defaults with this option.

Show Hidden Files

> When you need to see the hidden files on your computer, check this box. You probably will want to uncheck it after doing any administrative work that requires these files; otherwise, they may clutter up your view of your documents and folders.

Arrange Items

> This provides the same functionality as right-clicking on the file browser background and selecting Arrange Items. See the section "Selecting Items in Sequence" on page 174 to view the available arrangement options.

Clean Up by Name

> This option is enabled only when you have used Arrange Items to set manual arrangement as the default. In this case, a click on this option will order the items by name.

The Zoom Controls

> The options shown here are the same as the controls available when you right-click the file browser background. See the section "Zooming In and Out" on page 177 for details on how they work.

Icons, List, and Compact

> These options let you choose the way you want files and folders to be displayed. Just select the one you need.

The Go Menu

This menu handles navigating around the filesystem and provides quick access to your most important folders and documents, as well as the network. It also gives you convenient access to the files and documents you've used most recently, as shown in Figure 6-23.

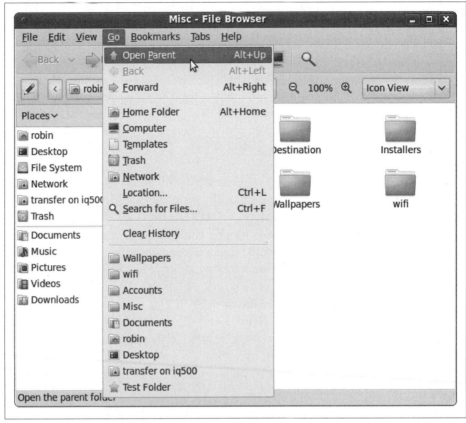

Figure 6-23. The file browser Go menu

Open Parent

This option in the Go menu replaces the current folder view with that of its parent. So, if the current folder is *Documents*, selecting this will take you back a level to your home folder.

Back and Forward

These two options in the Go menu are enabled when you have browsed through a directory structure. If you have clicked through from one folder to another, the Back option is enabled so you can return to the first folder. Once you use the Back option, the Forward option becomes enabled so you can move forward again.

Home Folder, Computer, Templates, Trash, and Network

These five options are duplicates of those on the desktop's main Places menu and take you directly to each of the listed folders or to the network.

Location…

>This option opens up an address bar into which you can type a path for the location you would like to go to. Figure 6-24 shows the path */home/robin/Desktop/Misc* being entered.

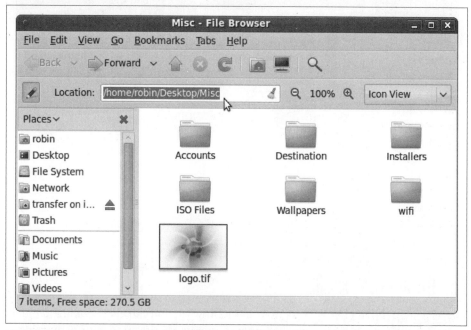

Figure 6-24. Entering a location manually into the address bar

Search for Files…

>When you use this option, a search input bar appears into which you can enter a piece of a filename to search for, starting at the current folder and searching all the folders within it. Figure 6-25 shows a search made for the term "tif" to find all TIF graphic image files.

Folder History

>Ubuntu keeps track of the folders you've recently visited, as it's likely you'll want to go back to them. These are all listed at the bottom of the Go menu. If you wish to clear that section, use the Clear History option. You can remove all of them at once, but you can't remove individual items.

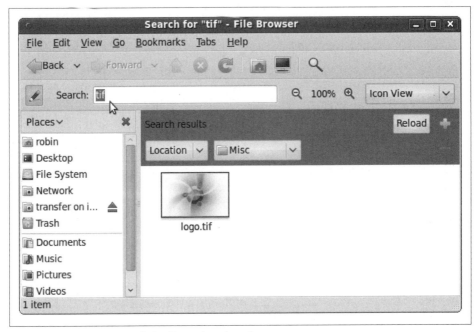

Figure 6-25. Searching for all the files with "tif" in their names

The Bookmarks Menu

Just as you can bookmark web pages in a web browser, you can also bookmark folders using Nautilus. By default, a few bookmarks are already set up to your main folders, as shown in Figure 6-26, and you can click any of the bookmarks shown at the bottom of the list to be taken straight there.

Add Bookmark
> You can add more bookmarks at any time you like. Just browse to the folder you want to bookmark, and then select this option. The bookmark will be added using the name of the current folder.

Edit Bookmarks
> Use this option to edit or remove bookmarks by scrolling through them in the lefthand pane and editing their details on the right, or clicking the Remove button. You can also use the "Jump to" button to view a bookmark's location while editing, as Figure 6-27 shows.

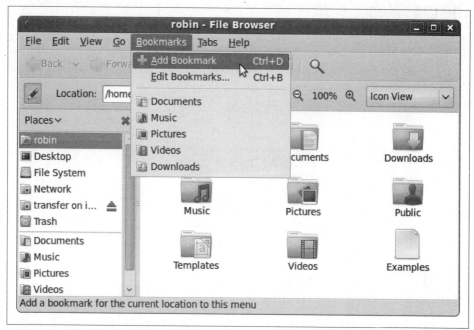

Figure 6-26. Using bookmarks in Nautilus

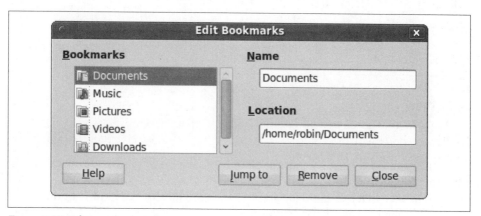

Figure 6-27. Editing a bookmark

The Tabs Menu

When you have open tabs in the file browser, you can navigate through them by using the Tabs menu, which is a very simple menu for moving back and forth through the various tabs. Available options will be shown in bold, and unavailable options will be grayed out, as can be seen in Figure 6-28. You can also click directly on the tab you want out of those shown at the bottom of the menu.

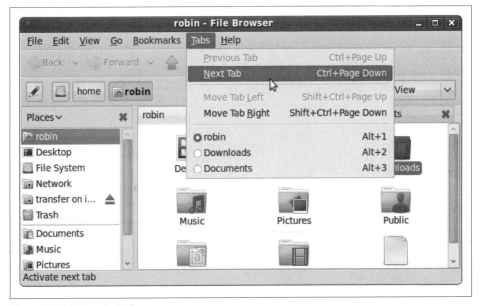

Figure 6-28. Using the Tabs menu

Help

In the file manager, as in most parts of Ubuntu, comprehensive help is available when you need it. Just press the F1 key or select Contents from the Help menu. You can also select Help → Get Help Online to ask a question at launchpad.net, or read the documentation online at *http://help.ubuntu.com*.

Context Menus

When you right-click a file or folder, a menu appears whose contents vary based on the item and the available activities (hence the term *context menu*). There will be options such as cut, copy, and paste, making symbolic links (shortcuts), encrypting, compressing, and more. Figure 6-29 shows a range of typical options for an image file.

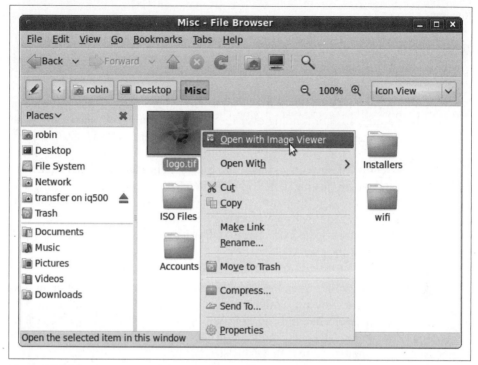

Figure 6-29. *The context menu for a typical image file*

Open with *programname*

> This option opens the file using the application named in the option.

Open With

> This lets you choose the application with which to open the file.

Cut

> This option cuts the file so that it can be pasted elsewhere. If you do not perform a paste operation, the file will be unchanged, but if you do a paste after a cut, the original item is deleted, which has the effect of moving it.

Copy

> This is similar to the Cut option, except that the original item is always retained, so a copy is made when you paste.

Make Link

> With this option, you can create a symbolic link, also known as a shortcut. The new linked file will be given the name *Link to <name>*, where *<name>* is the original file or folder's name. You can then drag and drop this link icon anywhere you like, and when it is accessed, the item it is linked to will be used. You can also change the name of the link, which has no effect on the original file or its name. An arrow on the top right of the icon indicates that it refers to a link.

Rename

This option lets you change a file or folder's name.

Move to Trash

This moves the file or folder to the trash.

Compress

This option compresses a file or folder (or a selected group) to save disk space or to reduce a file's size for sending over the Internet. Figure 6-30 shows the wide range of compressed file formats supported, including *.zip*, *.tar*, and *.gz*. Once you have a compressed file, you can navigate within it just as though it were an extension to the regular filesystem; just click and browse. You can even open a file from within an archive by clicking it, or add more items to the archive by dragging and dropping them into it at the correct location in the archive's file structure. To decompress files that are within an archive, first click it to open it, select the files to extract, and then click the Extract button. If you wish to extract everything, press Ctrl-A to select all and then click Extract.

Send To...

Using this option, you can send the selected item(s) to a number of different destinations or in different ways. Your choices of methods are: as an email, to the CD or DVD creator, over Bluetooth, as an instant message, or to a removable disk or shared folder. If you click the Compression checkbox, the item will be reduced (if possible) to a smaller, more manageable size.

Properties

This brings up the Properties window, as described in the section "Other File Attributes" on page 164.

Open

This and the following four options will appear only when one or more folders has been selected. This option does the same thing as clicking on the folder.

Open in New Tab

This option opens the folder or folders within tabs in the file browser.

Open in New Window

This option opens up each selected folder in a separate window.

Open with Other Application...

This allows you to open the folder or folders in a different application of your choosing.

Sharing Options

This last option opens up the folder-sharing window, in which you can share the folder's contents if the Sharing service has been installed. See Chapter 10 for more details.

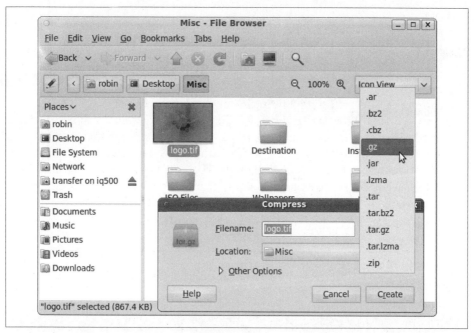

Figure 6-30. Compressing the logo.tif image to a .zip file

Template Files

In the previous section, I explained all the features that the file browser's context menu has to offer—with the exception of one. The feature I saved for now is *templating*, which I touched on in Chapter 5, in the section "The Directory Tree" on page 151.

With templates, you can configure the context menu to create a new file based on an existing template saved in the *Templates* folder of your home folder.

For example, if you frequently have to send out invoices, you can create a file with all the standard invoice details already typed and save it into the *Templates* folder. Figure 6-31 shows such a template file, *invoices.odt* (an OpenOffice.org document), which has been saved in this folder.

Once you have one or more template files stored in the *Templates* folder, you can start to use this extra functionality by right-clicking on the desktop or a folder background, and then selecting Create Document, followed by the name of the template. Figure 6-32 shows a new document being created using the template file (notice that in this case, it is shown using the filename *invoices*, without the extension *.odt*).

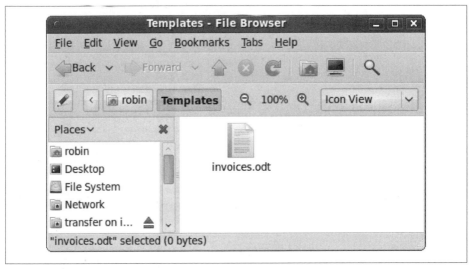

Figure 6-31. An OpenOffice.org template file in the Templates folder

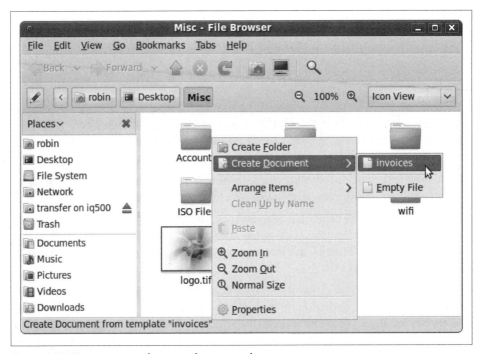

Figure 6-32. Creating a new document from a template

The new file will be given exactly the same filename and extension as the template file but with the filename part selected so that you can easily rename it, as shown in Figure 6-33.

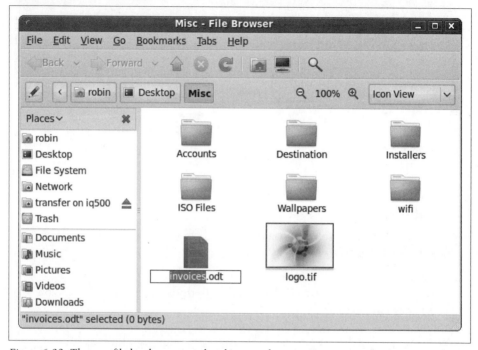

Figure 6-33. The new file has been created and just needs renaming

When you now open up the file, it will automatically launch OpenOffice.org and load it in, ready for you to edit, with all the default invoice details already in place. All you have to do now is add the specifics, save, and print.

This feature also works if you select File → Create Document from the file browser menu. You can also right-click the desktop to create new documents from template files.

The Toolbars

The top of the Nautilus file browser window features two toolbars called Main and Location, which appear as long as you are in Browser mode. If you are in Spatial mode, you will not see the top toolbars or the lefthand directory tree pane (see the section "Edit → Preferences → Behavior" on page 186 for how to change between modes). Figure 6-34 shows the toolbars displayed in a file browser window set to Browser mode.

Figure 6-34. Underneath the menu bar are two toolbars

The Main Toolbar

In order from left to right, the icons on this toolbar are all duplicated in the file browser menus, and are as follows:

Back and Forward
> When enabled, these move you back and forth through a path of folders you have previously navigated.

Up
> This icon takes you up to the level directly above the current folder.

Stop
> This icon stops the file browser when it is taking too long to return all the information.

Reload
> This icon refreshes the file browser window, updating it with any changes that have been made.

Home
> This icon takes you to your home folder.

Computer
> This icon takes you to the *Computer* folder, which shows everything on your local system, including connected devices such as CD drivers and USB devices.

Search
> This icon opens up the search bar.

The Location Bar

The first icon on the Location bar (which looks like a pencil and paper) toggles the bar between showing buttons for the folders and displaying a text box to type in a location. Just to its right is the location area itself, which, depending on the setting of the toggle, comprises either clickable buttons or a simple text input field.

Just to the right of the location area are the zoom in and out icons for enlarging and reducing icon sizes. Between them, you will see the current zoom level expressed as a percentage. If you click this zoom level indicator, the zoom level returns to the default, which is usually 100%.

The final item on this bar is the Icon view selector. With it, you can choose whether files and folders are to be displayed in Icon view, List view, or Compact view.

Configuration Editor

This is an editor available for modifying various GNOME settings, which works in much the same way as editing a Windows registry. Most of the settings available are quite advanced, and it's possible to mess up programs, even GNOME itself, if you make the wrong changes. However, there are some benign uses for the program, such as specifying the icons that should or should not display on the desktop.

To run the editor, press Alt-F2, enter `gconf-editor` into the input field that pops up, and click Run. This will bring up the window shown in Figure 6-35, in which I have used the lefthand pane to drill down to apps → nautilus → desktop.

To the left of the Configuration Editor window, on the desktop, you can see half a dozen icons that are similar to those you might see on a Windows computer. I achieved this by right-clicking *computer_icon_name* and other keys within the righthand frame, and entering string values for these keys. Then I checked *computer_icon_visible* and the other checkboxes to enable their display on the desktop.

You can also decide whether mounted volumes should have icons displayed on the desktop by checking or unchecking *volumes_visible*.

There are also many other options available in this Nautilus section, and they are all fairly safe to experiment with. But I recommend you don't alter settings for other programs unless you know what you're doing.

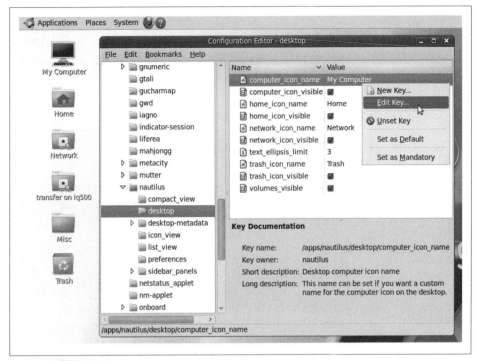

Figure 6-35. The Configuration Editor, in which a key is about to be edited

What's New in 10.04

Ubuntu 10.04 has a redesigned Nautilus File Manager in which the following changes have been made (as shown in Figure 6-36):

- The Zoom and Icon view controls have been moved from the directory bar to the main toolbar.
- The graphic presentation has been slightly enhanced with the addition of a single pixel border around the window panes.
- The lefthand pane has been enlarged by moving the Places title up to the directory bar and extending the pane all the way to the window bottom.
- The Pencil icon for toggling between the text and button-based address bars is removed, so now the only ways to manually enter a location are to select Go → Location or press either the / key or Ctrl-L.
- Most of these changes seem to have been made to enable a new split view option, which you can call up either by pressing F3 or by selecting View → Extra Pane. You then have two views open on the filesystem at the same time.

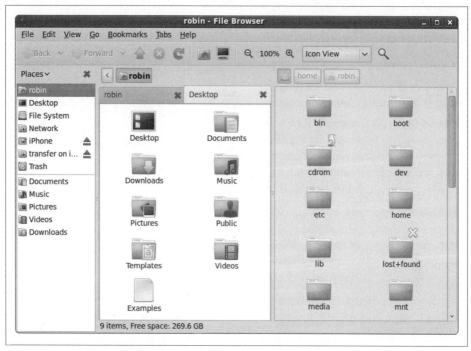

Figure 6-36. Ubuntu 10.04 introduces a few tweaks to Nautilus

Summary

At this point, you should be quite a proficient Ubuntu Linux user, so in the next chapter, I'll start to test your mettle by introducing the Terminal window and how to use the command line for issuing powerful commands as the *root* user, setting advanced file permissions, and monitoring the operating system's internal processes. But don't worry; it doesn't get too technical, I promise.

CHAPTER 7

The Command Line

As powerful as the GNOME desktop and Nautilus file manager are, there are still times when you will need to use a command line in Ubuntu. Fortunately, though, the days when you needed to learn enough stuff to fill an entire book before you could make good use of the command line are long gone.

Instead, you should be able to get by with just the information provided in this chapter, in which you'll learn how to start a command-line session, manage files and folders and their permission settings, run programs, and perform many other housekeeping tasks.

If you've never used a command line before, please don't be put off by this chapter. Unix, the operating system on which Linux is based, has been around a very long time, precisely because it's actually quite easy to use and, yes, even easy to learn, as you'll soon discover.

The Terminal

The main method you will use to enter command-line instructions into Ubuntu is via the Terminal program, which you call up by selecting Applications → Terminal. This results in a blank window capable of displaying 24 rows of 80 characters, as shown in Figure 7-1.

This resolution is used because it has been the standard size for text displays since the dawn of Unix. However, you can change it by dragging the window borders to suit your preferences and accommodate the text being displayed. Or select the Terminal menu and choose one of the four predefined resolutions. You can also zoom in and out, enlarging and decreasing both the window and font size, using the View menu.

Looking again at the screenshot, you'll see that the window's title shows *robin@linux-box: ~*. This indicates that the user *robin* on the computer *linux-box* is logged in, and the ~ means that the current folder (also known as the working directory) is the home

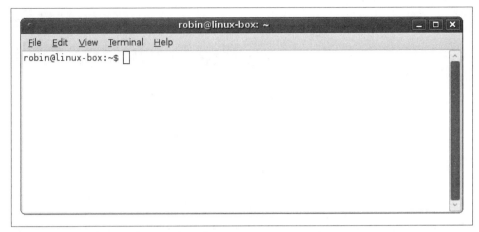

Figure 7-1. A newly opened terminal window

folder for *robin*, which is */home/robin*. By default, the command-line program used in the window will be *Bash*.

Bash

The Bash program is what is known as a shell program—a type of interface that provides access to the operating system's kernel. The name Bash is an acronym for "Bourne again shell," a free version of the earlier Unix shell written in the 1970s by Stephen Bourne. Bash is the default shell for the GNU project and most flavors of Linux, including Ubuntu. Interestingly, Bash is also used by Mac OS X, so if you have any recent Mac experience, you should be at home with it.

The Command-Line Editor

Before looking at the command-line instructions, I'd like to explore the various ways you can enter and edit text on the command line, because numerous options are available to make your life a lot easier.

For example, once you have entered one or more commands, you can scroll back and forth through the command history to reselect or edit previous commands by using the Up and Down cursor keys, or Ctrl-N for Next and Ctrl-P for Previous, as you can see from Table 7-1.

Table 7-1. Bash keyboard shortcuts

Shortcut	Equivalent to	Action
Ctrl-A	Home	Move the cursor to the start of the line.
Ctrl-E	End	Move the cursor to the end of the line.
Ctrl-D	Delete	Delete the character under the cursor. On a blank line, Ctrl-D (but not Delete) will cause the Terminal window to close.
Ctrl-H	Backspace	Delete the character to the left of the cursor.
Ctrl-J	Enter	Enter the current line.
Ctrl-B	Left arrow	Move the cursor back a character.
Ctrl-F	Right arrow	Move the cursor forward a character.
Ctrl-P	Up arrow	Recall the previous command (if any). See also Ctrl-N.
Ctrl-N	Down arrow	Recall the next command (if any). Using this and Ctrl-P, you can scroll back and forth through all the commands entered in a session.
Alt-B	Ctrl-left arrow	Move the cursor to the previous start of a word.
Shift-Alt-F	Ctrl-right arrow	Move the cursor to the first character following the end of the current word.
Shift-Ctrl-C		Copy the highlighted contents to the Ubuntu (not the Bash) clipboard.
Shift-Ctrl-V		Paste the contents of the Ubuntu (not the Bash) clipboard to the current cursor position.
Ctrl-C		Abort the current task or input.
Ctrl-K		Remove all the text from the current cursor position to the end of the line, saving it to the clipboard.
Ctrl-L		Clear the screen. Equivalent to the `clear` command, but keeps the contents of the current line.
Ctrl-U		Remove all the text before the cursor position, saving it to the Bash (not the Ubuntu) clipboard.
Ctrl-W		Remove the word before the cursor position to the Bash (not the Ubuntu) clipboard.
Ctrl-Y		Insert the Bash (not the Ubuntu) clipboard contents at the cursor position.
Ctrl-Z		If a program is currently running, this will suspend it and display a number and the word Stopped. To bring it back to the foreground again, you type `fg` followed by the number that was given.
Alt-C		Capitalize the character under the cursor, and then move the cursor to the character following the end of the current word.
Alt-D		Remove the word starting at the cursor position up to the first nonword character.
Alt-L		Lower the case of the character under the cursor and all those up to the end of the current word.
Alt-R		Cancel all changes made to a line and return it to its position in the history of commands.
Alt-Backspace		Delete the word immediately to the left of the cursor position.

Many of the Ctrl key shortcuts are holdovers from the days when keyboards didn't come with cursor keys, so unless you're also missing these keys, you can ignore them and use the equivalent arrow key and keypad shortcuts.

You may wish to try out the command line by entering some nonsense text, ensuring you start it with a # character to tell Ubuntu to ignore everything you type. You could even practice entering commands and scrolling back and forth through the history. A couple of minutes spent getting the hang of these shortcuts will make it much easier for you to work through the rest of this chapter.

A particular point to note while practicing is that Bash keeps its own clipboard, which you use with Ctrl-U, Ctrl-W, and Ctrl-Y. To paste from the Ubuntu clipboard into Bash, you use Shift-Ctrl-V or Edit → Paste, and to copy to the Ubuntu clipboard from Bash, you should highlight some text and either press Shift-Ctrl-C or select Edit → Copy.

Bash Commands

Running Bash commands is quite easy. For example, you can verify the location of the current folder simply by entering the command pwd, which stands for *print working directory*, to print out the full path of the current working folder. Or you can see which files and subfolders are in the current folder by entering ls, which stands for *list contents*. Table 7-2 details some of the more common commands relating to files and folders (along with what they do).

 Throughout this book I use the terms *folder* and *directory* interchangeably. *Directory* was the initial term for a folder in Unix, whereas *folder* is the term more commonly used on desktop systems such as Ubuntu, but they both refer to the same thing.

Table 7-2. File and folder commands

Command	Arguments	Action
cat	*file*	Display the contents of *file*.
cd	*folder*	Change the working directory (or folder) to *folder*.
chmod	{*various*} *fname*	Change the file or folder *fname*'s permissions, according to the options in {*various*}.
cp	*fname1 fname2*	Copy the file or folder *fname1* to *fname2*.
diff	*file1 file2*	Compare the contents of *file1* with *file2* and show the differences.
echo	*text*	Display the string *text*—generally used in shell scripts for providing feedback.
find	*where* -name *what*	Search the filesystem for filenames matching the string *what*, starting at the folder given in *where*.
grep	*what where*	Search the contents of the file or files supplied in *where* for occurrences of the string specified in *what*.

Command	Arguments	Action
ls		List all files and folders in the current folder (except hidden ones).
ls	*pattern*	List all files and folders (except hidden ones) matching *pattern*, which can be a file or folder name and may include wildcards.
ls	*-l*	Display all files and folders one line at a time with extended information (long form).
ls	*-a*	Display all files and folders (including hidden ones).
ls	*-la*	Display all files and folders (including hidden ones) in long form.
ls	*-la pattern*	Display the files or folders matching *pattern* (including hidden ones) in long form.
mkdir	*folder*	Create *folder*.
more	*file*	Display the contents of *file* one screen at a time, using the space bar to page and Q to quit.
mv	*fname1 fname2*	Rename or move the file or folder *fname1* to *fname2*.
nano	*file*	Open *file* in the Nano text editor (creating it if it doesn't exist).
pwd		Display the full path of the current working folder.
rm	*fname*	Remove the file or folder *fname*.
rm	*-rf folder*	Remove *folder* along with all subfolders and their files (this is a powerful command because you cannot retrieve the removed content; use it with caution, particularly on your home folder!).
rmdir	*folder*	Remove *folder* if it is empty (this will fail if *folder* contains any files or subfolders).
touch	*file*	Change the timestamp of *file* so that it looks like it has just been modified.
wc	*file*	Display the number of lines, words, and characters in *file*.

The cd, pwd, and ls Commands

By default, the prompt you see when you first open a Terminal window will be something like this:

user@computer:~$

In my case, my username is *robin* and the computer I am using is called *linux-box*, so the prompt I see is:

robin@linux-box:~$

The idea behind this is to remind you of the username and computer you are using, so you don't have to remember those details yourself, which is especially useful when managing multiple computers or logins.

Now let's look at some commands, starting with the **cd** command, which is used to *change directory* (or folder). In its simplest form, you just enter something like the following:

cd /home

This command makes the *home* folder the default working folder. Enter the text shown and press the Return or Enter key, and the Terminal prompt will change to show something like the following:

```
user@computer:/home$
```

Remember that the actual prompt you see will have your username and computer name in place of *user* and *computer*. Now try entering the following two commands:

```
cd /home
pwd
```

Ubuntu should report that you are now in the home folder by displaying the following:

```
/home
user@computer:/home$
```

You can try navigating back up a level to the / directory by entering this:

```
cd ..
```

 I often use the terms changing *up* and changing *down* a level in this book and realize that different people view them in different ways. I look at the filesystem as having the root directory at the top level of the root system of a tree (rather than the bottom level of the trunk and branches of a tree), and therefore when I say changing *up* it refers to going back a level toward the root, and changing *down* refers to moving to a deeper directory or folder.

The .. is a shorthand you use to represent the parent folder. Whatever the parent of the current folder is, Ubuntu will go to it automatically when this command is issued. Now try the following command to select your home folder:

```
cd ~
```

I have no way of knowing what your username is, but Ubuntu does, and when you use the ~ symbol, it is substituted with your home folder. So, enter the following to see which folder is now the working directory:

```
pwd
```

Now type the following to view the contents of this folder:

```
ls
```

The result should look something like Figure 7-2. Although you may have more or less items, you should have a very similar collection of subfolders, and unless you have deleted any of your default folders, you will at least see *Desktop*, *Documents*, *Downloads*, *example.desktop*, *Music*, *Pictures*, *Public*, *Templates*, *Ubuntu One*, and *Videos*.

You can also use -a option with the ls command to show all the files in the current folder, like this:

```
ls -a
```

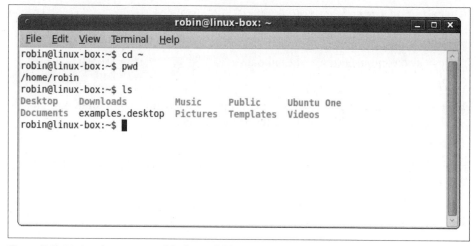

Figure 7-2. Listing the contents of the home folder

You will then be presented with a long list of files and folders that looks something like the following:

```
.                      .gnome2             .profile
..                     .gnome2_private     Public
.adobe                 .gnupg              .pulse
.apport-ignore.xml     .gstreamer-0.10     .pulse-cookie
.bash_history          .gtk-bookmarks      .qt
.bash_logout           .gvfs               .quicksynergy
.bashrc                .hplip              .recently-used
.cache                 .ICEauthority       .recently-used.xbel
.compiz                .icons              .ssh
.config                .kde                .sudo_as_admin_successful
.dbus                  .local              Templates
Desktop                .macromedia         test
   (etc...)
```

All the items beginning with a period are normally hidden, but the -a option has revealed them. Generally, though, you don't need to see these files.

To display the output in long form you can use another option, like this:

```
ls -l
```

And the result will then look something like this:

```
drwxr-xr-x  3 robin robin 4096 2009-10-05 14:12 Desktop
drwxr-xr-x  2 robin robin 4096 2009-09-07 15:29 Documents
drwx------  2 robin robin 4096 2009-09-02 10:15 Downloads
lrwxrwxrwx  1 robin robin   26 2009-04-16 17:56 Examples
                           -> /usr/share/example-content
drwxr-xr-x 12 robin robin 4096 2009-06-16 00:45 firefox
drwxr-xr-x  2 robin robin 4096 2009-04-16 18:07 Music
drwxr-xr-x  2 robin robin 4096 2009-10-05 13:45 My Projects
drwxr-xr-x  2 robin robin 4096 2009-04-16 18:07 Pictures
drwxr-xr-x  2 robin robin 4096 2009-04-16 18:07 Public
```

```
drwxr-xr-x  2 robin robin 4096 2009-09-23 15:13 Templates
drwxr-xr-x  2 robin robin 4096 2009-10-05 14:47 test
drwxr-xr-x  2 robin robin 4096 2009-04-16 18:07 Videos
```

You can also combine the switches like this:

```
ls -al
```

Anyway, getting back to the `cd` command, for the next example you should now change your working folder to *Pictures* by entering the following:

```
cd Pictures
```

Now enter `pwd` to verify that this has worked; you should see that you have switched to the *Pictures* folder.

So, let's see the `..` shortcut in action by changing up a level and back down again to the *Downloads* folder, all in a single command, like this:

```
cd ../Downloads
```

What you have given the `cd` command is a relative path, which will work no matter what your username is; see "Absolute and Relative Paths" on page 227.

 Windows users should remember to enter forward slashes (/), not backslashes (\), to represent folders in Bash. Bash follows the Unix and Linux convention of separating folders with forward slashes, which you should be comfortable with because URLs on the Web use the same character. Also remember that Linux is case-sensitive, which means the folder *Downloads* is different from the folder *downloads*.

The cp and mkdir Commands

The `cp` command takes two arguments: an existing file to copy and a destination. So, for example, if you have the file *accounts.txt* and would like to make a backup file, you can issue this command:

```
cp accounts.txt accounts.bak
```

This will create the new file *accounts.bak*, which will be an identical copy of the original file. You can also use this command to copy folders, and even entire filesystems and subsystems. If the second argument is a folder instead of a file, the files you copy go directly under the folder and are given the source file's filename.

For example, to create a copy of the */boot* folder within your home folder, you could ensure that you are in that folder and create a new one in which to copy the files by entering the following commands (the `mkdir` command standing for *make directory*):

```
cd ~
mkdir test
```

Then you would enter the following to perform the copy:

```
cp /boot/* test
```

What this does is tell Ubuntu to copy all the files it finds in the */boot* folder—achieved by use of the * wildcard character, which used this way means "any file at all"—into the *test* folder. It does not, however, copy any subfolders, and if there are any (such as the *grub* subfolder in this case), it will issue a message telling you that it has omitted them. To copy a folder and all its subfolders, you would add the -r argument for recursive copying, like this:

```
cp -r /boot/* test
```

The mv Command

Ubuntu considers renaming and moving items to be equivalent. If you rename a file, Ubuntu treats it as if you have moved it to a new location comprising the current folder and the new filename. Therefore, unlike DOS, instead of having both a MOVE and a RENAME command, Ubuntu provides just the mv command.

Renaming items

To rename a file in the current folder, you could issue a command such as this:

```
mv accounts.txt accounts.old
```

The file that was previously called *accounts.txt* will now have the name *accounts.old*. To move the file to a new location, you might use a command such as the following, which moves the file *accounts.txt* to the *backups* subfolder, if it exists (if not, the file will simply be renamed *backups*):

```
mv accounts.txt backups
```

Similarly, you can rename a folder by making that the first argument, like this:

```
mv oldfolder newfolder
```

Moving items

To move a file, you might enter something like the following, which moves the file *accounts.txt* into the *backups* folder:

```
mv accounts.txt backups
```

If the folder *backups* exists, then *accounts.txt* will be moved into it. Otherwise, *accounts.txt* will be renamed to *backups*.

To move and rename a file at the same time, you might enter something like the following, which moves the file *accounts.txt* into the *backups* folder, giving it the new name of *accounts.old*:

```
mv accounts.txt backups/accounts.old
```

If the backups folder doesn't exist, you will get an error message.

You can move an entire folder (and its files and subfolders) to another location by making that the first argument, like this:

```
mv oldfolder otherfolder
```

If *otherfolder* exists, then *oldfolder* will be moved into it. Otherwise, *oldfolder* will be renamed to *otherfolder*.

You can also move groups of files specified by wildcards, like this:

```
mv *.txt textfolder
```

This moves all files with the extension *.txt* into *textfolder*. If you like, you can provide multiple filenames to the mv command, like this:

```
mv *.txt *.jpg readme.doc destination
```

The final name is treated as the destination, and all the files preceding it are the sources. Other commands such as rm and cp also allow multiple arguments.

The diff Command

Using diff, you can quickly get a glimpse of the *differences* between two document files. The syntax to use is like this:

```
diff file1 file2
```

The program loads in the two files it is passed, synchronizes all the parts of text that are the same in each file, and then discards them. Whatever text remains from each file must be different from the other one. Then it is displayed, as shown in Figure 7-3.

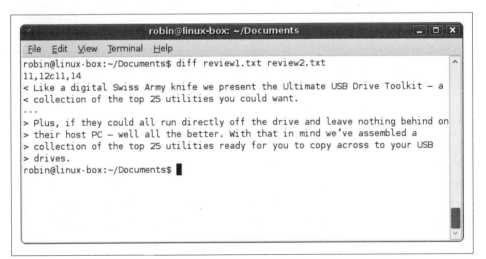

Figure 7-3. Displaying the differences between two files

If you want to create some text files to try out some commands such as diff, skip ahead to the section "Using Nano to Edit Files" on page 232.

Any text that exists in the first file but is not present in the second one is shown first, prefaced by a < symbol to remind you that the text is unique to the first file. Likewise, the text that occurs only in the second file comes next, but this time prefaced by a > symbol.

The screen grab shows that there are two extra lines in the file *review1.txt* and four in *review2.txt*. Using diff, it's clear to see that each file has been separately edited, with an extra paragraph added (or removed).

Programmers often use this program to highlight changes between various different versions of a program. You could use it to see changes made between versions of a report, a recipe, or anything that you save copies of as you go along.

The find Command

There are thousands of files in an Ubuntu installation (if not hundreds of thousands), so locating individual ones could be a nightmare without the find command. But with it, you can find almost any file within a few seconds.

The program supports many options, but at its most basic you use it by entering a command such as this:

```
find / -name blackjack
```

This command searches the entire filesystem for any files called *blackjack*. However, as you will see from Figure 7-4, folders that you do not have permission to access are skipped, with the error message "Permission denied."

At the top of the screen grab, you'll see that six files with the name *blackjack* have been found, and plenty of folders have not been searched due to permission settings. If you want to be given access to these folders, you can use the sudo command to temporarily become the *root* user (see the section "Using sudo" on page 252 for more information), like this (entering your password when prompted):

```
sudo find / -name blackjack
```

Either way, from the information returned, we can see that the likely location of the blackjack program is */usr/games/blackjack*, shown in the fourth line in the screenshot.

Of course, the default Ubuntu games are all available from the Applications → Games submenu, but if you ever delete any of these (or other) entries, this is how you can find out where the programs are located. And, indeed, if you type the following into the Terminal, the Blackjack game will open, as shown in Figure 7-5.

```
/usr/games/blackjack
```

```
                        robin@linux-box: ~/Documents                    _  □  x
  File  Edit  View  Terminal  Help
  /usr/share/gnome-games/blackjack
  /usr/share/gnome/help/blackjack
  /usr/share/omf/blackjack
  /usr/games/blackjack
  /home/robin/.gconf/apps/blackjack
  /home/robin/.gnome2/accels/blackjack
  find: `/var/spool/cups': Permission denied
  find: `/var/spool/cron/atjobs': Permission denied
  find: `/var/spool/cron/atspool': Permission denied
  find: `/var/spool/cron/crontabs': Permission denied
  find: `/var/lib/PolicyKit': Permission denied
  find: `/var/lib/gdm': Permission denied
  find: `/var/lib/php5': Permission denied
  find: `/var/lib/polkit-1': Permission denied
  find: `/var/cache/system-tools-backends/backup': Permission denied
  find: `/var/cache/ldconfig': Permission denied
  find: `/var/log/couchdb': Permission denied
  find: `/var/log/gdm': Permission denied
  find: `/var/log/samba/cores': Permission denied
  find: `/var/run/sudo': Permission denied
  find: `/var/run/cups/certs': Permission denied
  find: `/var/run/samba/winbindd_privileged': Permission denied
  find: `/var/run/PolicyKit': Permission denied
  robin@linux-box:~/Documents$ █
```

Figure 7-4. Searching for programs named blackjack

If you only know part of a file's name, you can also use the * and ? wildcard symbols. For more on this subject, see the section later in this chapter called "Wildcards, Sets, and Brace Expansion" on page 242. But for now all you need to know is that a ? represents a single wildcard character, and * represents zero or more unknown characters.

So, for example, all the following will locate the *blackjack* program file (and many others):

```
find / -name black*
find / -name *jack
find / -name bl?ck*
```

In fact, there may be so many entries that you want to page through them all, which you can do using the more command, explained in the next section.

You don't have to always search from the root folder. You can, for example, search for files only in the current folder and its subfolders, which you can do using the period character, like this:

```
find . -name invoice*
```

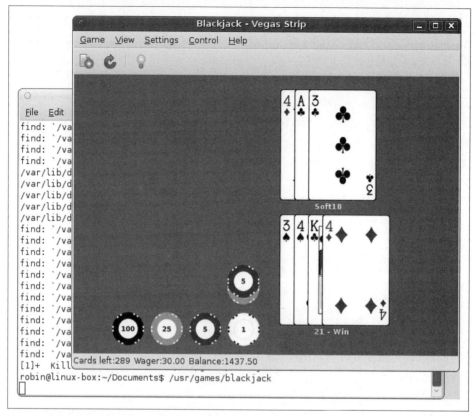

Figure 7-5. Running a program after determining its location

or starting from your home folder, like this:

```
find ~ -name invoice*
```

What's new in 10.04

The Blackjack game was removed from the default Ubuntu 10.04 distribution, but should still be on your computer if you upgraded from 9.10. However, if you don't have this game, you may wish to install it first before trying the previous and following examples. It wasn't in the 10.04 repositories at the time of publication, but you can always add it by entering the following URL into a web browser:

*http://mirrors.kernel.org/ubuntu/pool/main/g/gnome-games/gnome-blackjack_2.28
.0-0ubuntu1_i386.deb*

This is a single line that should be entered in its entirety, without pressing the space bar or Return until it has been typed in.

The cat and more Commands

The cat command takes a file and outputs it to the screen. To use it, enter a command such as the following:

    cat chapter7.txt

However, if there are more lines than will fit in the window, the text will scroll, which is where the more program comes in.

On its own, the more command is very useful for paging through text files that have more lines than can be displayed in the Terminal window. To use it, you enter the command's name followed by the name of the file to view, like this:

    more chapter7.txt

See Figure 7-6 for the result of using the program on an early draft of this chapter.

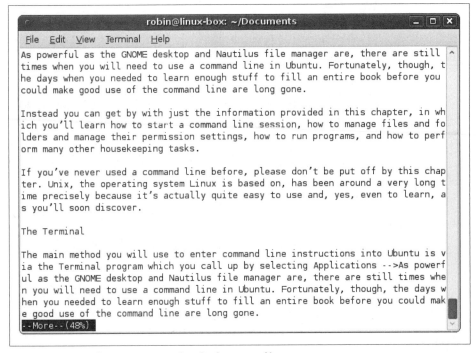

Figure 7-6. Using the more command to display a text file

As you can see, this is easier than loading the file into a text editor just for viewing it. You can scroll though the file a line at a time by pressing the Enter key, or a page at a time by pressing the space bar. To quit, press the q key.

The more command is, however, far more powerful than you might think, thanks to Ubuntu's ability to use pipes—a method by which the output from one program is passed as the input to another—which is fully explained later on in the sections "Using Redirection" on page 237 and "Using Pipes" on page 235. But more is such a useful feature that it's worth a quick look at now.

For example, in the previous section on using the find command, I promised we would see how we can combine it with more to page the output. And here's how you would do it:

```
find / -name bl?ck* |more
```

At the end of this command, I have added a | (pipe) symbol followed by a call to the more program. As you'll learn later, the | takes the output that would have been displayed and passes it to the more program to deal with instead.

What happens is that all the output (except for any error messages) is stored up, and when find exits, the more program takes over, displaying the stored-up output a page at a time. The first page displayed by more looks like Figure 7-7.

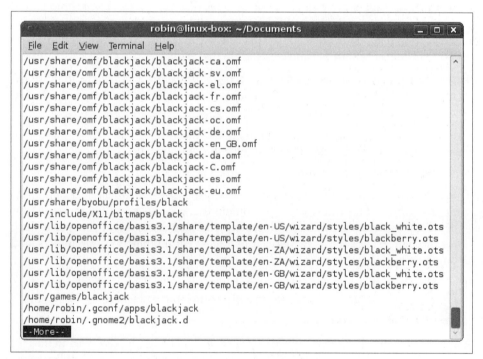

Figure 7-7. Using the more program to page the output from find

You can add the more command this way to almost any other Bash command where there is more output than will fit in the Terminal window. An odd little side effect of the pipe improves the value of the output from more: all the "Permission denied" error messages from find are displayed before more runs so that you get only the useful output all at the end. There are also ways to completely suppress error messages altogether, which I'll show later.

The grep Command

Using the grep command, you can take your searches a step further and look inside files for text to match. It is a very powerful command with some quite sophisticated features, such as choosing (or ignoring) case-sensitivity, matching only whole words, and much more. In fact, entire books have been written about the program. But most of us will generally use grep in its simplest form, in which a given set of files is searched for a particular word or phrase.

For example, to locate every file in your *Documents* folder containing the word *invoice*, you could issue the following command:

```
grep invoice ~/Documents/*
```

You should remember the ~ character from the earlier section on the cp command; it represents your home folder. Using it this way cuts out a step because you don't have to use cd to change to the home folder. Instead, by prefacing a file or folder name with ~, you tell Ubuntu to start a relative path from that point.

Therefore, if you have the username *fred*, then *~/Documents/* * will refer to all the documents within the folder */home/fred/Documents*.

So the previous command calls up the grep command, asking it to search for the word *invoice* in all the files within the given folder, and then displays those that match. To illustrate this, here's a command you can type in right now:

```
grep -r videos /usr/share/doc
```

This command specifies the -r option to search the */usr/share/doc* folder and all its subfolders for any files whose contents contain the word *videos*. (The option used is -r because programmers use the word *recursive* to describe a task that keeps on drilling down through levels, such as in this case of folders within folders within folders, and so on.)

If you don't care about the case of a match, you can use the -i option to choose a case-insensitive search, which will return even more results (but will take longer to perform):

```
grep -ri videos /usr/share/doc
```

And to only return documents where the word *videos* appears on its own and not, for example, as part of the string *videosettings*, you can use the -w option as follows, the result of which will look like Figure 7-8.

```
grep -rw videos /usr/share/doc
```

As with the more command, you can also use grep in conjunction with a pipe. So, for example, to narrow down the output from an ls command to display only certain files,

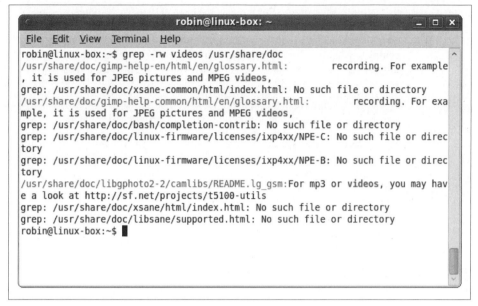

Figure 7-8. Searching for files containing the word videos

such as those containing the sequence *Do* within your home folder, you could enter this command:

```
ls ~ |grep Do
```

This will list at least your *Documents* and *Downloads* folders, as well as any others you have created that match the specified pattern.

The rm and rmdir Commands

To delete a file or folder, use the rm command, which stands for *remove*. For example, to erase the file *tempfile* in the current folder, use this command:

```
rm tempfile
```

Or to erase a file in your home folder, you could enter a command such as:

```
rm ~/oldfile
```

You can also delete an empty folder using rmdir, like this:

```
rmdir EmptyFolder
```

However, to remove a folder containing any files or subfolders, you need to use the rm command with the argument -rf, like this:

```
rm -rf FolderWithStuffIn
```

Be careful, as the previous line is one of the most destructive commands there is. If you execute it on the / folder using root privileges, it will wipe out your entire filesystem. Or, executing it on ~, your home folder, will completely remove that. Inserting an extra space character in an unfortunate place in the command can also cause you to lose directories you wanted to save.

So please, when using this command, look very hard at what you have typed before pressing Enter. And don't type an rm command someone on a bulletin board recommends without first checking to see which files and folders it will erase.

The wc Command

Using this command, you can quickly summarize the number of lines, words, and characters in a text file. You use it like this:

```
wc document
```

The program will then display a result such as this:

```
10  234 1319 document
```

This tells you that *document* has 10 lines, 234 words, and 1,319 characters. Actual lines within the document are counted, not the number of lines the file would use if displayed in the Terminal window. The character count will include one character for each end-of-line character, so it will be higher than the number of visible characters.

Using man

I've really only scratched the surface of the commands I've shown, giving you just enough information to get you started. But they all offer a wide range of options, providing additional control over how they work and the output displayed.

Using the man command, you can look up everything you could ever want to know about a Bash program. It's as easy as entering man followed by the command name, like this:

```
man wc
```

This displays the manual page for the wc command, which you can scroll through a line at a time by pressing the Enter key, or a page at a time with the space bar. You can also use the Up and Down cursor keys to scroll back and forth. To quit the program, press the q key.

If you have a scroll wheel on your mouse, you can also use that to scroll back and forth through a man page. Figure 7-9 shows the manpage for the wc command.

Ubuntu comes packed with masses of such information, so whenever you are in doubt about how to use a command or what it does, just call up its manpage. Some manpages

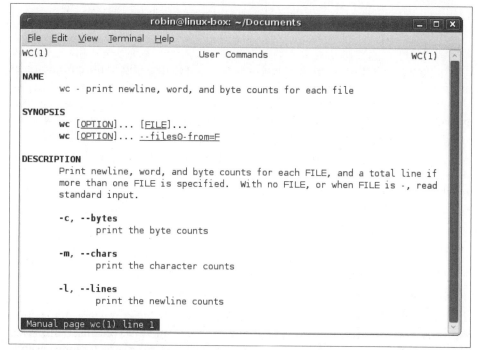

Figure 7-9. The manpage for the wc command

tell you that the command is documented in another page called an *info* page with more up-to-date or extended information. You call up an info page by substituting `info` for man.

Additionally, you can usually get a quick explanation of a command and its switches using `-help` in the following manner, which summarizes the options for the man command:

```
man -help
```

Absolute and Relative Paths

Although you may not realize it, you already have learned the difference between an absolute pathname and a relative one. But if you haven't come across these terms before, let me explain them to you, as they are very important when using the command line.

An absolute path is fixed, such as */home/robin/Documents*, and works the same way regardless of your working directory, whereas a relative path leaves out one or more parent folder names, either substituting them with the .. shortcut or referencing files and folders within the current one.

A path that uses parent folders without naming them might look like *../Videos*, or on a deeply nested folder something like *../../../Documents*. Each time the .. is encountered,

Ubuntu knows to go back up a level. A / is then required afterward if there is more in the path. If not, a relative path such as ../../.. is quite valid—it takes you to the folder three levels up.

The other type of relative path is where only files and folders within the current folder are referenced, such as *Documents/Reports* or *Vacation/Cancun/Photos*. In fact, although it would be pointless, a relative path such as *Vacation/Cancun/../Barbados* is perfectly valid because it actually represents the path *Vacation/Barbados*, unnecessarily visiting the *Cancun* folder on the way.

All you have to remember is that what differentiates a relative from an absolute path is the existence of a / at the front. Without an initial forward slash, a path is relative to the current location, but with the slash it is relative to the filesystem's root folder, which is more commonly known as an absolute path.

Using Quotation Marks

With the Nautilus file manager, it is easy to create files and folders that include spaces in their names. You can also copy and move these about by dragging and dropping them without any problem.

But when you come to access such files from the command line, you must remember to enclose them in quotation marks. For example, if your username is *jenny* and you have a folder called *My Projects* in your home folder that you would like to access from the command line, you cannot use the cd command in the normal way, like this:

```
cd /home/jenny/My Projects
```

The reason is that Ubuntu will think you want to change to a folder called */home/jenny/My* and will report the following error:

```
bash: cd: /home/jenny/My: No such file or directory
```

To prevent this, the correct way to change to such a folder is to enter the following, with double quotation marks (or you can use single quotation marks instead if you prefer):

```
cd "/home/jenny/My Projects"
```

Likewise, using any other Bash commands with spaces in file or folder names requires similar use of quotation marks. The following collection of commands all illustrate the correct way to handle spaces in folder and filenames:

```
mkdir "/home/jenny/My Projects"
cd ~/"My Projects"
ls -al "/home/jenny/My Projects/January"
rm "Backups/Old|Report.doc"
```

The fourth line doesn't have any spaces but it still requires the use of quotation marks. The reason is that the | character—which, like the space, is a normal character when used on the desktop—is a special operator when used in the command line. There are many more of these special operators, such as >, <, and ;.

If you omit the quotes when referencing files or folders that contain such characters, you will receive one of many different types of error message, depending on the characters used and their locations. Even worse, sometimes you may not get an error message at all, because such a string may look like a valid command that then gets executed, possibly even changing or erasing data!

As you can see by the second line in the previous code example, you do not have to surround the entire path in quotes, and sometimes should not if you want certain characters such as the ~ to be correctly acted upon. In fact, it is sufficient to simply surround just the nonalphanumeric characters in quotation marks. Therefore, the following commands are all equivalent to the previous four:

```
mkdir /home/jenny/"My Projects"
cd ~/My" "Projects
ls -al /home/jenny/"My Projects"/January
rm Backups/Old"|"Report.doc
```

The PATH Environment Variable

Many commands you enter at the command line require the use of an external program that is loaded from the filesystem. For example, commands such as mkdir and wc actually reside in the /bin folder.

Whenever you enter an instruction that Bash doesn't recognize, it tries executing it as a program and returns an error if no program of the same name is found. And this doesn't only include the main commands we've been looking at, because you can run almost any program from the command line.

But with a filesystem comprising thousands of files, how does Ubuntu know which programs to run and from which directories? The answer is that it uses a system environment variable to point to a subset of folders it must search upon receipt of an unknown command. This variable is called PATH, and it can be displayed using the echo command, like this (the $ symbol is required):

```
echo $PATH
```

The result of issuing this command will look something like the following seven absolute folder paths, separated by colons:

```
/usr/local/sbin:/usr/local/bin:/usr/sbin:/usr/bin:/sbin:/bin:/usr/games
```

Each time an unknown command is entered, Ubuntu will search each of the folders in the path in the order they are provided to try and find a program of the same name. If one is found, it is executed; otherwise, an error message is displayed.

These seven folders provide easy access to all the main programs in the operating system, including the games. But any programs that are not located in one of these folders cannot be executed by simply entering their names at the command line.

For example, let's say you have downloaded a utility program into your home folder called *diary*. If you enter its name at the command line, you will receive an error message because it is not located in the path. Instead, you would enter a command such as the following to run it (remembering that the ~ symbol is shorthand for your home folder):

```
~/diary
```

Or, if you have saved it to a folder outside of your path, you would have to enter the absolute path and filename in order to run it. Of course, this assumes that *diary* is a simple standalone program that doesn't require installation, because most major applications *will* place an executable program file somewhere in your path during the installation process.

Using the . Operator

Now let's look at a possibly confusing situation by assuming you have entered cd ~ to set your home folder as your working directory, and have saved into it a program called *find*. In this case you might think you can now enter find and the program will run, but actually it won't, because there's a program with the name *find* located in the */usr/ bin* folder, and Ubuntu will execute that file by default because it is in the path, and that gets searched before the current folder.

One solution is to reference the program with either an absolute or a relative path and filename, such as this:

```
~/find
```

However, when a program is in the current directory, you can use the single period operator to run it, like this:

```
./find
```

This turns the command into a relative pathname and tells the system to run the program exactly where you say it is, not to first search for the program in the path.

Alternatively, if you tried to run a program in your home folder (or any other not in the path) that *didn't* have a counterpart file with the same name somewhere in path, you would just receive a "command not found" error message, unless you properly identified the program's location with a ~, a ., or another relative or absolute prefix.

Other Environment Variables

Ubuntu also provides many other environment variables; some of the more common ones are listed in Table 7-3.

Table 7-3. Common environment variables

Environment variable	Contents
HOME	Your home folder
LANG	The default language
MANPATH	The path to the man program's manual pages
PATH	The system path
PWD	The current working directory
SHELL	The current shell
TZ	The time zone
USER	Your username

Each variable's contents can be displayed using the echo command, like this:

```
echo $HOME
```

 Most commands require you to preface variables with a $ sign to let the operating system know that you are referring to a variable and not just a string of letters.

You can also use environment variables in paths, so you could list the contents of the *Documents* folder within your home folder using this command:

```
ls $HOME/Documents
```

As you can see, $HOME and the ~ operator are interchangeable.

Alternative Shells

Unless you have changed it, until now you have been using Ubuntu's version of the Bash program called Dash (the Debian Almquist shell). Dash is based on the Ash shell by Kenneth Almquist and is almost identical to Bash in use—but is much smaller and faster.

Other shells are also available. For example, advanced users may sometimes encounter the slight differences between Dash and Bash, and so can choose to use Bash itself by entering chsh (for "choose shell"), entering your password, and then pressing Enter to accept the default new shell of */bin/bash*. To change back, enter chsh again, enter your password and select */bin/sh* for your default shell. If you wish to be certain that you are using Dash, you can enter chsh and select */bin/dash* as your shell.

You can view the list of available shells by entering the following command:

```
cat /etc/shells
```

If you are a seasoned Linux user and prefer to use a shell that isn't shown, from the desktop you can select System → Administration → Synaptic Package Manager and search for the term *shell* to list all those available. Normally, though, most users will want to stick with using the default shell.

Using Nano to Edit Files

Most of the time you'll probably edit files from the desktop using either the Gedit or OpenOffice.org program. But when you are already using a Terminal window, sometimes it's quicker and easier to use the Nano text editor. It's very easy to use, and unlike the Linux or Unix editors that programmers use for heavy text editing, Nano doesn't require learning a complex series of keyboard shortcuts.

To edit an already existing file, type nano followed by its path and filename. For example, to edit the document *chapter7.txt* in the *Documents* folder, I entered the following, resulting in the screen shown in Figure 7-10:

```
nano ~/Documents/chapter7.txt
```

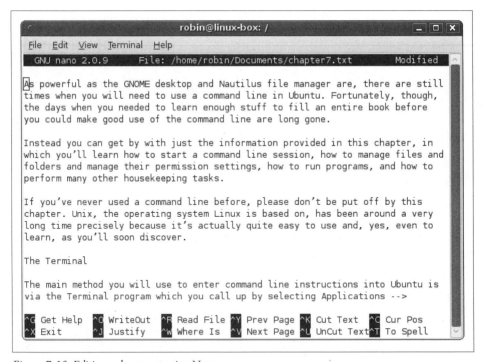

Figure 7-10. Editing a document using Nano

To navigate around the document, use the cursor keys. All the other actions you need are listed at the bottom of the screen, with the ^ character representing the Ctrl key.

So, to save a document, press Ctrl-O, edit the filename shown near the bottom of the screen (if necessary), and then press Enter. If you want to save a file and exit the program at the same time, you can press Ctrl-X, press the y key when asked to confirm the save, edit the filename if necessary, and then press Enter.

You can also create a brand new document by entering nano without any argument. You would then specify your document's path and filename upon saving it.

Shell Scripts

A shell script is a sequence of command-line commands brought together into a single file to work like a small program. Let's make a simple *Hello World* script by entering the following command to call up Nano ready to create the file *hello* in your home folder:

```
nano ~/hello
```

Now enter the following two lines into the editor, pressing Enter after each. Then press Ctrl-X, followed by y to confirm, and then Enter to save the file:

```
#!/bin/sh
echo "Hello World\n"
```

The first line, #!/bin/sh, tells Ubuntu to use the */bin/sh* shell program to execute the following commands. It could equally have requested */bin/bash* or another shell, but I have chosen to use */bin/sh* for this example. The second line prints the text *Hello World* followed by a blank line, specified by the \n at the end.

Once you have saved this file, you then need to make it executable by entering the following command:

```
chmod +x ~/hello
```

The chmod command stands for change mode, and +x tells Ubuntu to make the file executable. See the section "File and Folder Permissions" on page 246 for more details on this command.

You are now ready to run your script by entering the following. Afterward, you should see the welcoming message followed by a blank line, and then the command-line prompt:

```
~/hello
```

As I said, any commands you can enter at the command line can be used in a shell script, and that includes the use of environment variables, or even creating new variables of your own. For example, here's an improved version of the previous script that will ask you your name and then say hello to you:

```
#!/bin/sh
clear
echo -n "What is your name? "
read NAME
echo "\nHello $NAME\n"
```

The clear command clears the Terminal window, and the -n argument after the first echo command tells Ubuntu to suppress the carriage return so that the next text displayed will follow directly, rather than appearing underneath. That's why there's a space after the question mark—to leave a small gap.

The read command is used to request input from a user, and the word NAME after it is the name of the variable in which to place that input. In this instance, a $ symbol should not preface the variable name. When you type in your name, the text will appear directly following the preceding output.

In the final line, to tell the echo command that NAME is a variable (and not just a string of text), it is prefaced with a $ symbol. Figure 7-11 shows this script in action.

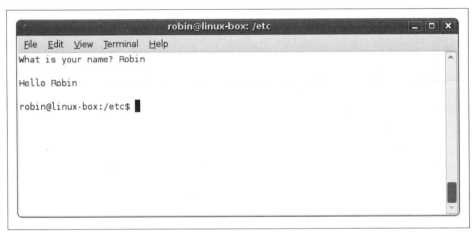

Figure 7-11. The output from the improved hello script

This is an interactive script, but usually you'll want your scripts to simply get on with a task quietly, for example, compressing and backing up weblog files, or deleting files from a temporary folder. If you want to learn more about the vast subject of shell scripting, I recommend the book *Classic Shell Scripting*, also from O'Reilly.

Using Backticks

The backtick is a special type of quotation mark that you'll usually find near the 1 key on your keyboard. You use it in a command line to tell Ubuntu to execute the contents between the ticks as a separate command, and then to paste the output in place of the backtick's contents.

For example, you can combine some text with a command to display the current date like this:

```
echo "Today is `date`"
```

Or, to list the current working directory in a friendly way, you could use this command:

```
echo "You are in `pwd`"
```

Or here's how you can list all the files in your home folder (and its subfolders) that have the file extension *.txt*:

```
echo -e "`clear`Your text files:\n\n`find ~ -name *.txt`";
```

As you can see, there are two uses of backticks here: once to clear the screen and again to search for the text files. The -e argument tells Ubuntu to allow escaped characters such as \n, which is used to display new lines.

Using Pipes

A little earlier we looked at alternative ways of using the more and grep commands by piping output through them using the | operator. Pipes are such a useful device that you will see them used in a variety of ways, often with multiple commands piped together to produce a final output. For example, take a look at the following composite command:

```
ps -ax | sort -k5 | less
```

The ps program, in conjunction with the argument -ax, displays all the background processes running on your computer, and is covered in more detail in the section "System Processes" on page 252. On its own, ps -ax will display many screens full of information; and the last few lines will look like Figure 7-12.

The processes are listed in order of when they were started (as indicated by the numbers in the first column). So, to quickly search through the list and find processes you may be interested in, you can use the sort command with the -k5 option. This causes a sort to occur on the fifth column (as defined by the end of a section of whitespace), which is the one containing the process path and filenames. This results in the screen grab shown in Figure 7-13.

This is an improvement, but we can do even better by also adding the less command, which is an enhanced version of more. The less command makes it easier to move back and forth in the output because it supports the cursor keys as well as Enter and the space bar.

So, the combined result is to list all the current processes alphabetically, displayed in a manner that supports scrolling through it in both directions, as shown in Figure 7-14.

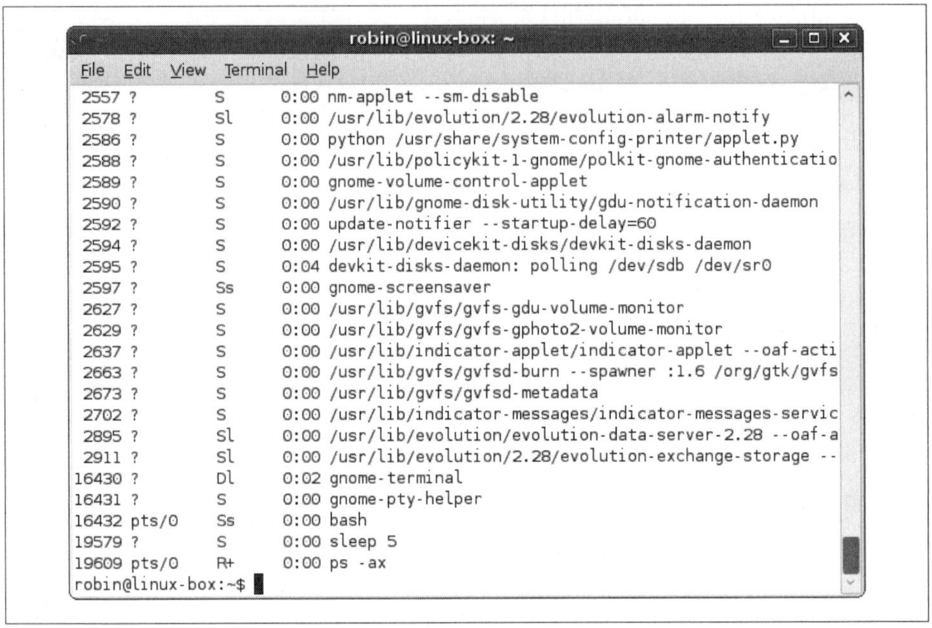

Figure 7-12. The result of issuing the command ps -ax

Figure 7-13. The result of the ps -ax command sorted at column 5

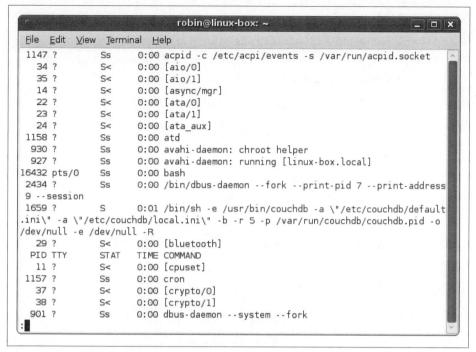

```
                      robin@linux-box: ~                        _ □ X
 File  Edit  View  Terminal  Help
  1147 ?         Ss     0:00 acpid -c /etc/acpi/events -s /var/run/acpid.socket
    34 ?         S<     0:00 [aio/0]
    35 ?         S<     0:00 [aio/1]
    14 ?         S<     0:00 [async/mgr]
    22 ?         S<     0:00 [ata/0]
    23 ?         S<     0:00 [ata/1]
    24 ?         S<     0:00 [ata_aux]
  1158 ?         Ss     0:00 atd
   930 ?         Ss     0:00 avahi-daemon: chroot helper
   927 ?         Ss     0:00 avahi-daemon: running [linux-box.local]
 16432 pts/0     Ss     0:00 bash
  2434 ?         Ss     0:00 /bin/dbus-daemon --fork --print-pid 7 --print-address
     9 --session
  1659 ?         S      0:01 /bin/sh -e /usr/bin/couchdb -a \"/etc/couchdb/default
 .ini\" -a \"/etc/couchdb/local.ini\" -b -r 5 -p /var/run/couchdb/couchdb.pid -o
 /dev/null -e /dev/null -R
    29 ?         S<     0:00 [bluetooth]
   PID TTY       STAT   TIME COMMAND
    11 ?         S<     0:00 [cpuset]
  1157 ?         Ss     0:00 cron
    37 ?         S<     0:00 [crypto/0]
    38 ?         S<     0:00 [crypto/1]
   901 ?         Ss     0:00 dbus-daemon --system --fork
 :
```

Figure 7-14. The final, scrollable output of the composite command

> I've used **sort** in a somewhat advanced manner here. As explained earlier, you can find quite powerful options for nearly any command through its manpage or info page.

How you use pipes is entirely down to the result you want to achieve. You can have as few or as many as you want, and there are many different ways to achieve the same result.

For example, you could even extend the composite command further by displaying only lines that match a search string, such as the following, which limits the output to processes with *gnome* somewhere in the string:

```
ps -ax | sort -k5 | grep gnome | less
```

Using Redirection

In addition to supporting pipes, Ubuntu allows you to redirect output using the > and < symbols. Using the first, you can, for example, send the output from a program directly to a file, whereas the second accepts input from a program.

Redirecting Output

The following command creates a file called *files.txt* in your home folder containing the output from ls -al:

```
ls -al > ~/files.txt
```

If *files.txt* already exists, it will be overwritten; otherwise, it will be created.

When you issue that command, you won't see anything on the screen, because the output that would have been displayed has been redirected to a file. But you can verify that the command worked by entering the following, which displays the file's contents:

```
cat ~/files.txt
```

The result of issuing this command will look something like Figure 7-15.

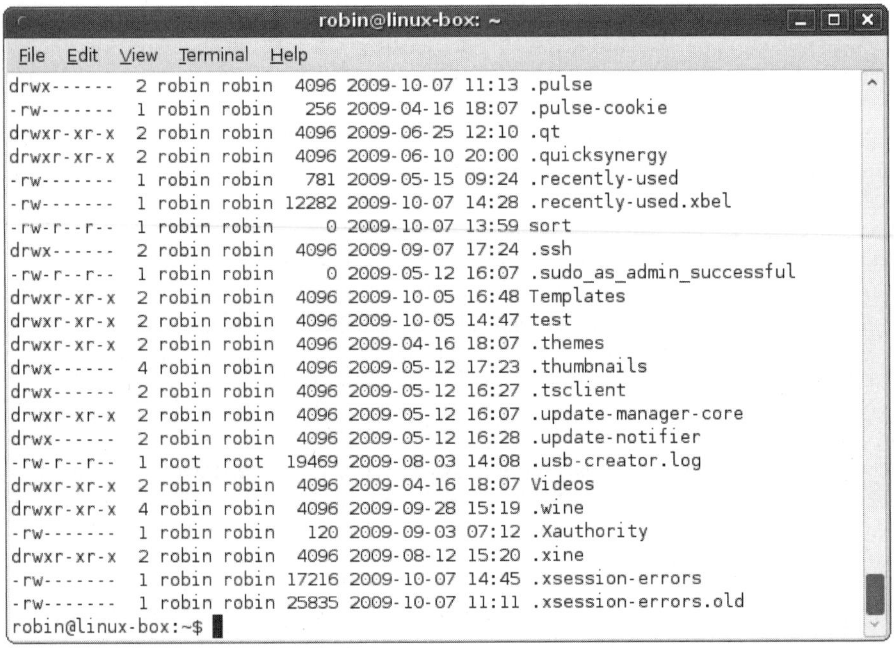

```
robin@linux-box: ~

File  Edit  View  Terminal  Help

drwx------    2 robin robin   4096 2009-10-07 11:13 .pulse
-rw-------    1 robin robin    256 2009-04-16 18:07 .pulse-cookie
drwxr-xr-x    2 robin robin   4096 2009-06-25 12:10 .qt
drwxr-xr-x    2 robin robin   4096 2009-06-10 20:00 .quicksynergy
-rw-------    1 robin robin    781 2009-05-15 09:24 .recently-used
-rw-------    1 robin robin  12282 2009-10-07 14:28 .recently-used.xbel
-rw-r--r--    1 robin robin      0 2009-10-07 13:59 sort
drwx------    2 robin robin   4096 2009-09-07 17:24 .ssh
-rw-r--r--    1 robin robin      0 2009-05-12 16:07 .sudo_as_admin_successful
drwxr-xr-x    2 robin robin   4096 2009-10-05 16:48 Templates
drwxr-xr-x    2 robin robin   4096 2009-10-05 14:47 test
drwxr-xr-x    2 robin robin   4096 2009-04-16 18:07 .themes
drwx------    4 robin robin   4096 2009-05-12 17:23 .thumbnails
drwx------    2 robin robin   4096 2009-05-12 16:27 .tsclient
drwxr-xr-x    2 robin robin   4096 2009-05-12 16:07 .update-manager-core
drwx------    2 robin robin   4096 2009-05-12 16:28 .update-notifier
-rw-r--r--    1 root  root   19469 2009-08-03 14:08 .usb-creator.log
drwxr-xr-x    2 robin robin   4096 2009-04-16 18:07 Videos
drwxr-xr-x    4 robin robin   4096 2009-09-28 15:19 .wine
-rw-------    1 robin robin    120 2009-09-03 07:12 .Xauthority
drwxr-xr-x    2 robin robin   4096 2009-08-12 15:20 .xine
-rw-------    1 robin robin  17216 2009-10-07 14:45 .xsession-errors
-rw-------    1 robin robin  25835 2009-10-07 11:11 .xsession-errors.old
robin@linux-box:~$
```

Figure 7-15. The result of displaying files.txt

But what if you want to know which files and folders were created first? The answer would be to sort them by column 6, and you *could* use this command to do it:

```
ls -al | sort -k6 > ~/files.txt
```

Redirecting Input

If you need to keep the file sorted alphabetically but still wish to sometimes view the lines in date order, you can issue the following command on it instead:

```
sort -k6 < ~/files.txt
```

This opens up *files.txt*, reads it in, and passes its contents to the command immediately preceding the < symbol.

You could even extend that to use the less command by adding the | operator:

```
sort -k6 < ~/files.txt | less
```

This works because the > and < operators work on files and devices, whereas the | operator creates pipes between commands. Therefore, sort -k6 < ~/files.txt is seen as a complete command in its own right, the output of which can be displayed or, as in this case, piped to another command.

The Difference Between Pipes and Redirections

You should now see that a pipe is the equivalent of combining two separate redirection commands. For example, take a look at the following simple command, which pages the output from a file listing:

```
ls -al | more
```

This is actually equivalent to these two lines:

```
ls -al > tempfile
more < tempfile
```

Actually, to make these commands fully identical in action, you should also add the following command afterward to remove the temporary file:

```
rm tempfile
```

So, all told, each pipe can represent the equivalent of three separate commands.

 Whenever you want to run a program but don't care, or even want, to see its output, you can redirect it to */dev/null*, which is a nonexistent, notional place in the filesystem, into which anything sent is simply discarded. You might use it like this:

```
./install-program >/dev/null
```

Appending to Files

You can also append to an existing file by stringing two > symbols together, like this:

```
ls -al >> ~/files.txt
```

If *files.txt* already exists, the output is appended to the end of it; otherwise, the file is created first.

Standard Input, Output, and Error

In the previous section, we were redirecting streams known as standard input and standard output. When using a < redirection operator, you are telling the operating system that for just this one command it should ignore the standard input device (which is your keyboard) and instead take its input from a file.

Likewise, when using the > operator you are telling Ubuntu to ignore the standard output device (which is your monitor or, more precisely, the Terminal window) and instead send its output to the supplied file.

You may recall from the section "The find Command" on page 219 that sometimes an error message would be displayed when access to a particular folder was not allowed, such as with the following command, in which some of the folders are not permitted to be searched by regular users:

```
find / -name blackjack
```

Try this command again now, and you'll see a whole bunch of error messages scroll past, obscuring the few matches we are interested in.

There's actually a simple solution for this, which is to strip out the error messages from the useable output. In the previous example we separated the error messages from the output we wanted by piping the output through the more command. But how did it do that?

Streams and Handles

The answer is that Ubuntu uses three different streams for input, output, and error messages, and when you use a > or | for redirection or piping, it affects only standard output, not standard error. This means that when you type this:

```
find / -name blackjack | more
```

only the standard output is redirected; the standard error stream is still displayed by the initial find command. However, after displaying the errors, the more program then pages through the standard output. So, although the display is a little untidy because the errors are still shown, at least the matching results are all shown together.

But you can clear up any messiness by telling Ubuntu *exactly* what should be redirected or piped by using stream handles. Table 7-4 lists the three streams, along with their handles and their short names, `stdin`, `stdout`, and `stderr`, which I'll use from now on.

Table 7-4. The three input and output streams

Name	Stream number	Description
stdin	0	Standard input
stdout	1	Standard output
stderr	2	Standard error

The way we force a particular stream to be used is to place it directly before a redirection or pipe operator. So, for example, we could send all the `stderr` error messages from a command directly to a different file like this:

```
find / -name blackjack 2> ignoreme.txt
```

However, this is not an optimal solution, because we end up creating a useless file that's not actually wanted or needed. But as I mentioned in the section "Using Redirection" on page 237, this scenario has already been covered by the operating system's programmers, who created an imaginary device called */dev/null*, which acts as a black hole for unwanted output. Therefore, a much more elegant solution would be to redirect all the output from `stderr` into that abyss, like this:

```
find / -name blackjack 2> /dev/null
```

If you try out this improved version, you'll have to wait before you see anything while all the various folders are searched. But sure as eggs are eggs, your patience will be rewarded, as one by one, matches for the search term *blackjack* are displayed. The output also can be piped to `more` or `less` if you like.

Redirecting One Stream to Another

Error messages can be very useful, though, so suppose you have decided you actually *do* want them included in a file created from a redirect. You can achieve this by merging the `stderr` and `stdout` streams like this:

```
find / -name blackjack > ~/results.txt 2>&1
```

This command redirects `stdout` using the default `>` operator to the file *~/results.txt*, and then redirects `stderr`, using its stream number of 2, to the unlikely looking recipient of `&1`. Note that there must be no space between the `>` and the `&`.

What the `2>&1` says to the operating system is "redirect the output for `stderr`, sending it to `stdout`," because `stdout` has the stream number 1.

By now you'll see that I wasn't entirely truthful when I implied earlier that you could redirect *all* the output from a program to */dev/null* with the following redirection:

```
./install-program >/dev/null
```

In fact, this only redirects stdout. As you should now realize, to fully redirect all output you would need to merge stdout and stderr together:

```
./install-program >/dev/null 2>&1
```

There's also a convenient shortcut that combines > with 2>&1; simply use >& instead:

```
find / -name blackjack >& ~/results.txt
```

Also, if you really want to get fancy, you can use the shortcut |& to pipe standard error and standard output together.

The tee Command

There are times when you want output to be sent to a file and also to the Terminal window, both at the same time. The way to do this is to pipe whichever output you desire (stdout or stderr, or even both if you create the proper redirects) to the tee command, and then supply the recipient filename, like this:

```
ls -al | tee ~/files.txt
```

This lists all the files in the current folder both to the screen and to *~/files.txt*. You can also use tee with the merged streams in the previous section, like this:

```
find / -name blackjack | tee ~/results.txt 2>&1
```

Wildcards, Sets, and Brace Expansion

We've already used wildcards in a few places in this chapter, but there's a lot more you can do with them than just using the * and ? operators to match strings and characters, respectively, as shown in Table 7-5.

Table 7-5. Wildcards and their meanings

Wildcard	Meaning
*	Any sequence of characters, except for a leading period
?	Any single character, except for a leading period
[set]	Any one of the characters in the set
[ch1-ch2]	Any one of the characters from ch1 through ch2
[^set]	Any single character not in the set
[^ch1-ch2]	Any single character not from ch1 through ch2
{ch,str,etc…}	Match all the characters and/or strings

Using Sets and Ranges

A set of characters placed within a pair of rectangular brackets can match a single character in a file or folder name. This is a more precise version of the ? single-character wildcard. For example, the set [abcdef] will match any of the six characters shown so that [abcdef]ark.txt will match the filenames *bark.txt* and *dark.txt*, as long as they both exist. You can also save on typing by using a hyphen to indicate a range of characters so that [a-f] is equivalent to [abcdef].

Another neat thing you can do with a set is force all upper- or all lowercase matches using the ranges [A-Z] or [a-z]. Or you can limit the matching to only alphabetical characters of either case (excluding digits and other characters) by using the set [a-zA-z]. And you can also use numbers in a range, as in [0-9].

Alternatively, you can exclude characters from matching by using the ^ operator. In this case, [^b]ark.txt would prevent the file *bark.txt* from being matched, but would let through *dark.txt, lark.txt*, and so on.

You can also use ranges with the ^ operator so that [^a-l]ark.txt will allow through only filenames starting from *mark.txt* onward, as all the first letters prior to m are excluded.

Using Brace Expansion

With brace expansion you can offer sets of alternatives strings of any length, so you aren't limited to the single characters of sets. For example, all three terms in the expression ca{ree,mpe,tere}rs.txt will be expanded, allowing all of the files *ca**ree**rs.txt*, *ca**mpe**rs.txt* and *ca**tere**rs.txt* through the filter (if they exist), with the matching portions shown in bold.

Unlike sets and wildcards, brace expansions are also supported in other parts of the command line, so the following echo command will show you the result of using the expression just shown:

```
echo ca{ree,mpe,tere}rs
```

The following is the displayed result:

```
careers campers caterers
```

By the way, did you notice that there are no quotation marks around the argument to the echo command (unlike previous examples in this chapter)? That's because quotation marks tell Ubuntu to use the exact contents of the string, rather than supporting brace expansion and other features. Therefore the following command results in displaying only the expression itself, so make sure you know when you do and when you don't need quotation marks:

```
echo "ca{ree,mpe,tere}rs"
```

The displayed result of entering this command is simply:

```
ca{ree,mpe,tere}rs
```

Using Aliases

You can make up your own command names to replace those used in Ubuntu. For example, if you're used to using the command md in Windows to create a directory and keep forgetting to enter mkdir, you can set an alias like this:

```
alias md="mkdir"
```

Thereafter both md and mkdir will refer to the mkdir command. Note that you can use either single or double quotation marks.

An even more common and powerful use of aliases is to add options to commands. For instance, many people make sure they know exactly which files are removed by rm (because its deletions are irreversible) by aliasing it as follows:

```
alias rm="rm -i"
```

The -i option causes rm to ask you whether it's OK before removing each file—a time-consuming addition, but a safe one.

And you're free to create your own commands, like this:

```
alias newf="find ~ -type d -mtime -3"
```

Now when you type newf you will see all files under your home directory that were created or modified within the past three days. This will include a lot of hidden files created by your browser and other programs you use.

To find out which aliases have been created, just type alias on its own, like this:

```
alias
```

If you do this you may see that, among others, the ls command has been aliased as follows (having the effect of allowing color to be used to display files with different file and folder attributes, where applicable):

```
alias ls='ls --color=auto'
```

To remove an alias, use the unalias command. So, if you like, you can remove the color display option from the ls command like this:

```
unalias ls
```

File Compression

Ubuntu Linux supports various file compression formats, many of which will automatically open when accessed via the desktop. The main compression file types you are likely to encounter are listed in Table 7-6.

Table 7-6. Common file and compression types

File type	Compress with	Decompress with
.bz2	bzip2	bunzip2
.gz	gzip	gunzip
.tar	tar	tar
.zip	zip	unzip
.tar.gz or .tgz	gzip and tar	gunzip and tar
.tar.bz2	bzip2 and tar	bunzip2 and tar

Some of the compression programs will handle other types of files too, but generally each is best compressed and decompressed using its own programs. For example, to compress the file *finances.doc* using `gzip`, you could enter the following:

```
gzip finances.doc
```

A new file called *finances.doc.gz* will then be created containing the compressed file, and the original will be removed. To keep your original file when creating a compressed copy, use the `-k` option (for keep), like this:

```
gzip -k finances.doc
```

Likewise, you can compress a file with `bzip2` in the same way using either of the following:

```
bzip2 finances.doc
bzip2 -k finances.doc
```

The first creates the compressed file *finances.doc.bz2* and removes the original file, whereas the second creates a compressed file but also keeps the original in place.

Extracting Files

To extract files from a `gzip` archive, enter a command such as the following:

```
gunzip finances.doc.gz
```

This extracts the file *finances.doc* and then removes the archive file. You can similarly extract files from a `bzip2` archive using a command such as this:

```
bunzip2 finances.doc.bz2
```

This will restore the compressed original file and remove the archive.

You can also use these and many other compression and decompression programs to manage multiple files and folders and provide a range of other archiving features. For example, you may come across *.tar* archive files, which combine multiple files or directories into a single file to facilitate backup and copying. The `tar` program is often combined with other compression programs to create *.tar.gz* or *.tar.bz2* files.

A beginner to Ubuntu really doesn't need to explore the intricacies of archive and compression utilities, thanks mainly to the GNOME desktop and the Nautilus file browser's ability to handle everything for you automatically. But if you wish to access advanced command-line file compression features, you should read the manpages by entering `man` followed by the compression program in question, such as `man tar`.

File and Folder Permissions

In Chapter 5, we looked at managing groups, users, and file permissions from the desktop. Here, you'll learn how to do all that and more from the command line. Let's recall the possible file attributes, which are:

0. No permissions
1. Execute only
2. Write only
3. Execute and Write
4. Read only
5. Execute and Read
6. Write and Read
7. Execute and Write and Read

I have numbered them from 0 to 7 because these values are used by the system to store the attributes in octal (base 8). Table 7-7 shows each of these attributes, with a checkmark indicating where an attribute is set.

Table 7-7. The eight possible file attribute values

Value	Read	Write	Execute
0			
1			✓
2		✓	
3		✓	✓
4	✓		
5	✓		✓
6	✓	✓	
7	✓	✓	✓

Looking at these checkmarks, you'll see that they actually represent the binary values for 0 through 7, like this:

```
0 = 000
1 = 001
2 = 010
3 = 011
4 = 100
5 = 101
6 = 110
7 = 111
```

The highest value that can be created from three binary digits is 7, and so this is how the octal system of file permissions came about.

But in Ubuntu Linux (as with Unix and other Linux distributions), there are actually three sets of attributes (known as permissions) for each file and folder: one for the owner of the file or folder, one for the group that is allowed to access it, and one for everybody else.

The Owner, Group, and World Attributes

With eight possible permutations of permissions (and three sets of them), there are 512 different possible permissions per file. So, how on earth does anyone, or even the computer, keep track of all this? Well, it's actually quite simple, as illustrated by Table 7-8, in which each of the *owner, group*, and *world* columns can have a value between 0 and 7, giving possible values between 000 and 777 in octal (the 0 through 511 permutations in decimal being the same as 0 through 777 in octal).

Table 7-8. All the possible permutations of file and folder permissions

Value	Owner			Group			World		
	Read	Write	Exec	Read	Write	Exec	Read	Write	Exec
0									
1			✓			✓			✓
2		✓			✓			✓	
3		✓	✓		✓	✓		✓	✓
4	✓			✓			✓		
5	✓		✓	✓		✓	✓		✓
6	✓	✓		✓	✓		✓	✓	
7	✓	✓	✓	✓	✓	✓	✓	✓	✓

Let's look at the most commonly used permission setting, which is 644. The value 644 corresponds to an *owner* setting of 6, and *group* and *world* settings of 4, such that a file with attributes set to this value can be written to and read from by the file's *owner*, but people in the file's *group* or anyone else (the *world*) can only read the file. This is the default setting applied to new files you create.

To see how this works, look at Table 7-8 and reference row 6, and then look up the checkmarks for this value in the *owner* column; both *read* and *write* are checked. Then look at the row where the value is 4, and you'll see that only *read* is checked.

An executable program file that you want to protect in a manner similar to a document should have permission settings of 755. This is the same as 644, except that the *exec* column is checked for each type of user (in other words, a 1 has to be added to each of the three parts).

Or, as another example, if you want to make a file so that only you can access it, but can do anything you want to it—write to, read from, or execute—you would set its permission value to 700. Any file with attributes ending in 00 is therefore 100% private to you—except that the superuser account, *root*, can also do anything it wants with such a file.

Using chmod

The chmod command is used to change a file or folder's attributes (the name refers to another term, *mode*, which is sometimes used for the set of attributes), as long as you are its owner. So, to set the file *filename* to readable and writable for yourself but only readable by all others, you would need to use a setting of 644, like this:

```
chmod 644 filename
```

If you don't want to be bothered with working out the octal number, you'll be glad to hear you can also use the following shorthand options:

u

> User (the owner)

g

> Group

o

> Others (neither u nor g)

a

> All users

+/-r

> Add or remove read permission

+/-w

> Add or remove write permission

+/-x

> Add or remove execute permission

The first four options specify which users (out of the owner, group, world, or all) the permission change should apply to, the default being a for all users. The final three are the permission(s) to change.

Therefore, to force a setting of 644 (regardless of a file's previous permissions), you could use these two commands:

```
chmod a+r-w-x filename
chmod u+w filename
```

The first command sets all of user, group, and others (a) as allowed to read but not to write or execute (+r-w-x) the file. The second enables the user (u) to write (+w) to the file.

To find out what the current attributes are, type:

```
ls -l filename
```

This will display a long line containing the meta information the system knows about the file. The first column will contain the attributes and will look like this:

```
-r--r--r--
```

The very first character on the line indicates whether an item is a file, a directory, or a symbolic link. Files show up as a hyphen (-), directories display the letter d, and links are represented by the letter l. So, ignoring that first character, there are nine remaining: three triplets of three, representing in turn the permissions for each of the owner, group, and world.

Therefore we can see from the example just shown that *filename* offers only read access to the owner, the group, and the world. To change this file so it is writable by the owner, all that needs to be done is add that one attribute, like this:

```
chmod u+w filename
```

For another example, if the file you are accessing needs to be set to executable so that it can be run by everyone, you could use this command:

```
chmod a+x filename
```

Alternatively, because the default always applies to all users, you could simply enter:

```
chmod +x filename
```

 Whether you choose to use octal or shorthand notation is up to you; there is no right or wrong way.

When you view a folder using the `ls -l` command, the output will look something like this:

```
drwxr-xr-x 2 robin robin 4096 2009-11-30 10:38 Desktop
drwxr-xr-x 2 robin robin 4096 2009-11-27 04:48 Documents
drwxr-xr-x 2 robin robin 4096 2009-11-27 04:48 Downloads
-rw-r--r-- 1 robin robin  167 2009-11-27 04:38 examples.desktop
drwxr-xr-x 2 robin robin 4096 2009-11-27 04:48 Music
drwxr-xr-x 2 robin robin 4096 2009-11-27 04:48 Pictures
drwxr-xr-x 2 robin robin 4096 2009-11-27 04:48 Public
drwxr-xr-x 2 robin robin 4096 2009-11-27 04:48 Templates
drwxrwxr-x 2 robin robin 4096 2009-11-27 12:49 Ubuntu One
drwxr-xr-x 2 robin robin 4096 2009-11-27 04:48 Videos
```

In turn, each of these columns displays the following information:

- File type and permissions
- Number of hard links (an old feature of files, rarely used)
- Owner
- Group owner
- Size (for text files, the number of characters in them)
- Date and time of creation or last modification
- Name

Using chown

The `chown` command allows the ownership of a file or folder to be changed. This is such a powerful command that it can be used only by the root user, which means you must preface it with a `sudo` command and will be prompted for your password.

So, for example, to change the ownership of a file to the user *mary*, you would use a command such as this (as long as the user *mary* already exists):

```
sudo chown mary filename
```

If you then perform an `ls -l` command on the file, you'll see that the file has changed ownership. If the file was one that you previously owned, changing its attributes now will require using `sudo`, unless you change the ownership back again.

Ubuntu comes with the ready-created user called *nobody*, so you can easily test this command out using the following sequence of instructions:

```
echo > testfile
ls -l testfile
sudo chown nobody testfile
ls -l testfile
sudo rm testfile
```

These lines create an empty file called *testfile* by redirecting a blank `echo` command. Then the file's attributes are viewed using the `ls` command, before then changing its ownership with `chown`. After that, the ownership is again displayed, showing that it has indeed changed, and finally, the test file is removed with the `rm` command. Figure 7-16 shows what you should see on your display if you enter these lines.

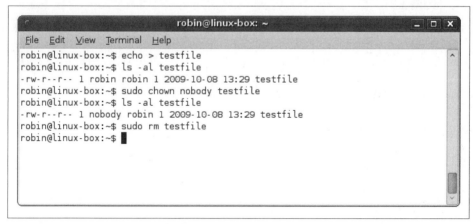

Figure 7-16. A test of changing a file's ownership

On the sixth line down in the screenshot you'll see that *robin* is no longer the owner of the file, as that privilege now belongs to *nobody*, although the group called *robin* retains its ownership.

Using chgrp

This command is similar to `chown` except that it works for groups. With it the group assigned to a file or folder can be changed to another one, and with the `sudo` command, you can do this without assuming the root user—as long as you are the owner of the item and also a member of new group that you wish to assign.

So, for example, if you are a member of the group *accounts*, you could change the group associated with a file to that group with this command:

    chgrp accounts filename

When you are not already a member of the group that you wish to change a file or folder to, or if you need to change the file of another user or group, you will need to assume *root* for the command with `sudo`, like this:

    sudo chgrp accounts filename

You can change owner and group in a single `chown` command by specifying the owner followed by a colon and group name:

    sudo chown mary:accounts filename

Using sudo

So, just what is all this talk of *root* and sudo? Well, *root* is the name given to the super user on an Ubuntu system. It is an all-powerful user with maximum privileges, allowing it to do anything.

For this reason, Ubuntu actually disables the *root* user and only allows you to assume it one command at a time. This is because permissions on the filesystem normally prevent you from running dangerous commands that are all too easy to enter accidentally during routine system use, and none of these permissions can hold back *root*. So, should you become the *root* user for a particular command but forget to change back, you could end up damaging your installation.

The Ubuntu viewpoint is "better safe than sorry," so you have to preface every command requiring root privileges with sudo. Thankfully, the developers realized it can be annoying to keep entering your password each time you do this, so after you use sudo and provide your password, you won't be asked for your password again for another 15 minutes. Hopefully this will be sufficient time to perform all your maintenance.

Logging in As root

That said, if you ever have a *lot* of work to perform as *root* or have a specific reason to do so, you can actually log in as root (and also bypass typing all the sudo commands) by entering the following:

```
sudo -i
```

This will log you in as the root user with all the dangers previously discussed, so don't do this unless you know exactly what you are up to. To log back out again, enter the command exit.

For more information on sudo, as with all commands, enter the following:

```
man sudo
```

System Processes

All operating systems comprise a main kernel and several different programs that all work together. Most of them wait patiently until you need the system to do a task for you, such as send documents to your printer or sound to your speakers. They handle the graphical desktop environment, keep track of the time, communicate with the network, and...well, handle everything that your computer needs to do.

These programs are referred to as processes (or tasks) and can be viewed by entering the following (with ps standing for *process status*):

```
ps -ax
```

Figure 7-12, shown earlier, shows typical output from this command. In it you can see that each process is assigned a unique number, and using these you can interact with processes by stopping or restarting them, and so on. As a beginner to Ubuntu, it is very unlikely you will have to manage your processes. However, there may be times when you at least need to take a look at them, if only to provide information for obtaining help on the Ubuntu bulletin boards.

So, this section is mainly intended to give you an overview and provide a couple of helpful pointers. For example, sometimes Ubuntu may not seem to perform as well as it should. When this happens, it's usually after you have accepted an update to one of its packages, or perhaps installed a new driver or other program. Problems you may encounter could be unusual slowdowns, or maybe the computer fan is making a loud noise because the processor is working harder than normal and getting hotter.

In such cases you can enter the command **top** to see all your processes in order of the amount of Central Processing Unit (CPU) time they are taking up. Figure 7-17 shows a typical display.

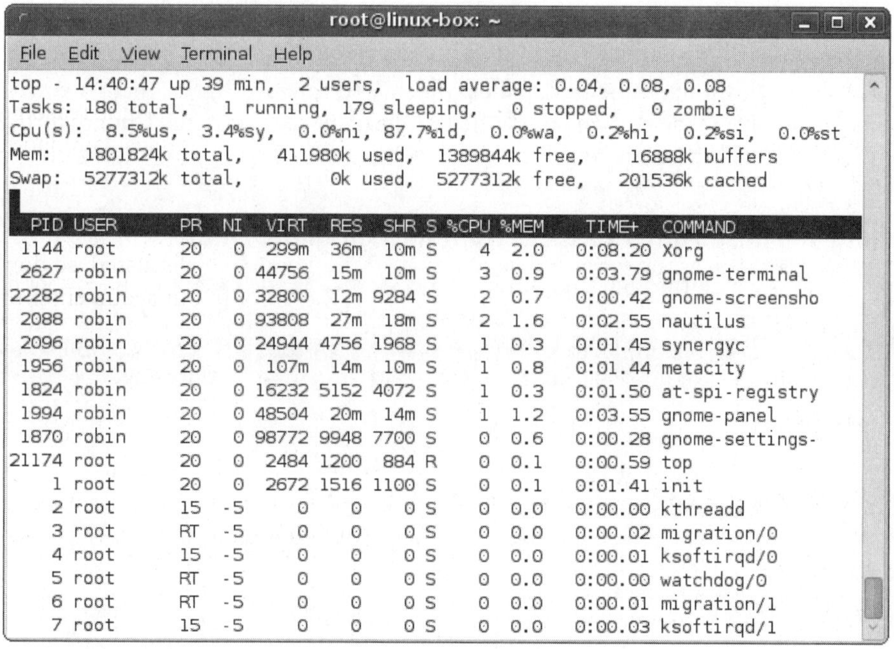

Figure 7-17. Using the top command to view running processes

In the bottom section, where the processes are listed, you can see that X.org, the software behind the graphics capabilities of Ubuntu, is using up the most processor time at just 4%, and the Terminal program is next at 3%. Then, because a screenshot is being taken, that process comes up third, Nautilus is fourth, and so on. If you then take a look in the top portion (on the third line down), you'll see that the "Cpu(s)" entry shows that Ubuntu is very efficient and currently has over 87.7% idle (or spare) processor capacity available for programs, which means only 12.3% is being used.

When you have a stuck program or one that is otherwise causing problems (like the fan whirring I mentioned), you will often find much more CPU time being used up, and the culprit will probably be listed somewhere near the top of this list of processes—usually in the first two or three entries. When it is acting up, the safest way to restart your computer is to use the built-in options in the desktop menus, but if that fails and if you know what you are doing (and it's best that you take advice from an expert who has confirmed that you have a problem before doing anything), it is possible to kill one of these tasks by pressing the K key and entering the process PID number, as shown in the first column.

Be warned, though, that doing this for an important process may make your computer unstable and could cause other problems requiring a reboot, and maybe even some corrective action after that. So, like I said, do this only when you know what you are up to.

That warning out of the way, if killing an offending process frees up your computer or slows your fan back down because the processor doesn't have to work so hard, then you have possibly found the cause of the problem and can investigate whether you can uninstall or reinstall the program in question. One of the experts in the Ubuntu forums may have further advice for you.

Killing and Restarting Processes from the Command Line

You can also search through the running processes using the `ps` command (generally using the options `-ax` to display all processes) and can terminate any of them using the `kill` command. For example, to kill a process with the process ID of 7662, you would enter:

```
kill 7662
```

This sends the process a signal requesting it to terminate. However, some processes may refuse (or be unable) to act on this signal, in which case wait a few seconds and try it again. If it still fails, you may need to reboot your computer. But before you give up and reboot your computer, try using a more powerful kill signal:

```
kill -9 7662
```

Again, please be aware that you should not issue such commands lightly, and ought to do so only if you know what you are up to or if a bona fide expert has suggested you do so.

Summary

Congratulations! You've just completed the hardest chapter in this book. I hope I have explained things clearly, but there was a lot of material to cover, and you may find it helpful to review it again in a few days. You should also find it a good reference for those cases when you need to use the command line, which hopefully won't be too often—unless you want to, of course.

Anyway, pat yourself on the back and get yourself a well-deserved cup of tea or coffee as we prepare to move on to the subject of installing and removing programs in the next chapter.

CHAPTER 8

Installing and Removing Software

If you're used to Windows or OS X, you're in for a pleasant surprise with Ubuntu because the developers have taken on the laborious task of assembling a collection of all the best software for the operating system.

Not only have they done that, it's all been brought together into a single location called the Ubuntu Software Center; with just a few mouse clicks, you can install any of several thousand programs.

That's right, you don't have to go trawling the Web looking for a program you need, and then wade through pages of information about how to install it. That's all a thing of the past with Ubuntu, as you'll see in this chapter.

The Ubuntu Software Center

To open up the Ubuntu Software Center, select Applications → Ubuntu Software Center from the main menus. A new window will then open up that looks like the one shown in Figure 8-1.

The application is very easy to use. To add a new program to your computer, browse through the righthand departments to locate what you are looking for. For example, if you want to install a game of chess, select the Games department and you'll see the program 3D Chess appears near the top, as shown in Figure 8-2.

At the bottom of the window, you can see that, on this occasion, there are actually 464 games listed, so there's a good chance that other versions of chess are also available. To check this, you can scroll down using the scroll bar, the up and down cursor keys (once you have highlighted an item), or your mouse's scroll wheel. And, indeed, as expected, at least another three versions of the game show up once you get to programs starting with the letter C.

But this is quite an inefficient way to look for a program. So instead you can enter a search string in the upper-right input box, as shown in Figure 8-3, where you will see that there are over 20 different versions of chess (or programs that have been tagged with that word) available for installation.

Figure 8-1. The Ubuntu Software Center

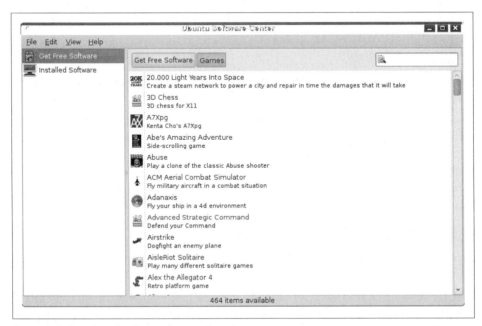

Figure 8-2. Browsing the Games department

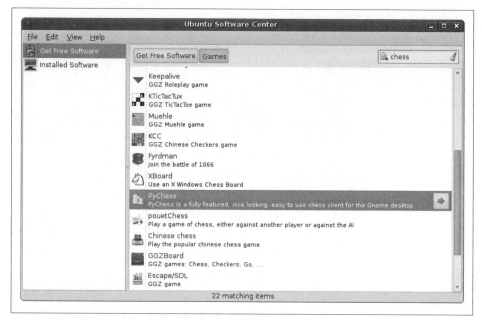

Figure 8-3. Searching for programs tagged with the keyword "chess"

Actually, you may find that sometimes the compilers of the Software Center have been a little overzealous in applying keywords because, as in this example, at least 10 of the results are not actual chess games. But hey, at least hundreds of programs have been narrowed down to a couple of dozen from which to choose.

Installing a Program

So, let's install one of these games. To do this, double-click on the first result returned, *Chess (gnome-chess)*, and you'll see the screen shown in Figure 8-4 in which the program is described, accompanied by a screenshot and the program's license details and price. At the time of this writing, all the programs in the Software Center are free, so I assume the latter information is there to support the addition of commercial programs in the future.

If after reading this page you don't wish to install the program, you can return to the main menu where you started browsing for software. Notice the button at the top of the main window called Chess, which shows you the current page you're on, and the button labeled Get Free Software right before it (above the picture of the chess knight). These show the sequence of windows you've opened, and the Get Free Software button returns you to that window.

The left pane also has a button labeled Get Free Software, but that refers to the whole collection you're in. The button under it, Installed Software, refers to the packages that your computer already has. We'll use that button later.

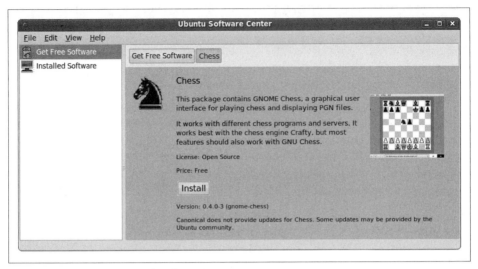

Figure 8-4. Viewing a program's information page

Let's install the Chess game on your computer. Click the Install button and enter your password when prompted by the Authenticate window that pops up. The lefthand pane will then show an additional item with the name In Progress, accompanied by a round icon with rotating arrows.

Once the installation has finished, the program's information page will return, but the Install button will now be replaced with a Remove button, indicating that it has been installed. So, let's verify that this is the case by clicking in the lefthand pane on the entry called Installed Software. You should now see the program listed in the righthand pane.

You can also check that the program has been installed by opening the Applications → Games menu, as shown in Figure 8-5, where you'll see that you are now able to run the program by selecting it from the menu.

Removing a Program

It's just as easy to remove a program you no longer need. Simply open up the Ubuntu Software Center and click the Installed Software heading in the lefthand pane. Then either search for the program to remove by name, or because you'll probably have a small number of installed programs, just scroll down the list until you find it.

Now double-click the program's name, which in this case is *Chess (gnome-chess)*, to display the information screen shown in Figure 8-6. This is the same as the initial screen in the Get Free Software section, except that the background color is different, the program is shown as having been installed, and there's a Remove button.

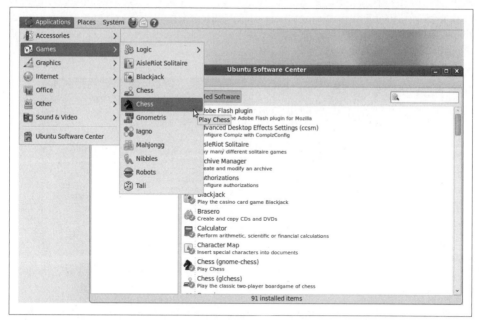

Figure 8-5. The chess game has now been installed

To remove the program, click the Remove button and enter your password in the Authentication window that pops up. The In Progress entry will then appear for a while in the lefthand pane, after which the information screen changes to show the list of installed software, and the recently removed program will no longer be in this list.

Advanced Features

The Software Center comes with a few extra features that are available from the menus. The first of these is Software Sources, available under the Edit menu. With it, you can choose the types of software to download and from which locations, among other things, as shown in Figure 8-7, which shows the contents of the Ubuntu Software Tab.

The Ubuntu Software Tab

When you call up the Software Sources window, you must first enter your password. Then you'll see a selection of five tabs, the first of which is Ubuntu Software. Under this tab, there are several checkboxes and a drop-down input, with which you can specify the types of software to display, as follows.

Canonical-supported and community-maintained software

Canonical-supported software is maintained by the programmers at Canonical, the company that publishes Ubuntu. Community-maintained software is maintained by members of the open source community at large. The only difference between the two is that non-Canonical programs have many different authors and maintainers and therefore they may not always have the same look and feel, or even the same level of testing, as Canonical programs.

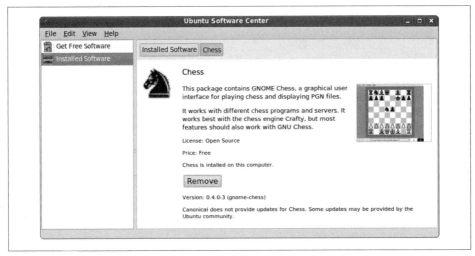

Figure 8-6. The information page of an installed program

Figure 8-7. The Software Sources window

Even so, don't be scared by the sound of this. Because the whole range of GNU and Linux software is continuously supported by the developers, bugs are quickly caught and corrected. Basically, this is Canonical's way of saying "we think the software that we list from third parties is of sufficiently high quality to promote it, but we don't maintain it or provide support for it."

Proprietary drivers

The proprietary drivers tend to be graphic or printer drivers that have been developed by the hardware manufacturer, rather than through open source developers, meaning there is a closed development approach that isn't scrutinized by the open source community. That said, all hardware manufacturers want their hardware to work, so it behooves them to release solid, professional drivers, just as they do for Windows or OS X.

Software restricted by copyright

Additionally, some of the software available may be restricted by copyright and other legal encumbrances so that, for example, you cannot reuse or reverse engineer it. But again, if you are just going to run software and don't intend to modify or redistribute it, I see no reason to uncheck this box.

Source code

If you are an advanced Linux user, you may be interested in viewing and compiling from source code, and can check this box to display such software. Otherwise, I recommend you leave it unchecked.

Download from

Depending on the country assigned to your Ubuntu account and your location in the world, the download server nearest to you will be selected by default. But you can change this to another one with this drop-down list. If the location you want isn't displayed, select the Other... option to browse through servers from all over the world, as shown in Figure 8-8.

Normally, you won't need to change this setting, but it can be useful if, for example, the default server appears unresponsive (perhaps because it is currently down), in which case, you can select an alternative to try.

In fact, you can click the Select Best Server button to test a range of servers and find the fastest one for you. But be prepared to wait for a while as each of over 300 servers is checked in turn. If it takes too long, you can always click Cancel and go back to selecting one manually.

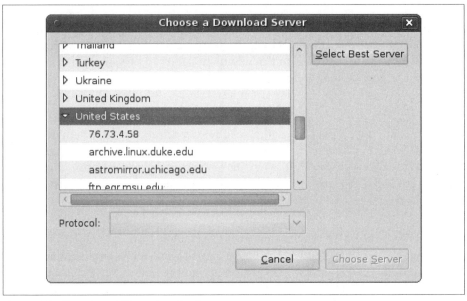

Figure 8-8. Choosing a different download server

The Other Software Tab

This tab allows you to include updates that are unsupported, as well as updated from other versions of Ubuntu. Unless you are an expert and know what you are doing, I recommend you leave all of the boxes unchecked, as shown in Figure 8-9.

The Updates Tab

The Updates tab lets you choose the types of updates you would like to receive, as shown in Figure 8-10.

Ubuntu updates

Generally, I recommend you keep the first two tabs checked. These refer to important and recommended updates for your current version of Ubuntu. The next two offer the ability to include prereleased and unsupported updates. I recommend you don't check these boxes, unless you are prepared to install updates that could crash your computer or make it work incorrectly.

Automatic updates

In this section, you can decide how often you would like Ubuntu to check for updates using a drop-down list with the options Daily, Every two days, Weekly, and Every two

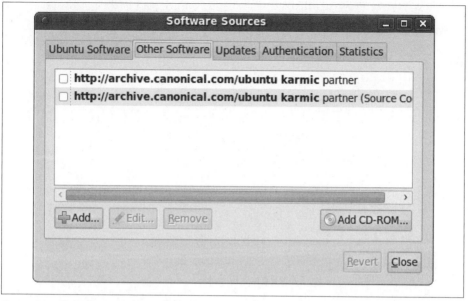

Figure 8-9. The Other Software tab

weeks. If you want your computer to be as secure and up-to-date as possible, I recommend the Daily option.

Underneath the drop-down list, there are three radio buttons, with "Only notify about available updates" as the default setting for the group. You can also choose to download updates in the background or install security updates without confirmation. I recommend you don't use the latter, as it could conflict with a document you are working on, requiring a system restart when you least expect it. In my view, it's best to know when your computer is installing updates so that you can close all applications in case a restart is required.

Release upgrade

The final drop-down list lets you choose which distribution releases you wish to upgrade. The options are:

Never
> Select this if you don't want your operating system to ever be upgraded. This is the best choice if you intend to manually upgrade only certain parts of your operating system.

Normal
> This will download every release of the types you have checked.

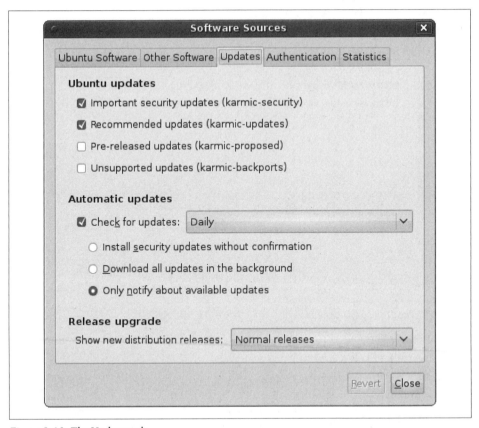

Figure 8-10. The Updates tab

Long term
> This limits downloads to releases that Canonical has declared to be Long Term Support (LTS). These releases are made every two years, and they are supported for three years for desktop and five years for server versions.

Generally, you will want to select the Normal option.

The Authentication Tab

This tab is best left completely alone. It lists all the trusted providers of software and their encrypted keys, which are used to identify them as being who they claim to be. Figure 8-11 shows some of the providers you will see if you click this tab. The screen grab includes *ubuntu.com*, *zend.com*, and *google.com*, but you may see others.

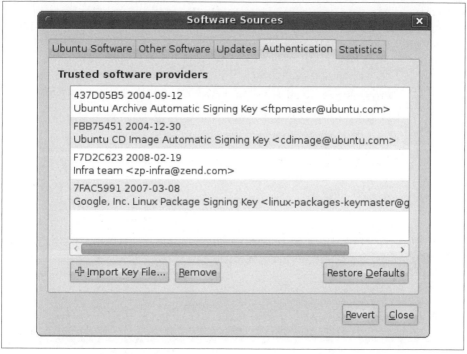

Figure 8-11. The Authentication tab

The Statistics Tab

This tab helps you give back to the Ubuntu community by reporting on which programs you have installed, as shown in Figure 8-12. The data supplied helps the developers see which programs are the most popular, and therefore select the ones deserving the most support and further development.

Don't worry about your privacy, though, because all the data is sent anonymously, and you and your machine will not be associated with the programs you use; only the program names are collected to add to the totals for each.

The View Menu

The View menu, as shown in Figure 8-13, is another means by which you can quickly change between viewing all available applications and viewing just the ones maintained by Canonical.

You'll notice that the total number of available items (displayed in the bottom status bar) drops sharply when only the Canonical-maintained ones are displayed.

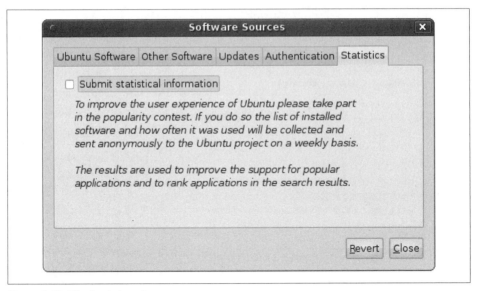

Figure 8-12. The Statistics tab

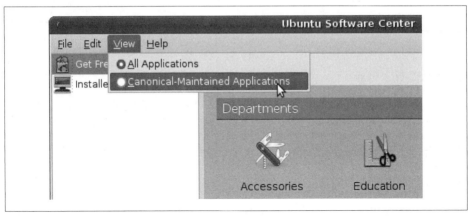

Figure 8-13. The View menu

The Remaining Menus

The other options in the menus mostly replicate actions you've already seen and that you can usually perform more quickly using the mouse to point, click, and select. So, there's no need to detail them any further, other than mentioning that there's additional help available in the Help menu, which may be useful if you are using a different version of Ubuntu, such as the Netbook Edition (or Remix).

The Synaptic Package Manager

The predecessor to the Ubuntu Software Center is the Synaptic Package Manager, which you can call up by selecting System → Administration → Synaptic Package Manager. After entering your password, you'll see a new window similar to Figure 8-14.

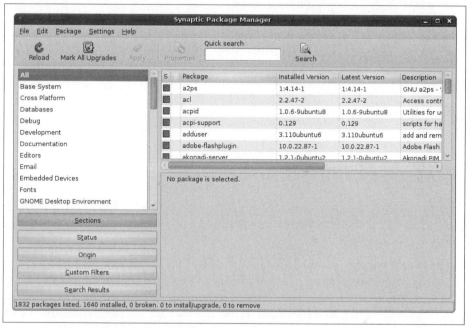

Figure 8-14. The Synaptic Package Manager main screen

You might need to use Synaptic because the Software Center is actually more of a work in progress that's transitioning from Synaptic to a more user-friendly experience. I say "work in progress" because not all possible Ubuntu programs have made it into the Software Center yet, and it may be some time before they do. Therefore, when you can't find the program you want in the Software Center, the next best place to look is the Synaptic Package Manager.

To ensure you are shown all the latest packages, it's always a good idea to click on the Reload button when you first run Synaptic. Then, in a similar way to using the Software Center, you can browse through the various departments listed in the lefthand pane to change the contents of the top-righthand one. For example, if you select Editors, then the top-righthand pane will list all the editors Synaptic knows about, including program editors and word processors, as shown in Figure 8-15.

Packages that haven't yet been installed have an empty checkbox next to them, whereas ones already installed have filled-in checkboxes, and Canonical applications have a little Ubuntu logo next to the checkbox.

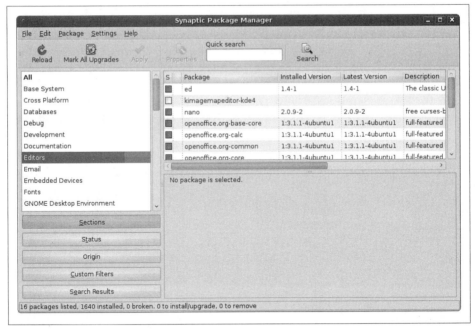

Figure 8-15. Viewing the Editors category

Figure 8-15 illustrates why the Software Center is being developed: the top-righthand pane lists all the programs with long-winded filenames, and it's not immediately clear which entry does what. Also, some entries have no explanation, such as the one for *kimagemapeditor-kde4*, although it can be surmised that the package is probably something to do with editing image maps for the KDE desktop.

Installing a Program

Anyway, let's persevere with finding a chess game using this system. There are a couple of ways to do this. First, click on the wide Status button at the lower left, and the upper-left pane will then let you choose the type of packages to display out of Installed, Not installed, and so on, as shown in Figure 8-16.

In the top-right pane I have selected the *3dchess* game, and its details have been displayed in the lower-right pane. At this point, you can see what the program looks like by clicking Get Screenshot, which, if one is available, will download an image and display it in place of the button.

Marking a program for installation

If you decide you want to install the program, you can then click on the checkbox next to its name in the upper-right pane, and then select the "Mark for Installation" option, as shown in the close-up in Figure 8-17.

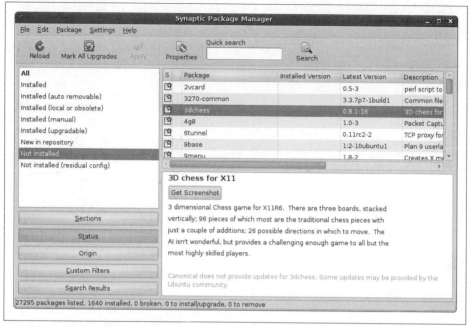

Figure 8-16. Selecting the "Not installed" packages

When you mark a program for installation, Ubuntu checks to see whether there are any other programs or data that also require downloading; if so, it pops up a window detailing them, as shown in Figure 8-18, where the additional item *xaw3dg* is also needed.

You should generally click the Mark button at this point to include the dependency in your installation. If you press Cancel, you can go ahead and try to install the program you want, but this dependency will not be installed with it, and the program will probably fail when you try to run it. When you click Mark, the checkbox icon will change to show the program has been selected (as will those of any additional items to be installed).

Activating the installation process

You are now ready to perform the installation by clicking the Apply button, which will pop up a confirmation window like the one shown in Figure 8-19.

It is actually possible to mark many different programs for installation, and then later select them all for installation at the same time using the Apply button. In this case, all the programs you marked since the previous installation you performed will be listed in the confirmation window.

By clicking the triangle at the left of the entries in the white area, you can list all the items in each of the categories. You can also click the Show Details button to get

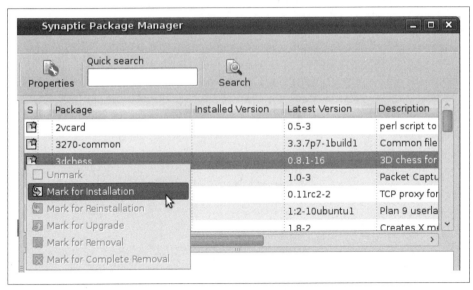

Figure 8-17. Marking the 3dchess program for installation

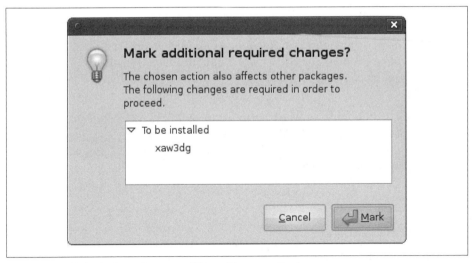

Figure 8-18. Click Mark to select any additional items required

additional information. I don't recommend clicking the "Download package files only" checkbox, as you would then have to locate and install the packages yourself.

So, just click Apply and the program (or programs) will be downloaded and installed for you. Afterward, the top-right pane will no longer show the program(s), as it is only displaying packages that haven't been installed.

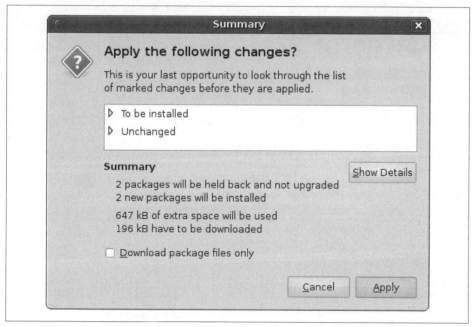

Figure 8-19. The confirmation dialog window

To verify that the installation has worked, select Applications → Games and you'll see *3D Chess* is there, ready to be run.

Using Search to Install a Program

Instead of browsing through the Synaptic categories, you can use the Quick Search input box. So, in the preceding example, just type chess into the box, and it will narrow down the packages displayed in the top-righthand pane to those whose filenames or descriptions match that word.

There will probably be many alternatives in the list, or some specialized programs that add extra functionality. You probably won't want all the items displayed, so just mark the packages you want, and then apply the installation as in the previous example.

Removing a Program

To remove a program, you can select the Installed category in the lefthand pane and browse for it in the top-righthand one. Alternatively, you can use the "Quick search" input box and type the program's name (or part of it) to narrow down the items displayed, as shown in Figure 8-20.

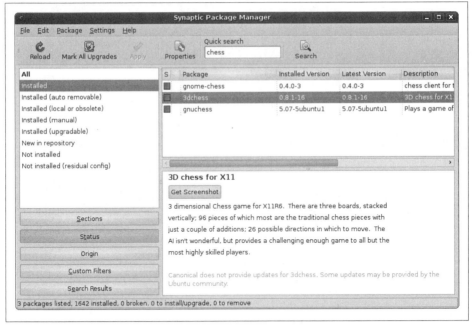

Figure 8-20. Selecting a program to remove

When you have found the program to remove, you can click on its name to display its details in the bottom-right frame. You can also look at the checkbox next to the name to ensure that it has already been installed. Once you are certain it's the right program, you can click the checkbox to call up a menu with a number of choices available to you, as shown in the close-up in Figure 8-21.

These choices will usually include Mark for Reinstallation, Mark for Removal, and Mark for Complete Removal. You may also see Mark for Upgrade if one is available. So just click Mark for Complete Removal to remove any configuration files along with the package.

The checkbox will then show a yellow x symbol to indicate that the package has been marked for complete removal. If you mark a package for normal removal (without deleting the configuration files), the x symbol will be red.

To finalize the package removal, click the Apply button to bring up the confirmation window shown in Figure 8-22.

Remember that before clicking the Apply button you are allowed to mark as many packages as you like for either installation or removal. This enables you to perform your housekeeping in one go. Therefore, any other actions you have chosen will be shown in this window, and you can view them by clicking the triangles shown next to each entry or by clicking the Show Details button.

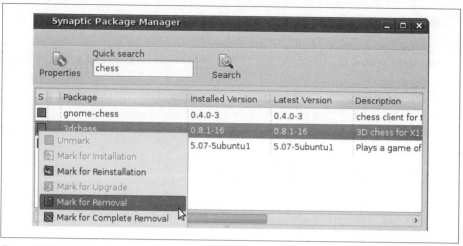

Figure 8-21. Marking a program for removal

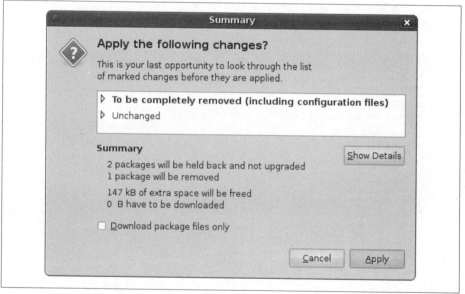

Figure 8-22. Confirming the removal of a package

So, when you are ready, click the Apply button to perform the removal (and any other selected actions). After the process has completed, you will be returned to Synaptic, with checkboxes newly filled for programs you just installed and cleared for those you've removed.

Other Synaptic Options

So far you've seen the Sections and Status buttons used to display the categories and installation statuses, but there are three other wide buttons at the bottom left: Origin, Custom Filters, and Search Results. With these, you can see where packages originate from, apply advanced filters for searching, and display the results from searches.

But as a new user to Ubuntu I wouldn't worry too much about them, as you can do practically everything you need with the commands I've shown you so far.

Synaptic's Menus

Synaptic's menus offer several additional features of interest that are worth mentioning.

The File Menu

Starting with the File menu, shown in Figure 8-23, you can save and read the markings you make, generate package download scripts, add download packages, or view the history of your use of Synaptic.

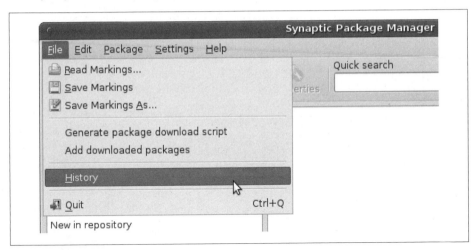

Figure 8-23. The File menu options

Only the last selection, History, is of use to you as a beginner to Ubuntu. With it you can view by month and year every change made to your system, which can be invaluable when you need to check exactly when you installed or removed a certain package.

The Edit Menu

The Edit menu mostly replicates buttons and features from elsewhere in the program, but it does include a very useful Fix Broken Packages facility, shown in Figure 8-24.

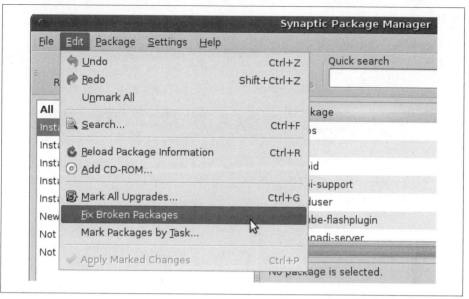

Figure 8-24. The Edit menu options

If any broken or corrupted packages are detected by Synaptic, it won't allow any further changes to your system until all the broken packages have been fixed. The way you're informed of this problem is an error message about "unsatisfied dependencies," meaning that parts of a package are missing. Should that ever happen to you, you now know to use this option in the hope that it can fix the dependency.

When you select the Fix option, all the broken packages will be marked to be fixed, but you must then also click the Apply button (or select Apply Marked Changes), which will then cause the broken packages to be fixed by downloading the missing parts.

The Package Menu

You probably won't need to use this menu, as it mostly replicates the effect of clicking on the checkboxes next to packages, although there are a couple of advanced features that seasoned users can utilize, as shown in Figure 8-25.

For example, you can lock a package so that it won't get upgraded when new versions become available. Also, Ubuntu installs many packages automatically because they are part of the default operating system. However, you can change this by checking and unchecking the "Automatically installed" checkbox.

There's also the Download Changelog option, which provides information about changes to, and bugs closed, in a package. The Properties option brings up the Properties information window for a package, in which you can view a wide range of information, including the description, dependencies on other packages, versions released, and more. This information is divided into five tabs, as shown in Figure 8-26.

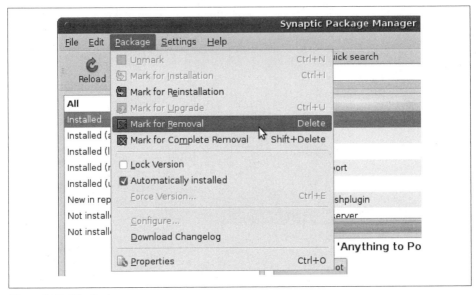

Figure 8-25. The Package menu

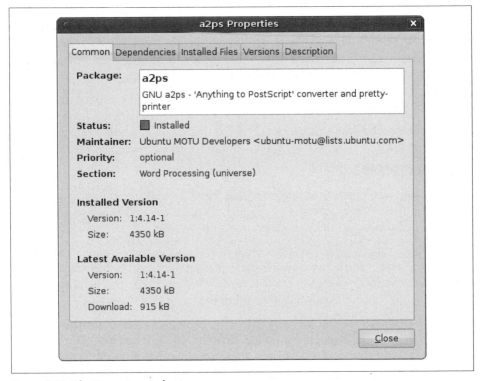

Figure 8-26. The Properties window

The Settings Menu

In the Settings menu, shown in Figure 8-27, the first entry, Preferences, can change settings in five different areas, with each assigned to its own tab.

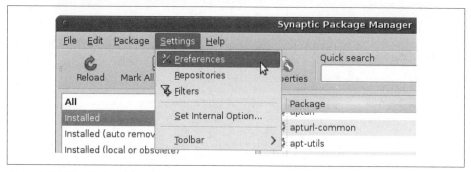

Figure 8-27. The Settings menu

Again, as a newcomer to Ubuntu I wouldn't recommend you change anything in this window, or you run the risk of rendering Synaptic incapable of correctly installing and updating packages.

That said, if you know what you are doing, you can use the Preferences window tabs, shown in Figure 8-28, to modify the confirmation options, set the default view of properties, change the columns, fonts, and colors of packages, decide what to do with temporary files, manage the history, set up a proxy, and change the package upgrade behavior.

The Settings menu also includes the Repositories option, which you saw earlier in Figure 8-7 in the discussion of the Ubuntu Software Center, where it was referred to by the name Software Sources. All the tabs shown are the same as in the Software Center Advanced Features section.

The Filters option brings up the window shown in Figure 8-29, in which you can specify exactly which packages will and won't be displayed by Synaptic. You probably won't need to use it, though, until (or unless) you become fully proficient in using Synaptic.

As the Set Internal Option states when you click it: "Only experts should use this." So, it's probably best left alone.

Finally, in the Settings menu, the Toolbar option lets you decide whether to display the icons, how they should look, whether to show accompanying text, and where to place it.

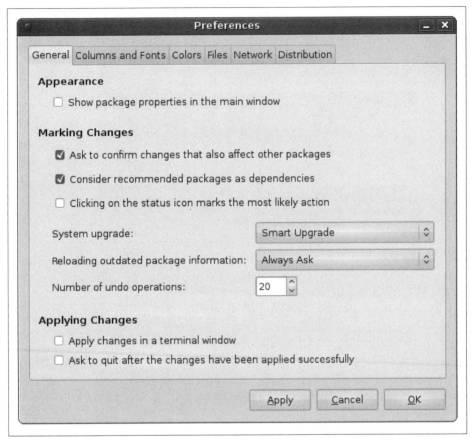

Figure 8-28. The Preferences window

The Help Menu

Of course, as you'd expect from Ubuntu, there's also plenty of assistance available in the Help menu. You can call it up by pressing F1 or by selecting Help → Contents. Or you can bring up a summary by selecting Help → Quick Introduction, or view the online help with Help → Get Help Online.

Using Aptitude

Another way to install and remove programs in Ubuntu is with the Aptitude Package Manager, a frontend for the Advanced Packaging Tool (APT), which you call up from a Terminal window command line like this:

```
sudo aptitude
```

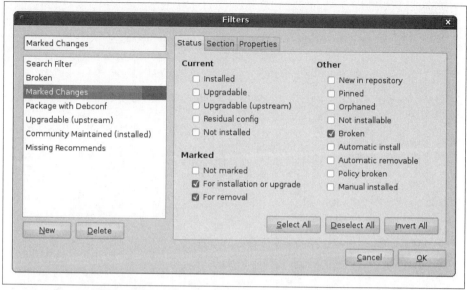

Figure 8-29. The Filters window

When asked, enter your password. Also, make sure that neither the Software Center nor Synaptic are running when you do this, or you'll get an error message. Once Aptitude is running, your Terminal window should look like Figure 8-30.

Personally, I don't recommend using Aptitude, now that both Synaptic and the Software Center are available as alternatives. However, if you happen to be logged into a Terminal window, it may be convenient to run the program.

You navigate around Aptitude using your cursor keys and the Enter key. For example, to list all the installed packages, highlight that option and press Enter. A list of all the packages will show up below. You can then move the cursor through the package list, and the description of each will appear in the bottom section. Press Enter again to close the list.

To perform actions on packages, such as installing or removing them, refer to the toolbar at the top. It explains that the ? key will display help, q quits the program, u updates a package, g either installs or removes a package, and so on. If you are presented with a dialog box (perhaps with "Yes" and "No" options), you can move between the options using the Tab key.

Instead of this menu-driven program, when I wish to perform an installation or other action on a package from the Terminal, I generally use the much quicker apt-get program, described in the following section.

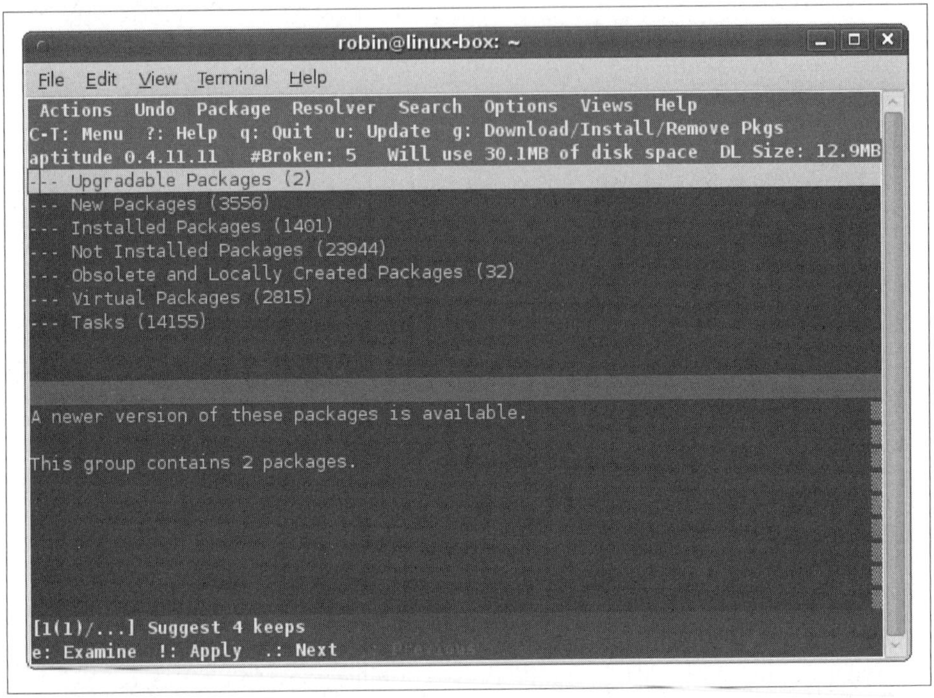

```
                         robin@linux-box: ~                    [_][□][X]
File   Edit   View   Terminal   Help
 Actions   Undo   Package   Resolver   Search   Options   Views   Help
 C-T: Menu   ?: Help   q: Quit   u: Update   g: Download/Install/Remove Pkgs
 aptitude 0.4.11.11    #Broken: 5    Will use 30.1MB of disk space   DL Size: 12.9MB
 --- Upgradable Packages (2)
 --- New Packages (3556)
 --- Installed Packages (1401)
 --- Not Installed Packages (23944)
 --- Obsolete and Locally Created Packages (32)
 --- Virtual Packages (2815)
 --- Tasks (14155)


 A newer version of these packages is available.

 This group contains 2 packages.




 [1(1)/...] Suggest 4 keeps
 e: Examine   !: Apply   .: Next
```

Figure 8-30. The Aptitude Package Manager

Using apt-get

This is the fourth and most precise way of performing an action on a package. Like Aptitude, it runs from the command line, and there are four main types of commands you will issue with it.

You are mostly likely to use one of these commands when following advice you have been given to install or remove a particular program. This is because it's much easier to provide you with a single line that you should type into the Terminal than to provide the step-by-step instructions needed to navigate through Synaptic or the Software Center, although most programs can also be installed through the latter two programs if you so choose.

Updating the package index

Before using apt-get, it's usually a good idea to enter the following, which will update your computer with the latest version information on all the packages it knows about (as well as adding packages that have recently been released):

```
sudo apt-get update
```

As ever, the sudo command starts the line to temporarily acquire super user privileges. The first time you use it, you'll have to enter your password, but you won't be prompted again for your password for another 15 minutes.

Upgrading packages

Once you have the system updated with all the latest package information, you may wish to enter the following command, which upgrades any packages you have installed that have newer versions available:

```
sudo apt-get upgrade
```

If any packages have unresolved dependencies and you get any error messages, you can use the dist-upgrade command instead, which intelligently handles dependencies that change with new versions of packages:

```
sudo apt-get dist-upgrade
```

Searching for packages

You can quickly search the cache for the names of new packages using a command such as the following, which returns all installable packages matching the word *chess*:

```
sudo apt-cache search chess
```

Installing a package

To install a package, as long as you know the right name for it, you can issue the following command, which will download and install the package with the name *packagename*:

```
sudo apt-get install packagename
```

Removing a package

To remove a package from your computer, enter the companion command to the previous one, which removes the package *packagename*:

```
sudo apt-get remove packagename
```

Getting help

For further help on using apt-get, you can enter the following to get a quick reminder of the available options:

```
apt-get help
```

Or for more comprehensive information, enter this:

```
man apt-get
```

Summary

Each of the four methods covered in this chapter for installing and removing programs has its pros and cons, and also its own supporters in the Ubuntu community.

Whichever you choose is entirely up to you, although I would recommend that you try to install new programs using the Ubuntu Software Center. Drivers and other packages that you cannot locate in the Software Center may well be installable using Synaptic.

The program you are least likely to run, and which I also recommend the least, is Aptitude. Although it's powerful and fast, it does take some getting used to, and in my view is superseded by the Software Center and Synaptic. On the other hand, whenever you are in an environment without access to a graphical desktop, Aptitude will do everything you need.

But I'm afraid there's no getting away from the command line and apt-get; sometimes this will be the only way for you to quickly install or remove a program without going through a whole lot of pointing and clicking. It's also the method most experts provide for installing packages when you ask them for advice. And once you've tried it, you'll probably find that the Ubuntu command line isn't that hard after all.

So, now that you have the tools for adding programs to your computer, the next chapter will cover maintaining it and keeping it secure.

CHAPTER 9

System Maintenance and Security

Now that you have your Ubuntu system up and running, it's time to look at how you can keep it that way by taking the proper security precautions and maintaining your computer in tip-top condition.

Don't worry that this chapter will be full of convoluted command-line statements and advanced Linux features, because you can actually do almost everything you need right from the desktop, with just a little mouse pointing and clicking.

Mostly, all you need to know is how to use a selection of programs and utilities that are accessible from Ubuntu's menu system, and how to install a couple of others that aren't. As you'll soon see, it's all quite easy.

System Maintenance

Proper maintenance includes power management to limit unnecessary wear on components when the computer isn't in use, configuring your preferred and startup applications, setting up how your removable media is treated, and various other system settings.

Preferences

The place to find most of your maintenance and administration tasks is in the System → Preferences menu (see Figure 9-1). Some of these programs offer fairly advanced options that you most likely won't need, but there are half a dozen of them with which you should acquaint yourself.

I'll run through these programs in the order in which they appear in the menu.

Power Management

This program is useful for extending the product life of the components used by your PC, by giving you the ability to turn some or all off when the computer is idle.

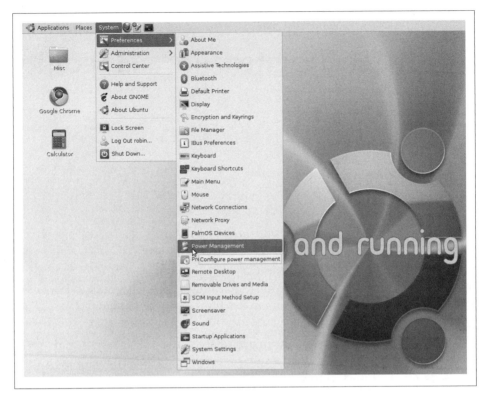

Figure 9-1. The System → Preferences menu

It displays differently depending on whether you're using a laptop or a desktop computer. Laptops will usually display items you won't see for a desktop, such as a battery power tab.

Figure 9-2 shows what the window looks like on a laptop. On a desktop PC there is no On Battery Power tab and no ability to set the display brightness.

The On AC Power tab. This is the first tab, which is shown on all computers. With it, you can choose whether to put your computer to sleep after a period of inactivity. This is good for cost savings, reducing wear on the computer, and ecological benefits—but obviously, if you make the time too short and cycle frequently between sleeping and waking, the effects will be both annoying and detrimental. You can also choose an interval after which, if no user input is detected, the display will go to sleep.

Another option makes hard disks spin down slowly, which can help the battery last longer on a laptop. Also on a laptop computer, you have the opportunity to choose your display's default brightness and to dim the display when your computer is idle.

The On Battery Power tab. This tab is available only on laptops or when a battery power source is detected. Its actions are similar to those on the AC power tab, as shown in Figure 9-3.

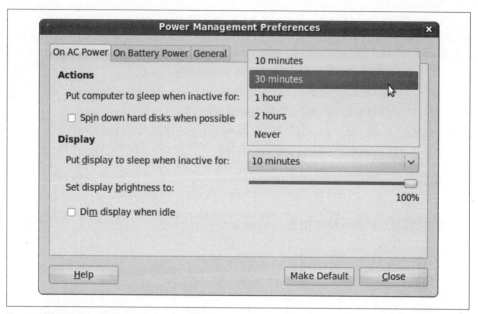

Figure 9-2. The Power Management Preferences window

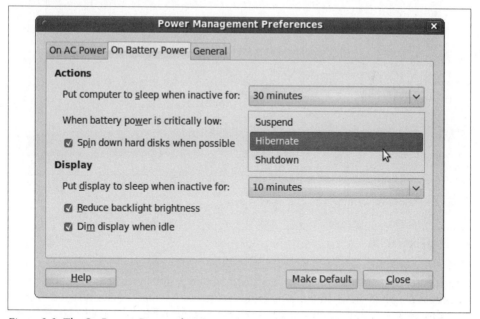

Figure 9-3. The On Battery Power tab

You also get some additional options, such as the ability to choose what to do—suspend, hibernate, or shut down your PC—if battery power becomes critically low.

A hibernated PC is a little safer because it can lose all power and yet return to where it left off when power resumes, including all documents and open programs, whereas a suspended PC will lose all of these once power is lost. On the other hand, a suspended PC starts up much more quickly than a hibernated one.

Finally, you can use this panel to reduce the backlight brightness from its AC power level when the laptop is running on battery power.

The General tab. Using this tab you can choose your preferred action (suspend, hibernate, shut down, or prompt the user with these choices) when either the power or suspend button is pressed, as shown in Figure 9-4. You can also choose which icon, if any, to display in the notification area.

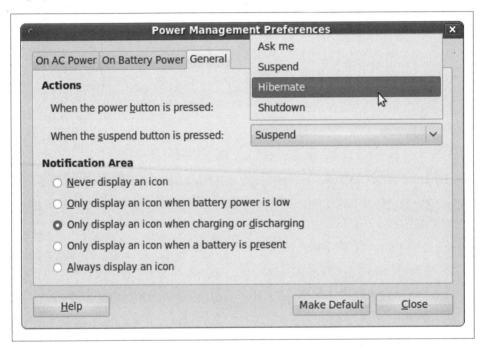

Figure 9-4. The General tab

Preferred Applications

Using this window, you can choose the programs to use for the most common computing tasks, such as web browsing and reading email. Whenever one program has to call another—such as when you open an attachment in email or download a PDF in your browser—the system checks your preferred applications to make its choice. Figure 9-5 shows what the Preferred Applications window looks like when you call it up.

Figure 9-5. The Preferred Applications window

The Internet tab. In this tab you can choose which programs to use as your preferred web browser and email reader. To change a program, you can click it and then select Custom, which will enable the Command input field. The concepts I laid out in Chapter 7 help you here. You can enter a program name, which you should normally follow with %s to allow files dropped onto the program's icon to be passed to it. If the program is not in your path, you'll need to provide its full path and program name.

You can also check the "Run in terminal" checkbox if the program runs in text output mode (in other words, if it uses standard output).

The Multimedia tab. This works in exactly the same way as the previous tab, but it sets your preferred multimedia player.

The System tab. This tab is for system commands and is similar to the previous two, except that the command you enter is split up into Command and "Execute flag" sections, as shown in Figure 9-6.

Most terminal applications have an option that causes them to treat the remaining command-line options as commands to run. This can be set by entering -x in the "Execute flag" field.

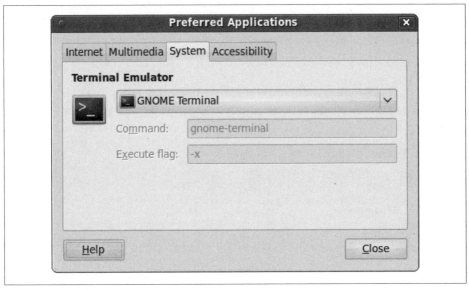

Figure 9-6. The Preferred Applications System tab

The Accessibility tab. The options in this tab are for visual and mobility aids. In addition to specifying the programs and commands to run, you can check a box called "Run at start" to ensure the utilities are always available.

Startup Applications

When Ubuntu boots up, there are a number of programs that get started by default, such as Bluetooth and network managers, the power manager, volume control, and so on (see Figure 9-7).

Using the Startup Applications utility, you can disable any of these or add new programs to the list using the Add, Remove, and Edit buttons. Remove and Edit will be grayed out until you select a program.

Be careful which programs you remove, as you could have difficulty restoring them if you need them later. The same goes for editing any of the default programs.

To add a program, click the Add button to bring up the dialog shown in Figure 9-8.

Here, I have chosen to add the program *synergyc* to run at startup. This is the client program of the Synergy utility, which lets me use a single keyboard and mouse on the computer named *robin* to operate all my Windows, OS X, and Ubuntu PCs. So now, each time this computer starts up, it will accept input from the *robin* computer's keyboard and mouse. Chapter 10 offers more details on setting up and using this great little program.

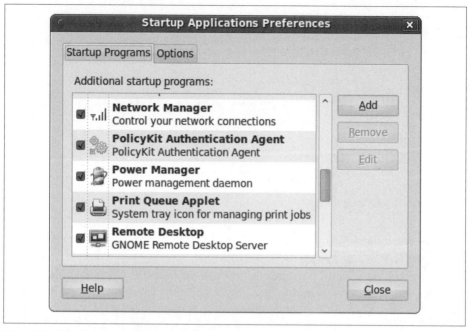

Figure 9-7. The Startup Applications Preferences window

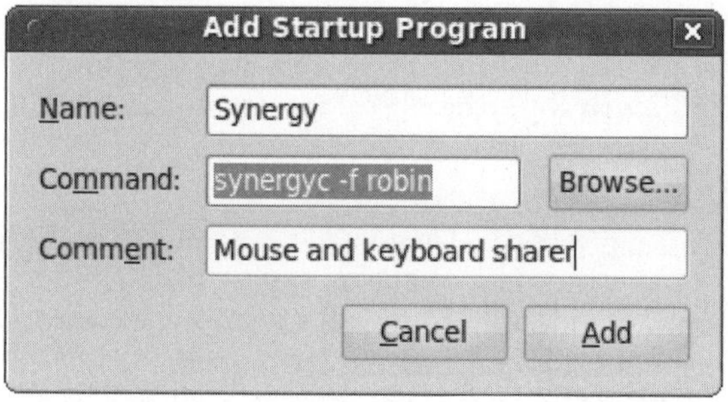

Figure 9-8. Adding a program to the startup list

If you don't know a program's name and/or location, you can click the Browse button and look for it.

Remember current applications. After you log out, all your programs will be closed. If you want Ubuntu to remember them and reload them for you when you next log in, you can click the Options tab and then check the box called "Automatically remember running applications when logging in," as shown in Figure 9-9.

Thereafter, all your programs will be reloaded each time you log in. If you close any programs before logging out, only those that remain open will be remembered.

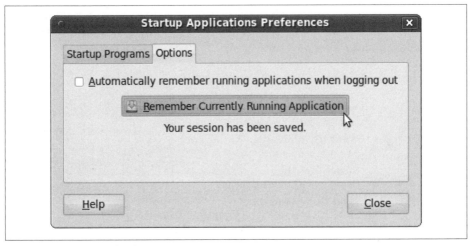

Figure 9-9. Automatically choosing startup programs

You can also have Ubuntu remember your open applications by clicking the button with the label Remember Currently Running Application (even though there is no final "s" on the end of the button label to indicate that the option potentially controls multiple applications), and they will be loaded in again each time you log in. To turn this behavior off, ensure all applications have been closed, and then click the Remember Currently Running Application button again.

 Ubuntu is not consistent in remembering all applications. For example, gedit and Terminal are remembered and restarted, but the Calculator is not.

Windows

The Window Preferences window allows you to control the way windows behave in conjunction with the mouse and keyboard (see Figure 9-10).

The window is divided into three main sections.

Window Selection. In this section, you can choose to make the desktop select a window when the mouse moves over it. This means that whichever window happens to be under the mouse will be focused, and therefore the target for mouse and keyboard actions.

Although a window becomes focused as soon as you pass a mouse over any portion of it, if any part of the window is obscured by another, you won't be able to access that portion unless you click the window to bring it to the front, also known as *raising* it.

For this reason, you can also choose an interval after which a newly selected window will automatically be raised, as long as the mouse stays over it. By default, the interval

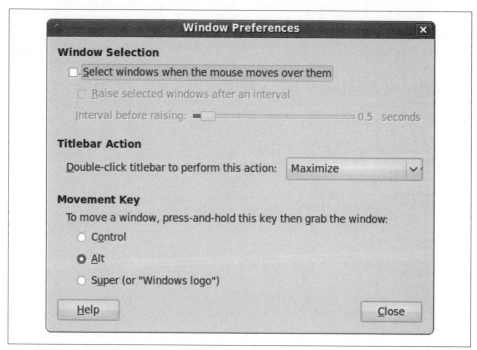

Figure 9-10. The Window Preferences window

is half a second, which is convenient for most users. If you pass over one window on the way to another, you won't be distracted by having it raised, but as soon as you hover for half a second, the window is raised. You can change the time to any value between 0 and 10 seconds.

Titlebar Action. Normally when you double-click a window's titlebar, it will cause the window to maximize. But with this pull-down menu, you can choose the action to associate with this event. The options are:

Maximize
Expand the window to fill the whole desktop.

Maximize Vertically
Expand the height of the window to the height of the desktop.

Maximize Horizontally
Expand the width of the window to the width of the desktop.

Minimize
Reduce the window to a tab on the bottom panel.

Roll up
Stop displaying the window's contents, but leave the titlebar in place.

None

Do nothing.

Double-clicking the title bar another time reverses the action, restoring a window to its previous state.

Movement Key. You can drag windows around by clicking and dragging their titlebars, but when a titlebar is off-screen, you can hold down the Alt key and then drag the window by clicking any visible part of it.

Using the Movement Key option, you can change this action from the Alt key to either the Ctrl key or the Windows logo key.

Administration

Moving on to the Administration menu next, there are several more maintenance options you may need.

Computer Janitor

The Computer Janitor helps you remove old files that are no longer needed. When you select it, you will be prompted for your password, and then a screen such as the one in Figure 9-11 will be displayed.

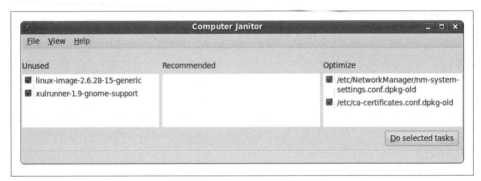

Figure 9-11. The Computer Janitor

In the lefthand frame, you can see that two old packages have been found and their checkboxes automatically checked. Clicking either of them will display more details and help you decide whether to uncheck it.

The central frame will list any recommended changes to make, whereas the righthand one lists changes you can make to optimize Ubuntu. Again, in each case you can click an entry to view more information about it.

Once you have selected all the changes you wish to make, click the "Do selected tasks" button and you'll be asked whether you are sure you want to clean up. If you are, click the "Clean up" button.

Sometimes after cleaning up, the program will discover one or more new items that can be optimized, and you can repeat the process. If the Computer Janitor can't find anything to clean up, it will pop up a window to tell you so and advise you to close the program.

Login Screen

With this utility, you can choose the action that should occur on login. By default, all users will be required to select their username and then enter their password. But if you click the Unlock button and enter your password, you can select one user who will be logged in automatically, as shown in Figure 9-12.

Figure 9-12. The Login Screen Settings window

You can either have that user logged in as soon as the computer starts or reboots, or set a time delay during which other users can select their usernames and log in. If the delay is passed without another account being chosen, then the automatic login of the selected user will proceed.

 Allowing automatic logins is an extremely unsafe option where security is an issue—for example, if you have access to sensitive data via a particular computer. Generally, I recommend using this setting only in a home environment in which you are certain there are no security issues. Even if you trust everyone with access to your computer, remember that they can always pull an annoying prank on you if you leave open access to your account.

Creating a password-free system

In our house, we keep a Netbook PC in the living room so that we can look things up and check our email and social networking sites from time to time. We used to have just one account on it that we all shared, but we decided it was annoying to keep logging in and out and entering passwords in the web browser each time when changing users.

So, I decided to create a completely unsecure environment on this machine, because ease and speed of use were much more important to us than privacy and security, particularly since it never leaves the house.

The Netbook now has multiple users, each with empty passwords that the system automatically accepts. Any user can now click the User Switch icon at the top right of the desktop, and then choose a username from the list shown to automatically log in as that user. As long as the PC hasn't been restarted, each of us now has all the programs we want open all the time, and which we can instantly return to—with all our settings and password details already entered.

If you want to create such a system, call up a Terminal window and then, for each user, enter the following:

```
sudo passwd -d username
```

The first time you do this you'll need to enter your own password, but for the next 15 minutes you won't be prompted. So, for example, if you have the users andy, brian, claire, and denise, you would enter the following:

```
sudo passwd -d andy
sudo passwd -d brian
sudo passwd -d claire
sudo passwd -d denise
```

This removes the password from all the users mentioned. You now need to edit a file to tell the system that users without passwords are allowed to log in automatically. To do this, enter the following:

```
sudo gedit /etc/pam.d/common-auth
```

The file will then be opened up in the editor, so move the cursor to the line (about 17 lines from the top) that looks like this:

```
auth    [success=1 default=ignore]    pam_unix.so nullok_secure
```

Now delete the _secure at the end of the line, click the Save button, log out, and enter your username to verify that you can now log in without a password. You will now have a completely open system, and even **sudo** commands will not require passwords.

 Remember that a fully open computer is completely unsecure, and that if it is lost or stolen, account information for each user could be easily extracted and used maliciously. Also, having no password for **sudo** means that it is very easy for someone careless (not even necessarily malicious) to seriously mess up or break your computer. So don't create such a system lightly.

System Monitor

The System Monitor is the place to go when you need to know how well your computer is handling its resources, such as memory, the network, hard disks, and so on. Figure 9-13 shows the program's first tab, the System summary screen.

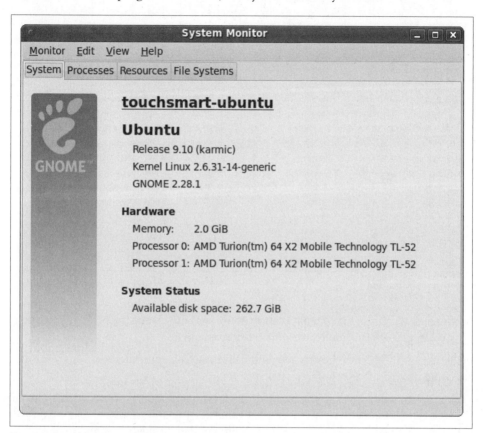

Figure 9-13. The System Monitor System tab

The System tab. This tab provides an at-a-glance summary of your computer, including the name it has been given, the versions of Ubuntu, Linux kernel, and GNOME desktop, the amount of memory, the processor(s) used, and available disk space.

The Processes tab. This tab provides full details on the processes currently running, as shown in Figure 9-14. You can click on any of the column titles to sort by the data in that column and determine, for example, which processes are consuming the most CPU time or memory.

To kill a process (in other words, to terminate its execution), highlight it and click the End Process button. But be careful—you may lose or corrupt data that the program was using, or disrupt another program that depends on the program you kill. Use this

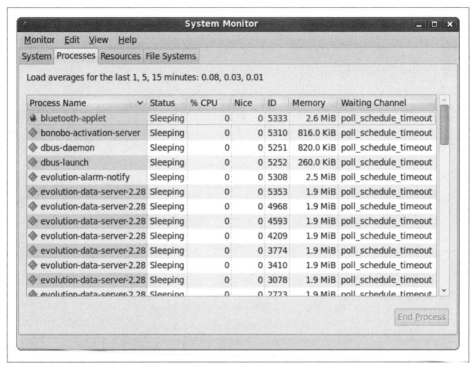

Figure 9-14. The System Monitor Processes tab

button only when you know what you are doing, and only when the program has hung or you can't close it normally for some other reason.

The Resources tab.   This tab shows you graphically how your computer's various resources are being used, as shown in Figure 9-15.

Each graph slowly moves to the left with the latest data point plotted on the right. In the figure you can see that the processors are averaging about 20% or less usage, the memory used is only in the region of 15% (with no use of a swap file), and the network graph shows four peaks, corresponding to web pages I called up in the Firefox web browser.

Compared to the Windows Vista operating system that this PC came with, these low levels are a tribute to the power and compactness of Linux. The fan on this PC also runs in its slowest and quietest mode under Ubuntu, but under Vista it whines away as it tries to diffuse the heat generated by the extensive CPU workload.

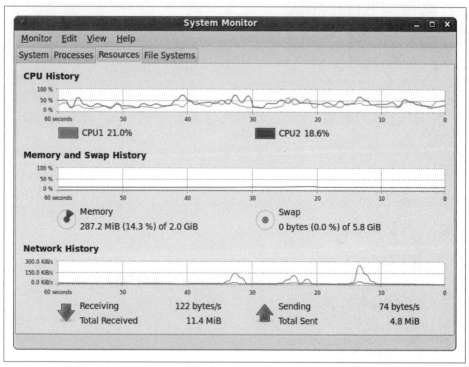

Figure 9-15. The System Monitor Resources tab

The File Systems tab. This final tab shows how your hard disks are doing. It lists the device name, location, and type, as well as its total, used, and free space, as shown in Figure 9-16.

The menus. The Monitor, Edit, and View menus are useful for choosing how the various options should be displayed, whether to display alerts when killing a process, the update intervals to use, and so on. Generally, these are advanced options that I recommend ignoring if you are a newcomer to Ubuntu.

System Testing

To thoroughly test your hardware, you can use the System Testing facility, as shown in Figure 9-17.

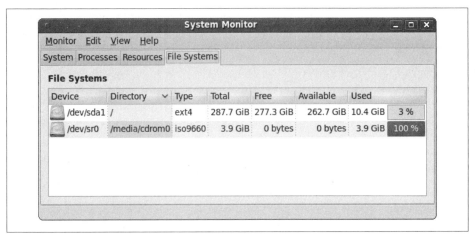

Figure 9-16. The System Monitor File Systems tab

Figure 9-17. The System Testing utility

Select the tests you would like made, and click Next. You will then be taken through various tests. For example, when testing the audio on your computer, you'll be asked to open the volume control application and make certain setting adjustments before clicking the Test button. The process will then continue for Bluetooth headsets, microphones, and USB audio devices.

Performing all the tests may take a while, but doing so will alert you to any problems with your computer that might need your attention.

Alpha and Beta Releases

Although I covered the Update Manager at the end of Chapter 2, there was one item I left out until you were ready, which is how you can upgrade to alpha and beta tests of new Ubuntu releases.

If your computer is used for important tasks or contains valuable data, you should never install beta software on it (let alone alpha). But if you have a computer on which you are prepared to lose all your data and reinstall the operating system if the worst should happen, it's a candidate machine on which you could play with prerelease versions of Ubuntu.

New editions of Ubuntu are released every six months, preceded by various alpha and beta tests available for people who are willing to test them and report any bugs found back to the developers. You can also install them purely out of curiosity if you wish, as there's no requirement to report bugs.

The new editions are usually released in April and October, so the alpha tests are generally available from about January to February and July to August. However, these will be the most unstable versions and are recommended only for seasoned Linux users.

But each March and September, the beta releases come out. These are much more stable and can be fun to install to see what's coming up in the forthcoming edition. So, bearing all my prior warnings in mind, if you still want to go ahead and check for an alpha or beta test, you can open up the Terminal and enter the following command:

```
sudo update-manager -d
```

After entering your password, the Update Manager will load, and if there are new versions or an alpha or a beta test, a button will appear offering the opportunity to upgrade to it. It will also tell you what type of upgrade is being offered (whether it's a full release, alpha, or beta), so you can decide whether or not to go ahead.

But remember that there's no easy way to go back if you proceed with an upgrade at this point. Anyone willing to run alpha or beta software should also be comfortable with completely restoring a system from a backup.

 ISO images for clean installs of the latest development versions of Ubuntu can always be downloaded from *http://iso.qa.ubuntu.com*.

System Security

On the security side, because it was built from the ground up as a multiuser operating system, Ubuntu suffers far less from virus attacks, but they still must be guarded against. You also need to lock your computer against intrusion, whether via the Internet or from physical access to your hardware.

Passwords

Passwords are one of the most important parts of securing any computer. Unfortunately, most people don't realize how easy it is these days for attackers to crack passwords based on dictionary words. In fact, even combinations of letters and numbers can be broken.

For example, one common way to save a password is to store it as a hash, which is a string of hexadecimal numbers derived from the original but which cannot be used to determine the password it came from—at least not in any practical timescale using current technology.

However, cunning hackers have spent years building huge databases of hashes for every password combination they can compute. These databases contain millions of combinations, so just imagine trying to think of an original combination of letters and numbers that won't be in such a database. It would have to be quite long (probably in excess of 20 characters) to stand a chance of being unique.

So, not only can hackers send repeated guesses to a password prompt by running through their dictionaries of passwords, whenever they manage to compromise a weakly protected computer, they can gain access to the password files and also try hash dictionaries against those.

For these and other reasons, your best bet for securing a computer is to create a password based on a combination of the following, all of which should be used:

- Uppercase letters
- Lowercase letters
- Digits
- Punctuation

At the same time, you need to be able to remember your password, so you can't just use a random string of characters, or you'll have to write it down—which is also a security risk. So the following three examples illustrate some passwords that are memorable but likely to remain unguessable and unique:

`{+}JaMeSO311MaRyO704{+}`

> This makes use of a repeated string of punctuation, surrounding the main password, which is built up using the names and birthdays of two people, but with alternating upper- and lowercase letters.

`disney112008LAND!!!!`

> This uses a vacation destination split into two words, one upper- and one lowercase, separated by the month and year of the vacation, and followed by four exclamation marks because it was a great time.

`kanye--TAYLOR++WEST--swift++`

> Here, I have mixed up two musicians' names and kept the password memorable because the two inner words are uppercase and the two outer are lowercase, while the names of one artist are followed by pairs of dashes and those of the other by pairs of plus signs.

Obviously, don't use these exact passwords or methods, because some cracker has already read them and added them to a database. Instead, spend a minute to be creative and make up your own. You should also think about changing your password from time to time, just in case.

Root Access

As I have mentioned a few times, there is one user that can access any and all files and programs, regardless of their file permissions and settings: the *root* user, or super user. On many operating systems, people who know the password can log into this account and use it to access any other user account. But this creates a huge security risk because absolutely any file can be accessed or deleted, and in the wrong hands such an account could be devastating.

Therefore, the developers of Ubuntu took the decision to disable the root account by default and allow access to it only one command at a time using the *sudo* command, which is covered in Chapter 7.

But you must remember that once a *sudo* command has been issued and you have provided your password, for the next 15 minutes your password will not be requested. So if you leave your computer unlocked for any reason during this time, someone else could come in and use your root access to create a new account or perform other mischief.

Also, if you ever use the `sudo -i` command to drop into a shell running as the root user, you must remember to exit from the shell before you leave your computer. Better still, don't use that particular option. Luckily, when you are in a root shell the command prompt will inform you by changing from `user@` to `root@`, as shown in Figure 9-18.

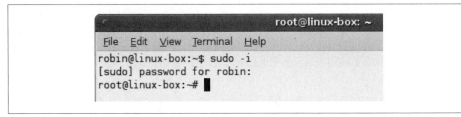

Figure 9-18. *When inside a root shell, the prompt changes*

Physical Access

While the developers of Ubuntu have made every attempt to securely isolate physically local users of a shared computer from one another, the standard Ubuntu installation is not intended to block an attacker with physical access.

In other words, a default Ubuntu installation is extremely secure when connected to via a network or the Internet. But Ubuntu is also a very user-friendly operating system, so the root user doesn't have a password by default.

This means that someone can walk up to your system, reboot it into a safe or recovery mode (which are provided to debug serious system problems), and log in as the root user without a password. Therefore, if local security is important, I strongly recommend that you issue the following command to give the root user its own password:

    sudo passwd root

You will then be prompted (twice) to "Enter a new UNIX password." Do so and make sure you remember the password you enter. Once a root password has been set, the safe and recovery modes will require the new password before proceeding.

To further increase security, you may also wish to look into setting your BIOS password to prevent someone forcing a boot up using a different device from the internal hard disk, and then copying or changing data on the main hard disk. However, details on changing the BIOS password are beyond the scope of this book, so please refer to the documentation that came with your computer.

Another good security measure is to use hard drive encryption so that even if someone gains access to your hard disk, they still won't be able to read it. This is also an advanced topic that I don't have enough room to cover in this book, but you can get further details from the following URL on the official Ubuntu website:

https://help.ubuntu.com/community/EncryptedFilesystemHowto

Firewall

It's a fact of life that most computers with Internet connections are probed daily by hoards of automated systems searching for exploitable weaknesses. Ideally, your computer will already be using a firewall, either at work or behind a home ADSL or cable router. Check the manual that came with your router or access point to see whether you have a firewall and, if so, how to change its settings to, for example, allow certain programs such as Skype or BitTorrent access through it.

Also, by default Ubuntu comes with no open ports on public interfaces, so port scans will only show closed ports.

 A port is just a number used to indicate connection to a particular service, such as the Web or email, but you can consider it as if it were a phone socket. Disconnecting a port is therefore like unplugging a phone plug from a phone socket—no signal can get through to your browser, email program, or whatever service uses the port.

This theoretically means that you don't actually need a firewall. However, if you should unintentionally install a server program that opened up a port, your computer could be compromised. Therefore, by installing a firewall, you can have the peace of mind of knowing that you are in ultimate control over your computer's ports, because the firewall will override any other installed program.

There's lots to learn when managing firewalls, but to at least get you up and running, you can enter the following sequence of commands into the Terminal to create a basic level of additional security:

```
sudo ufw allow ssh/tcp
sudo ufw logging on
sudo ufw enable
sudo ufw status
```

The result of issuing these commands should look like Figure 9-19, in which I have enabled the firewall on my *touchsmart-ubuntu* computer. Now all incoming connections are definitely denied, but all outgoing ones are allowed. A facility called *state tracking* lets in the responses to my outgoing connections, such as the web pages that my browser asks for, but a malicious intruder trying to exploit a bug in the browser cannot establish a new incoming connection.

For further details on using the firewall, including opening and closing individual ports, I recommend you visit the following URL:

https://wiki.ubuntu.com/UncomplicatedFirewall

Use Reliable Sources

Where possible, you should try to install software only via the Synaptic utility, the Ubuntu Software Center, or the apt-get program, all described in Chapter 8. That way at least you'll know that a program has been checked by the community and considered worthy of inclusion.

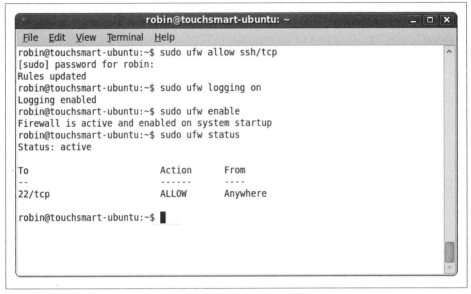

Figure 9-19. Enabling the Ubuntu firewall

But of course, not all software will be in these repositories, especially new programs that have yet to be evaluated, so sometimes you have no alternative other than to install software using instructions supplied by the developer. In such cases, I recommend you perform a couple of quick search engine checks on the program's filename, and perhaps also the developer's name, just to ensure there are no reports of problems associated with the software.

Don't Use Untrusted Commands

If you ask for advice or read the answer to someone else's question in an Internet forum, and you now have one or more commands to type in, make sure that they are not dangerous.

For example, any command with rm in it will try to remove something from your file-system. Likewise, mv commands will copy or move files and folders, possibly overwriting important ones, and so will commands that use the > symbol to redirect output.

In other words, use your common sense before arbitrarily typing in commands, just in case a hacker is trying to get you to compromise your computer, or a malicious person is trying to corrupt it. Above all, use the -r and -f arguments in conjunction with the rm command (they often appear as rm -rf) with the absolute utmost caution—together they could erase your entire filesystem.

Updating

Keeping your computer up-to-date is another important security measure you should get into the habit of taking. Not only will you ensure that you have all the latest features, you'll also be updating to the latest security measures.

The best way to do this is to call up the Update Manager, click the Settings button, and ensure that updates are checked for daily, as shown in Figure 9-20.

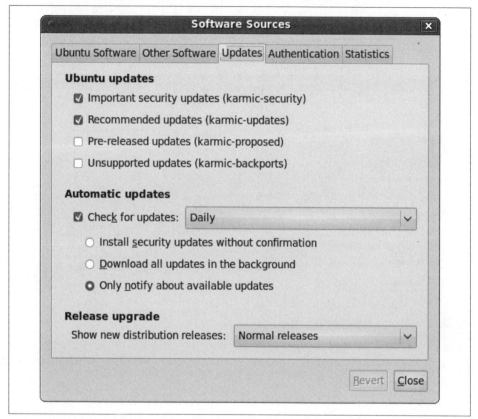

Figure 9-20. To keep your computer secure, check for updates daily

Viruses and Malware

Because the Linux desktop market is still quite small, and also because it is very secure, there are very few reports of viruses and other malware for it. Still, that doesn't mean you can relax your vigilance. Linux is growing in popularity, and hackers are bound to spend more time trying to hack it in the future.

You'll gain the most protection from malware just by sticking to repository software. But for extra protection, you may wish to install *ClamTk*, a graphical frontend for the *ClamAV* antivirus program.

You may also want to consider *rkhunter* and *chkrootkit* for detecting rootkits that try to take over your PC at its core, although, yet again, there have not been many reported instances of rootkits for Linux to date.

To install any or all of these programs, call up the Synaptic Package Manager and enter their names into the "Quick search" field. If you like, you can enter all three names at once, separated by spaces, and the results returned will be related to these items (see Figure 9-21).

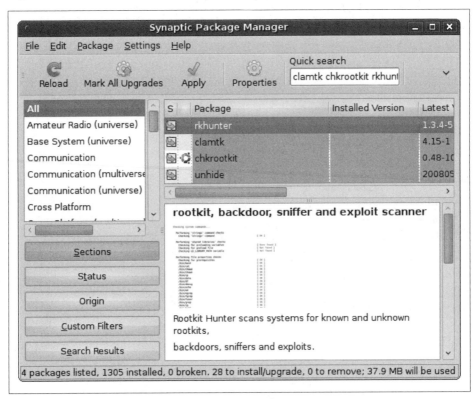

Figure 9-21. Installing antivirus and rootkit detection software

You can then click each of the accompanying checkboxes in turn and mark them for installation, along with other programs they depend on. When finished, click the Apply button to perform the installation. The required files will then be downloaded and installed.

You can now select Applications → System Tools → Virus Scanner to open up the program shown in Figure 9-22, with which you can scan for and fix viruses found on your

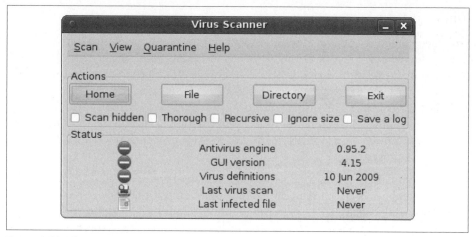

Figure 9-22. The Virus Scanner main screen

computer. Numerous options are available, but you can just click the Home button to scan your home folder. For a much longer but more thorough scan, check the Recursive checkbox, click the Directory button, and select File System to scan the entire filesystem.

Browsers and Email Clients

I sometimes worry that Linux users may be a little too complacent about the robustness of their operating system so that should an exploit be discovered and a virus spread, they will be less prepared than Windows users to deal with it.

Fortunately, browser exploits and email attachment malware mostly affect Windows users, and therefore the programs they try to install on a Linux computer will fail. But you must still be cautious about what you download, as you never know whether someone will succeed in writing a malicious program that exploits Ubuntu and other versions of Linux.

Generally, this means you should keep your browser updated so that it is aware of potential attack sites, and don't trust email attachments or web pages that are sent to you from people you don't know. In fact, don't trust them period, until you are sure they are safe to use. One technique that reduces your risk (although it doesn't eliminate it) is to save the attachments and run the virus checker over them before opening them.

 You should always remember that phishing and social engineering attacks can happen on any operating system, including Linux.

Wine

Let's face it, there is some very good software out there that hasn't made its way onto the Ubuntu or any Linux operating system. Even the OpenOffice.org suite, which is mostly compatible with Microsoft Word and other Office programs, doesn't entirely substitute for them in everyday use. "Mostly" is the key word here. Often you'll find that files get corrupted or display and print differently when transferred from one program to another. Therefore, the Wine Windows application interface is especially handy, as it can run a huge variety of Windows-only programs, including Word and other Office programs.

But this compatibility brings with it a security risk. True, it's not as great a risk as running Windows itself, particularly as long as you don't run Wine as *root*. But nevertheless, a risk exists, so all the preceding cautions should apply doubly whenever you run a Windows program using Wine. For further details on using Wine, please refer to Chapter 16.

Summary

This chapter discussed some of the best ways to keep your computer current and secure, but you should always remember that both maintenance and security are ever-evolving issues that you need to keep on top of.

Therefore, every time you upgrade your Ubuntu installation to a new version, which will generally be every six months (unless you are intentionally staying with a particular release), you should make a note of any new programs or features for properly maintaining and securing your computer.

You can also join one or more of the Ubuntu mailing lists to keep yourself informed. There are actually a couple of hundred lists available at *http://lists.ubuntu.com*, but don't be put off by that number. Unless you need very specific information, you'll probably only want to join one or two of the following lists:

Ubuntu Announcements
   http://lists.ubuntu.com/mailman/listinfo/ubuntu-announce

Ubuntu News
   http://lists.ubuntu.com/mailman/listinfo/ubuntu-news

Ubuntu Security Announcements
   http://lists.ubuntu.com/mailman/listinfo/ubuntu-security-announce

Ubuntu Users
   http://lists.ubuntu.com/mailman/listinfo/ubuntu-users

Kubuntu Users
   http://lists.ubuntu.com/mailman/listinfo/kubuntu-users

Xubuntu Users
   http://lists.ubuntu.com/mailman/listinfo/xubuntu-users

Edubuntu Users
   http://lists.ubuntu.com/mailman/listinfo/edubuntu-users

Ubuntu Studio Users
   http://lists.ubuntu.com/mailman/listinfo/Ubuntu-Studio-users

Now that you know how to keep your computer secure, in the next chapter, I'll explain how to network your computer with others for file sharing and remote access over local networks and the Internet.

CHAPTER 10

Networking Ubuntu

In this chapter, we'll look at how to connect your Ubuntu computer with others, whether they run Linux, Windows, or OS X. We'll cover file and folder sharing, using one keyboard and mouse to operate multiple computers, and logging into remote computers.

In the past, many of these operations took a lot of wrestling with highly technical configuration options. Getting the networking right could be a fiddly and time-consuming task. But nowadays advanced networking is nothing to be frightened of, because it's generally just a matter of using your mouse to click a few options, maybe entering the name of a computer to which you wish to connect, and clicking a Connect button.

This chapter assumes you can reach the local network that connects the computers in your home or office. Make sure you are connected to your local hub and the Internet, using the instructions in Chapter 3 as needed in your environment. To show you how easy it is, let's jump right in and start accessing one computer's desktop remotely via another one.

Remote Desktop

Ubuntu comes installed with a Virtual Network Computing (VNC) program with which you can echo another computer's desktop onto yours, either in a window or taking up the whole screen, as though you were at that machine. You can also operate that computer through VNC if you have been given that privilege.

You may wish to do this to provide assistance to other people remotely, or so you can work on different computers in different locations all from the one computer. If you don't have access to two computers, you may want to jump ahead to the section "Using Shared Folders" on page 324.

Enabling the VNC Server

To use this facility, you will need two computers, one of which should be running a VNC server and the other a VNC client. So, let's get an Ubuntu computer up and running as a server by selecting System → Preferences → Remote Desktop to bring up the window in Figure 10-1.

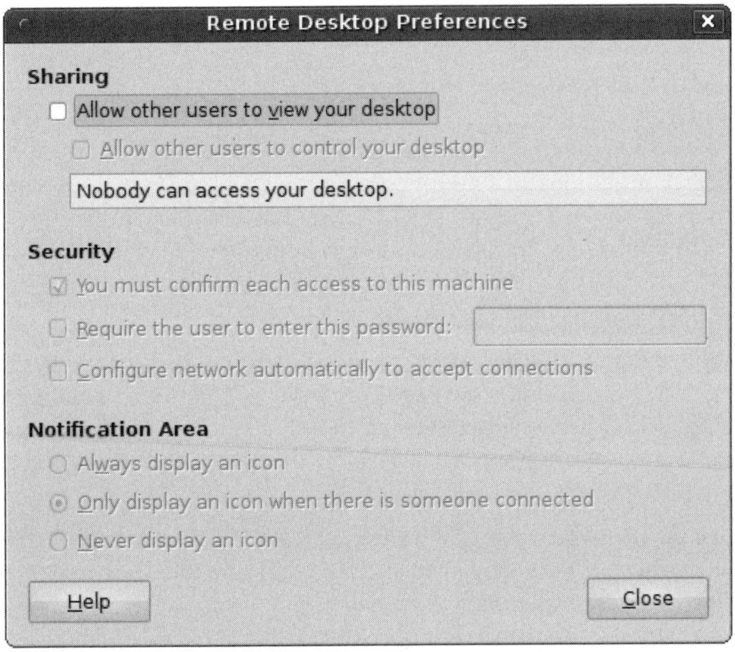

Figure 10-1. The Remote Desktop Preferences window

This is the default state in which, as the program says, "Nobody can access your desktop." But remember that as soon as you start using it, VNC may open up security risks, depending on what you do.

To enable the VNC client, click the checkbox next to "Allow other users to view your desktop" and wait a few seconds until the connectivity check completes. Then check the box "Allow other users to control your desktop," followed by "Configure network automatically to accept connections," and you'll be set to go.

However, it will be possible for anyone else to log into your computer at this point, so also check "Require the user to enter this password" and enter a password in the input field, and then you'll be set to go *and* secure. The program's window should now look something like the one shown in Figure 10-2.

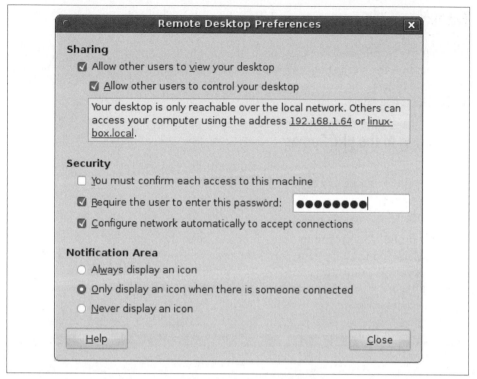

Figure 10-2. The computer is now configured for VNC connections

 Make sure to read the section "Passwords" on page 302 to help you choose a secure password. Usually the activities in this chapter open your system only to other systems on the local network in your home or office. Even so, every program you open to allow access to your computer creates an attack channel for malicious users, and thousands of programs roam the network daily looking for bugs that permit entry. So, good passwords are highly recommended.

As you can see in the figure, the local IP address the router has given this computer is *192.168.1.64*, and it can be accessed using the local name *linux-box.local*. I have also created an eight-character password.

The remaining options

You should note that checking the third option under the Security section causes the first one to become unchecked, since they are mutually exclusive. When the first is checked, you will need to be at the server computer whenever a request to start a VNC connection comes through, because you must then accept or deny the request.

However, seeing as you may be using VNC to connect computers in different rooms, I have set this VNC server up to allow all incoming requests, as long as the correct password is supplied. You may wish to change this back if you intend to allow only VNC connections under your immediate physical control.

I also left the Notification Area setting at the default. The way it is by default, an icon will appear on the status bar only when there is an active VNC connection. But you can choose to have the icon always displayed when the VNC server is running, or to never have it displayed.

Connecting to the VNC Server

I'll now show you three ways of connecting to the VNC server you've enabled: for Ubuntu, Windows, and OS X.

Using Ubuntu

To connect one Ubuntu computer to another one with an enabled VNC server, you need to select Applications → Internet → Remote Desktop Viewer on the computer that looks at or controls the other's desktop. This option calls up the Vinagre VNC program shown in Figure 10-3, which has been grabbed from another Ubuntu installation on the same local network.

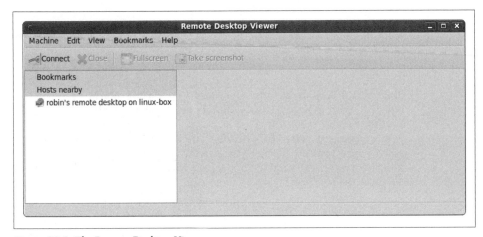

Figure 10-3. The Remote Desktop Viewer

You can now double-click any VNC servers shown in the lefthand pane to connect to them. In this case only one has been found, which is the machine on which I just enabled VNC in the previous section. Double-clicking it brings up the password prompt shown in Figure 10-4.

When entering the password, you can check the "Remember this credential" checkbox to remember the password in future (which you can do if you're in an environment you trust and don't have to worry about casual visitors playing with the computer). When ready, click the Authenticate button to establish the connection, which will make the

Figure 10-4. Enter the correct password when prompted

Remote Desktop Viewer's righthand pane display the contents of the VNC Server's desktop, as shown in Figure 10-5. Here, I have also clicked the magnifying glass icon to resize the desktop to fit exactly into the pane.

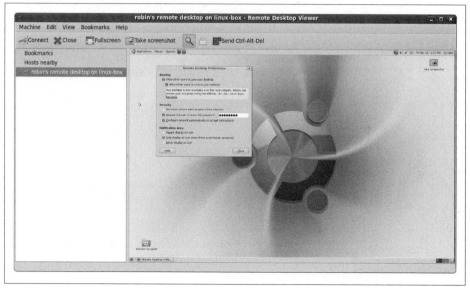

Figure 10-5. Accessing the remote VNC server's desktop

This resized view is great for seeing what's on the desktop. When you need to see more detail, click the magnifying glass icon again to return the display to normal size, but you'll have to use the scroll bars to move the contents around within the pane. You may also want to resize the lefthand pane and/or the whole window to get the best fit.

The View menu. Using the View menu, you can toggle the display of the top toolbar, the status bar, or the side panel, and can alternate between full screen and windowed view, as well as scale the display and control whether to just view the remote desktop without being able to modify it.

Fullscreen mode. By clicking the Fullscreen button or pressing the F11 key, you can also toggle between full screen and windowed mode, as shown by Figure 10-6. In full screen mode, you would never know that the desktop shown is that of another computer, except that the responsiveness will not be as fast as the local desktop.

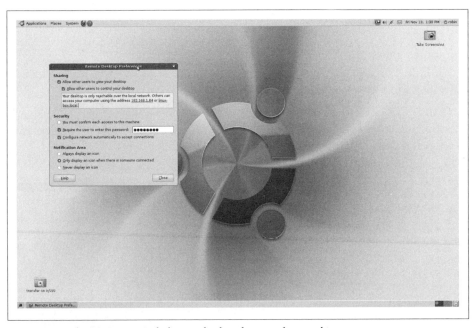

Figure 10-6. The VNC server's desktop redisplayed on another machine

Using Windows

With Windows, you will need to download and install a VNC client program such as RealVNC (available from *http://www.realvnc.com/products/download.html*). You can then run it in the usual way. Depending on the program you use, you will normally get a window such as Figure 10-7, in which the VNC server name or IP address is being requested.

Enter the IP address of your Ubuntu computer (which, in my case, is 192.168.1.64), select any options (which generally provide customization for the colors used and rate limiting of mouse movement events), and click OK. This should bring up a password prompt such as the one in Figure 10-8.

Once the password has been authenticated, the VNC connection is established and Windows will open up a view of the VNC server's desktop, which will be similar to Figure 10-9.

Figure 10-7. Connecting to a VNC server from Windows

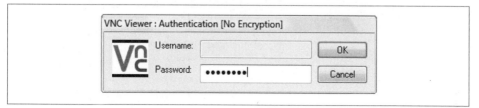

Figure 10-8. Entering the password

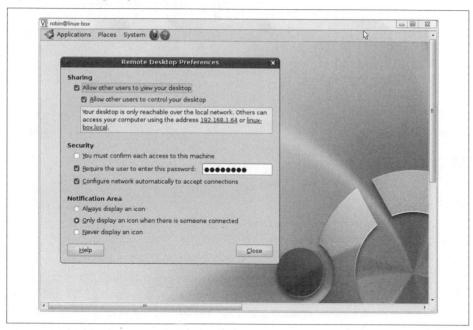

Figure 10-9. An Ubuntu desktop displayed on Windows via VNC

Depending on the features available with your VNC client, you should be able to move the view of the desktop around with the scroll bars and maximize the window to view the Ubuntu desktop in as much detail as possible.

Using Mac OS X

On a Mac computer, you can use a program such as Jollys Fast VNC (available from *http://www.jinx.de/JollysFastVNC.html*) as your VNC client. Simply download and install the program, and then run it to bring up a screen similar to Figure 10-10.

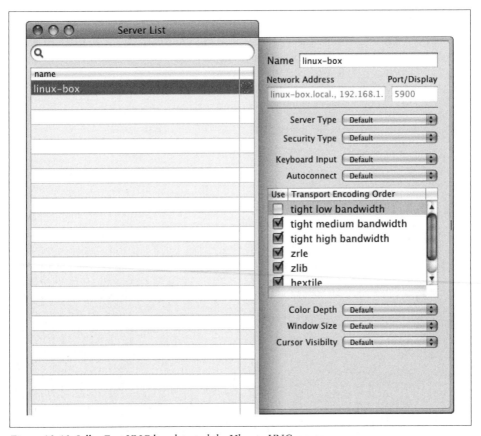

Figure 10-10. Jollys Fast VNC has detected the Ubuntu VNC server

As you'd expect, the VNC client will normally detect servers to which it is capable of connecting, and it has done so here. Now all you need to do is double-click the server to which you wish to connect, bringing up the password prompt shown in Figure 10-11.

Once the password has been verified, the VNC client starts communicating with the server and opens up a window similar to the one shown in Figure 10-12.

Interestingly, when the remote desktop is larger than the local window, this particular VNC client displays the area immediately surrounding the mouse pointer in full detail, and then shrinks areas of the desktop farther away, so you can still view the desktop in its entirety.

Figure 10-11. Entering a password into Jollys Fast VNC

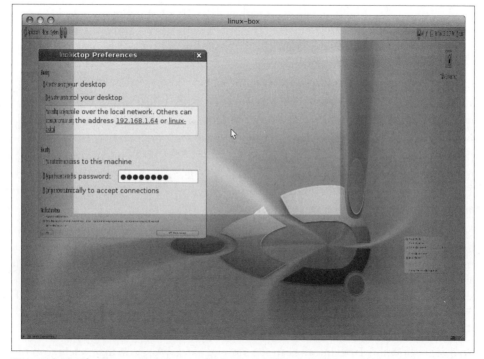

Figure 10-12. The Mac computer is now displaying the Ubuntu desktop

VNC Desktop Resolutions

When running a VNC server, it is helpful for other users (or yourself) who will be connecting to it if you choose a lower resolution. This substantially reduces the amount of data transferred across the network, and allows a client to show the remote desktop in a smaller window. I generally think a size of 1024 × 768 pixels is more than necessary, and 800 × 600 is probably optimal for both speed and productivity. You can change the desktop resolution using System → Preferences → Display. If you need a larger desktop, you could instead try changing your monitor's color depth to a small value such as 256, or even 16.

Using VNC over the Internet

Another use for VNC is to connect computers remotely over the Internet—for example, to access your work computer from home. But there are several security issues to consider, and doing so is not as easy as over a local network. Therefore, I suggest you refer to the official Ubuntu documentation at *https://help.ubuntu.com/community/VNC*, which explains in detail the procedures to follow.

Controlling Multiple Local Computers

Nowadays, with technology being so much cheaper, it's not uncommon to have two or even more computers on your desk. The only downside is that they all require their own keyboard and mouse to operate them, which leaves little room for much else on your desk.

Luckily, there's a very useful program called Synergy with which you can share a single keyboard and mouse across multiple computers. And, unlike using VNC, it's a remarkably responsive system because only the mouse and keyboard data is sent across the network, rather than large amounts of graphical data.

On Ubuntu you can download and install Synergy by selecting System → Administration → Synaptic Package Manager, and entering Synergy in the "Quick search" field. This highlights two packages, *synergy* and *quicksynergy*. Mark both for installation, and then click Apply to perform the installation.

Now you must choose which computer will be your master, i.e., the one whose keyboard and mouse will control the others, and make a note of its name. For example, mine is simply called *robin*. Then, on each Ubuntu computer you wish to control, you should select Applications → Accessories → QuickSynergy and then click the Use tab, shown in Figure 10-13. Here, you should enter the controlling computer's name in both fields. (The screen name just determines what name appears in the Synergy program.)

Once all your slave computers have been set up, you need to configure your master. To do this, download and install both *synergy* and *quicksynergy* on that machine in the previous manner using Synaptic. But then, when you call up the program (by selecting Applications → Accessories → QuickSynergy), use the Share tab to decide where each of your remote computers (slaves) should appear, relative to your main computer's screen. You can control up to four slaves.

So, for example, if you have two slaves, called *slave1* and *slave2*, I would recommend placing one monitor on the left and the other to the right of your main one. Then, in the fields showing Left and Right, enter the names of the two slave computers, as shown in Figure 10-14.

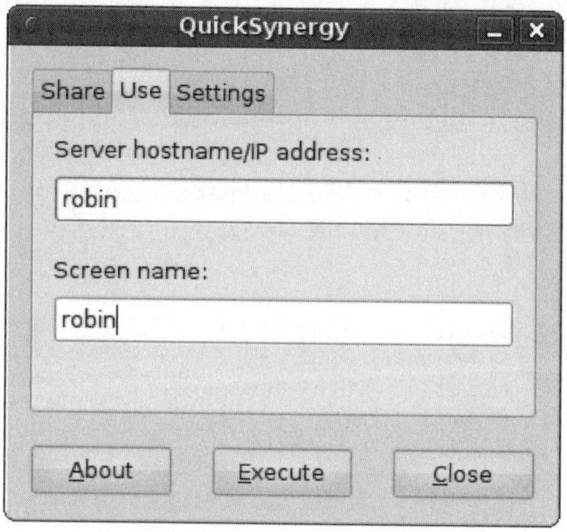

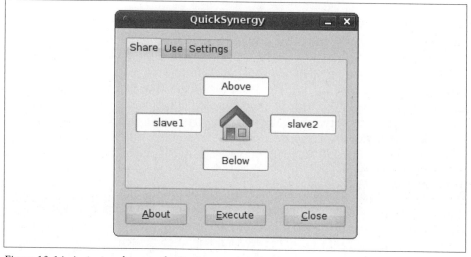

Figure 10-13. Setting a Synergy slave to use a master computer's keyboard and mouse

Figure 10-14. Assigning slaves to the Synergy master computer

You are now ready to click the Execute button on each of your computers, and you'll find that your main computer will allow your mouse pointer to travel all the way from the far left of the lefthand monitor, past your main monitor, and all the way through to the far edge of the righthand one. With each monitor it enters, your main computer's mouse and keyboard will take over control of that computer.

Once you have verified that it's all working, you can tuck the spare keyboards and mice away behind the monitors. Don't move them too far, though, as you may need them for logging in again after a reboot, or if the master machine plays up.

If you decide you like this setup and want the convenience of having your slave computers start up automatically with each reboot, you can select System → Preferences → Startup Applications, and then enter the details shown in Figure 10-15, replacing the word *master* with the name of your master computer. After the next reboot you won't need to run QuickSynergy again, although you'll still need the keyboard and mouse to log in, unless you have chosen automatic logins. On my setup, I've chosen automatic logins because the slave machines are on my desk in a secure environment.

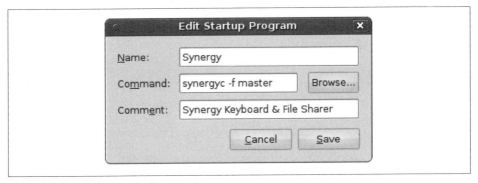

Figure 10-15. Configuring the Synergy client to run at startup

Synergy is also available for Windows and Mac OS X, but its configuration can be convoluted compared to the ease of QuickSynergy on Linux. If you would like to network Ubuntu with these types of computers, the details you need are on the program's home page at *http://synergy2.sourceforge.net*. For example, using the information there, I have been able to connect a Mac, a Windows Vista and 7 computers, and some Ubuntu machines all together.

Because these are all different computers (and not several monitors connected to a single computer), you cannot drag windows or files between them, but Synergy does retain the clipboard buffer, so you can copy and paste between computers. For transferring entire files and directories between a group of computers, I usually open up a server connection, as described in the following section.

Using Shared Folders

When you wish to access a folder that has been previously shared by another computer in your network, you can manually choose Places → Connect to Server and enter that folder's details, as shown in Figure 10-16. Here, the folder *transfer* is being opened up on the computer *iq500*.

If prompted, enter any password that has been set, and the folder will open up on your desktop, along with an icon representing it. If you don't know which resources are where on your network, you can also select Places → Network and then browse through

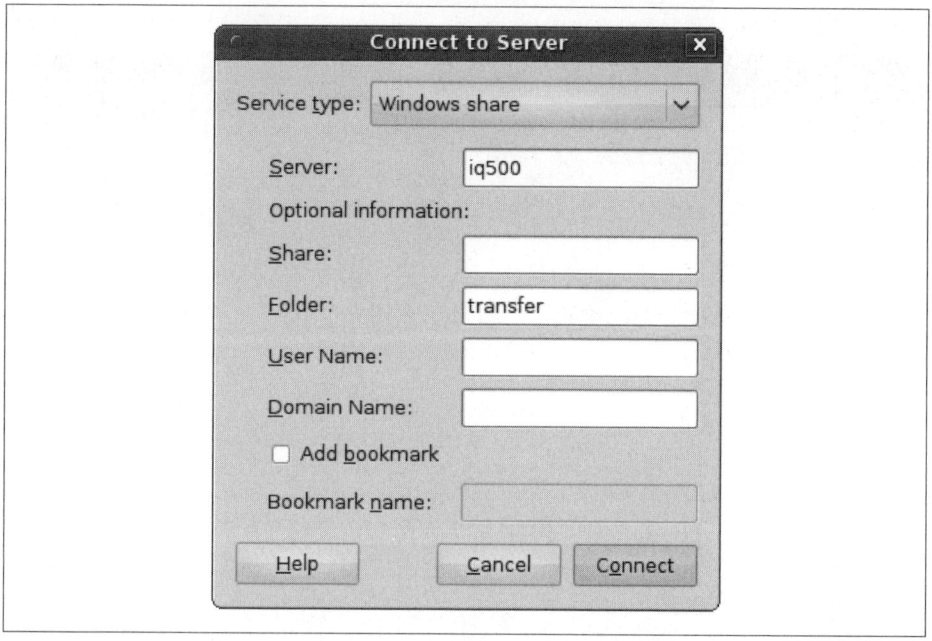

![Connect to Server dialog box]

Connect to Server ✕

Service <u>t</u>ype: | Windows share ▾ |

<u>S</u>erver: | iq500 |

Optional information:

<u>S</u>hare: | |

<u>F</u>older: | transfer |

<u>U</u>ser Name: | |

<u>D</u>omain Name: | |

☐ Add <u>b</u>ookmark

Bookmark <u>n</u>ame: | |

[<u>H</u>elp] [<u>C</u>ancel] [C<u>o</u>nnect]

Figure 10-16. Connecting to a network-shared folder

the computers and folders shown in the righthand pane. Figure 10-17 shows what it will look like.

Unlike other operating systems, Ubuntu doesn't remember network shares between reboots. However, it is possible to create a launcher to reconnect to them. To do this, right-click the desktop and choose Create Launcher. When the window pops up, provide a name for the launcher, and then enter the following in the Command field, where *computer* and *folder* are the names of the computer and folder to which you wish to connect:

```
nautilus smb://computer/folder
```

Then click OK, and you can instantly re-establish a connection by double-clicking the new icon on your desktop. This works by calling up the Nautilus file browser and passing it the details for creating a Samba networking protocol connection. So, in the previous example case, you would enter the command:

```
nautilus smb://iq500/transfer
```

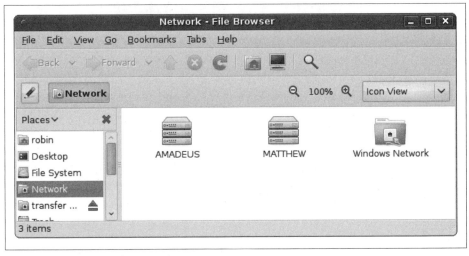

Figure 10-17. Browsing the network

Sharing Your Folders

To share files on your Ubuntu Computer with other systems, you first need to turn on the Sharing service, which is disabled by default. The easiest way to do this is wait until you have something to share, and then right-click its folder and select Sharing Options, as shown in Figure 10-18.

A new window will then pop up with the sharing options available, shown in Figure 10-19.

The first time you click the "Share this folder" checkbox, another window will pop up (see Figure 10-20) informing you that the Sharing service is not yet enabled, and giving you the option to close the window or install the service. So click "Install service," and enter your password when prompted.

Some package files will then be downloaded and installed, which may take a couple of minutes. When the process is complete, you will be prompted to click "Restart session" to continue. So make sure your work is saved, and then click the button. You won't have to repeat this procedure again.

The Folder Sharing window will now change and offer you its options, which you can use to confer creation and deletion capabilities (on top of having read access), and whether guests can access the folder. Once you have decided what to allow, click Create Share.

The first thing you should notice now is that the icon of the folder you have shared has a small emblem at its top right that shows two arrows facing in different directions. This indicates that the folder has been shared and can now be accessed from other computers.

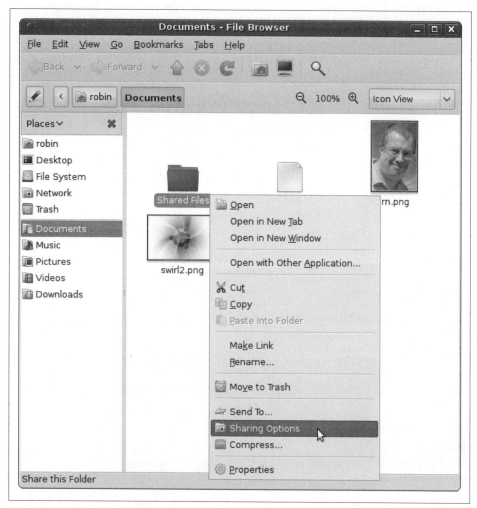

Figure 10-18. Selecting a folder's Sharing options

Sharing folders on other operating systems

Most operating systems, including Windows and OS X, use either the Windows domain protocol or the Samba protocol (which is fully Windows compatible). Therefore, you should be able to refer to your operating system's user documentation to see how to share folders, which generally involves the same steps, regardless of the operating system used by the remote computer.

Figure 10-19. The Folder Sharing window

Figure 10-20. Click "Install service" to enable sharing

Using Keyrings

When working with Ubuntu and network shares, WiFi connections, and so on, you will sometimes be asked for your keyring password. Don't be confused by this. Simply enter your main Ubuntu password.

There's a lot more to the Keyring, though. Ubuntu can remember all your passwords and prompt you just once, the first time you need one of those passwords, to enter your keyring password. The idea is clever in that you can have several passwords for different things, and yet only have to remember one master password. But it's not always clear to new users what is going on. It can also be annoying when you don't actually want to use the keyring feature.

So here's how it works. If you don't want to use the keyring, whenever you are prompted by a keyring request, just press Enter. As long as you haven't already set a keyring password for the particular type of access you want, you shouldn't be prompted again for that item.

Otherwise, if you do want to use the keyring system, think up one password you would like as a master password, and enter that whenever asked for your keyring password. You can then supply the actual passwords just the once for each item. They will then be remembered by Ubuntu, which will prompt only for the keyring password in future, and only once per session.

Managing Your Keyring

You can manage your keyring by selecting Applications → Accessories → Passwords and Encryption Keys. This will bring up a window similar to the one shown in Figure 10-21.

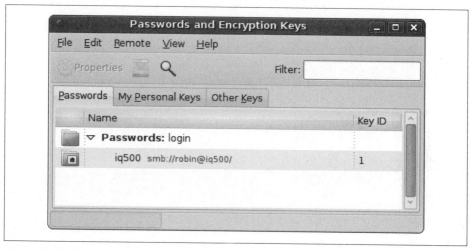

Figure 10-21. The Passwords and Encryption Keys window

Here, you can see there is currently only a single password in use, which is one I created for accessing another computer with the name *iq500*. Instead of having to remember the correct password for the *iq500* computer, I now only have to enter the keyring password.

Should you decide you don't want to use a particular keyring password anymore, you can right-click it and select Delete. You will then have to confirm any prompts you are given, and the key will be removed. If you still have problems, delete the keyring itself (it will normally be called *Passwords: default* or *Passwords: login*). You can then choose an empty password next time you are requested to, and you won't be prompted again.

Summary

This marks the last of the "How to use Ubuntu" chapters. Congratulations—you are now an experienced Ubuntu user! In the remaining chapters, I'll take you through some of the things you can do *with* your new operating system, such as playing games, running Windows programs, working with OpenOffice.org, or, as in the next chapter, using the Internet.

CHAPTER 11

The Internet

One of the computer's biggest functions these days is Internet connectivity, whether for browsing websites, exchanging emails, sending family photos to relatives, making use of free Internet phone calls, using cloud servers for offline storage, or any number of other things.

And Ubuntu is no shirker when it comes to the horsepower needed for some of these tasks. It is light on system resources, leaving plenty of memory and processor power for use by programs such as browsers and instant messengers, and it's fast, so your use of the Internet will be as streamlined as possible.

What's more, Ubuntu comes with all the software you could want to get you up and running, and there's plenty more you can easily install using the Ubuntu Software Center or Synaptic Package Manager. In this chapter, I'll take you through some of the main installed programs, and detail others you might want to add.

Web Browsing

We all use browsers nowadays as if they were extensions of ourselves. Whenever we need the facts about something, we turn to our computers and Google it. Some developers have even written browser operating systems, with which you hardly ever need to leave your browser. And productivity suites such as Google Apps bring cloud computing ever closer.

By default, the browser installed with Ubuntu is Mozilla Firefox (see Figure 11-1). Like most of the other applications in this chapter, you will find the launcher for Firefox in the Applications → Internet menu. It's such an important program that there's also an icon for it on the top status bar.

If you've never used Firefox before (for example, if your previous browser was Microsoft Internet Explorer, which is not available for Linux), then you may find it takes a little getting used to. So here's a brief introduction.

Figure 11-1. The default Firefox home page

The Menus

Most of the menus are very similar to those in other browsers, so I won't go into them in detail. However, a couple of features are in different places, such as the Options menu, which is under Tools → Internet options in Internet Explorer or Tools → Options in other versions of Firefox. But in Ubuntu, you'll find it under Edit → Preferences.

Also, the Check for Updates option in the Help menu of other versions of Firefox is not included on Ubuntu. Instead, you will be informed about new versions either by Firefox itself or by the Update manager.

The Bookmarks Toolbar

In Ubuntu, this toolbar is enabled by default and features three items:

Most Visited
　　A drop-down menu of the pages you frequent the most

Getting Started
　　Takes you to the "Getting started with Firefox" web page

Latest Headlines
　　A drop-down menu of the latest news from the BBC World News website

Tabs and Windows

Firefox supports tabbed windows, which you can open up either by clicking the New Tab button (the + symbol to the right of the existing tabs), by holding down the Ctrl key when clicking on a link to open it in a new tab, or by pressing Ctrl-T. Sometimes the middle scroll button on a mouse will also do this if there is one.

If more tabs are open than can be displayed, the right side of the New Tab button will feature a drop-down list, with which you can jump to any tab.

You can also right-click on the tab bar for additional options, and to open or close tabs. If your mouse has a middle button, you can middle-click on a tab to close it.

You can open new windows by selecting New Window from the File menu or by holding down the Shift key when you click a link. These should be closed by clicking the X button, as with any other window, or by pressing Alt-F4.

Searching

The Google search on the Firefox home page is a great place to start Internet browsing, but if you are already viewing a page and need to look something up, the best thing to do is click on the New Tab icon to open a new window, and then either click the Home button or simply type your search query into the top-right search box. You can also change your search provider by clicking the drop-down menu next to this input field.

Other Browsers

A number of other browsers are available for Ubuntu, of which my favorite alternative is Opera (see Figure 11-2). The Google Chrome browser (available at *http://google.com/chrome/*) also looks very promising and should be out of beta test sometime in 2010.

To install Opera using Firefox, visit the following page, check the version required, and click Download Opera:

> *http://www.opera.com/download/index.dml?platform=linux*

This type of installation is a special case. Normally you use the official repositories to install programs. However, Opera is not among the repository entries, and rather than going to the trouble of adding the Opera repository and then using Synaptic, it is sometimes much easier to simply provide the location of a downloadable *.deb* package where available, as in this case.

Figure 11-2. The Opera browser is a good alternative to Firefox

When Firefox asks you what to do with the file, select "Open with GDebi Package Installer" and click OK. After the download is complete, click the Install Package button, enter your password, and wait for the installation to finish. Opera will now show up as an entry in the Applications → Internet menu.

Email

The default Ubuntu email program is Evolution Mail (see Figure 11-3), which you can access from the Applications → Internet menu or by clicking the envelope icon in the top status bar.

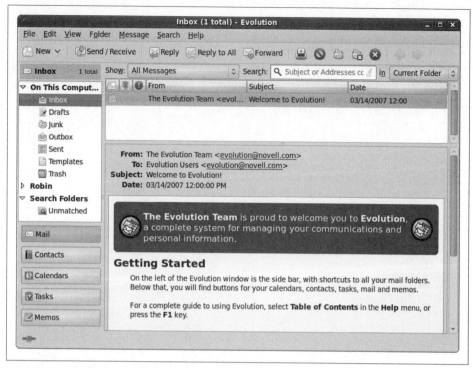

Figure 11-3. The Evolution Mail application

The first time you use Evolution you'll need to set up one or more email accounts. So after you've read the Welcome screen, click the Forward button to get to the Restore screen.

So far you won't have made a backup, so there is nothing to restore. But once you start using Evolution, it's a good idea to make backups from time to time, and if you do, this is where you can restore them. You can, at this point, restore a backup made on another computer if you wish. Otherwise, click the Forward button.

On the next screen, you should enter your full name and email address on the top two lines, and (optionally) your reply-to email address and organization name (see Figure 11-4).

You can also uncheck the box "Make this my default account" if you don't want it to be the default. Click Forward when you are ready to go to the screen for setting up the collection of email, shown in Figure 11-5.

If in doubt on what to select for this screen, try the default IMAP option for Server Type. Other options you can select by clicking the pull-down list include Microsoft Exchange, Novell GroupWise, POP, Usenet News, Local Delivery, and more.

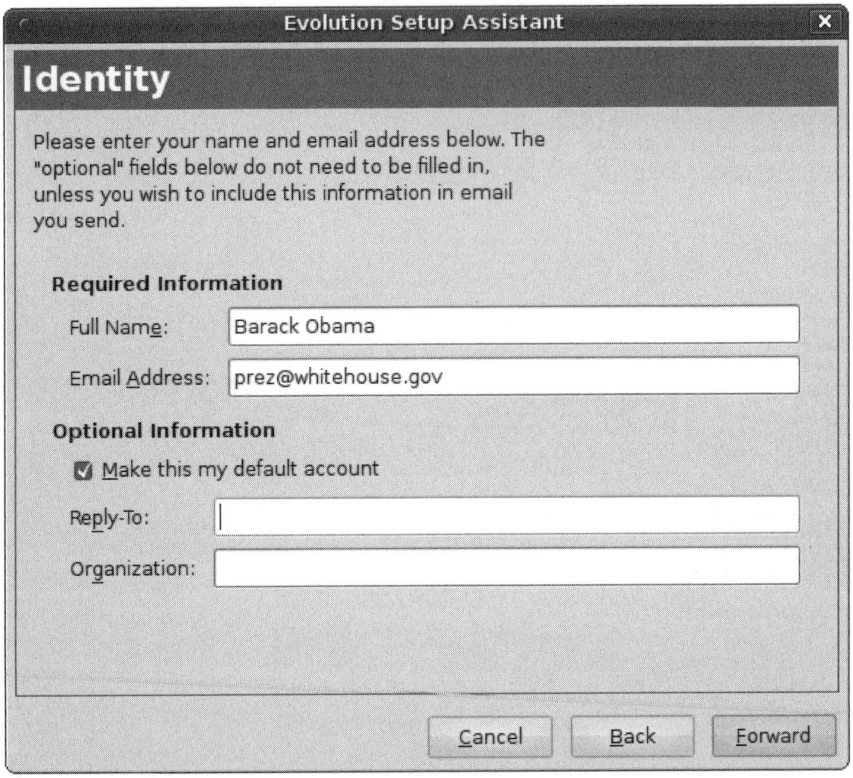

Figure 11-4. Enter your name and email address

You need to then enter the domain name of your email server and the username you are known by on that server. Normally, the username will be the same as the first half of your email address, the part before the @ character.

You can also enable a secure connection at this point, choose authentication types, and configure Evolution to remember your password. If you do the latter, you will be prompted for your password only the first time it is needed. When you are finished, click Forward to call up the Receiving Options screen (see Figure 11-6).

This screen lets you choose whether and how often to check for new messages. If you don't check any of the options on this screen, you will have to click a button whenever you want to see if you have any new messages.

Using this screen, you can also enter custom commands the mail server may require, designate mail folders to view or check for messages, and choose whether and how to apply filters, such as checking for junk messages. When you are ready, click Forward to go to the Sending Email screen (see Figure 11-7).

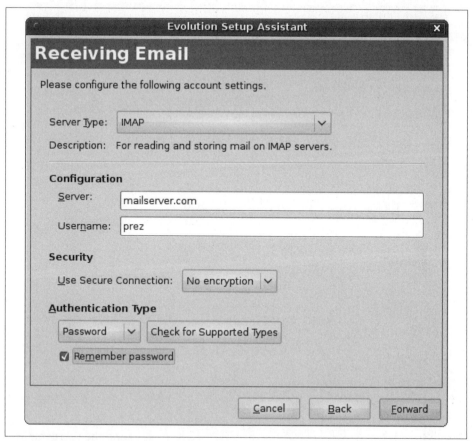

Figure 11-5. Configuring the receiving of email

On this screen you can choose between SMTP and Sendmail for Server Type, and set a different server for sending email if necessary. If the same server does both sending and receiving, leave the default name as is.

If the server requires authentication, click the box, and then tell Evolution whether to use a secure connection. When you are ready, click Forward to enter the Account Management screen, shown in Figure 11-8.

On this screen you can choose the default name supplied, which will be your email address. But if you would like to name the account differently, you are free to do so. When done, click the Forward button to go to the congratulations message, and then click Apply to finish. Evolution will then open up, with a welcome message waiting for you in the inbox that you can click to view.

The menus and icons used by the program are pretty self-explanatory, but to get you going, just click the Send/Receive button to make your first email collection, and any

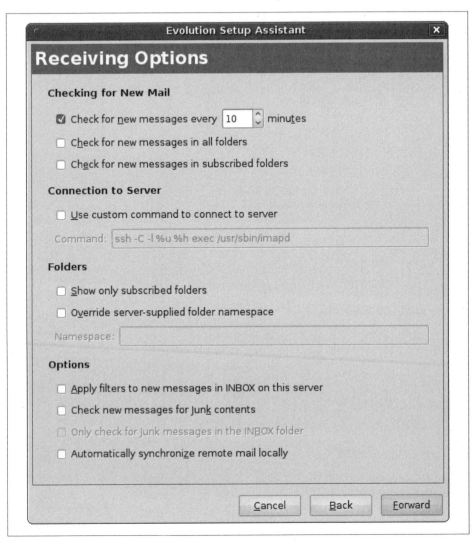

Figure 11-6. Setting the various receive options

emails waiting for you on the server will then be fetched. To write a new message, click the New button, to reply to a message click Reply, and so on. For further details on using the program, select Help → Contents from Evolution's menus.

Instant Messaging

Since version 9.10 (named Karmic Koala), Ubuntu's default instant messaging (IM) client is Empathy, but I have found it to be rather buggy. For example, it doesn't check

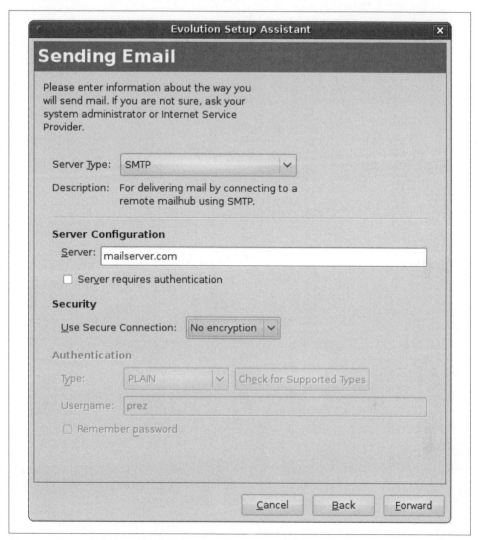

Figure 11-7. *Configuring email sending options*

whether a new account has been created properly or whether an existing one has been entered successfully, error reporting is minimal, and there appears to be no means of removing accounts once they are created. There's also a lot more besides that just doesn't work right or seems incomplete, but if you're curious, try it for yourself—some people really rave about it.

Until these issues are resolved I recommend you use Pidgin, the previous default IM program that used to be included with Ubuntu but was unceremoniously dropped— and not even installed alongside Empathy to allow for continuity.

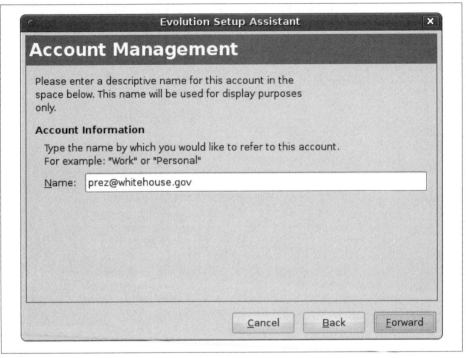

Figure 11-8. Give your email account an identifying name

Therefore, you'll need to install the program by visiting the Ubuntu Software Center and entering "pidgin" in the search field. Then, double-click Pidgin Internet Messenger, click the Install button, and enter your password when prompted to do so, and the program will be downloaded and installed.

While using the Software Center, if you wish you can also remove Empathy from your PC to save resources by clicking Installed Software in the lefthand pane and entering "empathy" in the search field to bring up the Uninstall button.

 If you upgraded from a version of Ubuntu earlier than 9.10 and already had Pidgin installed, you shouldn't need to install it again, because it will have been left in place. However, you still might want to uninstall Empathy if you don't plan on using it.

Using Pidgin

Once installed, you can run Pidgin by selecting Applications → Internet → Pidgin Instant Messenger, or click the envelope icon on the top status bar. The first time you use it, a welcome screen will be displayed, in which you should click the Add button to bring up the Add Account window shown in Figure 11-9.

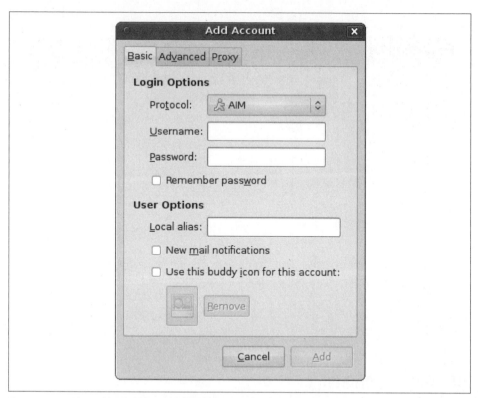

Figure 11-9. The Pidgin Add Account window

Here, you can click the Protocol drop-down list to select any of 17 different IM services, so your favorites are sure to be supported. Then enter your username and password for that service, check "Remember password" if you'd like it saved, and configure any of the User Options that you'd like. The "Local alias" is just a name you'll see for yourself in Pidgin; it isn't displayed to the people you communicate with. If you need them, various advanced and proxy settings can also be managed via the tabs at the top of the window.

When you've finished entering your IM account details, you can add other accounts by clicking the Add button, or click Close to finish.

Adding buddies

You're now ready to start adding your buddies to your Buddy List, which may be minimized to the bottom status bar. Once you've called it up, the window will look like Figure 11-10, in which I have already added one buddy.

Figure 11-10. The Pidgin Buddy List

Using Pidgin is simplicity itself, and if you've used any other IM program, you'll be right at home with it. To add a buddy, click Buddies followed by Add Buddy; to join a chat, click Buddies followed by Join a Chat; and so on. And, once you have buddies listed, you can also right-click them to call up an extensive menu of options.

All that's left for you now is to start communicating.

Internet Telephony

Ekiga Softphone used to be Ubuntu's default Voice Over Internet Protocol (VOIP) application, but it is no longer included by default. However, you can still install it from the Ubuntu Software Center if you'd like to try it out. Instead, the Empathy program is intended to be the replacement VOIP program, but for reasons previously stated, I would not recommend it.

Therefore, I suggest going with the most popular program in place of Empathy, and that means Skype, although you won't find it in either the Software Center or the Synaptic Package Manager because it is proprietary software. Instead, you need to visit *http://skype.com/download* in your browser and then click the version you would like to download, either 32-bit or 64-bit.

The latest version may be a couple behind the current version of Ubuntu, but it will still run just fine. After downloading, open your *Downloads* folder and double-click the downloaded file to call up the Package Installer (unless you set the download facility to automatically do so). When it opens, click Install Package, and after entering your password, the program will be installed. When installation finishes, click the Close button and exit the Package Installer.

You will now be able to run Skype from the Applications → Internet menu, and the first time you do so you must select your language and accept the license agreement. You will then be ready to enter your Skype name and password (see Figure 11-11).

Figure 11-11. Skype asks for your details the first time it runs

If you don't have a Skype name, click "Don't have a Skype Name yet?" and you'll be taken through the free signup process. Otherwise, using the program is the same as on any other platform, and that includes video support, so you'll be right at home.

 When Skype is running, an icon will be displayed in the top status bar that you can click to call up the Buddy List, or right-click to change your status and configure other settings.

Peer-to-Peer File Sharing

In case you haven't come across them yet, peer-to-peer (P2P) programs are ones that allow computers all over the world to connect with each other and exchange files.

With P2P you can add a data file to your local file-sharing client (known as seeding), and its details will then be passed to the tracker servers that you choose. Using these servers, other users can then discover the file and start to download it from you.

If more than one user wants the file, they will all fetch different parts of it from your computer and then exchange the various pieces they get with each other, which means you don't have to serve up the entire file for every downloader—keeping your bandwidth usage to the minimum.

 When large files such as the Ubuntu operating system ISO images are released, rather than consuming all of the available bandwidth at *http: //ubuntu.com*, they are also listed on file-sharing trackers so that the images can be downloaded using P2P clients that share the required bandwidth between all downloaders (because they are also all uploaders, too).

Probably one of the best-known P2P file-sharing programs is BitTorrent, which you can access by selecting Applications → Internet → Transmission BitTorrent Client. But the most common way to call it up is by clicking a link to a *torrent* file.

The easiest way to find torrents is to use a search engine with a query that includes the word "torrent." When you have located one that you want, click it and your browser should prompt you to open the torrent using the Transmission BitTorrent Client. Click OK to accept, and the Torrent Options window, shown in Figure 11-12, will open up.

Using this window, you can check that you have selected the right file, choose the download folder, and if the torrent is made up of separate files, opt out of downloading any files you don't need. When you are ready, click Add to start the process.

The program's main window will then be displayed, showing the torrents you have in your folder and their status. For example, you may have some torrents you previously downloaded but are leaving in place to seed for other users to download. This is a great way of paying back the community for all the bandwidth you benefited from during the download. You will also see the most recent torrent you selected, as shown in Figure 11-13, in which an Ubuntu ISO is being downloaded from 36 out of a possible 52 different locations.

 Some broadband providers throttle torrent bandwidth at certain times of day, which is the case in Figure 11-13, where it is running at only 31.4 KB/s. This is because I started the download during a peak usage period. If that happens to you, you may find that times before 6 p.m. and after midnight are better for downloading large files.

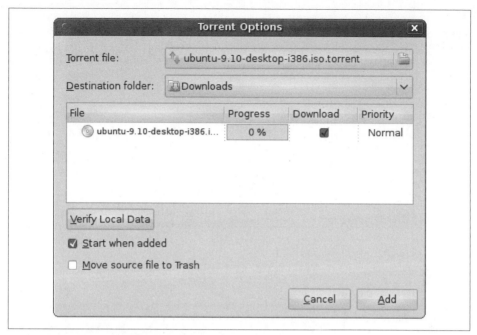

Figure 11-12. The Torrent Options window

Telnet and SSH

Sometimes you need to log directly into a command-line shell on a remote computer, and the best way to do this is via Telnet or SSH (Secure Shell). SSH is far preferable because it's secure, whereas Telnet isn't, although on a local network behind a suitable firewall Telnet is perfectly OK.

The best program I have seen for performing these functions is the PuTTY application, which you can install from the Ubuntu Software Center by entering "putty" in the search field and then double-clicking Putty SSH Client, followed by clicking Install on the following screen. After entering your password, the program will be downloaded and installed, and will become available under the Applications → Internet menu. When you first run PuTTY, it will look like Figure 11-14.

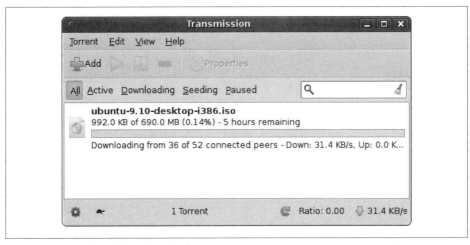

Figure 11-13. A torrent being downloaded

Figure 11-14. The PuTTY main screen

To connect to a remote computer, enter its IP address or domain name in the Host Name field, and choose the kind of connection from the radio buttons underneath—by default this will be SSH. You can, if you wish, enter a session name in the Saved Sessions field and click the Save button to store those details for future use. After choosing the window behavior on exit (from the "Close window on exit" section), click the Open button to establish a connection.

Once connected, a new window will open like the one shown in Figure 11-15, in which I have logged into a web server on which I keep my websites.

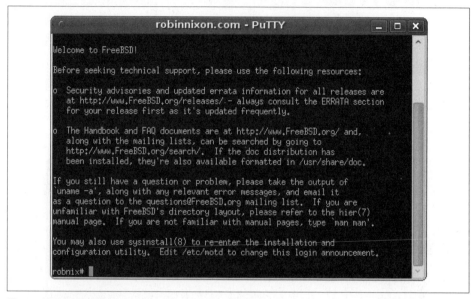

Figure 11-15. An SSH connection has been established

Ubuntu One

Ubuntu One is a new service from Canonical, the publishers of Ubuntu, that provides you with 2 GB of free offline, or cloud, storage for backing up and transferring your files. If this free storage isn't enough for you, you can also upgrade to a much larger 50 GB of space for a monthly fee.

Joining and Logging In

To get started with Ubuntu One, select Applications → Internet → Ubuntu One. The first time you do so, you'll be taken to the Launchpad Login Service page shown in Figure 11-16.

Here, you can use a previous Launchpad login (if you have one) or create a new account. Either way, enter a valid email address first, and then click Continue.

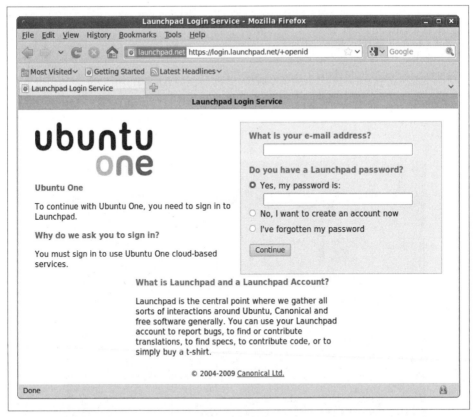

Figure 11-16. The Launchpad Login Service

If you are creating an account, a confirmation email will be sent to the address you gave, giving you a link you should follow. You will then be taken to a web page where you can choose your Display Name and decide whether to hide your email address. Then enter a password twice and click the Continue button.

Once you have created an account, you can simply enter your email address and password at the Login Service screen and click Continue. If a computer is new to Ubuntu One, you will be asked whether to add the computer you are using to your Ubuntu One account, so click Subscribe and then Add This Computer.

Using Ubuntu One

Once you have created an account, you will see a new icon in the top status bar that looks like a cloud, depicting Ubuntu One as what is known as a cloud service. You can connect to the service by clicking the icon and selecting Connect.

If you wish to view your Ubuntu One account's folders and files, you can right-click the cloud icon and select "Go to Web," which will open up a screen similar to Figure 11-17 in your browser.

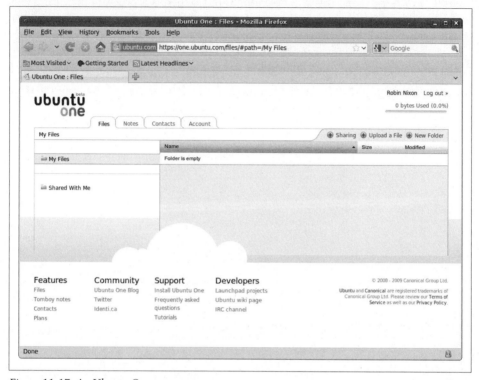

Figure 11-17. An Ubuntu One user page

You can also copy files into and out of your Ubuntu One folder, which is under your home folder and is also available by selecting Places → Ubuntu One. Any files that you copy into the folder will be uploaded to the remote cloud storage (up to your allowance limit). And any files you copy from that folder will be downloaded from the cloud storage.

You can learn about a number of other Ubuntu One features, such as sharing files with friends and colleagues, via the following link:

https://wiki.ubuntu.com/UbuntuOne/Tutorials

Summary

This chapter covered a number of things that you can do over the Internet using Ubuntu. For most users, this will be enough. But if there's a program or feature you want that I haven't mentioned, you will almost certainly be able to find it (or another program that provides a reasonable approximation of the feature) by searching either the Synaptic Package Manger or the Ubuntu Software Center.

One of the best examples of the power and capability of open source software is the OpenOffice.org productivity suite of programs, which we'll take a look at in the next chapter.

CHAPTER 12

Using OpenOffice.org

One of the great things about Ubuntu is that it comes with a wide range of ready-to-use software. And one of the best of these is the OpenOffice.org productivity suite, which comprises all the major applications you find in other office suites, such as Microsoft Office.

Not only do you get a word processor, spreadsheet, and presentation maker, Open-Office.org also includes a drawing application, a database program, and a utility for creating mathematical formulas.

What's more, OpenOffice.org can read and write files in many formats, including Microsoft's familiar *.xls*, *.doc*, and *.ppt*, and it can even export PDF files. This means you can share and collaborate on documents with users of other operating systems and office suites. And like Ubuntu, OpenOffice.org is a free program with no purchase, upgrade, or license fees to pay, eliminating both up-front and ongoing costs.

Preparing the Example Files

You will recall from earlier chapters that your home folder contains an *Examples* folder with several example documents. Actually, *Examples* is a shortcut that points to the folder */usr/share/example-content*, and all the files in it were created by the user *root*. This means that they can be read but not edited or saved. You'll be able to tell this when you open a file because the title bar at the top will say "(read-only)" next to the name of the document, and you won't be able to add or change anything.

So if you want to try out the various OpenOffice.org programs and modify the examples, you will need to make the files writable by opening the Terminal and copying the folder of examples to your desktop with the following command:

```
cp -r /usr/share/example-content ~/Desktop
```

This will create a new folder on your desktop called *example-content*, in which all the example files can be read from and written to. It also means the original example files will remain untouched, should you wish to refer back to them.

Writer

The OpenOffice.org word processor is a fast and easy-to-use application called Writer, and it's packed with every conceivable feature you could need. To run it, you can select Applications → Office → OpenOffice.org Word Processor or double-click any file that's associated with it, such as those with the extension *.odt* (the standard format used by OpenOffice.org and other free programs) or *.doc*. For example, Figure 12-1 shows the result of opening the file *Welcome_to_Ubuntu.odt* from within the *example-content* folder you just copied to your desktop.

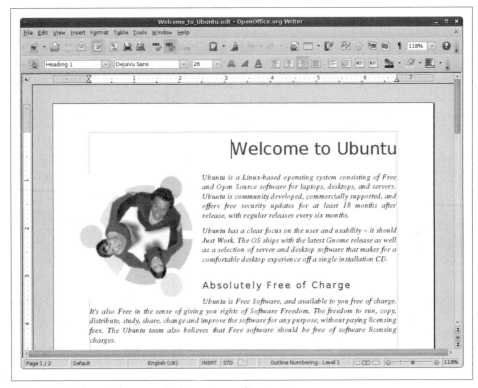

Figure 12-1. Editing a document in the Writer application

 Although Writer can handle Microsoft Word files (like all parts of the OpenOffice.org suite), files with some complicated formatting elements do strange things if you move between Writer and Word. These problems are unpredictable and can range from strange page layouts to missing text. That said, different versions of OpenOffice.org are much more compatible than different versions of Word, which often have difficulty with files from Word running on other systems.

If you have used any popular word processing package, you should find that Writer is very easy to learn, as it follows a lot of standard conventions. For example, the menus at the top are logical, and just browsing through them you'll be able to find many of the features you need.

And, of course, there's always the Help menu, which contains complete descriptions of all the features, along with a comprehensive index of topics.

This book doesn't have room for a tutorial on using the word processor, but to get you started I'll show you a few things, such as the Standard and Formatting toolbars, which are directly underneath the menus.

The Standard Toolbar

Figure 12-2 shows the left half of the Standard toolbar, which contains buttons for main features such as loading, saving, and printing files, and so on.

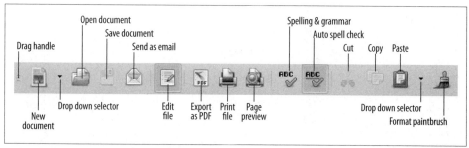

Figure 12-2. The left half of the Standard toolbar

The first small icon, made up of three horizontal lines, is the drag handle, which you can use to drag and drop the bar elsewhere within the program's window. If you drag it to any of the four window edges, it will align with that edge, and if you drop it elsewhere it will be released from the main window so that you can move it to anywhere you like on your desktop.

The next icon, which looks like a printed page, is for creating new documents. By default, a new word processor document will be started, or you can click the downward-pointing triangle next to it to select from the many other types of documents supported by OpenOffice.org.

After that comes the Open button (which looks like a document in a folder), the Save button (which looks like a 3.5" disk and is highlighted only when there are changes to be saved), and the E-mail button (for sending the current document as an email attachment using the default email client).

Next, standing off on its own between two separators, is the Edit file button, which toggles between edit and read-only modes. When you open a read-only document and click this button, you can then edit the document if you have sufficient privileges or will be offered the option of editing a copy of the document. Or if you click the button while editing a document, you can place it into a read-only (or preview) mode (see Figure 12-3). In this mode the document becomes read-only, and items you cannot use, such as the Formatting toolbar, are hidden.

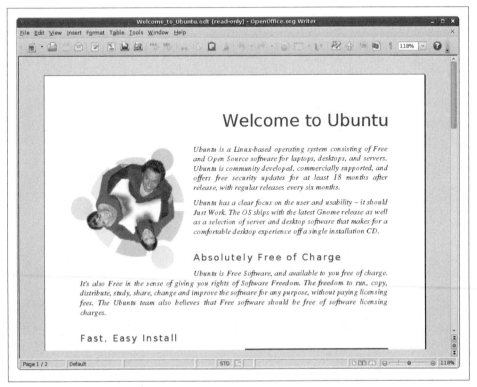

Figure 12-3. In Preview mode, the Rulers and Formatting toolbar are removed

The next three buttons are for outputting a document as a Portable Document Format (PDF) file, to a printer, or in Print Preview mode, which will show more than one page at a time if there's enough space.

The two following buttons let you spellcheck a document interactively and enable automatic spellchecking as you type, respectively. If the latter is enabled, any unrecognized words will be underlined with a wavy line.

The next three buttons are for cutting, copying, and pasting, and are grayed out when they can't be used (for example, if there is no highlighted text to cut or copy, or there is nothing in the clipboard for pasting). The final button, which looks like a paintbrush, allows you to paint a formatting style in the document by dragging the mouse over the portion to transform.

The right half of the Standard toolbar is shown in Figure 12-4, and starts with two curved arrows that provide undo and redo functionality. In lower resolutions or in a

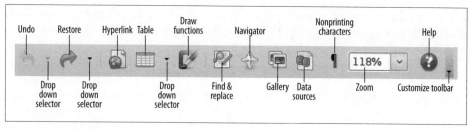

Figure 12-4. The right half of the Standard toolbar

nonmaximized window, you may not see all these icons at once, but you can call up any hidden ones by clicking the >> icon that will appear on the far right of the toolbar.

The next two icons, in turn looking like the world on a document and a spreadsheet, let you insert hyperlinks and tables. The next icon, which looks like a paintbrush drawing a rounded corner, calls up the drawing functions toolbar.

After these, the button that looks like a magnifying glass calls up a search (and optional replace) dialog, the four-pointed star brings up a handy navigator for moving throughout a document, and the button that looks like two photographs brings up a toolbar of graphic images.

The button following the photographs is for managing your data sources, and the one with a ¶ symbol toggles the display of nonprinting characters. The final two main buttons let you change the zoom level of the document and call up the help pages, respectively.

At the far right of the toolbar there's a downward-pointing triangle you can use to customize the toolbar by adding and removing buttons or locking it in place.

The Formatting Toolbar

The other main toolbar you'll use in Writer is the Formatting toolbar, the left half of which is shown in Figure 12-5.

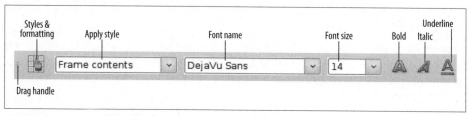

Figure 12-5. The left half of the Formatting toolbar

This part of the Formatting toolbar starts with another drag handle for moving the toolbar about. It works in exactly the same way as the Standard toolbar. After this, a button that looks like a finger pointing to a cell in a table brings up the Styles and formatting menu.

The rest of this part of the toolbar deals with the style, font name, and font size of text, and the three letter A buttons at the end are for toggling the use of bold, italic, and underlined text.

Figure 12-6 shows the other half of the toolbar.

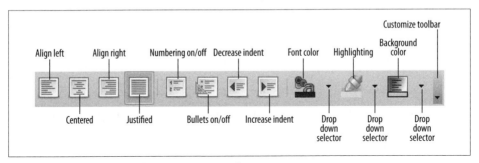

Figure 12-6. The right half of the Formatting toolbar

The first four buttons in this half of the toolbar let you select left, centered, right, and full justification. The next two buttons turn numbering and bullets on and off, and the ones after those, with left- and right-pointing triangles, are for decreasing and increasing indents.

The multicolored button with several letters on it changes the color of a font. Clicking the button directly changes selected text to the currently selected color, which you can further change to another color by clicking the downward-pointing triangle to the button's right. The next button, which looks like a highlighter pen, works in the same way but alters the highlighting, and the final main button also works in the same way but controls the background color.

Again, at the end there's a button with a downward-pointing triangle with which you can customize the toolbar.

Using Styles

Although you can create your document's various styles as you go along by pushing buttons for indentation, bullets, and so on, you may find it much easier to apply styles instead, which will change the look of a feature (such as a bulleted list) throughout an entire document.

To create or edit a style, select an area of text, and then click the Styles and Formatting button in the Formatting toolbar. A menu will appear in which you can select the type of style (out of character, paragraph, frame, page, and list).

You can then right-click a style to modify it, or click the "New style from selection" button (at the top right) to create a new one. Or you can simply double-click a style of your choice to apply it to the selection. Your most recently used styles are displayed in a drop-down menu next to the Styles and Formatting button so you can easily apply them.

About Word Completion

There's a clever feature in Writer that can help you auto-complete words you frequently use. Enabled by default, it's called Word Completion, and it can help experienced users be more productive. However, many people find this feature intrusive and annoying, particularly when learning the ins and outs of Writer.

If you feel the same way, you can disable Word Completion by selecting Tools → AutoCorrect Options, and then click the Word Completion tab. Finally, uncheck "Enable word completion," and the feature will be turned off. Or if you prefer, you can set Word Completion to accept the Tab key instead of Enter (matching the Nick Completion setting of the Pidgin program). To do this, click the "Accept with" drop-down menu in the AutoCorrect settings window, and then select Tab.

Calc

The OpenOffice.org spreadsheet program is called Calc, and you'll find it works in much the same way as other major spreadsheets, such as Microsoft Excel. As with Writer, there's not enough room in this book to teach you how to use the program, but I at least can get you up and running by pointing out where the main options are.

To try out the Calc program, you can double-click the spreadsheet file *Payment_schedule.ods* in the *example-content* folder of your desktop, as shown in Figure 12-7.

The Standard Toolbar

The first thing you should notice is that the Standard and Formatting toolbars are quite similar to those in Writer, so I don't need to explain them to you again in detail. This is the great thing about the integrated suite; the look and feel and functionality transfer between the various parts. Once you've learned one of the programs, you already know most of the other parts, too.

However, a few of the buttons do work slightly differently from their effects in text documents, and there are a couple of additional or replacement buttons as well, as shown in Figure 12-8.

So, for example, in the Standard toolbar the Table button in Writer is now replaced with two buttons in Calc that feature the letters A and Z, which are for sorting in either ascending or descending order, respectively. There is also a new button that looks like a pie chart and calls up the Chart Wizard (see Figure 12-9), and the nonprinting characters button is removed, as it's not applicable to spreadsheets.

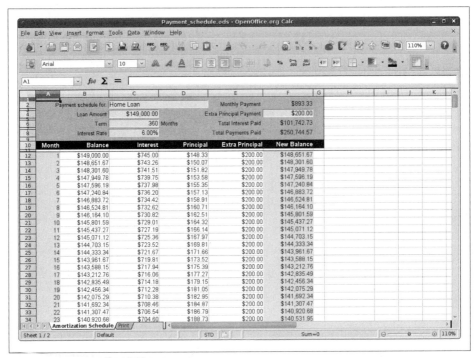

Figure 12-7. Editing a spreadsheet in Calc

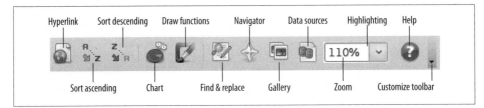

Figure 12-8. The righthand icons are slightly different in Calc than they are in Writer

The Formatting Toolbar

In the left half of the Formatting toolbar, the style field has been removed, but styles can still be selected by clicking the very first button, which calls up the Style and Formatting menu, so there's not a lot of change there.

However, there are a few differences in the right half, as shown in Figure 12-10.

The first icon in the right half of the Formatting toolbar is for merging and centering cells. The next four buttons, starting with a pile of coins, select the number format, with the choices being currency, percent, adding a decimal place, and deleting a decimal place (which automatically rounds a fraction to the nearest whole number).

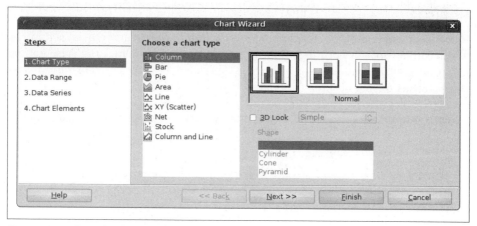

Figure 12-9. The Calc Chart Wizard

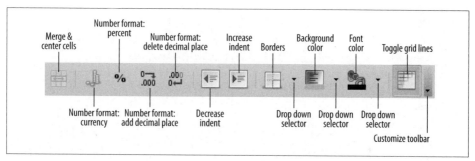

Figure 12-10. There are several differences in the right half of the Formatting toolbar

After the decrease and increase indent buttons, which are the same as in Writer, there's a new button for placing borders around cells. The very last main button toggles the display of grid lines.

Viewing and setting data types

As well as using the Formatting toolbar buttons to change the data type of a cell or selection, when a highlighted section of a spreadsheet contains the same type of data, that information will be highlighted in the Formatting toolbar. For example, if a cell contains currency data and you click within it, the currency button will be highlighted. The same goes for a selected group of cells containing currency data, or even whole (or multiple) columns.

And if the highlighted cells contain percent data, that will be highlighted, and so on. By right-clicking the toolbar and selecting Visible Buttons, you can also add more Number Format buttons, since there are seven types available.

Impress

OpenOffice.org is also great for creating presentations. The program to use is Impress, which you can open by selecting Applications → Office → OpenOffice.org Presentation. Or you can call up a presentation file such as *Presenting_Ubuntu.odp* from the *example-content* folder of your desktop (see Figure 12-11).

Figure 12-11. Editing a presentation in Impress

The Standard Toolbar

The functions in the Standard toolbar are mostly the same as the rest of the suite, but a new Presentation toolbar is available to its right, as shown in Figure 12-12.

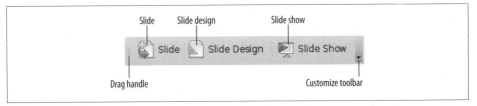

Figure 12-12. The Presentation toolbar

There are three buttons in the toolbar, the first of which inserts a new slide in the current location with the currently selected slide design. The second calls up the Slide design window for selecting other designs, and the third button starts a presentation slide show.

The Line and Filling Toolbar

Instead of placing the Formatting toolbar underneath the Standard toolbar, Impress gives you the Line and Filling toolbar, which looks like Figure 12-13.

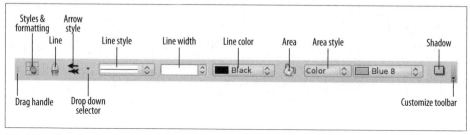

Figure 12-13. The Line and Filling toolbar

After the grab handle, the next button is the familiar Style and Formatting button, followed by the Line button, which calls up a window with which to select a line style. Following that is the Arrow style button, which is a drop-down menu. After that come the Line style, Line width, and Line color drop-down fields.

The next button, which looks like a can of paint, is the Area button for handling a wide range of area fills, followed by the area Color and Styling fields. Finally, the button with a shadowed rectangle represents toggling shadows on or off. Like all the other toolbars, you can customize this one by clicking the downward-pointing triangle at the far right.

A mini toolbar, called the Slide Sorter, is placed to the right. Its two buttons either select objects or start a slide show. Underneath the toolbars, the Impress program is divided into three main frames: Slides, Workspace, and Tasks.

The Slides Frame

This frame contains a scrollable view of all the slides in a presentation. You can use the scroll bar or middle mouse wheel to move backward and forward through the stack of slides and click one to display it in the center frame.

The Workspace Frame

This is where you do all of your slide designing and editing. Every object in a slide is smart so that clicking on it will call up the correct toolbars for editing it above the frame, including some toolbars I haven't detailed.

Right-clicking an object element will also bring up a context-sensitive menu with additional options.

The Tasks Frame

This frame features a variety of tasks, such as Layouts, Table Design, and so on. Click one of the headings to expand its contents, which are then selectable. Just as with toolbars, you can drag and drop this and other frames into the main window, after which you can then leave it floating over your content or move it out and onto your main Ubuntu desktop.

The Drawing Toolbar

Underneath these frames is the Drawing toolbar, which provides a range of shapes, lines, fonts, and many other tools with which you can fully customize your presentations to their best effect.

The Master Slide

One way to develop slides is to lay out the first one exactly the way you want it, including font, size, layout of elements, and so on, and just duplicate it over and over, changing what you want on each slide.

However, every presentation has a master slide that can be used as the default for slides in the presentation. You view the master by selecting View → Master → Slide Master, which opens up the master view, in which only that slide is edited. Now you can edit the header, footer, background, and any other constant features to use throughout a presentation.

Every new slide you make will then have these attributes. When you have finished editing the master, click Close Master View in the Master View toolbar.

Draw

OpenOffice.org comes with a powerful drawing program called Draw, which you can open by selecting Applications → Graphics → OpenOffice.org Drawing. Figure 12-14 shows the program editing a photo from the *example-content* folder.

Describing the features available in the different OpenOffice.org modules becomes easier with each one. For example, Draw has many of the same toolbars as Impress, and its drawing features work in the same way.

The program has powerful style and formatting features, 2D and 3D object rotation, photorealistic rendering, smart connectors for creating charts, and much more. The best way to find out what it can do for you is to play with it.

Figure 12-14. The OpenOffice.org Draw program

The Draw program will save only file types that can be read by Open-Office.org programs, so it's not suitable for creating images for use in other programs. But there's always the GIMP image editor (the Ubuntu equivalent of Photoshop), the F-Spot photo manager, and the XSane image scanner (or the more user friendly Simple Scan if you are using Ubuntu 10.04), all of which are available from the Applications → Graphics menu in Ubuntu 9.10. So, if OpenOffice.org's Draw doesn't have exactly the features you want, one or more of the other programs probably will.

Base

The Base database program started off as added functionality for the other OpenOffice.org applications, but eventually evolved into a powerful database application in its own right.

Ubuntu doesn't install the program by default, but you can easily install it yourself by going to the Ubuntu Software Center and entering "openoffice" in the search field, as shown in Figure 12-15.

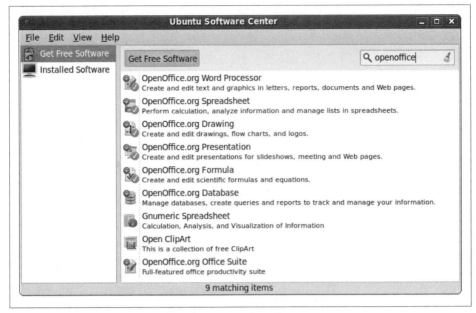

Figure 12-15. Install OpenOffice.org Database via the Software Center

You will see that the other parts of the suite have a checkmark on their icons, indicating that they are installed, but the sixth entry doesn't. This is the one you want, so double-click it, and then click the Install button on the following screen. After entering your password, the program will be downloaded and installed. When finished, it will be accessible from the Applications → Office menu.

When you run Base you'll be prompted to either create a new database or open an existing one (or you can connect to an existing database connection). Once you have chosen what to do, you'll be taken to the main screen, as shown in Figure 12-16.

In Base you can use a variety of tools for inserting or editing data, ranging from handy wizards for creating tables, queries, forms, and reports, to a powerful design view interface for entering data.

Whether you simply want to catalogue your CD collection or need to produce monthly departmental sales reports, Base has the features you need. It's also extremely fast, even with large databases.

Math

The OpenOffice.org Math program helps you to create advanced mathematical formulas, using the right symbols properly aligned in the correct places. It comes preinstalled with Ubuntu, but for some reason its menu option has been set to hidden.

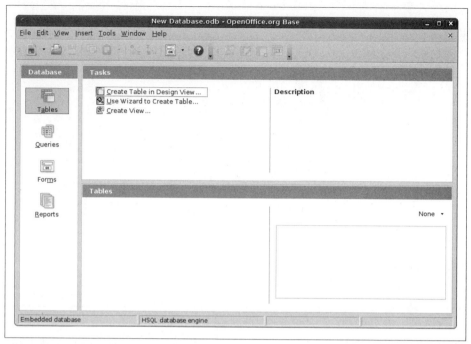

Figure 12-16. The OpenOffice.org Base main screen

You can access it either by opening any other OpenOffice.org application and then selecting File → New → Formula or by right-clicking on the top-left Ubuntu menus and selecting Edit Menus to bring up the menu editor, as shown in Figure 12-17. In the menu editor, select Office in the lefthand pane to open the Office menu in the righthand one. Then, after you check the box next to OpenOffice.org Formula and click Close, the program will become available from the Applications → Office menu.

Using Math, there are three main ways of entering a formula. You can type markup directly into the equation editor, right-click on the equation editor and select the symbol from the context menu, or select a symbol from the Selection toolbox.

Figure 12-18 shows an equation that has been entered as text into the equation editor, with its corresponding formula displayed in the top pane.

Built-in Help

If you can't figure out what an OpenOffice.org button does, select Help → What's This from the program's menus, and then hover your mouse over it to be shown a brief description of its function.

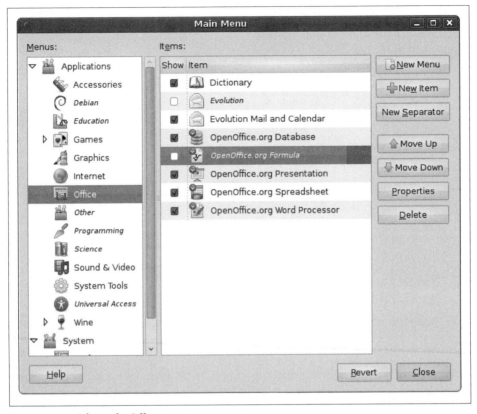

Figure 12-17. Editing the Office menu

Evolution Calendar

Although not a part of the OpenOffice.org suite, don't forget that you can always click the date at the right of the top desktop status bar to pull up a calendar. From here, you can then double-click any date to enter the Evolution Calendars program, which features appointments, reminders, contacts, memos, and more (including subscribing to other calendars and publishing your schedule), as shown in Figure 12-19.

What's New in 10.04?

As Ubuntu has grown in size, due to new features being constantly added, not everything the developers would like can fit on a 700 MB CD-ROM. Therefore, for each release decisions have to be made about what to include. As you've already discovered in this chapter, a couple of releases ago the Base program was dropped from the CD, and for 10.04 it's the GIMP program's turn.

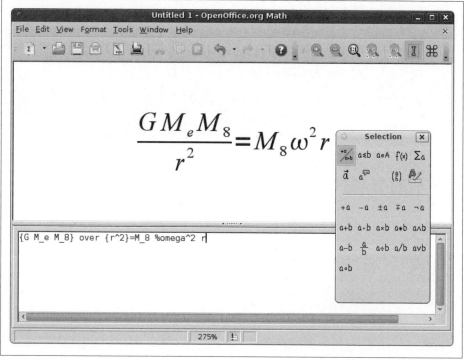

Figure 12-18. Creating formulas is easy with OpenOffice.org Math

Both applications remain in the Ubuntu repositories, are easy to install with the Ubuntu Software Center, and remain under development. But they are not used as much as the other bundled programs, so they have made way for other features that will be used by more users to be installed by default.

Therefore, seeing as this book went to press before the final release of 10.04, it is possible that other parts of OpenOffice.org may have been moved off the installation ISO file. If this is the case, remember that you can always install them from Synaptic or the Ubuntu Software Center.

Summary

The OpenOffice.org suite is a powerful match for any other commercial suite. Because it's open source, and therefore under continuous development by a wide range of programmers, bugs are fixed, features are added, and updates are released much more frequently than the every three years or so of other suites. In fact, since 2006 there have been at least four updates to the suite each year. Because of this, it has the solid support of millions of users all over the world, and you can be sure that your time spent learning OpenOffice.org will be well invested.

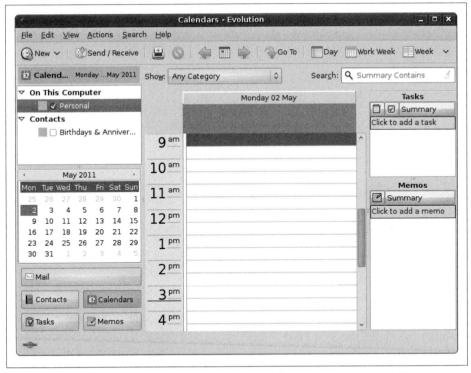

Figure 12-19. The Evolution Calendars program is the perfect companion to OpenOffice.org

Now that you have the office applications under your belt, in the next chapter, we'll take things a little easier and look at the world of Ubuntu gaming.

CHAPTER 13

Playing Games

Although Windows and OS X computers make up about 99% of desktop operating systems, there is still a vast amount of software available for Linux, and games are no exception. The reason for this may be that historically Linux users have tended to be programmers, so they would naturally want to port the games they write to Linux.

But Linux is also a very powerful OS with the ability to emulate other operating systems at virtually full speed. This means that a large number of Windows-only games can now be played on Linux.

In other words, just because you use Ubuntu, it doesn't mean that you'll be missing out on great software, as I'll demonstrate in this chapter.

Built-in Games

A default Ubuntu installation comes with over a dozen fun games that you can run straight away from the Applications → Games menu, as shown in Figure 13-1. The main games are in the *Games* folder, whereas more logic-oriented games can be found in the *Logic* subfolder.

If you're a migrant from Windows, you'll be pleased to see the AisleRiot Solitaire game, which is similar to Windows Solitaire, although you'll need to use the game's Klondike menu and check the "Three card deals" box to make the game play the same as the Windows default version (see Figure 13-2).

There's also a Mines game, which is the equivalent of Windows Minesweeper, shown in Figure 13-3.

Windows Vista and Windows 7 users will also be pleased to see the *Mahjongg* game already installed in Ubuntu (see Figure 13-4).

In addition to these, there are versions of Chess, Four-in-a-row, Sudoku, and many more games that will keep you occupied for hours. But when you have worked your way through them all and are thirsty for more gaming action, I recommend you next take a look at PlayDeb.

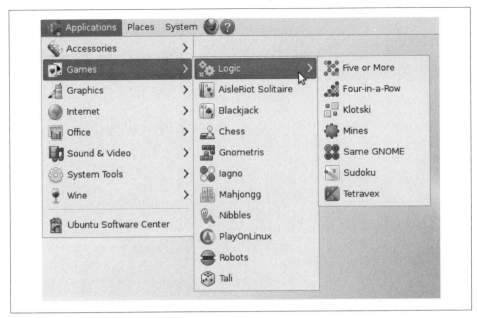

Figure 13-1. Ubuntu comes with several games preinstalled

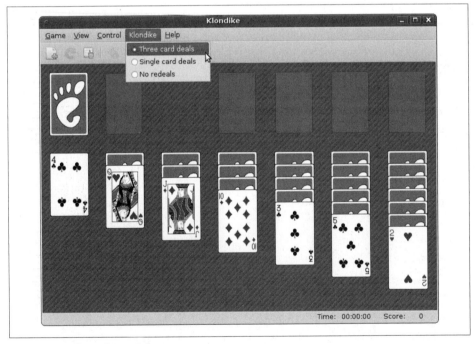

Figure 13-2. The AisleRiot Solitaire game

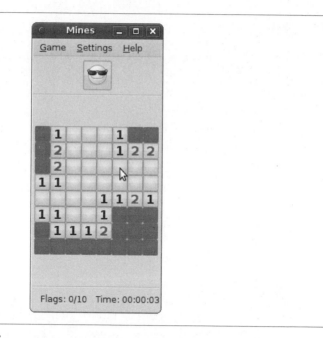

Figure 13-3. The Mines game

Figure 13-4. The Mahjongg game

PlayDeb

PlayDeb provides a repository of some of the best open source and freeware games available for Ubuntu. Unlike Ubuntu's twice-yearly schedule, PlayDeb's repositories are updated whenever new programs or updates are available, so it's worth bookmarking and checking the site regularly.

To make use of the site's simple download and installation process, you'll need to add its repository to your computer by entering the following URL into your web browser:

http://archive.getdeb.net/install_deb/playdeb_0.3-1~getdeb1_all.deb

 The wavy character after the 0.3-1 part is a tilde, which is often on the top-left backtick key of a U.S. keyboard, or on the # key of a UK keyboard next to the big Return key, although it can vary.

After entering that URL, you should see the window in Figure 13-5 pop up, prompting you to open the URL in the GDebi Package Installer. If that option isn't shown, select it from the drop-down list. Then click OK to install PlayDeb.

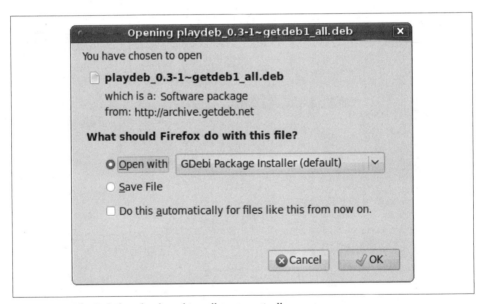

Figure 13-5. PlayDeb downloads and installs automatically

You are now ready to visit any of the pages on the *http://playdeb.net* website. Wherever you see a button or link that says "Install this now," you can click it to directly install the chosen program, as shown in Figure 13-6.

Figure 13-6. Install programs by clicking "Install this now"

When you do so, a new window will pop up suggesting that the application *apturl* should be used to handle the link (see Figure 13-7). If you wish, you can check the "Remember my choice for apt links" checkbox, to make that the default in future. But regardless of whether you check it, click OK to perform the installation.

After entering your password, the program will be downloaded, and any dependencies the program relies on or recommends will be suggested as additional installations. I recommend you also click Install for any of these dependencies.

Installation may take some time with larger programs, such as the brilliant first-person shooter game Blood Frontier. After installation, the new game will be added to the Applications → Games menu.

Other Linux Games

Of course, there are thousands more Linux games that will run under Ubuntu, and the following URLs detail some of the most popular of them:

http://help.ubuntu.com/community/Games
http://linux.about.com/od/ubuntu_doc/a/ubuntu_games.htm
http://linuxgames07.blogspot.com/2007/11/top-ubuntu-linux-games.html
http://gwos.org/doku.php

Make sure you read the instructions supplied with a game for details on how to install and play it.

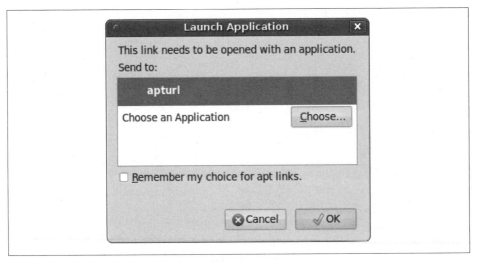

Figure 13-7. Use apturl to perform the installation

PlayOnLinux

The PlayOnLinux program is an implementation of the Wine Windows interface (see Chapter 16 for more on Wine). With it you can play a wide range of free, shareware, open source, and commercial Windows games.

To get the program installed, you will need to add information to the Ubuntu repository, so open the Terminal program and enter the following command. Although it takes up two lines here, it must be entered as a single command, with a space on either side of the -0. Enter your password when prompted.

```
sudo wget http://deb.playonlinux.com/playonlinux_karmic.list -O
/etc/apt/sources.list.d/playonlinux.list
```

 If you are running a version of Ubuntu newer than Karmic Koala, such as Lucid Lynx, replace the word karmic with lucid, or whatever the release name is.

Once the command has completed, you should then enter the two following lines to perform the installation:

```
sudo apt-get update
sudo apt-get install playonlinux
```

Upon completion, there will be a new entry in the Applications → Games menu called PlayOnLinux that you can select to call up the program, which will look like Figure 13-8.

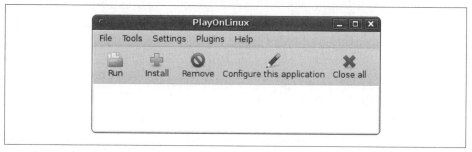

Figure 13-8. The PlayOnLinux main window

To get started adding games (and other programs) to Ubuntu, click the Install button to bring up the new window shown in Figure 13-9, in which the Games category has been selected and the program Crayon Physics highlighted.

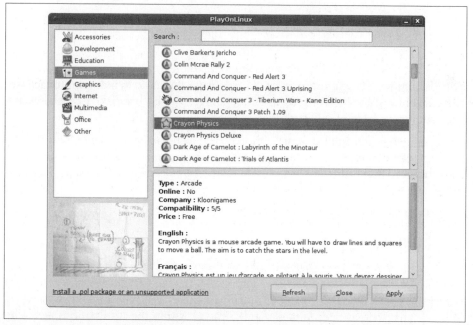

Figure 13-9. Installing a PlayOnLinux game

Where a game is commercial or there are licensing requirements, the program will properly configure itself to optimally run that game, but you will then have to supply your original discs that you purchased in order to install it.

However, many of the programs are free and can be installed from PlayOnLinux directly, without having to get hold of them separately. Crayon Physics, selected in Figure 13-9, is such a game, and it can be installed by clicking Apply. You will then be taken to an installation wizard that will help you install the program.

Once complete, the game will be available as an icon within the PlayOnLinux main window, as shown in Figure 13-10. Here, I have also opted to install Internet Explorer 7 to test the compatibility of PlayOnLinux, which actually runs it perfectly well.

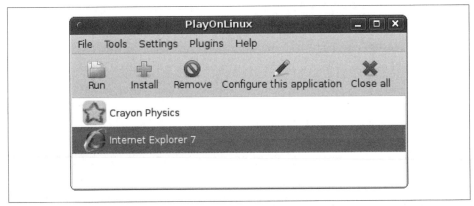

Figure 13-10. The PlayOnLinux window with two installed programs

PlayOnLinux is powerful enough to run more than one program at a time, each in its own Ubuntu window, so they can be treated just as if they were native Linux applications. Figure 13-11 shows the program running alongside both IE7 and Crayon Physics, which is a great game of skill and strategy I highly recommend you try.

If you have chosen the appropriate option during installation, you will now also have icons on your desktop with which you can start a program. The first time you use one you'll be asked to confirm whether it's safe. If you say that it is, the default PlayOnLinux icon image will be replaced with the program's proper icon.

KDE Games

If you choose to install the KDE desktop environment, as covered in Chapter 15, and also add the free KDE Games pack (see Figure 13-12), you will gain easy access to many more games that you can use in KDE, and in Gnome as well. These will then be added to submenus, such as *Arcade*, *Board* and *Strategy* within the Applications → Games menu, bringing the total number of games on your computer to more than 50.

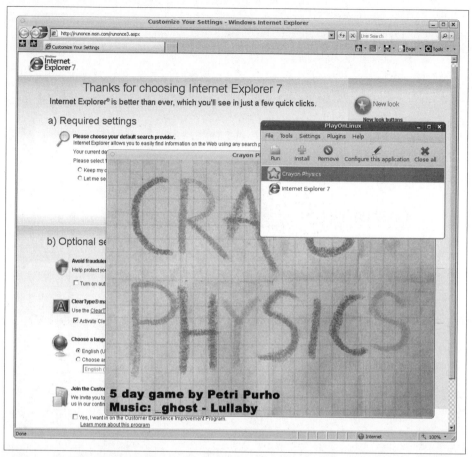

Figure 13-11. Multiple programs can be run simultaneously

Browser-Based Games

In-browser games, such as those written in Flash, JavaScript, or Java, should work with any Ubuntu web browser. Just use your favorite search engine and submit a query such as "flash games" to find them.

Ubuntu Easter Eggs

Although not strictly in the games category, it's fun to see what the Ubuntu developers have been up to in their spare time—for example, hiding commands in the operating system, which are commonly known as Easter eggs.

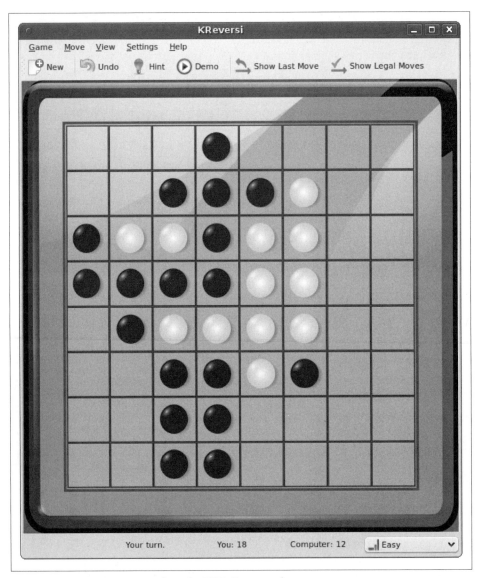

Figure 13-12. KReversi, a game from the KDE Games pack

The Ubuntu Fish

If you press Alt-F2 and enter the following in response to the prompt that's displayed, you'll release a fish (see Figure 13-13) onto your desktop that will swim around, leaving and entering the screen at random intervals:

```
free the fish
```

Figure 13-13. Wanda the fish

When you click Wanda, she will change direction and rapidly swim away. When you've had enough of the little creature, you can banish her by pressing Alt-F2 and entering the following command to restart Gnome's panels:

```
killall gnome-panel
```

This Easter egg will run only in Gnome, not KDE or Xfce.

OpenOffice.org StarWars

Next time you're frustrated because you're having trouble organizing your spreadsheet data in OpenOffice.org Calc, enter the following into any cell to enjoy a Space Invaders-style game called StarWars (see Figure 13-14):

```
=Game("StarWars")
```

Aptitude Silliness

There's also a bit of fun to be had with the apt-get and aptitude commands. Open a Terminal window and enter all the following commands, one at a time, viewing the response you get to each:

```
apt-get moo
aptitude help
aptitude moo
aptitude -v moo
aptitude -vv moo
aptitude -vvv moo
aptitude -vvvv moo
aptitude -vvvvv moo
aptitude -vvvvvv moo
```

I won't reveal what happens here—you can find out for yourself!

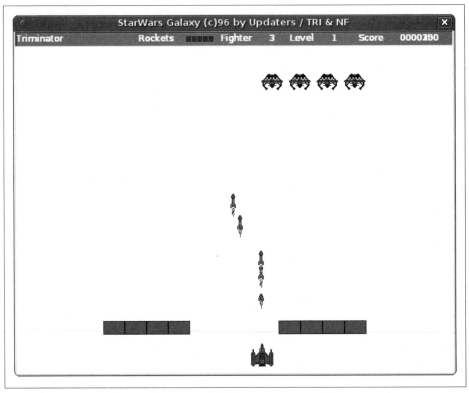

Figure 13-14. That's right, StarWars in OpenOffice.org!

What's New in 10.04

As it grows, the developers of Ubuntu continually need to remove items from the main distribution to enable everything to fit on a single CD, and until the decision is taken to move onto DVD installation media as the default, this will continue to be the case. Unfortunately, this means a few games didn't make it, with only AisleRiot Solitaire, Gnometris, Mahjongg, Mines, and Sudoku remaining in the Applications → Games menu. But now that you've read this chapter you know how easy it is to get all the games you could want, including those that used to be installed by default.

 If you upgrade to Ubuntu 10.04 from a previous version, your installed games will not be affected. Only new installations of 10.04 have the reduced number of installed games.

Summary

As you've seen in this and the previous chapters, Ubuntu isn't just a powerful work-horse for providing web server and database functionality; it's also an incredibly flexible and user-friendly desktop operating system that can run the latest office suites, multi-media applications, games programs, and much, much more.

In the next chapter, we'll look at something else Ubuntu is good at: interfacing with other devices such as cameras, scanners, USB hard drives, and the like.

CHAPTER 14

Pictures, Sound, and Video

When it comes to multimedia, Ubuntu is definitely no slacker. In fact, the Ubuntu Studio edition is absolutely brimming with programs for handling all types of multimedia. But you don't need to install Ubuntu Studio to be able to retouch and print photographs, edit home movies, or play your MP3s, because the standard Ubuntu edition comes with programs for these tasks, either preinstalled or available for download and installation with a few mouse clicks.

Even better, because Ubuntu is extremely efficient and can run quickly using a lot less processor power and system memory than other operating systems, you should find that manipulating media using Ubuntu is quicker and easier than ever.

Whether you just want to listen to your MP3s or watch videos, or you need to create or edit your own media, this chapter introduces a range of professional and fully featured programs that are as good as, or better than, those you'll find on other platforms. What's more, they won't cost you a cent to install and use.

Movie Player

The Movie Player program is supplied with Ubuntu as the default application for playing movies and audio files. You can open it from the Applications → Sound & Video menu, or by default, it will be called up when you double-click a movie or audio file. Figure 14-1 shows the program displaying the file *water-and-wind.ogv*, one of the samples in the folder */usr/share/example-content* (which you may also have copied to your desktop if you followed the examples in Chapter 12).

To view a movie in full-screen mode, you can double-click the player window; double-click it again to return to normal view. You can also use the slider, as well as the backward and forward buttons, to move about within a movie.

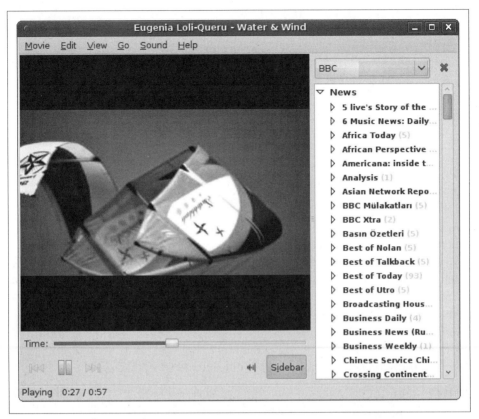

Figure 14-1. Movie Player displaying a sample movie

To the right of the window is the sidebar, which displays the properties of the current video, the playlist, a selection of BBC audio podcasts, or a YouTube video search application—all selectable from the drop-down menu above it. The Sidebar button underneath the video can be used to toggle the sidebar on and off.

At the time of this writing, the BBC audio podcasts were working, but as this book went to press, they were not, and an error of "Could not connect to server" was returned. Hopefully, they will be up and running again by the time you read this.

Adding Plug-ins

In order to play the wide range of audio and video formats in which artists release their work (MP3, WAV, and QuickTime, just to mention a few), programs such as Movie Player depend on related programs called *codecs*, available as plug-ins. Whenever you play a video for which your system lacks the required codec, the window shown in Figure 14-2 will pop up, and you will need to click the Search button.

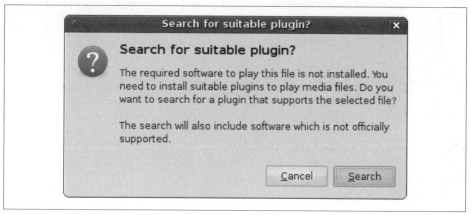

Figure 14-2. The "Search for suitable plugin" prompt

The window will then be replaced with the Install Multimedia Plugins window, which will spend a few seconds searching for the plug-ins and then display those it finds. To install them, click the Install button (see Figure 14-3), and then click Confirm in response to the following prompt. Finally, enter your password when asked to initiate the installation process.

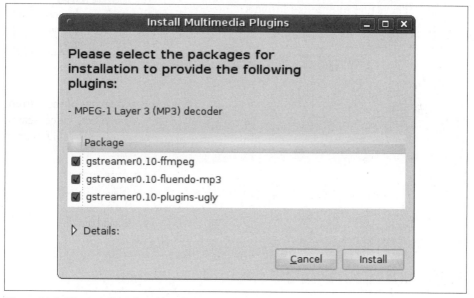

Figure 14-3. The Install Multimedia Plugins window

The plug-ins are then downloaded and installed, and you will then return to the Movie Player window, which you should restart in order to take advantage of the new plug-ins. You may have to go through this process the first few times you try to play different types of content. But once a plug-in has been installed, you won't be prompted for it again, and that includes any other programs that might use the same plug-ins.

 The United States and some other countries have responded to the complaints of copyright holders by passing laws that make it illegal to download some plug-ins. I won't launch into a legal discussion here, but the practical effect of such laws is to discriminate against Linux and other free software users. I will leave it up to your discretion about whether to install the plug-ins. Life would certainly be easier for users of all systems if artists moved to formats unaffected by these laws.

VLC Media Player

The Ubuntu Movie Player is great for a basic program, but if you want bells and whistles you may wish to try the VLC Media Player, which you can download and install in the usual way by entering "vlc" in the search field of the Ubuntu Software Center. Once installed, it becomes available in the Applications → Sound & Video menu.

Figure 14-4 shows the minimal window that appears when you run it. But don't be fooled by its modest appearance, because VLC is packed with powerful features for playing just about any kind of media, including DVDs and network streams. It can even convert and save files in different formats.

Figure 14-4. The VLC media player

It's well worth your time to browse through the various menus to discover the features that VLC offers, which also include a graphic equalizer and spatializer, as well as image transformation effects such as sharpening, rotation, cropping, and more.

 To open files in VLC, you can right-click them and select Open With → VLC media player. To associate VLC as the default player for a file type, right-click a file and select Properties, click the Open With tab, and then click the radio button next to "VLC media player."

Rhythmbox Music Player

You can open Rhythmbox by selecting it from the Applications → Sound & Video menu. It may not immediately open a window, though; instead, a new icon (looking like a loudspeaker cabinet with one large and either one or two small speakers depending on the version) will be placed on the top status bar, as shown in Figure 14-5.

Figure 14-5. Rhythmbox is the icon that looks like a speaker cabinet

To open the program, click the icon, and a window like the one in Figure 14-6 will appear, although if you haven't imported any music yet, there will be nothing displayed in the various panes.

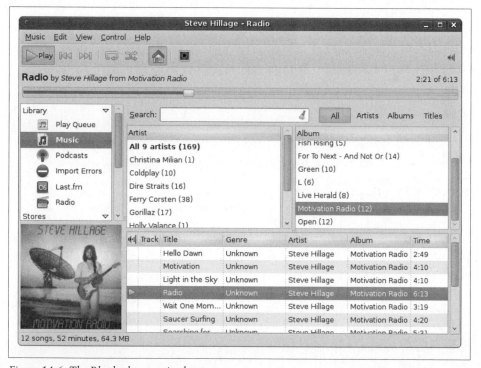

Figure 14-6. The Rhythmbox music player

Importing Tracks

To import music into Rhythmbox, select Music → Import Folder from its menus and locate the root folder of your music collection. You can also drag and drop files and folders from the File Manager into Rhythmbox.

Imported tracks will then appear in the three righthand panes, sorted by artist, album, and track names. In Figure 14-6, *Radio*, the fourth track of the album *Motivation Radio*, is currently playing. You can also see that, where available, album covers are also shown.

Playing Music

To play a track, double-click it, or double-click an album to play all the tracks in the album. When a track is playing, the speaker cabinet icon in the top status bar will either display a circle around it, or simply become darker and bolder, depending on the version.

You can control playing and pausing as well as track skipping, looping, randomizing, and the master volume from the top toolbar. The Library pane lets you create a play queue and play podcasts and live radio. It also informs you of any errors encountered while importing your music collection.

Using the Search field, you can quickly find any track. Or you can browse your collection by artist, album, or title by clicking the relevant button above the Album pane. The bottom pane lists the tracks matching your selection, which you can further sort by clicking any heading

Unlike some other Linux audio players, Rhythmbox plays a wide variety of formats, including *.wma* (Windows Media Audio) and *.m4a* (Apple's iTunes format), so you shouldn't need to convert your music collection.

 When you click the Rhythmbox player's close icon, the program doesn't actually close; it just makes the window go away so that you can play your music without cluttering the desktop. You can click the Rhythmbox icon in the top status bar at any time to bring back or hide the display of the main program window.

Last.fm

If you are a member of the popular online music streaming service Last.fm, you can access it from Rhythmbox by clicking Last.fm in the lefthand pane and then clicking the Account Settings button to enter your username and password.

What's New in 10.04

At the time of this writing, a music store called the Ubuntu One Music Store was slated for inclusion within the Rhythmbox program in Ubuntu 10.04. So, if you have upgraded Rhythmbox to the latest version, and if everything has gone as planned, by now you may be able to access this store from the Stores section, in a similar manner to the free and listen-before-you-buy stores Jamendo and Magnatune. Presumably, you will have to create an account with a designated credit card in order to purchase tracks, and hopefully they will be free of Digital Rights Management (DRM).

There was also talk of adding an audio equalizer to Ubuntu in order to make your music sound as good as possible by tailoring it to the acoustics of the room your computer is in. If it has made it into the final release, you will most likely be able to access the graphic equalizer by clicking (or right-clicking) the sound icon in the desktop's top panel.

Another major new feature in 10.04 is the ability of Rhythmbox to access your iPhone or iPod media. Simply connect it to your computer by USB and it should be immediately recognized and mounted on the desktop, and also listed as a device in Rhythmbox. You can then play media directly from the device, or copy it back and forth between your player and computer. I have confirmed this using a 32 Gb unjailbroken iPhone 3GS with version 1.3.1 firmware. However, it is always possible that future firmware upgrades from Apple could change this, requiring an update to Rhythmbox to restore interoperability.

The GIMP Image Editor

The GIMP image editor, available from the Applications → Graphics menu (but see the section "What's New in 10.04?" on page 390), is an incredibly well-featured and powerful image editor, championed by many people as the Linux equivalent of Adobe Photoshop. It does take a little getting used to, not least because it divides its components up into separate windows on your desktop (see Figure 14-7).

But if you are used to an environment in which your graphic editor takes up the entire desktop, and prefer not to be distracted by any other open windows, you may wish to click the bottom-left icon of your desktop to hide all open windows, and then click the tab in the bottom status bar representing the GIMP. This will ensure only GIMP windows are visible.

Learning How to Use It

Teaching you how to use an image editor as powerful as the GIMP is beyond the scope of this book, so you'll need to browse through the various menus and try out options to acquaint yourself with the program's full capabilities.

Figure 14-7. The GIMP opens several windows on the desktop

Having said that, though, the Help menu brings up a comprehensive tutorial that takes you through every aspect of the program (see Figure 14-8). Because the GIMP shares the desktop with other windows and doesn't hog the whole monitor to itself, you can open up the help next to the GIMP editor and try out features as you read.

There's also a very popular GIMP community at *http://gimptalk.com*, which is dedicated to helping new and seasoned users alike, and where they share tips, techniques, and images created using the program. The GIMP program is also easily extensible using plug-ins available from *http://registry.gimp.org*, and there are some handy tutorials at *http://gimp.org/tutorials*.

What's New in 10.04?

Starting with Ubuntu version 10.04, the decision was taken to remove the GIMP from the standard Ubuntu installation in order to return space to other new features that are deemed to be useful to a greater number of users. As the distribution expands, this is the kind of difficult decision that the team will keep having to make.

But by no means has the program been dropped, nor is it considered old or obsolete— far from it. The GIMP remains one of the jewels in the Linux crown, is still in the Ubuntu repository, and is easily installed by typing "gimp" into the Ubuntu Software Center search field, and may also be available in a planned new section of the Ubuntu Software Center called Staff Picks.

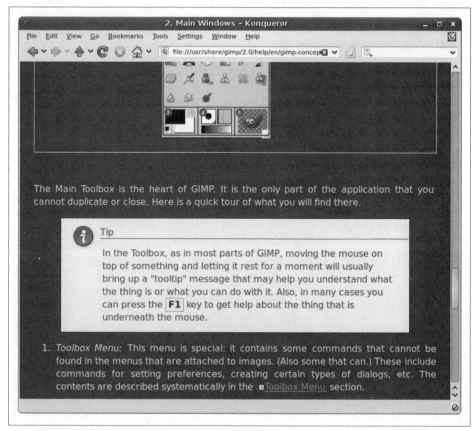

Figure 14-8. The GIMP help pages are the best place to start

As you might imagine, there was a lot of discussion about this on the Ubuntu bulletin boards as this book was going to press, and therefore I believe that there is a slight possibility that the decision to drop the GIMP from the ISO could be reversed (although this would likely be at the expense of something else being dropped), in which case, disregard this section. Also, if you installed Ubuntu 9.10 from the DVD supplied with this book and then upgraded to version 10.04 or higher, GIMP will be grandfathered in on your computer, and will not have been removed.

F-Spot Photo Manager

The F-Spot photo manager, available from the Applications → Graphics menu, is a handy editor designed for touching up your photographs (see Figure 14-9).

With F-Stop, you can crop images to size, reduce or remove the red from people's eyes, modify the color balance and saturation of an image, and a whole lot more. Select these

Figure 14-9. The F-Spot photo manager

features by clicking buttons in the lefthand pane, and then use them in the righthand main pane.

The top toolbar lets you import photos, rotate them left or right, browse multiple images, view photos full screen, and display them in a slide show. At the bottom left, you can get details such as an image's histogram, the date a photo was taken, its size, and the exposure setting used. The slider at the bottom right lets you easily zoom in and out of a picture you are working on.

For more details on using the program, click the Help menu to bring up a comprehensive manual.

Audacity Audio Editor

Audacity is a multitrack digital audio editing application. It's not bundled with Ubuntu, but you can easily install it by entering "audacity" in the search field of the Ubuntu Software Center. Once installed, it will be available in the Applications → Sound & Video menu. You can also open it by right-clicking an audio file and selecting Open

With → Audacity, which is exactly what has been done in Figure 14-10 using the file *InTheCircle.oga*, one of the supplied example media files.

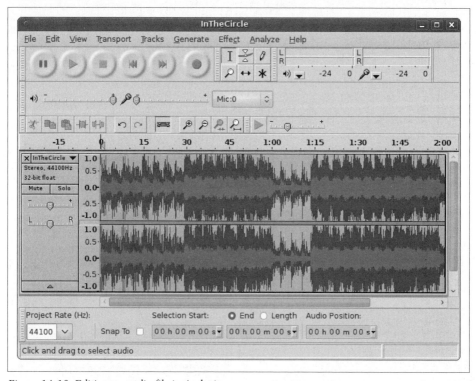

Figure 14-10. Editing an audio file in Audacity

As you can see, the file being edited is in stereo because the left and right parts are both shown. Mono files have only a single track.

To edit sounds using the program, think of them like the tape of an old fashioned reel-to-reel recorder. Using the mouse, you can highlight segments of the "tape" and then perform actions on them, such as copy, delete, and paste, or any one of the huge range of effects, such as echo, fade, reverse, pitch, and so on, all available from the Effect menu.

You can even add more tracks to the editor by dragging and dropping them into the program, or by using the File → Import function. You can then edit them individually or as a group, from which you can create a final stereo mix. Resampling, overdubbing, and many other options are also available, as well as over a 100 specialist plug-ins, including comb filter, valve rectifier, harmonic generator, and more.

The Help menu provides links to both a quick reference and the complete online manual for the program.

Rosegarden

If you want to use MIDI to create and edit music, Rosegarden is one of the best programs available for Linux. It's a complete sequencer, along with a multitrack editor, and supports both piano-roll and score notation. Figure 14-11 shows the program editing *aveverum.rg*, one of the sample files that comes with it.

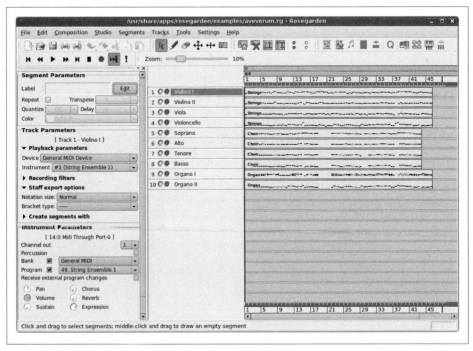

Figure 14-11. Editing a MIDI file with Rosegarden

On the left of the window are three panes for controlling one or more of the current track segment's parameters, the parameters of the whole track, or the instruments used. In the center, the instruments used are shown, with round checkboxes next to them for selecting muting or recording.

The righthand pane shows a piano roll representing the entire track. Using the slider above it, you can zoom in and out of the track to see more or less detail. The buttons in the top toolbar offer many powerful extra options, such as calling up the MIDI Mixer shown in Figure 14-12.

Other features include a percussion matrix editor, an audio mixer, and a musical notation editor, as shown in Figure 14-13, with which you can make beautiful-looking scores. Because of all these powerful features, the application takes a little while to learn, but the rewards are well worth the time spent doing so.

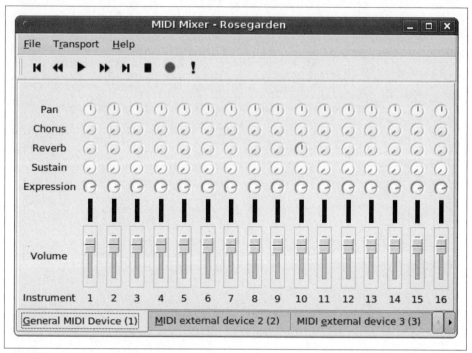

Figure 14-12. The Rosegarden MIDI Mixer

In addition to playing around with the features to see what they do, use the Help menu to bring up a link to a complete online manual, which has all the information you need to master Rosegarden and make music like a professional.

PiTiVi Video Editor

When it comes to video editing, Ubuntu also comes up with the goods, and one of the best applications is the PiTiVi program, which is not installed by default (but see the section "What's New in 10.04?" on page 396). However, you can easily install it by entering "pitivi" into the search field of the Ubuntu Software Center.

I have found that the best way to use the program is to drag and drop all the source files (which can be movies, audio, and still images) into the lefthand frame. From there you can drag and drop them into the compositing pane at the bottom, where you can insert scenes, images, and audio exactly where you need them (see Figure 14-14).

You can also place extra tracks underneath each other, which can be of any media type. So, for example, you can overlay sound effects and music, as well as add captions. Using the controller buttons under the movie pane, you can then play your movie or step through it to see how it's progressing.

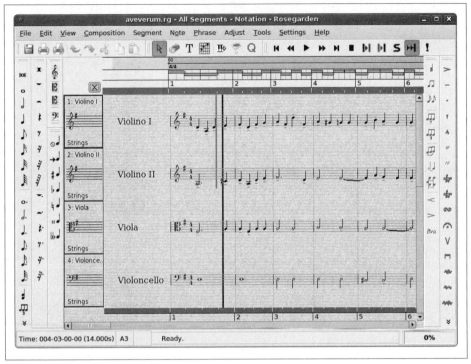

Figure 14-13. The Rosegarden Notation editor

The top toolbar lets you save the movie project, import clips, view the movie on the whole screen, and render the project to a new movie file. Depending on the complexity of a project, rendering can take some time, but you can leave it to run in the background.

Again, unfortunately, there's no room to teach you how to make movies, but all the help you could want, including a complete manual, is available at *http://pitivi.org*.

What's New in 10.04?

Starting with version 10.04 of Ubuntu, PiTiVi is now installed by default, and so you will not need to install it from the Software Center. This is a good decision because video editing is becoming ever more popular, and PiTiVi is one of the easiest and fastest programs of its type out there.

Figure 14-14. Editing a movie with PiTiVi

The Take Screenshot Program

Ubuntu comes with a handy utility for grabbing all or part of a screen, aptly called Take Screenshot. It's the program I used for the majority of the screen grabs in this book, and is available from the Applications menu. When run, it opens the window shown in Figure 14-15.

The main choices it offers include grabbing the whole desktop, the currently selected window, or an area of the screen. The first and second choices occur after the delay shown, which can be between 0 and 99 seconds. The delay gives you a chance to set up any options or menus to grab and then move the mouse pointer out of the way of the area you want to focus on.

When the current window choice is selected, only its contents will be grabbed, unless you select "Include the window border," in which case, it will also include the title bar. The available effects for grabbing a window are drop shadow and border.

Figure 14-15. The Take Screenshot program

The third choice lets you select an area to grab, which you do by dragging a rectangle around the part of the screen that you want. When you release the mouse button, that area is then grabbed.

In all cases, a window then pops up, offering to save the grabbed image as *Screenshot.png* (followed by *Screenshot-1.png*, and so on, for subsequent grabs). You can change the filename offered if you wish, as well as the destination folder. When you are ready, click Save to save the grabbed image.

Summary

Never let anyone tell you that Ubuntu doesn't have the multimedia tools that are available for Windows and Mac computers, because you've now seen just some of the amazing programs that either are provided by default or are available with just a few mouse clicks. And there are many more quality programs; there simply wasn't room to include them all in this chapter. I recommend you spend a little time browsing the Software Center to find other programs. However, be prepared to try out a few in each category before you settle on one you like.

Anyway, this chapter marks the end of everything strictly Ubuntu in this book. In the remaining two chapters, we'll look at some other flavors of the operating system, such as Kubuntu and Xubuntu, as well as the Wine program for running Windows software under Linux.

CHAPTER 15

Other Ubuntu Distributions

One of the great things about Linux, when compared with proprietary operating systems such as OS X and Windows, is that the licenses under which it is released allow developers to modify it and create new versions suited to their particular needs. Because of this, there are hundreds of varieties of Linux available, most of them tuned to very specific and niche requirements, while a small subset of distributions (or distros) have become very popular.

Of course, the most successful of these is Ubuntu, which itself is based upon another well-liked distro called Debian. But some developers have now taken Ubuntu and created derivatives of *it* for their own needs. For example, there's Ubuntu Studio for creating media, Edubuntu for use in education, Mythbuntu for using as a personal video recorder, and so on.

In this chapter, we'll look at a range of alternate Ubuntu distros and how to install and use them. Some are included on the DVD supplied with this book, so you won't even have to download them.

Installation

You have a few options when it comes to installing Ubuntu distributions, as described in Chapter 2, ranging from installing one as your main operating system to adding it alongside another operating system or even within a virtual machine. But whichever method you choose, you'll need the original ISO file.

For your convenience, the most popular Ubuntu derivative ISO files are included in the *distros* folder of the DVD supplied with this book, and their filenames are listed in Table 15-1.

Table 15-1. The Ubuntu distributions on the companion DVD

Distribution	Filename
Kubuntu 9.10	*kubuntu-9.10-desktop-i386.iso*
Mythbuntu 9.10	*mythbuntu-9.10-desktop-i386.iso*
Ubuntu 9.10	*ubuntu-9.10-desktop-i386.iso*
Ubuntu Netbook Remix 9.10	*ubuntu-9.10-netbook-remix-i386.iso*
Xubuntu 9.10	*xubuntu-9.10-desktop-i386.iso*

The original Ubuntu ISO is also there so that it can be used in conjunction with the *wubi.exe* program (in the same folder) to create an installation of Ubuntu within Windows (see Chapter 2). It can also be used to burn a CD-ROM for use on older computers that cannot read DVDs.

If you need the installer for any other distro, visit the following URL to choose the edition you need and download its ISO file:

> *http://ubuntu.com/products/whatisubuntu/derivatives*

To install a distro, you will need to burn its ISO to a blank disc, either using the Ubuntu Brasero program by right-clicking the file or using any similar program available for other operating systems. If you are using Windows, the *distros* folder also contains the Active ISO Burner program, which you can install and use to burn ISO files.

Once you have burned an ISO file to disc, you can insert the disc into your target computer and reboot it to perform an installation. Although the different editions vary slightly, they will mostly follow the same process outlined in Chapter 2.

Installing Distributions Alongside Ubuntu

If you have already installed one of the Ubuntu editions and have a reasonably fast Internet connection, there's an easy way to add other distros to your operating system, in such a way that you can choose which desktop environment to use each time you log in.

One of the benefits of this approach is that the core parts of Ubuntu don't have to be downloaded again. Instead, just the packages relevant to the edition you are adding are fetched, saving on your bandwidth and the amount of time it takes to install.

And there's nothing preventing you from creating your own "Megabuntu" edition by adding all the extra distros, giving yourself the maximum amount of flexibility and the greatest number of applications to use.

The only edition I don't show you how to add is the Netbook Remix (known as Netbook Edition from version 10.04 onward), because it's vastly different from all other editions in terms of design, usability, and layout, and would change your desktop in a number of ways you might not like.

Installing additional editions may have the unwanted effect of changing the logos and colors used for the splash and login screens. The easiest way to ensure you have the look and feel you want is to add the distro whose graphics you like the most last, and those settings will then be your defaults.

Adding Kubuntu

To add the Kubuntu desktop to your computer, open up a Terminal window and enter the following command, followed by your password when asked:

```
sudo apt-get install kubuntu-desktop
```

You will then be prompted for input a few times by the installer, but you can press Enter each time to accept the default inputs offered (as shown in Figure 15-1).

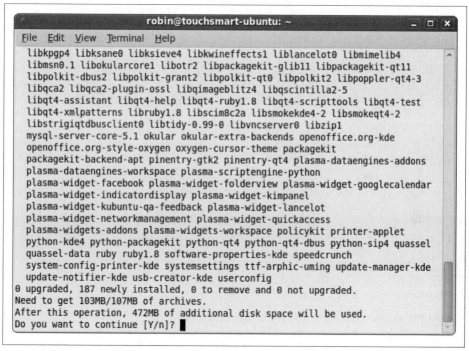

Figure 15-1. Adding Kubuntu to an Ubuntu installation

As a rough guide, at around 100 MB, on a 2 Mb broadband connection, the download process should take under five minutes. Once done, the screen in Figure 15-2 will appear. This is the start of the KDM configuration section, so press Enter to continue.

Next, you will need to decide which display manager you would like to be your default (see Figure 15-3). If you want GNOME to be the default, select gdm, or if you want KDE, select kdm. Don't worry about making the wrong choice, because you can easily change

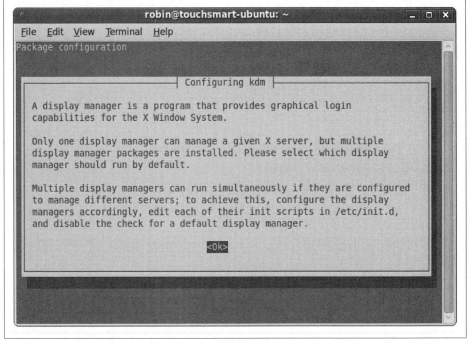

Figure 15-2. Configuring KDM after downloading Kubuntu

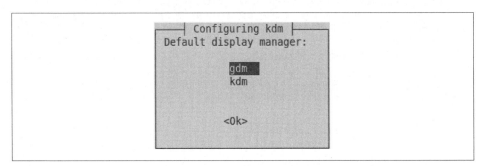

Figure 15-3. Choose your default display manager out of gdm and kdm

the default whenever you log in. After making the decision, press Enter to continue with the installation.

The installer will then proceed to unpack and set up all the packages it just downloaded, which will take a few more minutes. When it has finished, the installer will return control to the command line, and you'll be ready to try out Kubuntu by first logging out of your current session.

When you log back in again, select your username. Then, in the Sessions input at the bottom of the screen, you can now choose between GNOME and KDE for your desktop. Finally, enter your password and you'll be taken to the default KDE desktop.

Adding Xubuntu

You can add the Xubuntu desktop to your computer in almost the same way as Kubuntu, by opening a Terminal window and entering this command, followed by your password:

```
sudo apt-get install xubuntu-desktop
```

A similar download process to that shown in Figure 15-1 will then take place. This installation, however, will not pause to ask you which display manager to use as your default.

When the installation has finished and returned to the command prompt, you can log out and then back in again by selecting either GNOME or Xfce (or KDE if you installed Kubuntu) from the Sessions field at the bottom of the login screen.

Adding Mythbuntu

The procedure for adding the Mythbuntu software to your computer is similar to the previous ones. Simply enter this command in a Terminal window, followed by your password when asked:

```
sudo apt-get install mythbuntu-desktop
```

You will be prompted for input a few times during installation; if in doubt, accept the defaults offered. Once installation has finished, all the various Mythbuntu applications will be added to your desktop. You can then log out and in again, but first select Mythbuntu from the Sessions field at the bottom of the login screen.

Adding Edubuntu

The procedure for adding the Edubuntu software to your computer is similar to the ones already shown. Simply enter this command in a Terminal window, followed by your password when prompted:

```
sudo apt-get install edubuntu-desktop
```

This is a larger distribution, and as a rule of thumb, may take about 10 minutes to download on a 2 Mb connection. It will also take another 10 minutes or so to unpack and install the packages. Once installation has finished, you will be able to use the Edubuntu programs right away, without having to log out and in again first.

Adding Ubuntu Studio

The procedure for adding the Ubuntu Studio software to your computer is also similar. Just enter this command in a Terminal window, followed by your password when prompted:

```
sudo apt-get install ubuntustudio-desktop
```

After installation is complete, which will proceed without any questions being asked, you can use the newly installed programs immediately. There's no need to log out and back in again, although if you do, you'll get to see your desktop using the Ubuntu Studio theme.

Adding Ubuntu

To add the standard Ubuntu desktop to a computer that doesn't have it (but that does have another edition installed), type the following command into a Terminal window, and enter your password when prompted:

```
sudo apt-get install ubuntu-desktop
```

You should accept any defaults if prompted. When the installation has finished, log out and back in again to use the Ubuntu desktop. Select GNOME from the Sessions field at the bottom of the login screen.

 You may also wish to use this command to reinstall an Ubuntu desktop that has become corrupted or doesn't behave correctly. For example, occasionally the Quit menu has disappeared when I have been testing a beta version of Ubuntu, and running this command has restored it.

Kubuntu

This distribution is officially supported by Canonical, which means that it is thoroughly tested and support is available throughout the life of a release. Some other distributions are officially recognized but are not tested or supported by Canonical, and there are still other derivatives that are neither recognized nor supported.

The main thing about Kubuntu is that it uses KDE, the K Desktop Environment, instead of the GNOME environment of Ubuntu. But there's more to it than just that, because it also comes with a whole host of other programs, and some of the default applications are different from those in GNOME. With its Kickoff Application Launcher at the bottom left of the desktop, it's also reminiscent of the Windows Start menu (see Figure 15-4).

To access most things using KDE, click the K menu at the bottom left of the desktop (see Figure 15-5), from which you can select your favorites (files you have accessed a lot recently), the various available applications, the filesystem, and recently used files.

Figure 15-4. A typical Kubuntu desktop

Figure 15-5. The Kickoff application launcher

You can also call up the Quit menu for logging out, suspending the computer, and so on. If you can't find the program you need, you can always enter its name into the search field at the top of the launcher, and all matching applications will be shown.

The rest of the desktop is pretty self explanatory, seeing as by default there is only one toolbar at the bottom, which contains items such as the workspace switcher, volume control, network connectivity, and so on.

For further information on using Kubuntu, you should visit *http://kubuntuguide.org*, which features a comprehensive guide with a handy search facility.

Xubuntu

Xubuntu is not a supported edition of Ubuntu, but it is a recognized derivative, which means that Canonical evaluates and assists with its development but doesn't provide support for it. Luckily, you probably won't need much support, as it's just as easy to use as the other editions, if not more so due to the simplicity of its design.

Figure 15-6 shows a typical Xubuntu desktop, which is similar to GNOME (having the Applications and Places menus at the top left), but is actually based on the Xfce desktop manager.

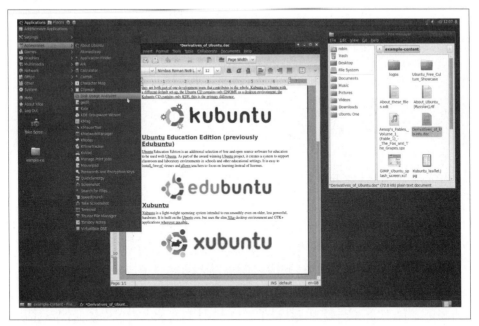

Figure 15-6. A typical Xubuntu desktop

Did you notice that there is no System menu shown in the screen grab? This is deliberate, because the developers of Xubuntu have decided to make this edition as fast and easy to use as possible, and also difficult for users to modify settings accidentally. This makes it ideal for installing on the computer of a novice user or on older computers with less powerful hardware.

Now that you know how to use Ubuntu from reading previous chapters, you'll find that you also already know Xubuntu. But if you need any further information on this edition, you can visit the home page at *http://xubuntu.org*.

Mythbuntu

Mythbuntu is an officially recognized derivative of Ubuntu, but it is not supported by Canonical. Its main focus is on setting up a standalone personal video recorder (PVR), but you can simply add it to any other edition of Ubuntu to benefit from its TV integration features.

I covered setting up the MythTV program in detail in Chapter 3, so there's no need to repeat that information here, other than to mention that the full Mythbuntu installation uses the Xfce desktop (see Figure 15-7) and doesn't come with applications such as OpenOffice.org. If you need further information, you can get it from the website at *http://mythbuntu.org*.

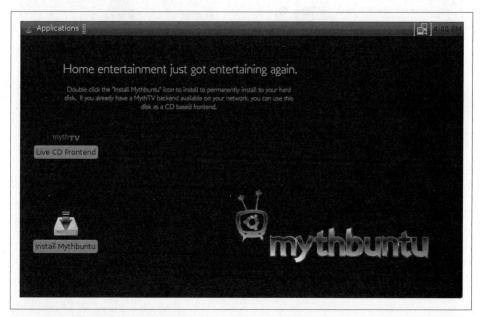

Figure 15-7. The Mythbuntu desktop

Edubuntu

Edubuntu is an officially supported edition of Ubuntu created to fulfill the needs of children, students, parents, teachers, and schools. The full ISO is so large (at over 3 GB) that you have to burn it onto a DVD (or a high-capacity USB thumb drive, as long as you make it bootable) instead of a CD.

However, using the process outlined at the start of this chapter, in the section "Adding Edubuntu" on page 403, you can opt to just install the main programs from the distribution, which are only an extra 200 MB or so to download.

The distribution comes with over a dozen educational programs, such as Tux Paint (see Figure 15-8), which you can access from the Applications → Education menu.

Figure 15-8. Tux Paint makes digital painting easy and fun

The full edition supports the Linux Terminal Server Project (LTSP), for networking students' computers with a teacher's in a classroom environment. Explaining how to use it is beyond this book's scope, but full details are available at *http://edubuntu.org*.

If you have young children, I definitely recommend installing the Edubuntu programs.

Ubuntu Netbook Edition

This edition of Ubuntu (known as Netbook Remix in versions of Ubuntu prior to 10.04) is a different kettle of fish altogether, because it's been totally redesigned specifically for use on Netbook PCs (see Figure 15-9), which generally have less processing power and smaller screens. If you have such a device and find your current operating system to be slow and somewhat unresponsive, the Netbook Edition may be just what you need.

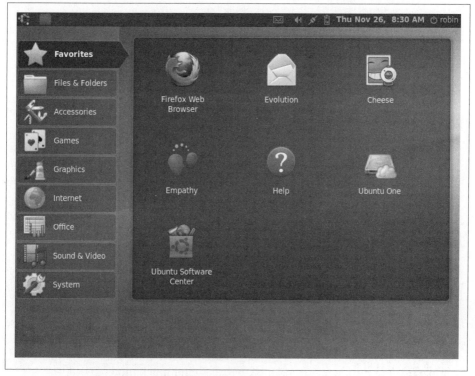

Figure 15-9. The Ubuntu Netbook Remix desktop

As you can see, the icons and menus of the Netbook Edition have been enlarged to take account of the small screens on Netbooks, with the main applications you are likely to use already placed on the desktop in the Favorites menu.

Using the Netbook Edition is similar to Ubuntu, except the menus from the top left of the desktop are no longer there. Instead, each item you select from the lefthand menu displays its contents on the desktop to the right, making for a very easy interface.

To install the Netbook Edition, you will need to burn the ISO image in the *distros* directory of the DVD supplied with this book to a blank disc, or to a bootable USB drive if your Netbook doesn't have an optical drive. Installation is quite easy because you just follow the prompts to tell it about your location and keyboard, and the installer then gets on with the rest.

I think that if you try it, you'll find this edition of Ubuntu to be an excellent alternative to your original operating system.

 If you choose to replace your current operating system, rather than setting the Netbook Edition up alongside it as part of a dual boot setup, I recommend that you make sure you have backed up the hard disk using a disk imaging application such as the free Macrium Reflect program, which is available at *http://macrium.com/reflectfree.asp*. This is just a precaution in case you experience problems and need to restore your computer to its original state. Remember that if you don't want to install Ubuntu Netbook Edition on your Netbook without testing it out first, you can always install it in a virtual machine using a program such as Sun's VirtualBox. Details on how to do this are in Chapter 2.

What's New in 10.04

Starting with Ubuntu 10.04, Ubuntu Netbook Edition is the new name for Ubuntu Netbook Remix. The name change is in recognition of the distribution now being much more than a simple remix. However, since the ISO file on the DVD supplied with this book is for version 9.10, it is called by its old name, Netbook Remix.

Ubuntu Server Edition

The Server edition of Ubuntu is officially supported by Canonical for 18 months with non-Long Term Support (LTS) releases, and a full five years for an LTS release, such as 10.04.

This edition comes with a range of rugged and reliable programs for fast and secure serving of web pages and applications. These include the Apache and Tomcat web servers, the MySQL and PostgreSQL database management systems, the PHP, Perl, Python, GCC, and Ruby programming languages, and much more.

Setting up and running a production web server is by no means an easy task, even when you have the support of a powerful operating system like Ubuntu Server. Therefore, I recommend you visit the following URL for further details:

http://www.ubuntu.com/products/whatisubuntu/serveredition

 By default, no graphical user interface is installed with the Server Edition, as it is unlikely to be required, although you can easily add one if desired using the information supplied in the section "Installing Distributions Alongside Ubuntu" on page 400.

Ubuntu Studio

The Ubuntu Studio edition is officially recognized by Canonical, but the company doesn't support it. The operating system consists of regular Ubuntu with the addition of audio, graphics, and video editing capabilities, such as the Kino video editor shown in Figure 15-10.

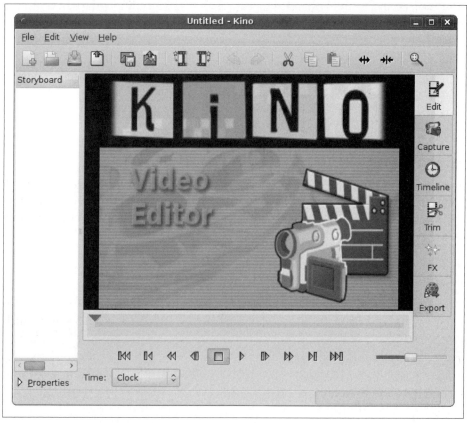

Figure 15-10. The Kino video editing program

This distribution also features a different version of the Linux kernel that has been optimized for real-time processing of audio, the PulseAudio sound server, and the JACK sound system. This makes it an amazingly powerful tool for editing sound and creating real-time audio and visual effects. But these features come only with the full install, not with the quick install I outlined at the start of this chapter, which simply adds programs used by the distro.

The ISO file for this distribution is over 1.4 GB in size, so you'll need to burn it to a DVD or a bootable USB thumb drive rather than a CD, or just perform the quick installation described at the start of this chapter if you want only the programs.

Visit *http://ubuntustudio.org* for full details on this edition of Ubuntu, including the hardware needed to run it at its best, and for comprehensive documentation.

Eeebuntu

If you are dissatisfied with either the Windows XP or Xandros Linux installation on your Asus Eee PC, you'll be pleased to learn that there's an edition of Ubuntu just for you, called Eeebuntu. Although not officially supported (or recognized) by Canonical, I have found that it runs better than regular Ubuntu "out of the box" on an Eee PC, with no tweaking required (see Figure 15-11). It comes in three flavors:

Standard (about 860 MB)
> This edition includes a full suite of Internet applications, including Firefox for browsing, Pidgin for IM chat, Thunderbird for mail, OpenOffice.org for office documents, and a selection of multimedia applications, including VLC for watching movies and Banshee for listening to music.

NBR (about 860 MB)
> This is the Netbook Remix version of Eeebuntu, which is similar to the Standard version except that it uses the Netbook Launcher, specially customized for the small screen of Eee PCs. Also, instead of the usual desktop, the main launcher provides a tabbed environment with easy to access icons for all your applications and documents. It also comes with a complete set of applications.

Base (about 560 MB)
> This is the smallest and most stripped down of the versions. Basically it consists of Firefox and some configuration applications, and not much else. But this makes it ultra sleek and fast for people who mainly use their Eee PC for web browsing. You can, of course, install any additional Ubuntu programs you need via Synaptic.

You can download the ISO image file of your choice from the distribution's website at *http://eeebuntu.org*. To create a bootable USB thumb drive for installing the operating system on your Eee PC, use a regular Ubuntu installation and select System → Administration → USB Startup Disk Creator.

 Because development of Eeebuntu lags behind Ubuntu by a version or so, you should only ever use the Install Updates button in Update Manager, and not the Upgrade button if it's offered. If you are informed that a new version of Ubuntu is available, don't be tempted to try and upgrade to it, or you may find your wireless and other features stop working correctly. Instead, wait until a new Eeebuntu (as opposed to Ubuntu) release is available, to which you can then safely upgrade. Note that Eeebuntu version numbers are much lower than Ubuntu ones by about a value of 6 (for example, Eeebuntu 3.0 is based on Ubuntu 9.04), so you can easily tell them apart.

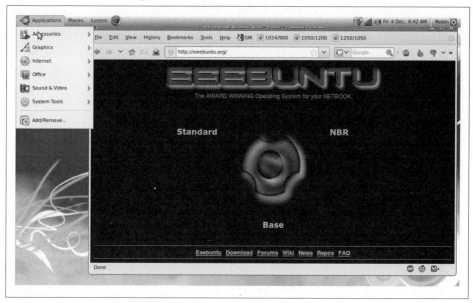

Figure 15-11. Eeebuntu with the panels set to auto hide to give more screen space to programs

Even More Distributions

Believe it or not, although I've outlined the main Ubuntu editions in this chapter, they comprise only a fraction of the complete set of distros; last time I counted, there were over 50, including versions for kids, security and bioinformatics workers, certain localized versions for the visually impaired, and more.

So, if you still haven't found the edition you want in the language of your choice and with the features you need, then I recommend the following URL, which lists every edition and derivative of Ubuntu there is and how to get it:

http://wiki.ubuntu.com/DerivativeTeam/Derivatives

Summary

In this chapter, you learned how to install the full versions of (or just extract the programs from) various releases and editions of Ubuntu. But no matter which you settle on in the end, if you have migrated from Windows, there may still be applications or utilities you miss or need access to for compatibility with your data. So, in the final chapter, we'll look at installing and using the Wine program, which you can use to run almost all Windows programs directly from Ubuntu.

CHAPTER 16
Using Wine

Although Ubuntu supports a wealth of different applications, spanning just about any subject you can think of, there are still occasions when it may not completely meet your needs. For example, OpenOffice.org is a fully featured office suite, providing all the functions you would expect and that exist in other similar applications such as Microsoft Office. And it can even read and write Office files. But it isn't totally compatible with Office, because many documents display and print differently in the two packages.

And why *should* OpenOffice.org be fully compatible? It's a completely different program that's been independently developed and approaches things in different ways that are completely logical in its own frame of reference. Once you get used to it, you can produce documents, spreadsheets, and presentations that are easily the equal of any you can create in Office.

But what if you have to collaborate on documents with someone who uses Office, while you use OpenOffice.org? You will almost certainly find that you both introduce changes that don't display correctly on each other's computers. They may be little things like changed tab settings, different page lengths, and so on, but these little things are also time-consuming to fix.

The simple solution to this problem is to install Office on Ubuntu using the Wine program (see Figure 16-1), which stands for Wine Is Not an Emulator—a typically recursive acronym, much loved by software developers. And the same goes for any other Windows applications whose documents you may need to handle using Ubuntu. If you have Wine, you'll usually be able to install the Windows program required to process such documents.

Or you may just miss some Windows programs that you feel you can't do without, at least until you have become more used to the Ubuntu operating system. But whatever the reasons, the fact remains that in conjunction with Wine, Ubuntu is capable of running almost all your Windows applications.

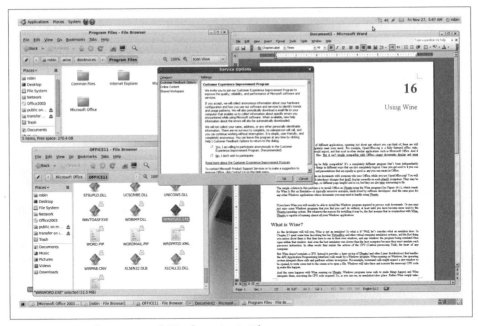

Figure 16-1. Yes, that's Microsoft Word running in Ubuntu

What Is Wine?

As the developers will tell you, Wine is not an emulator! So, what is it? Well, let's consider what an emulator does. In Chapter 2, I spent some time describing the Sun VirtualBox (and other virtual computer emulation systems). The first thing you notice about them is that they have to run in their own windows, which in turn contain the windows running the programs they emulate.

And even the best virtual machines run slower than the host computer because they must emulate each processor instruction. In other words, they mimic the actions of the central processing unit (CPU), the hardware at the heart of any computer.

But Wine doesn't emulate a CPU. Instead, it provides a layer on top of Ubuntu (and other Linux distributions) that handles the application programming interface (API) calls made by a Windows program. When running on Windows, the operating system interprets these calls and performs actions in response. For example, calls might request a new window to be opened, to write some text to the screen, or to open a file, and Windows will interpret these and execute the necessary CPU machine code to make this happen.

And the same happens with Wine when running on Ubuntu. Windows programs issue calls to make things happen and Wine interprets them, executing the CPU code required, and no emulation takes place. Rather, Wine simply takes the place of Windows in providing resources to Windows programs running on Ubuntu. And because of this, Wine can run these programs natively, at the fastest possible speed.

The Benefits of Wine

Wine offers many benefits compared to running Windows within a virtual machine emulator such as VirtualBox, the first being cost. With an emulator you must install a full version of a Windows operating system, which requires you to pay for a license. On the other hand, Wine is free to use. (However, if you use Microsoft Office or other commercial programs in Wine, you need licenses for those programs to run them legally.)

Another benefit of Wine is that it integrates with the Ubuntu desktop, which means that you can run Windows and Linux programs alongside one another, both as full-speed native applications, and with full copy and paste integration between the two.

If you look again at Figure 16-1, you'll see that the top-left window contains the Ubuntu File Browser, which is currently displaying the folders in a new *C:* drive that Wine has created. Below this, the *OFFICE11* folder on that drive is also being displayed, showing *WINWORD.EXE*, which has just been clicked, calling up the Microsoft Word program shown in the window to the right.

The small window on top of them all is for Microsoft's Customer Experience Improvement program. It has been called up by clicking the icon that was added to the top status bar, which normally would have been added to a Windows computer's system tray. So as you can see, Ubuntu and Windows programs integrate with each other seamlessly when Wine is installed.

 You may be interested to know that a version of Wine is also available for Mac OS X, which means that you can use Wine to create a very high level of compatibility between all three of the major operating systems: Linux, OS X, and Windows.

Wine's Limitations

Wine is still in development, and as long as there are new versions of Windows, it probably always will be, so there are known issues with the application. Although the majority of Windows software will run correctly with it, there are some programs that you may have problems with or that will simply refuse to work. Among these are various versions of iTunes, some games that rely on obscure Windows features, and so on.

The only way of knowing for certain whether a particular Windows program will work with Wine is to install it and test it for yourself. If it doesn't run correctly, maybe a future release of Wine will fix the problem. Just try another program instead, and consider that it's pretty amazing that Wine can run the number of programs it does.

Installing Wine

To install Wine, call up the Ubuntu Software Center and enter "wine" into the search field. This should result in three or so matching applications. You should double-click the first one, Wine Microsoft Windows Compatibility Layer, as shown in Figure 16-2.

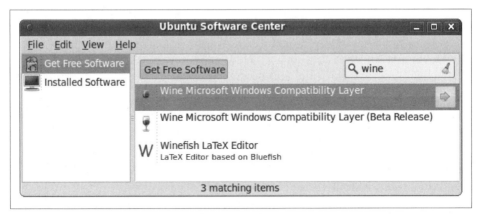

Figure 16-2. Installing Wine from the Software Center

 Unless you wish to become a beta tester, you should not install any version marked as a beta release, because it could be unstable and may crash.

This will bring up the description shown in Figure 16-3. When you are ready to install the program, click the Install button and enter your password if prompted. The installation process may take a while, depending on the speed of your Internet connection, and the progress bar may appear to stall, but be patient and wait for it to complete.

When finished, you can now install your Windows programs. For example, to install Microsoft Office, insert the disc into the drive, and it will be mounted onto the desktop. Double-click the mounted disc, and then double-click *SETUPPRO.EXE* (or whatever the setup file in your version is called). You can then follow through with the installation, in the same way as if you are using Windows.

Once installed, you can run a program from its folder or use the Applications → Wine → Programs menu to open it (see Figure 16-4), although you may need to restart your computer to make new entries appear there.

There's no Add/Remove Programs control panel, because Wine is not a full implementation of Windows. Just use Applications → Wine → Uninstall Wine Software to uninstall any Windows programs you no longer need.

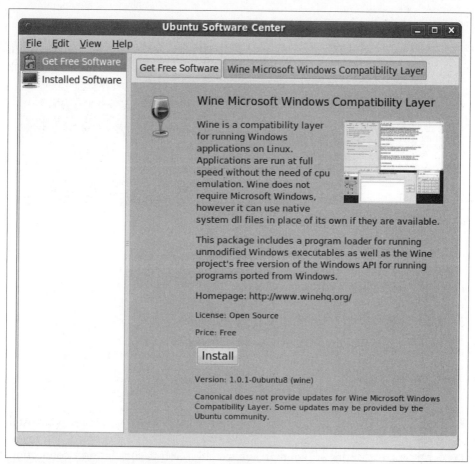

Figure 16-3. Read the description, and then click Install when ready

Installing Microsoft Fonts

If the fonts used by Windows programs don't look right to you, you might not have the Microsoft core fonts installed. This is easy enough to fix by entering the following command into a Terminal window, and then entering your password when prompted:

```
sudo apt-get install msttcorefonts
```

Either the fonts will install and you can now close and reopen your Windows programs to use them, or you'll be informed that you already have them.

Figure 16-4. Microsoft Office is now fully installed

 Microsoft originally licensed these core fonts for anyone to use freely, regardless of their operating system. This *Web Fontpack*, as it was called, was meant to help boost the market share of Internet Explorer. However, after IE became the dominant browser, these files were removed from the Microsoft website. Nevertheless, the End User License Agreement (EULA) continues to allow redistribution as long as the packages are kept in their original format and are not sold for profit. The license details are viewable on Microsoft's website at *http://microsoft.com/ty pography/fontpack/eula.htm.*

Configuring Wine

You can configure Wine to your preferences by selecting Applications → Wine → Configure Wine. This will open up the window shown in Figure 16-5, which is actually a Windows application itself running under Wine.

The utility displays seven tabs offering many options, including adding and removing applications, adding Dynamic Link Libraries (DLLs) to override Wine libraries, handling DirectX and Direct3D, managing themes, mapping disc drives, configuring audio, and more.

Some of these functions, such as adding DLLs, require a solid knowledge of how Windows works, so you shouldn't use them unless you know why you are doing so.

Accessing the Windows C: Drive

Wine emulates a Windows computer's C: drive by creating a collection of folders within your home folder, starting with the subfolder *.wine*. So, C:\ is actually located at *~/.wine/ dosdevices/c:.*

Figure 16-5. The Wine configuration window

So, for example, to change to the emulated *c:\Program Files* folder using the Terminal, you would enter the following command (remembering that you need quotation marks around any nonalphanumeric characters):

```
cd ~/.wine/dosdevices/c:/"Program Files"
```

You can also use the Nautilus file manager to browse the emulated drive by selecting Applications → Wine → Browse C:\ Drive.

Further Information

Wine is maintained and developed by the Wine Project (*http://winehq.org*). There, you can get assistance, report bugs, and make suggestions. I also recommend you view the wiki at *http://wiki.winehq.org*, which details everything you could want to know about the program and the project.

Summary

You have now come to the end of your journey to get Ubuntu up and running. I hope you have enjoyed the ride and will tell your friends, family, and colleagues just how easy and yet how powerful Ubuntu is.

If you like, come and visit this book's web page at *http://ubuntubook.net*, where you can also leave your comments about Ubuntu and this book. I'm always pleased to hear from readers, and do my best to help with any problems.

Index

Symbols

" " (quotation marks)
  using with filenames containing spaces, 228
  using with names containing special characters, 229
$ (dollar sign), prefacing variable names, 229, 231
* (asterisk)
  wildcard character, 242
  wildcard symbol, using in filenames, 220
. (dot)
  . operator, 230
  filenames beginning with, 157
/ (slash)
  filesystem root, 151
  path names in Bash, 216
; (semicolon), enclosing with quotation marks, 229
< (left angle bracket)
  enclosing in quotation marks, 229
  redirection operator, 239, 240
> (right angle bracket)
  >>, appending to existing files, 240
  enclosing in quotation marks, 229
  redirection operator, 237, 240
    using & with, 241
? (question mark)
  wildcard character, 242
  wildcard symbol, using in filenames, 220
[ ] (square brackets), enclosing sets, 243
\ (backslash), escaping characters, 235
^ operator, using in matching, 243
` (backticks), using on command line, 234

{ } (curly braces), brace expansion, 243
| (pipe character)
  enclosing with quotation marks, 229
  pipes versus redirections, 239
  using pipes with composite commands, 235
  using with grep command, 225
~ (tilde), representing home folder, 230

A

absolute paths, 227
AC power source, 286
accessibility
  Accessibility tab, Preferred Applications, 290
  calling up options, 105
  function key option, 18
  keyboard options for, 62
  keyboard settings, 67
Active ISO Burner, 26
  using on Windows, 26
Administration menu, 115, 294
  Computer Janitor, 294
  creating a password-free system, 295
  Login Screen, 295
  System Monitor, 297
  System Testing, 299
AisleRiot Solitaire game, 369
aliases, 244
  removing with unalias command, 244
alpha and beta releases, 301
antivirus software, 308
Appearance Preferences window, 127
  Background tab, 129
  Fonts tab, 131

We'd like to hear your suggestions for improving our indexes. Send email to *index@oreilly.com*.

Interface tab, 133
    changes in Ubuntu 10.04, 134
Theme tab, 128
visual effects, 134
appending to existing files, 240
Applications menu, 106
apt-get, 282
    fun with, 379
    help with, 283
    installing a package, 283
    removing a package, 283
    searching for packages, 283
    updating package index, 282
    upgrading packages, 283
aptitude command, 379
Aptitude Package Manager, 280
arrow keys, 212
Assistive Technology Support, 67
Asus Eee PCs, 412
Audacity audio editor, 393
audio, 79
    (see also sound)
    PulseAudio and JACK in Ubuntu Studio,
       411
audio editor, Audacity, 393
Authentication tab (Software Center), 266

B

background
    colors for, 128
    desktop, 129
    editing for folders, 182
Base (database program), 363
Bash shell, 210
    commands, 212–226
    keyboard shortcuts, 210
    quotation marks for spaces or special
      characters, 228
Basic (file attribute), 165
battery power source, 286
Behavior tab (File Management Preferences),
    186
beta releases, 301
BIOS password, 304
BIOS settings, allowing booting from CD/DVD
    drive, 16
BitTorrent (P2P file sharing), 344
Blackjack game, 219

removal from default Ubuntu 10.04
    distribution, 221
Bluetooth desktop icon, 121
Bookmarks menu (Nautilus file browser), 196
Bourne again shell (see Bash shell)
brace expansion, 243
browsers
    alternatives to Firefox for Ubuntu, 333
    games based on, 377
    system security and, 309
bunzip2 command, 245
burning CDs or DVDs, 26–28
    burning ISO image to thumb drive, 28
    burning ISO image using OS X, 27
    burning ISO image using Ubuntu, 28
    using Active ISO Burner for Windows, 26
bzip2 command, 245

C

C: drive (Windows), accessing, 420
Calc spreadsheet program, 357–359
    Formatting toolbar, 358
    Standard toolbar, 357
Calculator launcher, adding to top-left icon
    panel, 116
calendar (desktop), 120
Calendars program (Evolution), 366
canonical software, 262
capture cards, TV tuner, 92
case sensitivity in file and folder names, 154
cat command, 222
cd command, 213
    . . option (parent folder), 214
    using relative path name, 216
    ~ (home folder) option, 214
CD/DVD drive, booting from, 16
Chart Wizard (Calc), 357
Chess game, 369
chmod command, 233, 248
chown command, 250
chsh (choose shell) command, 231
clear command, 234
click behavior, changing from double- to single-
    click, 186
cloud service (Ubuntu One), 347
codecs, 384
colors
    choosing for desktop background, 130
    Theme option, 128

Windows
   browsing computer's Windows partition,
      109
   connecting to VNC server, 318
   full installation of Ubuntu as dual or multi-
      boot OS, 38–41
   network folders, 156
   network printer, configuring for Ubuntu,
      90
   networking with Ubuntu using Synergy,
      324
   path names in Bash, 216
   using Active ISO Burner, 26
   verifying checksums for distribution files,
      24
   Wine application interface, 310
windows, controlling open windows, 126
Wine (Windows application interface), 310,
      415–422
   accessing Windows C: drive, 420
   benefits of, 417
   configuring, 420
   definition and description of, 416
   installing, 418
   installing Microsoft core fonts, 419
   limitations of, 417
   resources for further information, 421
wired network connections, 85
wireless network connections, 87
   using Ethernet bridge, 87
word processor, OpenOffice.org (see Writer)
workgroups, display on network, 110
workspace switcher desktop icon, 123
world (file attribute), 247
write permission, 160
Writer application, 352–357
   Formatting toolbar, 355
   Standard toolbar, 353
   using styles, 356
   word completion, 357
Wubi, 38
   important considerations when using, 38

X

X Window System, 6
Xfce desktop environment, 8
   use with Mythbuntu, 407
   use with Xubuntu, 406
Xubuntu, 6, 406

installing alongside Ubuntu, 403

Z

zooming in and out with Nautilus file browser,
   177

About the Author

Robin Nixon has worked with and written about computers since the early 1980s (his first computer was a Tandy TRS 80 Model 1 with a massive 4 KB of RAM!). He has written in excess of 500 articles for many of the UK's top computer magazines.

Robin started his computing career in the Cheshire homes for disabled people, where he was responsible for setting up computer rooms in a number of residential homes and evaluating and tailoring hardware and software so that disabled people could use the new technology—sometimes by means of only a single switch operated by mouth or finger.

After writing articles for computer magazines about his work with disabled people, he eventually worked full time for one of the country's main IT magazine publishers, where he held several roles, including in editorial, promotions, and cover disc editing.

With the dawn of the Internet in the 1990s, Robin branched out into developing websites. One of these presented the world's first radio station licensed by the music copyright holders and was featured in several news reports on TV and radio networks in the United Kingdom. In order to enable people to continue to surf while listening, Robin also developed the first known pop-up windows.

Robin lives on the southeast coast of England with his wife, Julie, a trained nurse, and his five children. He also finds time to foster three disabled children, as well as work full time from home as a technical author.

Colophon

The animal on the cover of *Ubuntu: Up and Running* is an addax (*Addax nasomaculatus*). It is more commonly known as the screwhorn antelope because of the crooked horns that adorn both sexes of this endangered species. Females' horns can grow to be more than 2.5 feet high, while males' horns can reach as high as 4 feet.

The addax's coat changes colors with the seasons; in the winter, it is a grayish-brown and its hind legs are white, and in the summer, its coat is completely white or sandyblond. Its beard and red nostrils are also characteristic of its appearance. Its hooves are flat with strong *dewclaws*—vestigial digits on the feet of many mammals, birds, and reptiles—that help them walk on, rather than sink into, the sand.

The addax lives in isolated sections of the Sahara desert and is nocturnal, as temperatures are coolest at night. During the day, it rests in a bed it has dug with its forefeet, ideally hidden in the shade provided by boulders or bushes. It feeds on Aristida and Parnicum grasses, eating only specific parts of each. Aristida grass thrives with only the slightest bit of humidity and rain, so it is a dependable resource for the addax, and the seeds of the Parnicum grass are high in protein. Able to survive in the drastic desert conditions, addax can live without water almost indefinitely. In fact, they rarely, if ever, drink water; they get sufficient moisture from their food.

Addax herds can contain as many as 20 animals, both male and female. Its hierarchy appears to be based on age, as herds are characteristically led by the eldest male.

There are fewer than 500 addax in the wild. Much of their habitat was destroyed for commercial purposes and the animal itself is hunted for leather. The addax is much slower than other antelope species and is thus an easy target for hunters with motorized vehicles.

The cover image is from Wood's *Animate Creatures*, Volume I. The cover font is Adobe ITC Garamond. The text font is Linotype Birka; the heading font is Adobe Myriad Condensed; and the code font is LucasFont's TheSansMonoCondensed.

Buy this book and get access to the online edition for 45 days—for free!